First World War

and Army of Occupation

War Diary

France, Belgium and Germany

28 DIVISION
Headquarters, Branches and Services
Commander Royal Artillery
15 December 1914 - 31 October 1915

WO95/2269/2

The Naval & Military Press Ltd
www.nmarchive.com
Published in association with The National Archives

Published by

The Naval & Military Press Ltd

Unit 10 Ridgewood Industrial Park,

Uckfield, East Sussex,

TN22 5QE England

Tel: +44 (0) 1825 749494

www.naval-military-press.com

www.nmarchive.com

Contents

Document type	Place/Title	Date From	Date To
Heading	28 Div Adjutant & Quarter Master		
Heading	28th Division 'A' & 'Q' Branch Dec 1914-Oct 1915		
Heading	Headquarters (A & Q) 28th Division Vol I & II 1.12.14-31.1.15		
Heading	War Diary of Administrative Staff (A G & Q M G Branches) 28th Division From 1/12/14-31/12/14 Volume I		
War Diary	Winchester	15/12/1914	31/12/1914
Miscellaneous	C Form (Original.) Messages & Signals.		
Heading	Headquarters (A & Q) 28th Division Vol III 1-28.2.15		
Heading	War Diary of The Administrative Staff (A.G. & Q.M.G. Branches) From 1st January 1915 To 31st Jany 1915 Vol II		
Heading	War Diary of The Administrative Staff 28 Division From 1st Feb. 1915 To 28th Feb. 1915		
War Diary	Winchester	01/01/1915	18/01/1915
War Diary	Havre	18/01/1915	18/01/1915
War Diary	Hazebruck & Stomer	18/01/1915	18/01/1915
War Diary	France	19/01/1915	20/01/1915
War Diary	Pradelle	21/01/1915	31/01/1915
Miscellaneous	Post Office Telegraphs App 1		
Miscellaneous	To Confirm Telegram. App 2		
Miscellaneous	To Confirm Telegram.		
Miscellaneous	Post Office Telegraphs Appendix 3		
Miscellaneous	Post Office Telegraphs		
Miscellaneous	Post Office Telegraphs App. 5		
Miscellaneous	Post Office Telegraphs Appendix 6		
Miscellaneous	Post Office Telegraphs		
Miscellaneous	Post Office Telegraphs App. 7		
Miscellaneous	A Form Messages And Signals		
Miscellaneous	1st Bn Suffolk Regt.		
Diagram etc	Appendix 8		
Diagram etc	83rd Bde. Billeting Area		
Diagram etc			
Miscellaneous	31st Bde R.F.A.		
Miscellaneous	1st Bn Welch. Regt. In Merris		
Miscellaneous	2nd Bn Cheshire Regt.		
Miscellaneous	2nd Northd Fusiliers		
Miscellaneous	3rd London R.E. In Strazeele		
Diagram etc	Appendix I 5 February 1915		
Diagram etc	Poperinghe		
Miscellaneous	Messages And Signals App. 2		
Diagram etc	Not To Scale Traffic Control		
Miscellaneous	Further Arrangements For Transfer of Brigade Companion of 28th And 5th Divisional Trains. Appendix 4	23/02/1915	23/02/1915
War Diary	Pradelle	01/02/1915	01/02/1915
War Diary	Vlamertinghe	01/02/1915	02/02/1915
War Diary	Brandhoek	03/02/1915	05/02/1915
War Diary	Poperinghe	05/02/1915	28/02/1915

Heading	Headquarters (A & Q) 28th Division Vol IV 1-31.3.15		
Heading	War Diary of The Administrative Staff 28th Division From 1st March 1915 To 31st March 1915 Volume IV		
War Diary	Poperinghe	01/03/1915	31/03/1915
Miscellaneous	A Form Messages And Signals		
Miscellaneous	C Form (Original) Messages And Signals		
Miscellaneous	Water Supply Hutments Vlamertinghe-Ouderdom Road.	25/03/1915	25/03/1915
Diagram etc	Appendix 4		
Heading	War Diary Administrative Staff 28 Div From 1st April 1915 To 30 April 1915 Volume V		
War Diary	Poperinghe	01/04/1915	21/04/1915
War Diary	Vlamertinghe Chateau	21/04/1915	22/04/1915
War Diary	Vlamertinghe	22/04/1915	30/04/1915
Miscellaneous	Number of Officers And Other Ranks Sick And Wounded Admitted To Field Ambulances, Killed, Missing And Returned To Duty During The Month of March 1915 Appendix I Administrative Staff Diary 1st April 1915	01/04/1915	01/04/1915
Miscellaneous	28th Division Appendix 3	28/04/1915	28/04/1915
Diagram etc	Elverdinghe		
Heading	28th Division Administrative War Diary Head Quarters Staff 28 Division B.E.F. From 1st May 1915 To 31st May 1915 Volume VI		
War Diary	Vlamertinghe	01/05/1915	03/05/1915
War Diary	Chateau Couthove	04/05/1915	05/05/1915
War Diary	Vlamertinghe	05/05/1915	05/05/1915
War Diary	Chateau Couthove	05/05/1915	31/05/1915
Miscellaneous	War Diary Administrative Staff 28 Div App I May 1915		
Miscellaneous	28th Division. Appendix 2	06/05/1915	06/05/1915
Miscellaneous	Administrative War Diary 28 Div Appendix III	09/05/1915	09/05/1915
Miscellaneous	Administrative War Diary 28th Division. Appendix IV	07/05/1915	07/05/1915
Miscellaneous	List of Reserve Return Issued To Units of 28th Division Appendix V	11/05/1915	11/05/1915
Miscellaneous	28th Divisional Order No. 1 App. VI	13/05/1915	13/05/1915
Miscellaneous	March Table Route		
Miscellaneous	28th Division Casualties April 22 To May 13. 1915 Appendix VII	20/05/1915	20/05/1915
Heading	28th Division Head Quarters (A & Q) 28th Division Vol VII 1-30.6.15		
Heading	War Diary of Administrative Staff 28th Division From 1st June 1915 To 30th June 1915		
War Diary	Watou	01/06/1915	13/06/1915
War Diary	Westoutre	14/06/1915	30/06/1915
Miscellaneous	List of Refilling Points And Units Refilled 2/6/1915 Appendix I	02/06/1915	02/06/1915
Miscellaneous	Refilling Points-17th June 1915 Appendix II	17/06/1915	17/06/1915
Heading	28th Division Head Quarters (A & Q) 28th Division Vol VIII 1-31.7.15		
Heading	War Diary of Administrative Staff 28th Division From 1st July 1915 To 31st July 1915 Volume No 8		
War Diary	Westoutre	01/07/1915	31/07/1915
Miscellaneous	Report On Area Brigade Order S/820	19/07/1915	19/07/1915
Miscellaneous	85 Bde Area Ref Sheet 28 1/40000		
Diagram etc	Tracing From Map 28 1/20000		
Miscellaneous	Reference of Tracing	19/07/1915	19/07/1915
Diagram etc			

Miscellaneous	85th Infy Brigade.	26/07/1915	26/07/1915
Miscellaneous	Infantry Brigade Return Showing Ammunition Allowed By. And In Excess of. War Establishment Held At Trenches		
Miscellaneous			
Miscellaneous	85th Infantry Brigade		
Miscellaneous	A Form Messages And Signals		
Miscellaneous	Refilling Points And Units Refilled July 11th 1915 Appendix A		
Miscellaneous	Refilling Points & Units Refilled July 14th/15 Appendix B		
Miscellaneous	Consolidated Casualty Return Feb 2 To July 18 1915 Appendix C		
Miscellaneous	28th Division Expeditionary Force.	19/07/1915	19/07/1915
Miscellaneous	Refilling Points And Units Refilled July 20th Appendix D		
Miscellaneous	85th Brigade The Following Amount of Small Arm Ammunition Will Be Kept With Battalions	26/07/1915	26/07/1915
Miscellaneous	85th Infantry Brigade.	26/07/1915	26/07/1915
Heading	August 1915		
Heading	War Diary of 28th Division, Administrative Staff. From 1st Aug 1915 To 31st Aug 1915 Volume 9		
War Diary	Westoutre	01/08/1915	31/08/1915
Miscellaneous	85th Infantry Brigade	04/08/1915	04/08/1915
Miscellaneous	85th Brigade	03/08/1915	03/08/1915
Miscellaneous	Refilling Points, And Units Refilled, August 10th 1915 Appendix A		
Miscellaneous	Refilling Points, And Units Refilled, August 27th 15 Appendix B		
Miscellaneous	Number of rounds of S.A.A on Charge of Regiment.		
Miscellaneous	Number of Round Small Arms Ammunition On Charge of Brigade At 12 noon. Sunday-August Brigade of Battalion Each of strength 1000 Rifles And 20 Machine Guns. Three Battalion In Trenches And Two Resting.		
Heading	28th Division Head Quarters (A & Q) 28th Division Vol X Sept. 15		
Heading	War Diary (Original) of Administrative Staff 28th Division From Sept 1st To Sept 30th 1915 Volume X		
War Diary	Westoutre	01/09/1915	22/09/1915
War Diary	Merris	23/09/1915	25/09/1915
War Diary	Bethune	26/09/1915	27/09/1915
War Diary	Chateau Des Pres Sailly La Bourse	28/09/1915	28/09/1915
War Diary	Sailly La Bourse	29/09/1915	30/09/1915
Miscellaneous	Refilling Points And Units Rcfilled September 18th Appendix A		
Miscellaneous	Refilling Points And Units Refilled September 22nd 1915 Appendix B		
Miscellaneous	Refilling Points And Units Refilled September 24th 1915 Appendix C		
Miscellaneous	Refilling Points And Units Refilled September 26th 1915 Appendix D		
Miscellaneous	Refilling Points And Units Refilled September 29th 1915 Appendix E		

Miscellaneous	The Following Is The System For Getting Bombs Up As Far As Infantry Brigade Ammunition Reserves. Beyond That Point The Responsibility For Their Supply Lies With Brigades. Appendix I.	30/09/1915	30/09/1915
Miscellaneous	Refilling Points And Units Refilled September 30th 1915 Appendix G	30/09/1915	30/09/1915
Miscellaneous	Appendix To Diary Appendix H	29/09/1915	29/09/1915
Heading	War Diary Headquarters 28th Division (A & 2) October 1915 Vol XI		
Heading	War Diary of 28th Div Administrative Staff From Oct 1st To Oct. 31st 1915 Volume XI		
War Diary	Sailly La Bourse	01/10/1915	05/10/1915
War Diary	Busnes	06/10/1915	16/10/1915
War Diary	Bethune	17/10/1915	31/10/1915
Miscellaneous	Casualties 1st Corps 28th Division From Midnight 26/27th September To Morning 6th October. Appendix A		
Miscellaneous	Trench Mortar Batteries Attached To 28th Division Appendix B.	04/10/1915	04/10/1915
Miscellaneous	Accessories For Trench Mortar Ammunition & Hand Grenades Appendix C		
Miscellaneous	. The Following Is The System For Getting Bombs Up As Far As Infantry Brigade Ammunition Reserves. Appendix D.		
Miscellaneous	List of Refilling Points And Units Refilled October 4th 1915. Appendix E	04/10/1915	04/10/1915
Operation(al) Order(s)	28th Division Operation Order No. 60. Appendix F	05/10/1915	05/10/1915
Miscellaneous			
Miscellaneous	List of Refilling Points And Units Refilled 7/10/15 Appendix G	07/10/1915	07/10/1915
Miscellaneous	Method of Supply Of Grenades, Lights, And Trench Mortar Ammunition. Appendix H	15/10/1915	15/10/1915
Miscellaneous	The Following Instructions Are Issued To Govern The Move of 28th Division From The 1st Army Area On 21st. Appendix I	19/10/1915	19/10/1915
Miscellaneous	28th Division. Programme of Entraining Lillers Station. Appendix J		
Miscellaneous	28th Division. Programme of Entraining Fouquereuil Station.		
Heading	War Diary Headquarters 28th Divn (A. & Q.) Dec 1915 Vol XI		
Map	First Army Area Administrative Map.		

28 DIV
ADJUTANT & QUARTER MASTER

28TH DIVISION

'A' & 'Q' BRANCH

DEC 1914-OCT 1915

121
4327

Headquarters (A & Q) 28th Division.

Vols I & II. 1.12.14 — 31.1.15.

Dec 14
Oct 15

Vol. II

Dec 13th — Useful hints on Mobilization

27th — Institution of [illegible] company as formerly used —

Confidential
War Diary
of
ADMINISTRATIVE STAFF
(AG & QMG Branches)
28th Division

From 1/12/14 —— 31/12/14

Volume I

A. A. McHardy
Major DAQMG 28 D

Instructions regarding War Diaries and Intelligence Summaries are contained in F. S. Regs., Part II. and the Staff Manual respectively. Title pages will be prepared in manuscript.

WAR DIARY
or
~~INTELLIGENCE SUMMARY.~~

(*Erase heading not required.*)

Army Form C. 2118.

Hour, Date, Place	Summary of Events and Information	Remarks and references to Appendices
W. 3.30 P.M. 15.12.14 WINCHESTER	Major McHardy DAQMG 28th Div. Established himself as D.A.Q.M.G 28th Div at Black Swan Hotel and opened H.Q. office 28th Div. having previously notified Post Office; W.O.; & HQ Salisbury that this would be done.	
4.12 p.m. " "	Wires numbers 297 . 300 : 301 : 302 : 303 A.G. 2 d/14.12.14 received & acknowledged.	
5.45 pm. " "	Pte Caun reported for duty as an A.S.C. Clerk ~~at~~ Div HQ.	
7.45 pm. " "	No 5172 from Seemliness. London notifies appointment of Lt Col Atcherley as A.Q.M.G. 28th Div:	
6.30 pm " "	Written confirmation to see W.O. notifying that Div HQ has been established.	
" " "	~~Verbally~~ informed, by 27 Div that Major Ferguson RA ~~Bde Maj R~~ has been appointed Bde Maj RA 28th Div. Communicated with Maj Ferguson and asked him to call tomorrow afternoon –	
7.15 pm. " "	~~to~~ Capt Hamilton RA the local Remount officer reported and discussed question of RA Horses.	
" " "	S. QMS Lass A.S.C. & L/C Glisson A.S.C. reported for duty as Div HQ Clerks and were billeted.	
" " "	By request established Telephonic Communication with Capt Wells in A.G.(2) W.O. (Tel 88. W.O.)	
9.10 pm " "	Established Tel Communication with. Col Atcherley at Bedford –	

(73989) W4141—463. 400,000. 9/14. H.&J.Ltd. Forms/C. 2118/10.

Instructions regarding War Diaries and Intelligence Summaries are contained in F. S. Regs., Part II. and the Staff Manual respectively. Title pages will be prepared in manuscript.

WAR DIARY
or
INTELLIGENCE SUMMARY.

(*Erase heading not required.*)

Army Form C. 2118.

Hour, Date, Place	Summary of Events and Information	Remarks and references to Appendices
9.15 pm. 15.12.14 WINCHESTER	Conference with Captain Wetherall DAQMG. So Command on Camps and Local arrangements.	
10.45 pm. 15.12.14 " "	5172 from Secmiliness. W.O. notifies appointment of Captain W. Miller Mx Regt as APM.	
— " " " "	W.O. letter 121/Staff/466 (AG 4a) received thro' So Command notifying appointment of Lord Loch Gren: Guards as GSO 1st Grade.	
— " " " "	During Evening Senior official letter received from RA 27 Div suggesting 28th Div RA take over RA details of 27 Div who left behind. Objection raised to this. Weather wet then fine.	

(73989) W4141—463. 400,000. 9/14. H.&J.Ltd. Forms/C. 2118/10.

Instructions regarding War Diaries and Intelligence Summaries are contained in F. S. Regs., Part II. and the Staff Manual respectively. Title pages will be prepared in manuscript.

WAR DIARY
or
INTELLIGENCE SUMMARY.
(Erase heading not required.)

Army Form C. 2118.

Hour, Date, Place	Summary of Events and Information	Remarks and references to Appendices
8.30 a.m. 16/Dec/14 WINCHESTER	DAQMG 28 Div proceeded with DAQMG Southern Command to visit ~~Hor~~ Camps at HURSLEY PARK and VICINITY: Found following units in Camp. 1/KOYLI: 1/Suffolk. Detachment Div: Train: Camps in occupation very muddy.	
11. a.m. " "	W.O. letter P.M.1/2029 (A.G.7) received notifying appointment of Captain G. Master Royal Engineers as adjutant Div: Engineers.	
11.15 a.m. " "	Major C H Saunders reported as DADOS 28: Div:	
3 p.m. " "	Major Ferguson R.F.A. reported as Bde Major RA 28: Div:	
4.10 p.m. " "	Wire Q 1498 received from Brachician Salisbury ordering 3: FA Bde and attached Batteries into billets at WINCHESTER. Forthwith arrangements made and commenced could not be completed owing to handing over of barracks to 27: ~~FA Bde~~ Div: This will be completed 17th Dec:	
6 p.m. – 7.30 " " "	Following action taken by DAQMG. Authority ~~reqr~~ asked from Salisbury to billet Div HQ in Winchester. Police notified that Signal Coy will billet on arrival. Salisbury requested to push on medical inspection of KOYLI and inoculation of KOYLI and Suffolks. RA 28: Div directed to assist KOYLI & Suffolks in fitting collars on 1st Line T. Salisbury requested to arrange despatch of Heavy Baggage not required by units from overseas direct to place of Storage.	
8.20 p.m. " "	M.T. Camberwell notifies despatch of 2 motor Cars for Train.	
9 p.m.	Col Cairns OC Div Train reported. His motor Cars arrived later.	

(73989) W4141—463. 400,000. 9/14. H.&J.Ltd. Forms/C. 2118/10.

Instructions regarding War Diaries and Intelligence Summaries are contained in F. S. Regs., Part II. and the Staff Manual respectively. Title pages will be prepared in manuscript.

WAR DIARY
or
INTELLIGENCE SUMMARY.
(*Erase heading not required.*)

Army Form C. 2118.

Hour, Date, Place		Summary of Events and Information	Remarks and references to Appendices
8 am	17·12·14 WINCHESTER	DAQMG visited Magdalen Hill camp with D.A.Q.M.G. S.C. & Pater discussed arrangements for meeting troops ~~with~~ on arrival by rail – with R.T.O. HQ 27th Div: and Police latter promised assistance with guides.	
11 am	" " "	1 Pte (Cook) arrived on posting to HQ 28th Div:	
1 pm	" " "	Captain T.W. Cumberbatch YH&R reported as A.D.C. to GOC. 28th Div:	
3 "	" " "	Rev T.H. Royse C.F. reported for duty.	
4–5 pm.	" " "	1 Sgt. AOC & 3 Privates reported for duty with Div HQ.	
5·30 pm	" " "	AG(2) WO. informs by Telephone (a) that harness ~~[illegible]~~ and all Equipment will not be issued till 27th Div are clear of Winchester (b) That there may be delay in issue of 4 M.G. per Bn: (c) That no serving soldiers can be employed as Batmen. (d) That 2 Med: Offrs are being sent to the Bns	
6·30 pm	" " "	Major Genl Bulfin CVO. CB arrived to command 28th Div: Lt Col Atcherley M.V.O. also arrived.	
7· pm.	" " "	Captain Miller Middlesex Regt. reported as APM.	
"	" " "	GOC held Conference of Staff Officers & heads of departments.	
"		Weather fine then wet.	

Instructions regarding War Diaries and Intelligence Summaries are contained in F. S. Regs., Part II. and the Staff Manual respectively. Title pages will be prepared in manuscript.

WAR DIARY
or
INTELLIGENCE SUMMARY.
(Erase heading not required.)

Army Form C. 2118.

Hour, Date, Place	Summary of Events and Information	Remarks and references to Appendices
8.15 AM. 18.12.14 WINCHESTER.	1 Staff Sergt AOC reported and later 1 Sgt and 3 men AOC for duty with HQ.	
9.40 AM " "	Captain Cherry RAMC joined and ~~posted~~ attached to 1/KOYLI.	
	Lieut. McNeil do " " " " 1/Suffolks.	
10.50 am " "	Colonel W.H. Jerome CB RE Bilton Hall York reported as CRE. also Captain G. Master RE as his adjutant.	
11-15 am — " "	DADMS inspects Magdalen Hill Camps for 1 Field Amb and 1 Inf Bde in Coy with DADMS. S.C.	
4.45 pm " "	Major de Brett DSO RA reports for duty as GSO 2nd Grade.	
5 pm. " "	10 Mounted Police report.	
7.15 pm " "	4 Motor Cars arrived 2 for Div HQ 2 for train.	
7.30 pm " "	4 Mes AOD reported for duty with Div HQ & later 4 more —	
9.30 pm " "	Captain Tapley A.V.D reported for duty as A.D.V.S. 28th Div.	
" "	During day a draft of 162 Officers and men arrived for Div Train and 185 for Suffolks. Very wet all day. Mud in camps very bad.	
10 pm " "	4 Motor Cars reported distribution at Present uncertain.	

Instructions regarding War Diaries and Intelligence Summaries are contained in F. S. Regs., Part II. and the Staff Manual respectively. Title pages will be prepared in manuscript.

WAR DIARY
or
INTELLIGENCE SUMMARY.
(*Erase heading not required.*)

Army Form C. 2118.

Hour, Date, Place	Summary of Events and Information	Remarks and references to Appendices
8.15 a.m. 19.12.14 Winchester	Wire 1748 from WO orders Lt. E. Bradley 1/KOYLI to G'Staff for Signal Service	
9. a.m. 19.12.14 "	Information recd from HQ Salisbury that Div Train would arrive 21st Dec.	
10.30 a.m. " "	DAQMG – GSO 2nd Grade – ADVS – ADASC met at Hursley Park and arranged all detail for incoming Bdes –	
12. noon " "	Corporal Lane – L/Cpl Duncan – Pte Clayton reported for G.S. duty.	
12.30 pm " "	Rev Scott reported as Church of England Chaplain vice Rev: Laffan.	
2.30 pm " "	AQMG & other Staff officers inspected Vacated Camp Magdalen Hill found it in bad state of mud & refuse arrangements made for working party of 500 details from 60 Rifle Depot – Hamps: Yeomanry & Hamps Regt T.F. under offrs with transport to clean camp and to improve ~~Staff~~ approaches	
3.30 pm " "	AQMG ~~to~~ made telephonic arrangements with WO that Inf Units arriving from India were to be clothed in suits of ~~to~~ thick Khaki before landing – fitting of suits & ~~boots~~ to be very easy (also woollen drawers socks & cap –	
6 pm " "	Draft of some 162 all ranks arrived for KOYLI.	
7 pm " "	Orders received to take over certain garrison guards necessary arrangements made.	
7.30 pm " "	Wire MGO Salisbury asking that arrangements be made for units arriving from India to fit Service Dress & take warm clothing & boots – 2 pair socks	
10 pm " "	AQMG held conference of transport officers with a view to getting best cooperation.	
	Weather very wet all day.	

(73989) W4141—463. 400,000. 9/14. H.&J.Ltd. Forms/C. 2118/10.

Instructions regarding War Diaries and Intelligence Summaries are contained in F. S. Regs., Part II. and the Staff Manual respectively. Title pages will be prepared in manuscript.

WAR DIARY
or
INTELLIGENCE SUMMARY.
(Erase heading not required.)

Army Form C. 2118.

Hour, Date, Place			Summary of Events and Information	Remarks and references to Appendices
8 am.	20.12.14	W'chester	W.O. notifies that 1 Sqn of E. Surrey Yeomanry is held in readiness by Centre Force to join 28th Div:	
9.30 am	"	"	DAQMG & ESO2 visit Hursley Camp to ascertain if watering arrangements complete, latrines and other details.	
10. am	"	"	W.O. wire further regarding inoculation of RE. Reply sent to effect that all men from India have been inoculated at some time. No Med: officer.	
10.15 am	"	"	Working parties on clearing up Morne hill Camp (under offrs) reported shorthanded. Work progressing but Camp still v. bad.	
12.30 pm	"	"	Arrangements made to leave any S.A.A. not required by units of Inf from India in the Trucks at the Rlway Stn.	
1.30 pm	"	"	Centre Force notifies that 85 & 86 Fd Amb arrive Tuesday 21st all arrangts made.	
2.15 pm	"	"	The RE guard posted on SAA at Rlway Stn relieved.	
2.20 pm	"	"	3 Cars arrived 2 for HQ 1 for RE completing Establishment.	
3 pm	"	"	DAQMG & ESO2 inspected Drummond Jubilee & Morne Hill Camps. latter still v. bad but improving. Roads v. bad – up till now there had been a frost at now rain began ~~completely~~ to fall heavily.	
"	"	"	Conference between AQMG S.C. GOC & AQMG 28th Div:	
4.30 pm	"	"	Considerable difficulties are being experienced in ~~loading~~ finding Transport. There are many services on hand and 27th Div still requires a good deal. AQMG rang up ASC at Southampton and obtained 12 ~~wagons fully~~ pairs of horses	
8 pm	"	"	Conference of administrative Staff and Transport officers regarding work on 21st.	
10.10 pm.			Asked WO ~~for~~ to send the Sqn E. Surrey Yeo: & 4 units RE on Tuesday also wired Centre Force.	

(73989) W4141—463. 400,000. 9/14. H.&J.Ltd. Forms/C. 2118/10.

Army Form C. 2118.

Instructions regarding War Diaries and Intelligence Summaries are contained in F.S. Regs., Part II. and the Staff Manual respectively. Title pages will be prepared in manuscript.

WAR DIARY
or
INTELLIGENCE SUMMARY.

(*Erase heading not required.*)

Hour, Date, Place			Summary of Events and Information	Remarks and references to Appendices
10.45pm	20.12.14	Winchester	Wire advice wire to ~~[illegible]~~ H.Q. Salisbury asking for units disembarking to be warned to fit clothing sufficiently large to take warm clothes underneath and boots to take 2 pr socks.	
9 a.m.	~~21.12.14~~ 21.12.14	"	W/18 wire to Embarking Staff Officer Plymouth warning units to bring haversack ration.	
9.50am.	"	"	R.T.O. calls for working party arrangements made with depot. But these calls for working parties when there are no troops have made things very trying.	
10am.	"	"	DADMS makes final arrangements with R.T.O. — [illegible] & supplies for reception of troops.	
11 am	"	"	arrangements made to move all Rest tents to Pitt Corner tomorrow morning so that the Camp [illegible] go in when they like marquees to be pitched & C.S.L. tents stored in them.	
12.50 pm	"	"	Notification received of arrival of 2/ Northumbrian Ambulance tomorrow evening.	
1.49 pm	"	"	2/London Div Field Amb. arrive strength 6 offs. 160 OR 29 horses and proceeded to Hursley Camp. About 4½ tons of [illegible] Equipment brought with unit.	
2.42 pm.	"	"	Troops of Train arrive total strength 6 offrs. 148 OR. 108 Horses and proceed to Hursley	
4.41 pm	"	"	H.Q. Coy of Train arrives and joins remainder. Strength 7 offs. ~~131~~ 192 OR. ~~82~~ 54 horses.	
5. pm	"	"	Working parties from this ~~[illegible]~~ Coy. Clear the surplus kit left by 1st Ambs. ADMS takes in hand and organises fatigues which have not been satisfactorily for the last 2 or 3 days.	

(73989) W4141—463. 400,000. 9/14. H.&J.Ltd. Forms/C. 2118/10.

Instructions regarding War Diaries and Intelligence Summaries are contained in F. S. Regs., Part II. and the Staff Manual respectively. Title pages will be prepared in manuscript.

WAR DIARY
or
INTELLIGENCE SUMMARY.
(Erase heading not required.)

Army Form C. 2118.

Hour, Date, Place	Summary of Events and Information	Remarks and references to Appendices
5.20pm. 21.12.14 Winchester	3/Lond Fd Amb arrives Strength 7 offrs 131 OR. 82 Horses ~~car~~ about 5 tons of surplus Stores all cleared off by the train.	
10pm. " " " "	2/Northumbrian Fd Amb: Strength 10 offrs 241 OR 50 Horses arrived. Train v. late was due 8.26 pm.	
	Weather Wet ~~cold~~ at first - then cleared up. Hard frost at night.	

(73989) W4141—463. 400,000. 9/14. H.&J.Ltd. Forms/C. 2118/10.

Instructions regarding War Diaries and Intelligence Summaries are contained in F. S. Regs., Part II. and the Staff Manual respectively. Title pages will be prepared in manuscript.

WAR DIARY
or
INTELLIGENCE SUMMARY.
(Erase heading not required.)

Army Form C. 2118.

Hour, Date, Place		Summary of Events and Information	Remarks and references to Appendices
8. am	22.12.14. W'chester	Frost has disappeared leaving camps in very muddy condition.	
12.30 pm	" "	G.O.C. wires W.O. asking for Brigade Staffs Divn	
10.30 am	" "	A.Q.M.G. asks W.O. for R.S. to be sent earlier than Saturday and points out M.D.S. will be affected – W.O. notifies unofficially that Div amm Col is mobilising at Slough and that A.S.C. L of C units will get ready at a'shot.	
11.30 am.	" "	G.O.C. visits Supply Camp at Magdalen Hill – & inspects water supply – issues instructions for tanks to be cleaned out.	
5 pm.	" "	1 Sqn. (B) Surrey Yeomanry arrive. Strength 5 offs. 125 O.R. 121 horses 2 wagons and proceed to Pitt Hill Camp.	
7.44 pm	" "	Information had been received that Infantry units would arrive during night. This was now cancelled. Weather dull.	
		HQ 28th Div: moved to George Hotel.	

(73989) W4141—463. 400,000. 9/14. H.&J.Ltd. Forms/C. 2118/10.

Instructions regarding War Diaries and Intelligence Summaries are contained in F. S. Regs., Part II. and the Staff Manual respectively. Title pages will be prepared in manuscript.

WAR DIARY
or
INTELLIGENCE SUMMARY.
(Erase heading not required.)

Hour, Date, Place			Summary of Events and Information	Remarks and references to Appendices
2.5 pm ~~28-12-14~~	23-12-14	W'chester	1 train with ½ Bn 2/Buffs arrived and proceeded to Magdalen Hill Camp.	
3.30 pm	"	"	Train with ½ Bn. 2/Buffs " " " to Camp. Total Strength 23 offs: 968 OR.	
1.21 ~~4.3~~ pm	"	"	Train with 2/R. Lancs ~~Northumb. Fus arrived~~ Total Strength	
2.20 ~~4.40~~ pm	"	"	" " 2/Kings own R. Lancs 27 offs. 977 OR & proceeded to Hursley Camp.	
4.3 pm. 4.40 "	" "	" "	2/Northumb Fus arrived strength offs: 26 OR 903 arrived & proceeded to Hursley	
5.15 " 6.3 "	" "	" "	1/Welsh Regt arrived 27 offs: 758 OR for Hursley	
6.30 "	"	"	The three B. Inf Bde Majors reported.	
7. pm. 7.45 "	" "	" "	2/E. Yorks arrived & proceeded to Hursley 25 offs. 1027 OR. V. Fine weather	
1.10 am 2.5 "	24/12/14 "	" "	3/Middlesex arrived 23 offs 903 OR for Magdalen Hill	
2.5 " 2.45 "	" "	" "	2/E. Surrey arrived for Magdalen Hill 20 offs 966 OR	
3.45 " 4.25 "	" "	" "	3/R. Fus " " " 25 " 948 "	

Instructions regarding War Diaries and Intelligence Summaries are contained in F. S. Regs., Part II. and the Staff Manual respectively. Title pages will be prepared in manuscript.

WAR DIARY
or
INTELLIGENCE SUMMARY.
(Erase heading not required.)

Army Form C. 2118.

Hour, Date, Place	Summary of Events and Information	Remarks and references to Appendices
2.10 pm 24.12.14 W'Chester 3.35 " " "	} 2/ Cheshire R. arrived 21 off. 895 OR for Hursley	
5. pm " "	Bdr Gen Wintour departed.	
5.30 pm " " 6.30 " " "	} 1/4 Lancs arrived 24 off 967 OR. for Hursley. also Rear Party of 2/E. Yorks.	
10 pm. " "	Capt Lebb. Staff Capt 83rd Inf. Bde arrived.	
	Weather fine.	
	onwards from 5 pm 25% of troops from India proceeded on furlough for 3 clear days.	

(73989) W4141—463. 400,000. 9/14. H.&J.Ltd. Forms/C. 2118/10.

Army Form C. 2118.

WAR DIARY
or
INTELLIGENCE SUMMARY.
(*Erase heading not required.*)

Instructions regarding War Diaries and Intelligence Summaries are contained in F. S. Regs., Part II. and the Staff Manual respectively. Title pages will be prepared in manuscript.

Hour, Date, Place	Summary of Events and Information	Remarks and references to Appendices
— 25.12.14 W'Chester	Xmas Day – owing to heavy work during last 3 days Motor Transport given a rest as far as practicable. Several wires and letters from WO received during day pointed to possibility of raid in immediate future – and that anything up to 8000 men required in that case from 28th Div. Following arrangements made – Personnel.. Inf Bdes held in readiness in following order 85: 84: 83: To move with new Rifles – 100 Rnds Mk VII 1 Blanket 1 days Pres: Rations for 7000 men necessary arrangements made. ADMG. used S'hampton and Reading for supplies as there were insufficient at W'chester – 2 days for 7000 supervised by S'hampton to reach W'chester by morning – Sufficient S.A. Amn already at Camps – Rifles actually issued – Transport warned and organised for the move – necessary Staff arrangements made for warning Heads of departments arrangements completed about 10.30pm.	
12 noon 25.12.14 "	GOC telephoned to AG2 WO pointing out necessity of allowing officers extra weight on a/c of warm clothing as R&F had been allowed blankets	
5 pm " "	notification received from WO of dispatch of Artillery & Infantry drafts – also of guns & amn waggons.	
10 pm " "	weather dull & inclined to rain	

(73989) W4141—463. 400,000. 9/14. H.&J.Ltd. Forms/C. 2118/10.

Instructions regarding War Diaries and Intelligence Summaries are contained in F. S. Regs., Part II. and the Staff Manual respectively. Title pages will be prepared in manuscript.

WAR DIARY
or
INTELLIGENCE SUMMARY.
(Erase heading not required.)

Army Form C. 2118.

Hour, Date, Place	Summary of Events and Information	Remarks and references to Appendices
2.5 am. 26-12-14 W'chester	9-18 Prs and some 50 waggons with unfused Amn arrived. From numbers on waggons it appears that these were intended for Leamington. Question referred to DGA –	
2-20 pm. " " "	173 Rfles arrived for 1/Welsh R.	
2.36 " " " "	3/London Fd Coy RE arrived. 6 Offrs: 236 OR 76 horses with waggons and proceeded to Pitt Corner.	
— " " –	During afternoon following reported Brig Genl Boyle for 83 Inf Bde – Major Sir Grogan as GSO 3rd grade – General Chapman reported 26th: Total Brigadiers are now Complete.	
9-55 pm " " –	Following drafts arrived. 32 Rfles for Buffs: 62 for R. Fus: 30 for E. Surrey.	
11-15 pm " " "	" " " Y&L 36 : Middlesex 86.	
" "	Instructions issued to Yeomanry & RE to proceed with rearming with new Rifles –	
	GOC informed verbally by Telephone that he would receive a T.F. Bn in France (from Malta) fully equipped.	
	Weather Wet	

(73989) W4141—463. 400,000. 9/14. H.&J.Ltd. Forms/C. 2118/10.

Instructions regarding War Diaries and Intelligence Summaries are contained in F. S. Regs., Part II. and the Staff Manual respectively. Title pages will be prepared in manuscript.

WAR DIARY
or
INTELLIGENCE SUMMARY.
(Erase heading not required.)

Army Form C. 2118.

Hour, Date, Place			Summary of Events and Information	Remarks and references to Appendices
9 a.m.	27-12-14	W'chester	Information recd from D of A [illegible] G.S. that the guns & waggons which arrived yesterday would be kept by the here & that an expert would be sent to assist	
11 am	"	"	Rev. C. Bateson Lee of R.A.T.A. Called reference formation of Institutes of (A.T.A) in Camps at Hursley. situation explained.	
12 noon	"	"	Information received that advance Sub: Equipment would now arrive continuously arrangements made accordingly but about 2 pm transport ~~broke down~~ became insufficient	
2 pm	"	"	HQ of Bdes Inf Bdes drew Equipment. Div HQ drew yesterday.	
6 pm.	"	"	A.O.D receive notice of despatch of the 4 Vickers M.G.s. ammn.	
"	"	"	Telephones 88 Wo asking where unfit soldiers are to go — also procedure in case of unfit officer. asks for authority to Equip officers same as men. Hastens despatch of Batteries. Replies promised	
7.30 pm	"	"	77 Rcts join for Welsh Regt.	
10 pm	"	"	DADOS reports waggons arriving for the arrangements made to draw them. also reports he is about 100 waggons short. arrangements made for the mounted patrol to go over the ground and report what they can find.	
"	"	"	In 31 to [illegible] Fire reporting Yeomen [illegible] Weather dull - Thaw & wet - warm.	

(73989) W4141—463. 400,000. 9/14. H.&J.Ltd. Forms/C. 2118/10.

Army Form C. 2118.

Instructions regarding War Diaries and Intelligence Summaries are contained in F. S. Regs., Part II. and the Staff Manual respectively. Title pages will be prepared in manuscript.

WAR DIARY
or
INTELLIGENCE SUMMARY.
(Erase heading not required.)

Hour, Date, Place			Summary of Events and Information	Remarks and references to Appendices
8 am.	28-12-14	W'chester.	Drawing of Stores by Bde & Div Hd Qrs continued also by K.O.R. Lancs and 4 Buffs and 24 Waggons by R. Artillery.	
11am.	"	"	G.O.C. visited Magdalen Hill and Hursley Camps.	
12 noon	"	"	A.Q.M.G. ascertained from W.O. that tent equipment is allowed for for Officers and is accounted for in the tables.	
7.30 pm	"	"	A violent Squall which blew down part of Camp Hospital at Hursley also part of Morne Hill Camp. Patients evacuated from Hursley to Red X Hosp: Winchester. Considerable number of men (nearly 300) from Morne Hill Camp billetted in Guild Hall.	
			During day Div Train armed with Rifles.	
			4 Vickers M.G. arrived.	

(73989) W4141—463. 400,000. 9/14. H.&J.Ltd. Forms/C. 2118/10.

Instructions regarding War Diaries and Intelligence Summaries are contained in F. S. Regs., Part II. and the Staff Manual respectively. Title pages will be prepared in manuscript.

Army Form C. 2118.

WAR DIARY
or
INTELLIGENCE SUMMARY.

(*Erase heading not required.*)

Hour, Date, Place	Summary of Events and Information	Remarks and references to Appendices
28-12-14 - 2.45am. W'chester	Draft of 233 RE arrived from Ireland.	
9.30am. 28-12-14 "	DAQMG visited Hursley Camps to ascertain extent of damage & if anything could be done to remedy matters found that practically all marquees were down especially office tents. Everyone however cheerful. The weather was very fine and sun shining which helped to improve matters v. much.	
4.25pm " "	as asked by AQMG. ~~WO despatch~~ 3 Sunbeam cars received from WO to replace others.	
" " "	WO Formations called upon to ~~return~~ render return of Horses in possession.	
6pm " "	accurate State of personnel rendered by units.	
4pm " "	WO Telephone that Staff Capts from 84 & 85 Inf Bdes must be selected from Inf Bdes — and that 2 more Field Coys will ~~come~~ arrive shortly.	
6.30pm " "	Draft of 98 men arrive for 3/Middlesex During the day following units progressed in mobilisation as follows — Div HQ: Bde HQ 83, 84, 85: KOYLI. Practically completed Suffolks - E. Surrey. 3/Bde HQ RFA. Complete except Tech: Stores. 366 Batty completed all G1098. 2/18 Batty and 75 Completed. also 3/4 of Buffs. weather fine & sunny.	

Instructions regarding War Diaries and Intelligence Summaries are contained in F. S. Regs., Part II. and the Staff Manual respectively. Title pages will be prepared in manuscript.

Army Form C. 2118.

WAR DIARY
or
INTELLIGENCE SUMMARY.
(Erase heading not required.)

Hour, Date, Place			Summary of Events and Information	Remarks and references to Appendices
9 am.	30.12.14	W'chester	Mobilisation Progressing.	
11 am	" "	"	Owing to apparent delay in issue of Remounts AQMG interviewed OC Remounts Winchester and it was finally arranged that issue of Remounts should commence tomorrow: with [illegible] & RA.	
2 pm	"	"	Information received that the Div Sig Coy will proceed abroad at present strength and we will have 1 additional Cable Section trained & sent after it.	
3 pm	"	"	GOC visited Western Camps.	
			During the day the following progress was made in Mobn: Div HQ completed. HQ 83, 84, 85 Inf Bdes completed Blankets. KOR Lancs: KOYLI: 1/Suffolk 3/R. Fus: 366 Batty completed Blankets & 1/8 other Stores. 2/Buffs: 3/Bde RA: 18th Batty: 365th Batty: 69th Batty: ~~100th~~ 103rd Batty 366th & 367th all blankets & 7/8 other Stores: 2/R. Fus: 81st Fa Bde 100th & 103rd Battys also received Stores. On the whole Stores coming in well. Weather fine then wet. Mobile Vety Section arrived also 80 Batmen.	

(73989) W4141—463. 400,000. 9/14. H.&J.Ltd. Forms/C. 2118/10.

Instructions regarding War Diaries and Intelligence Summaries are contained in F. S. Regs., Part II. and the Staff Manual respectively. Title pages will be prepared in manuscript.

WAR DIARY
or
INTELLIGENCE SUMMARY.
(Erase heading not required.)

Army Form C. 2118.

Hour, Date, Place	Summary of Events and Information	Remarks and references to Appendices
9.45 am. 31-12-14 W'chester	Notification of arrivals ~~noted~~ from RTO including 6 offrs: 120 OR: 3 Wagons: 1 Cart: 15 horses from Christchurch unit unknown.	
" " "	~~Sat~~ HQ S.C. authorised whole of mangy horses total 32 viz 16 from Tutts Yd. 2 RE, 2 London Fd A: 16 Train: to be sent to Fareham ~~with~~ by rail 1st Jan: in charge of Mobile Vety Sec: now at Winchester. Also later ~~horses~~ authorised horses of 3/London Fd Amb. to be moved too	All documents referred to are stored at WINCHESTER
1.18 am " "	The troops notified for 1.18 pm turned out to be horses required for 27th Div: details.	
3.30 pm " "	1/N. M. Fd Coy strength 6 offs 229 other ranks. 8 - 4 wheeled vehicles. 6 - 2 wheeled. 33 bikes arrived & encamped at Hursley.	
	Weather wet.	

3/1/15

A. Allen-Stand
Major
D.A.Q.M.G. 28th Div.

(73989) W4141—463. 400,000. 9/14. H.&J.Ltd. Forms/C. 2118/10.

(5825) Wt. W 7504-1562. 15,000 Pads. Wy. & S., Ltd. Sch. 19. 329. 2 10 am Army Form C 2123.

C Form. (Original.) **MESSAGES & ~~SIGNALS.~~** No. of Message

Rec^d from | Prefix | Code | Words | Sent, or sent out At .M. | Office Stamp.

Delivery. Means | Distance | Charges for Delivery. Collected | Paid out | By | Returned at .M.

By

Service Instructions. 11-5 [illegible]

Handed in at the [illegible] *Office at* .M. *Received here at* .M.

TO 28 Div HQ

*Sender's Number | *Day of Month* | *In reply to Number* | **A. A. A.**

your Message G. 34 AAA 5244 rounds of pistol ammunition sent for practice purposes

FROM D A D O S 28 Div
PLACE
TIME

All Porterage, Redirection, or other charges collected on delivery are to be brought to account by means of Stamps affixed to the face of the form, and the particulars of such charges and of amounts paid out are to be set forth in writing above, in the space headed "Delivery" and "Charges for Delivery."
* This line should be erased if not required.

121 / 4505

Headquarters (A & Q) 28th Division

Vol III. 1 – 28.2.15

Feb 13th – Remarks on casualties from swollen feet and frost bite –

" 14th – Formation of 4 gun batteries.

" 23rd–24th – Difficulty of obtaining R E Stores –

" 25th – Arrival of Detachment of "Kickers" (not horses) –

" – Arrival of Motor M.G. battery

Confidential
War Diary
of the
ADMINISTRATIVE STAFF
(A.G. & Q.M.G. Branches)
28th Division

From 1st January 1915 to 31st Jany 1915

Vol II

[illegible]
Maj DAQMG
28 Div

I/15

<u>Confidential</u>

War Diary of the
Administrative Staff
28th Division

From 1st Feb 1915 to 28th Feb 1915

Instructions regarding War Diaries and Intelligence Summaries are contained in F. S. Regs., Part II. and the Staff Manual respectively. Title pages will be prepared in manuscript.

WAR DIARY
or
INTELLIGENCE SUMMARY.
(Erase heading not required.)

Army Form C. 2118.

Hour, Date, Place			Summary of Events and Information	Remarks and references to Appendices
11.30am.	1.1.15	W'chester	207 ~~mangy~~ horses of which 46 affected with mange despatched to Fareham.	
1pm	"	"	G.O.C. decides to billet 83rd Inf: Bde owing to state of Camp now under water owing to incessant rain which today is very heavy – Chief of City Police and Borough Sanitary Engineer ~~Officer~~ also ~~M.O.H.~~ Medical Officer of Health brought to H.Q. – whole question discussed and rapidly arranged &	
3pm	"	"	orders issued. At 3pm. orders issued for 85th Bde to move into billets – ~~B~~ areas in Winchester as follows. 83rd Inf Bde South of High St – 85th N of High Street & East of Jewry Street. E of L.&S.W.R.)	
7.15pm	"	"	83 Inf Bde in billets W'chester.	
8.30pm	"	"	85 " " " " "	
			In spite of the foregoing mobilisation progressed as usual –	
			During the day the following drafts arrived –	
			4 Suffolks 2 Offrs & 61 O.R.	
			4 Buffs " 17	
			E. Surrey " 11	
			Weather v. wet – a semi tropical downpour combined with cold wind. Camps practically under water.	

(73989) W4141—463. 400,000. 9/14. H.&J.Ltd. Forms/C. 2118/10.

Instructions regarding War Diaries and Intelligence Summaries are contained in F. S. Regs., Part II. and the Staff Manual respectively. Title pages will be prepared in manuscript.

WAR DIARY
or
INTELLIGENCE SUMMARY.
(Erase heading not required.)

Army Form C. 2118.

Hour, Date, Place			Summary of Events and Information	Remarks and references to Appendices
9 am	2·1·15	W'chester	Transport employed chiefly in moving in Stock Equipment from Camps of 83rd & 84th Inf. Bdes to Billets.	
			83 & 85 Inf Bdes expanded into more buildings – the principle being to use large buildings then empty houses.	
			Drawing of Stores by hand continued.	
			Area reconnoitred for billets in the adjacent Country.	
11 am	"	"	Draft of 18 men arrived for 3/R. Fus.	
3·30pm	"	"	Arrangements made to bring Coys of Train allotted to 83 & 85 Inf Bdes into their Bde areas – & to move the Hd Qr and 84th Bde Coys into billets at Horsley this was completed by 6pm.	
"	"	"	Draft of 158 men arrived for 2/Cheers:	
"	"	"	Arrangements made to bring ee 1/North: Fd Amb and 2/London Fd Amb:	
			Weather fine then wet.	

(73989) W4141—463. 400,000. 9/14. H.&J.Ltd. Forms/C. 2118/10.

WAR DIARY
or
INTELLIGENCE SUMMARY.
(Erase heading not required.)

Army Form C. 2118.

Instructions regarding War Diaries and Intelligence Summaries are contained in F. S. Regs., Part II. and the Staff Manual respectively. Title pages will be prepared in manuscript.

Hour, Date, Place			Summary of Events and Information	Remarks and references to Appendices
10 am.	3-1-15	W'chester	It had been raining all night and as heavy rain was still falling it was decided to bring in ~~the~~ the 4/Ches & 1/Welsh into billets in the afternoon.	
2 pm	"	"	The Two Bns began to move into billets – also the 2/London & Northumbrian Fd Ambs.	
8 am	"	"	The 1/Northumbrian Fd Coy RE arrived Strength 6 officers 232 OR. 72 horses and 5 vehicles also 15 Tons baggage & camped at Hensley	
"	"	"	Draft of 57 men for 4 K.O.R. Lancs also arrived	
10.8 am	"	"	Draft of 65 R[illegible] arrived for 2/North: Fus:	
			Considerable difficulty experienced with Transport.	
			The following ~~being under~~ work being all in hand at same time – i moving M.T. Equipment of ~~Fd Ambs~~ 83 & 85 Inf Bdes into Winchester	
			ii " in ~~Stores~~ Kits & blankets of 2 Bns of 84th also 2/Lond F.A. and 2/North F.A.	
			iii Distribution of M.T. Equipment	
			iv ordinary Services	
6 pm	"	"	4/Ches: and 1/Welsh: in billets by 6.15 pm.	
			Evening wet & Snowy	

(73989) W4141—463. 400,000. 9/14. H.&J.Ltd. Forms/C. 2118/10.

Instructions regarding War Diaries and Intelligence Summaries are contained in F. S. Regs., Part II. and the Staff Manual respectively. Title pages will be prepared in manuscript.

WAR DIARY
or
INTELLIGENCE SUMMARY.
(Erase heading not required.)

Army Form C. 2118.

Hour, Date, Place	Summary of Events and Information	Remarks and references to Appendices
10 am 4.1.15 W'chester	Orders issued for the HQ 84 Inf Bde & 2/1 Suffolks and 2/Norths Fus to move into Billets at Winchester also 3/Lond Fd. Coy Horses. Considerable difficulty about transport owing to the various services on hand viz. (i) movement of Inf Stores 83 Inf Bde into W'chester. (ii) " " Equipment 84 " " " (iii) Drawing Equipment	
12 noon 4.1.15 "	Question brought up by Corresp Surveyor as to difficulty of increasing Latrine accomodation in billets especially as the local CRE has withdrawn the Municipal Contractor Perry's men from the work in order to continue hutting for 29th Division – eventually after a long discussion between Local HQ authorities – HQ 28 Div and So Command arranged that R.E.T.F. Coy should carry on the work commencing tomorrow 5th.	
5 pm 4.1.15 "	HQ 84 Inf Bde. 1/Suffolks, 2/Norths Fus came in to Billets. Weather V. fine.	

Instructions regarding War Diaries and Intelligence Summaries are contained in F. S. Regs., Part II. and the Staff Manual respectively. Title pages will be prepared in manuscript.

WAR DIARY
or
INTELLIGENCE SUMMARY.
(Erase heading not required.)

Army Form C. 2118.

Hour, Date, Place			Summary of Events and Information	Remarks and references to Appendices
8am.	5.1.15	W'chester	Movement of ~~Bags~~ Units Equipment into W'chester from Hursley continued – Many Vehicles arrived during the night also S.A.A. These are being issued. The improvement of Sanitary arrangements & Cooking facilities in billets progressing satisfactorily.	
2.15pm	"	"	Home Counties Div Sig Coy arrived in strength 5 offrs 166 OR 90 horses 12 Vehicles & proceeded into billets at St Cross.	
2-30pm	"	"	Drawing of Units ~~Am~~ S.A.A. Commenced with 88 Inf Bde.	
12 noon	"	"	Draft of 75 Drivers arrived for R.A.	
6.15pm	"	"	" " " 33 Ptes arrived for 3/Middlesex.	
9 pm	"	"	AA&QMG held Conference of Staff officers to discuss doubtful points remaining regarding mobilisation – also movement overseas.	
			During day mobilisation proceeded. Work done chiefly clearing mobilisation Stores accumulated during the night at the Corn Exchange also the S.A.A. & certain Vehicles.	
			Weather fine but wet for one hour in the afternoon.	

(73989) W4141—463. 400,000. 9/14. H.&J.Ltd. Forms/C. 2118/10.

Instructions regarding War Diaries and Intelligence Summaries are contained in F. S. Regs., Part II. and the Staff Manual respectively. Title pages will be prepared in manuscript.

WAR DIARY
or
INTELLIGENCE SUMMARY.
(Erase heading not required.)

Army Form C. 2118.

Hour, Date, Place	Summary of Events and Information	Remarks and references to Appendices
9.30 am 6.1.15 W'chester	Remounts Suspended all other work to remount 3:7a Bde. for Emergency duty.	
	Work proceeded satisfactorily — Whole of 3:F.A. Bde. Completed with Horses —	
	Following Drafts arrived during the day	
10.30 am " "	1 officer & 24 O.R. R.F.A.	
1.20 pm " "	1 " " 51 " "	
1.20 pm " "	" 11 " "	
3.30 pm " "	1 " 27 " "	
3.45 pm " "	1 " 31 " "	
4.30 " " "	2 " 95 " "	
5.5 pm " "	1 " 27 " 2/S. Yorks	
5.5 pm " "	1 " 55 " K.O.Y.L.I.	
7.59 pm " "	" 73 " Y&L.	
	Weather Fine — wet in Evening.	

(73989) W4141—463. 400,000. 9/14. H.&J.Ltd. Forms/C. 2118/10.

Instructions regarding War Diaries and Intelligence Summaries are contained in F. S. Regs., Part II. and the Staff Manual respectively. Title pages will be prepared in manuscript.

WAR DIARY
or
INTELLIGENCE SUMMARY.
(Erase heading not required.)

Army Form C. 2118.

Hour, Date, Place	Summary of Events and Information	Remarks and references to Appendices
10 am – 7·1·15 W'chester	12 Plts arrived for 2/ North'd Fus.	
3·55 pm – 7·1·15 ..	13 .. .. .. 2/ Buffs.	
9· pm –	A conference of all Qr Masters ~~was held~~ with A.A. & Q.M.G. & DADOS was held. At conference any rulings not generally understood were given out & explained – all compared notes as to deficiencies and surpluses. In fact a sort of clearing house was formed. The great difficulty is to get in actual deficiencies	
	Weather fine – not ~~very~~ cold.	

(73989) W4141—463. 400,000. 9/14. H.&J.Ltd. Forms/C. 2118/10.

Instructions regarding War Diaries and Intelligence Summaries are contained in F. S. Regs., Part II. and the Staff Manual respectively. Title pages will be prepared in manuscript.

WAR DIARY
or
INTELLIGENCE SUMMARY.
(*Erase heading not required.*)

Army Form C. 2118.

Hour, Date, Place			Summary of Events and Information	Remarks and references to Appendices
12.25 pm	8-1-15	W'ter	22 Privates arrived for R.O.R. Lancs.	
5.49 "	"	"	3 offrs & 139 OR arrived for R.F.A.	
6.41 "	"	"	Draft arrived for 1/9 DL.	
9 pm	"	"	Conference of Qr Masters DAQMG & DADOS.	
10 pm	"	"	8.8 W.O. by telephone explained that a statement of deficiencies in Stationery of units to be sent by post to D of MB on Q[?] – Probably no difficulty in obtaining Rifles for officers. Probably no siege lamps ~~for~~ available for night firing by M. Guns.	
12 mn.	"	"	Special orderly to Ordnance Portsmouth with list of deficiencies – Weather v. fine.	

(73989) W4141—463. 400,000. 9/14. H.&J.Ltd. Forms/C. 2118/10.

Instructions regarding War Diaries and Intelligence Summaries are contained in F. S. Regs., Part II. and the Staff Manual respectively. Title pages will be prepared in manuscript.

WAR DIARY
or
INTELLIGENCE SUMMARY.
(Erase heading not required.)

Army Form C. 2118.

Hour, Date, Place	Summary of Events and Information	Remarks and references to Appendices
9 am. 9 - 1 - 15 W'chester	Mobilisation Proceeding - units handing in surplus harness - and blankets - ~~St~~ Certain harness - Longer Web Equip belts issued - Ammunition Reserve. ~~Horses~~ Remounts continue to issue horses.	
9 pm " " "	Conference of Quartermasters - one main point being carrying of Rifles by officers - Water Parties or Drummers. Weather Fine	

Instructions regarding War Diaries and Intelligence Summaries are contained in F. S. Regs., Part II. and the Staff Manual respectively. Title pages will be prepared in manuscript.

WAR DIARY
or
INTELLIGENCE SUMMARY.
(Erase heading not required.)

Army Form C. 2118.

Hour, Date, Place			Summary of Events and Information	Remarks and references to Appendices
–	10.1.15	W'chester	Mobilisation progressing in some details but very little came in by night. No stationery yet – and many deficiencies in harness.	
2pm.	"	"	GOC ruled officers not to carry rifles but drummers and water parties to carry them except Reserve.	
3pm	"	"	GOC organised massed band performance of Sacred Tunes and National Anthems	
6pm	"	"	Conference of Quartermasters who were urged to hand in surpluses —	
			Wire received at 3pm asking GOC when he would be ready to start.	Appendix I
			GOC replied 14th partially. 15th the Bulk – 17th all ready. Later wire ordered Entraining officers & 6 others to proceed.	Appendix II
11.38pm	"	"	They did so. Major Sir Grogan – Major Reeves & others.	
			Weather Fine & wet in evening	

(73989) W4141—463. 400,000. 9/14. H.&J.Ltd. Forms/C. 2118/10.

Instructions regarding War Diaries and Intelligence Summaries are contained in F. S. Regs., Part II. and the Staff Manual respectively. Title pages will be prepared in manuscript.

WAR DIARY
or
INTELLIGENCE SUMMARY.
(Erase heading not required.)

Army Form C. 2118.

Hour, Date, Place	Summary of Events and Information	Remarks and references to Appendices
9 am. 11.1.15 W'chester	~~Necessary~~ Preparations being made at CHEESEFOOT HEAD-Fawley Down for H.M. the Kings inspection of the Divn	
10.30 am " "	GOC inspected horses considered unsuitable.	
4.30 pm " "	Wire advising Division to move 15th Received	Appendix 3
5.30 pm " "	" " ~~Billetting~~ Billetting Party to move Received.	
	~~Weather~~ Mobilisation Proceeding more rapidly — Deficiencies are mainly unimportant.	
	Weather. Fine. Then wet.	

Instructions regarding War Diaries and Intelligence Summaries are contained in F. S. Regs., Part II. and the Staff Manual respectively. Title pages will be prepared in manuscript.

WAR DIARY
or
INTELLIGENCE SUMMARY.
(Erase heading not required.)

Army Form C. 2118.

Hour, Date, Place	Summary of Events and Information	Remarks and references to Appendices
7am - 12 - 1 - 15 W'chester	Billeting Party of DAA & QMG & Staff Capts left for Boulogne via Folkestone with 4 Cars –.	
10.40am " "	H.M. the King and Lord Kitchener inspected the Division at Fawley Down – Parade 13000 Strong. RA Firing Batteries only. RAMC. ASC. Personnel only.	
11am " "	WO notifies movements & Ports of Embarkation of certain L of C Units. e.g. ~~1st Bakery, 1st Butchery~~ Div Supply Col: Ammtn Park. RAMC Motors and Workshop. Cas: Clearing Stn ~~also~~ Sanitary Sec and Div Amm Col.	
7pm " "	Meeting of Bde Majors and Adjutants to clear up question of deficiency of Personnel – During day DADRT S'thampton submitted details of 1st day Embarkation. Telephoned later ~~regarding~~ to say now uncertain on a/c of fact that only 9 troop trains were allowed in transfer diem –	Appendix IV
	Weather v. fine.	

(73989) W4141—463. 400,000. 9/14. H.&J.Ltd. Forms/C. 2118/10.

Instructions regarding War Diaries and Intelligence Summaries are contained in F. S. Regs., Part II. and the Staff Manual respectively. Title pages will be prepared in manuscript.

WAR DIARY
or
INTELLIGENCE SUMMARY.
(*Erase heading not required.*)

Army Form C. 2118.

Hour, Date, Place	Summary of Events and Information	Remarks and references to Appendices
2pm. 13 ~~14~~·1·15 Winchester	R.A. reported 1100 Rounds Ammunition deficient for the first time. AA&QMG. made arrangements with W.O. to complete the first 2 FA Bdes to 90 a gun rate.	
4pm 13 ~~14~~-1-16 "	Received programme of Embarkation of units for 1st and 2nd days Embarkation Mobilisation nearly completed – Horses complete on 12th except for Casualties. Following Points have been learnt for future. (i) Wrong attempt to mobilise in Camp in winter in England – (ii) It appears faulty to address consignments of Stores to units as it takes the matter out of the hands of the DADOS and leads to duplication of indents. (iii) Moreover owing to lack of packing cases – with 28 Div many cases arrived marked with the description of stores they did not contain units read the description and discarded cases – Following drafts arrived 30 for 1/Suffolks 15 for 8. Yorks. 25 for North Lanc. Weather V. fine.	

(73989) W4141—463. 400,000. 9/14. H.&J.Ltd. Forms/C. 2118/10.

Instructions regarding War Diaries and Intelligence Summaries are contained in F. S. Regs., Part II. and the Staff Manual respectively. Title pages will be prepared in manuscript.

WAR DIARY
or
INTELLIGENCE SUMMARY

(Erase heading not required.)

Army Form C. 2118.

Hour, Date, Place	Summary of Events and Information	Remarks and references to Appendices
12.1 am. 14.1.15 W'chester	Major Grogan GSO from HAVRE asks if EOC intends to draw full scale of warm clothing as laid down or only skin waistcoats. EOC replies skin waistcoats only & wishes them drawn in bulk.	
5 pm " "	By WO letter QMG 2/123 d/ 11.1.15. 118 SW were directed to order 21 motor ambs to await orders - but as none had arrived here telephonic enquiries were made to WO with the result that WO replied that these field ambs had been ordered to leave London for Avonmouth by the W.O. itself.	appendix 5 –
7 pm " "	Wire from Havre asks for billeting parties of 1 off 5 NCOs & 1 bike per unit to be sent tomorrow - action taken	
	Weather fine –	
		AAW(?)

44

1247 W 3299 200,000 (E) 8/14 J.B.C. & A. Forms/C. 2118/11.

Army Form C. 2118.

Instructions regarding War Diaries and Intelligence Summaries are contained in F. S. Regs., Part II. and the Staff Manual respectively. Title pages will be prepared in manuscript.

WAR DIARY
or
INTELLIGENCE SUMMARY
(Erase heading not required.)

Hour, Date, Place		Summary of Events and Information	Remarks and references to Appendices
8.30 am	15.1.15 W'r	The Division commenced move to Southampton for Embarkation – units moving are shown below.	
2 pm	15.1.15 "	Reference appendix 5 Major Grogan wires warm clothing can be issued in bulk & accompany first few trains each day – remainder must ~~entrain~~ distribute before Entrainment.	appendix 6
	15.1.15 "	The following units of 83 Inf Bde – 3rd Bde RFA – HQ, HQ Coy & No 2 Coy Div Train. No 2 Lndn F. Amb – HQ & 1 Sec Signal Coy HQ 28 Div Unit – arrived at Southampton Docks by 3pm 15/1/15 – 15 minutes before time without incident & 4 vessels put to sea before 5.30pm. The remaining 2 later – of these latter one vessel the Trafford Hall was slow supplying to the very steep "brows" unsuitable for any horse especially H.D. Horses	
10 pm	" "	Following Drafts arrived & proceeded to Southampton for Embarkation tomorrow. 65 R Lancs – 15 YL – their Bns having sailed today –	
		Weather Fine till 5 pm Then v. wet.	A.A. McH.

1247 W 3299 200,000 (E) 8/14 J.B.C. & A. Forms/C. 2118/11.

Instructions regarding War Diaries and Intelligence Summaries are contained in F. S. Regs., Part II. and the Staff Manual respectively. Title pages will be prepared in manuscript.

WAR DIARY
or
INTELLIGENCE SUMMARY
(Erase heading not required.)

Army Form C. 2118.

Hour, Date, Place	Summary of Events and Information	Remarks and references to Appendices
8.30 am 16.1.15 W'chester	The second portion of the Division commenced to march from Winchester for Southampton — all units arrived well up to time the first ship being loaded by 3.30 am the last about 5 pm. The following units embarked by Sqn Surrey Yeo; 84th Inf Bde; 31st Bde R.F.A. No 3 Sec Div Sig Coy — No 3 Coy Div Train; 31 London Fd Amb.	
6.15 pm 16.1.15 [illegible]	405 men arrived for 3/ Middlesex R.	
7.45 pm 16.1.15 W'chester	Information received from RE that the 1200 Rounds of ammunition of which they were short had arrived at Winchester Station. Arrangements made to send on to Southampton for loading tomorrow.	
7 pm " "	6875 QMG 2 wire received from W.O. that owing to bad weather ships couldn't sail and that only 2 trains load tomorrow — received Spoke D.A.D.R.T. on Telephone who said only No 4 Sec Div Sig Coy — Buffs & No 4 Coy Div Train would embark tomorrow — necessary arrangements made — Spoke H.Q. So Command on Telephone — ~~Weather Fine~~ Wire from QMG 2; 6861 reships 1 off 874 OR of Ammunition Park with 200 lorries Ammunition will reach Newhaven for embarkation tomorrow. Weather Fine till 5 pm then wet	Appendix 7

a a M H:

Instructions regarding War Diaries and Intelligence Summaries are contained in F. S. Regs., Part II. and the Staff Manual respectively. Title pages will be prepared in manuscript.

WAR DIARY
or
INTELLIGENCE SUMMARY
(Erase heading not required.)

Army Form C. 2118.

Hour, Date, Place			Summary of Events and Information	Remarks and references to Appendices
8-25 am	17-1-15	W'chester	Further units of the Division proceeded to Southampton for embarkation as follows. No 4 Sec. Div Sig Coy. 2/Buffs. No 4 Coy Div Train. The Div Amm. Col arrived by train from Slough & embarked. L of C units have embarked as follows. 28th Field Baky, Field Butchery – No 16 Rlway Supply Det. No 38 & 39 Depot units of Supply all on 14th Jan. The Div Amm Park and Supply Col: is embarking from AVONMOUTH. The Reserve Park does not proceed.	
2.20 pm	"	"	GOC accompanied by G.S.O 1st Grade and A.A. & Q.M.G. proceeded to France via Boulogne.—	
7 pm	"	"	The ammunition (RA) reported deficient on 13th reached W'chester last night and is now alongside the embarking jetty for 146 Bde Amm: Col:	See 13th Jan
		France.	Following troops arrived in billeting areas: 2/E. Yorks: 18th Batty RFA; HQ 23rd Bde 62nd Batty RFA; 2 Platoons 2/E Yorks Weather Fine	

1247 W 3299 200,000 (E) 8/14 J.B.C. & A. Forms/C. 2118/11.

Instructions regarding War Diaries and Intelligence Summaries are contained in F. S. Regs., Part II. and the Staff Manual respectively. Title pages will be prepared in manuscript.

WAR DIARY
or
INTELLIGENCE SUMMARY
(Erase heading not required.)

Army Form C. 2118.

Hour, Date, Place		Summary of Events and Information	Remarks and references to Appendices
8.20 am	18.1.15 Winchester	Remaining Troops 28th Div marched from WINCHESTER for Southampton and embarked. Troops as follows; 28 Cyclist Coy: HQ & 5th Inf Bde. 1/2 Surreys, 3rd Middlesex 3rd Royal Fus: 146th ~~Fa~~ Brigade RFA: 1/N. Mid Fd Coy: 2nd Lond & 3rd Lond: Fd Coys R.E. 2/Northumbrian Fd Amb: HQ, RA & RE: also Rear party consisting of GSO2, DADMS, A.P.M. DADSC ~~& dets~~ DADOS & details of other ranks – The troops left in good order and the last unit completed its march 10 minutes before allotted time – Weather v. fine and frosty	
	" HAVRE	Troops continuing to arrive were met by RTOs both permanent and [illegible] detailed from 28th Div:– Most of units were entrained direct from the landing Jetties – The Buffs and Div Ammn Col proceeded to Rest Camp the entrainment was assisted by Major Sir E. Grogan GSO3 and Major Reeves the Buffs.	
	" HAZEBRUCK & St OMER	As troops arrived they were met by Capt Troyte, A.A. & Q.M.G. at St OMER the Regulating Station. Capt Troyte had previously allotted Billetting areas + directed trains accordingly. Troops were met ~~[illegible]~~ by Staff Captains who conducted troops to their areas. The Billetting parties proved very useful except that they arrived too late to be of use to the 83rd Inf Bde – Following troops arrived in billetting areas 1/K.O.Y.L.I: HQ & No 1 Sec Sig Coy: HQ & one Coy Div Train: 2 Platoons K.O.Y.L.I: 3rd Bde Ammn Col RFA: 2/London Fd Amb: 1/K.O.R. Lancs 365th Batty R.F.A: ~~2 Platoons~~ 1/4 Lanc R.	
	19.1.15 ~~[illegible]~~	Weather Showery	
	19.1.15 France.	Entrainment at HAVRE continuing. Following units arrived in the billetting area — BAILLEUL — OULTERSTEEN — BORRE — CAESTRE — METEREN —	

1247 W 3299 200,000 (E) 8/14 J.B.C. & A. Forms/C. 2118/11.

Instructions regarding War Diaries and Intelligence Summaries are contained in F. S. Regs., Part II. and the Staff Manual respectively. Title pages will be prepared in manuscript.

WAR DIARY
or
INTELLIGENCE SUMMARY
(Erase heading not required.)

Army Form C. 2118.

Hour, Date, Place	Summary of Events and Information	Remarks and references to Appendices
19.1.15 France	The forward move of the Division has been interfered with consequent on rough weather in the channel on night of the 17th–18th and many of 18th during which Pilots would not leave Havre harbour to bring ships in. Weather Showery.	
20.1.15 France	The following units arrived in the concentration area 2/Suffolk: 100 Batty R.F.A.: 1/Welsh and 2/Ches R. 103rd Batty R.F.A. 2/London Fd Amb: Part of 28th Div Train: 75th Batty R.F.A.: 2/Buffs. Weather Fine till 4 pm. Then wet.	
21.1.15 PRADELLES	Following units arrived in Concentration area: North Midland Cav. R.E.: 3/R. Fus: 146th Bde R.F.A. 3/Middlesex R. HQ R.E.: 28 Cyclist Coy. ~~Cas Clearing Station~~. 2/~~Northumbrian Fd Amb~~: HQ 85th Bde & ~~2/E Surrey~~. Div HQ. Snow fell during night of 20th 21st. Consequently units arriving late at Hazebrouck had rather a severe march in the dark to billets. V wet all day.	
22.1.15 PRADELLES	Following units arrived during the day. 2nd Northumbrian Field Amb. Cas: Clearing Station. 1/East Surrey. Div Ammn Column. The concentration of the Division was completed by 4 pm. Units being distributed in billets as shown in Appendix	Appendix 8
6 pm 22.1.15 "	G.O.C. institutes a conference every evening till further orders attended by Bde Majors or Staff Capts & a representative of each of administrative Services. Weather V. wet	

1247 W 3299 200,000 (E) 8/14 J.B.C. & A. Forms/C. 2118/11.

Army Form C. 2118.

Instructions regarding War Diaries and Intelligence Summaries are contained in F. S. Regs., Part II. and the Staff Manual respectively. Title pages will be prepared in manuscript.

WAR DIARY
or
INTELLIGENCE SUMMARY
(Erase heading not required.)

Hour, Date, Place	Summary of Events and Information	Remarks and references to Appendices
20.1.15 PRADELLE	Railheads at present are. Food EBBLINGHEM – Ammunition STRAZEELE – Supply at present carried out by Supply Column (M.T.) lent to the Corps bringing supplies direct to Train Vehicles in the Brigade areas.	
" "	~~This is the first day on which~~ The 27th Div Supply Col ~~has fed the Div – This Column~~ of 63 Vehicles crossed from AVONMOUTH and carrying one days supply for the Division reached HESDIN 22nd and HAZEBRUCK 23rd. Weather V. Fine.	
10.8 am 24.1.15 PRADELLE	Ascertained that extensions to gun shields will be provided after all, & these will be indented for by DADOS and put on by an expert when received	
12 noon " "	No 181 Coy M.T. the Supply Col of the 28th Div fed the Division for the first time today – 63 Lorries.	
10 pm " "	Instruction issued that the ones days reserve ration carried on train waggons to be eaten on 26th. GOC decided to endeavour to obtain and issue the following 50 flat irons per Bde for ironing shirts of men coming out of Trenches so that eggs of vermin may be killed. 36 pails per Bde for bailing Trenches – Soap & The second towel for use of men leaving trenches but units must arrange until this can be provided. Weather V Fine	

1247 W 3299 200,000 (E) 8/14 J.B.C. & A. Forms/C. 2118/11.

Instructions regarding War Diaries and Intelligence Summaries are contained in F. S. Regs., Part II. and the Staff Manual respectively. Title pages will be prepared in manuscript.

WAR DIARY
or
INTELLIGENCE SUMMARY
(Erase heading not required.)

Army Form C. 2118.

Hour, Date, Place	Summary of Events and Information	Remarks and references to Appendices
26.1.15 Pradelle	Halted Pradelle. Supply Railhead HAZEBRUCK	
9.25 pm " "	Wastage from Sickness during last seven days — Officers one; Ranks one hundred & twenty. Feeding Strength of Division, personnel 17014 — HD horses 814; Others 3238.	
11. pm " "	Fifth Corps notifies that indents for Stores from the RE Park at STRAZEELE must be countersigned by ~~the~~ the CE of the Corps or CRE 28th Div — weather fine	
27.1.15 PRADELLE	Division remained at same billets. Reconnoitred YPRES for billeting accommodation (2000) found same but considered the same somewhat insanitary. Unable to find sufficient accommodation South of Vlamertinghe for Reserve Bde on this date owing to difficulty from want of information from French Commander. At 9 pm was informed by 5th Corps that some part already allotted to 28th Div in Ypres would then be wanted for Cav Division.	

1247 W 3299 200,000 (E) 8/14 J.B.C. & A. Forms/C. 2118/11.

Instructions regarding War Diaries and Intelligence Summaries are contained in F. S. Regs., Part II. and the Staff Manual respectively. Title pages will be prepared in manuscript.

WAR DIARY
or
INTELLIGENCE SUMMARY
(Erase heading not required.)

Army Form C. 2118.

Hour, Date, Place	Summary of Events and Information	Remarks and references to Appendices
5 pm.	conference with representatives of Brigades at 5.30 pm. Endeavoured to organise a small Transport unit to carry French mortars, Grenades, etc. This will be done by the R.E Field Companies who will detach one section to each Infantry Brigade. One platoon in each Battalion to be selected as Grenadiers. These men to be specially selected and trained.	
28.1.15 Pradelle	5th Corps wires promising extra Transport up to 4 lorries per Bde to carry the large quantity of Stores accumulated by the ~~Bns~~ Bdes since arrival – Such as Trench Mortars – Sacks – Sandbags up to 1000 per Bn – Hand grenades – During the day D of R L of C (Abbeville) reports despatch of Remounts due ~~29~~ 30th for 3rd Bde R.F.A. 83rd Inf Bde. Weather v. fine.	
29.1.15 PRADELLE	arrival of 12th Lancers R.T.E. at Hazebrouck notified by V Corps en route to join Division. arrangements made for to billet it at Hazebrouck for the night and for it to proceed to STRAZEELE 30th.	

1247 W 3299 200,000 (E) 8/14 J.B.C. & A. Forms/C. 2118/11.

Instructions regarding War Diaries and Intelligence Summaries are contained in F. S. Regs., Part II. and the Staff Manual respectively. Title pages will be prepared in manuscript.

WAR DIARY
or
INTELLIGENCE SUMMARY
(Erase heading not required.)

Army Form C. 2118.

Hour, Date, Place	Summary of Events and Information	Remarks and references to Appendices
29.1.15 PRADELLE	during the day several conferences were held with the French authorities to consolidate billeting arrangements and a further reconnaissance made of billeting facilities — weather v. fine.	
30.1.15 PRADELLE	Division remains halted in existing billeting areas	
	one Private Welsh regiment committed suicide.	
	Hutting material being taken from CAESTRE (where it has been collected) to the VLAMERTINGE – YPRES. area	
	The 1st batch of Remounts arrived for the 28th Division at HAZEBRUCK at 2.30. viz for 3rd Bde R.F.A. — 1 Offr R — 6 R — 36 D — 24 D for HQ 83rd Inf Bde — 1 — — — 2 — 1	
	and were distributed at the Station by badges.	
11.2.am " "	5th Corps notifies that water at YPRES is badly contaminated and can be rendered fit for drinking by boiling for which purpose coal is being provided. Weather Fine — The 12 London R. T.F. arrived and billeted at STRAZEELE.	

1247 W 3299 200,000 (E) 8/14 J.B.C. & A. Forms/C. 2118/11.

Instructions regarding War Diaries and Intelligence Summaries are contained in F. S. Regs., Part II. and the Staff Manual respectively. Title pages will be prepared in manuscript.

WAR DIARY *or* INTELLIGENCE SUMMARY

(Erase heading not required.)

Army Form C. 2118.

Hour, Date, Place	Summary of Events and Information	Remarks and references to Appendices
11.30 a.m. 31. 1. 15 PRADELLE	3 Batteries RHA joined from Indian Corps & billetted in 83rd Inf Bde Area.	
2.30 p.m. 31. 1. 15 "	The ~~Second~~ Batch of Remounts for 28th Div arrived HAZEBRUCK and were distributed at the ground by the DAQMG. Total 11 offrs R — 18 R — 41 D — 46 HD — 3 Pack. The light draught horses were really ex Cavalry horses.	
"	Wastage from sickness during past 7 days 5 offrs. 296 OR. 1 about 60 horses dead chiefly Pneumonia.	
"	Ammunition Railhead for today is ARQUES. Supply HAZEBRUCK.	
9 p.m. 31. 1. 15 9 p.m. "	Following marched for VLAMERTINGHE. 1st line Transport 83rd Inf Bde. 1/ No. 1 Fd Coy RE. 2/ Lond: Fd Amb. 2 Supply & 2 Blanket wagons per Bn Weather - High N. wind with heavy snowstorm until 12 - bitterly cold - Then followed Thaw till 6 p.m. - after which came frost	

R A Hardy
Major DAQMG

1247 W 3299 200,000 (E) 8/14 J.B.C. & A. Forms/C. 2118/11.

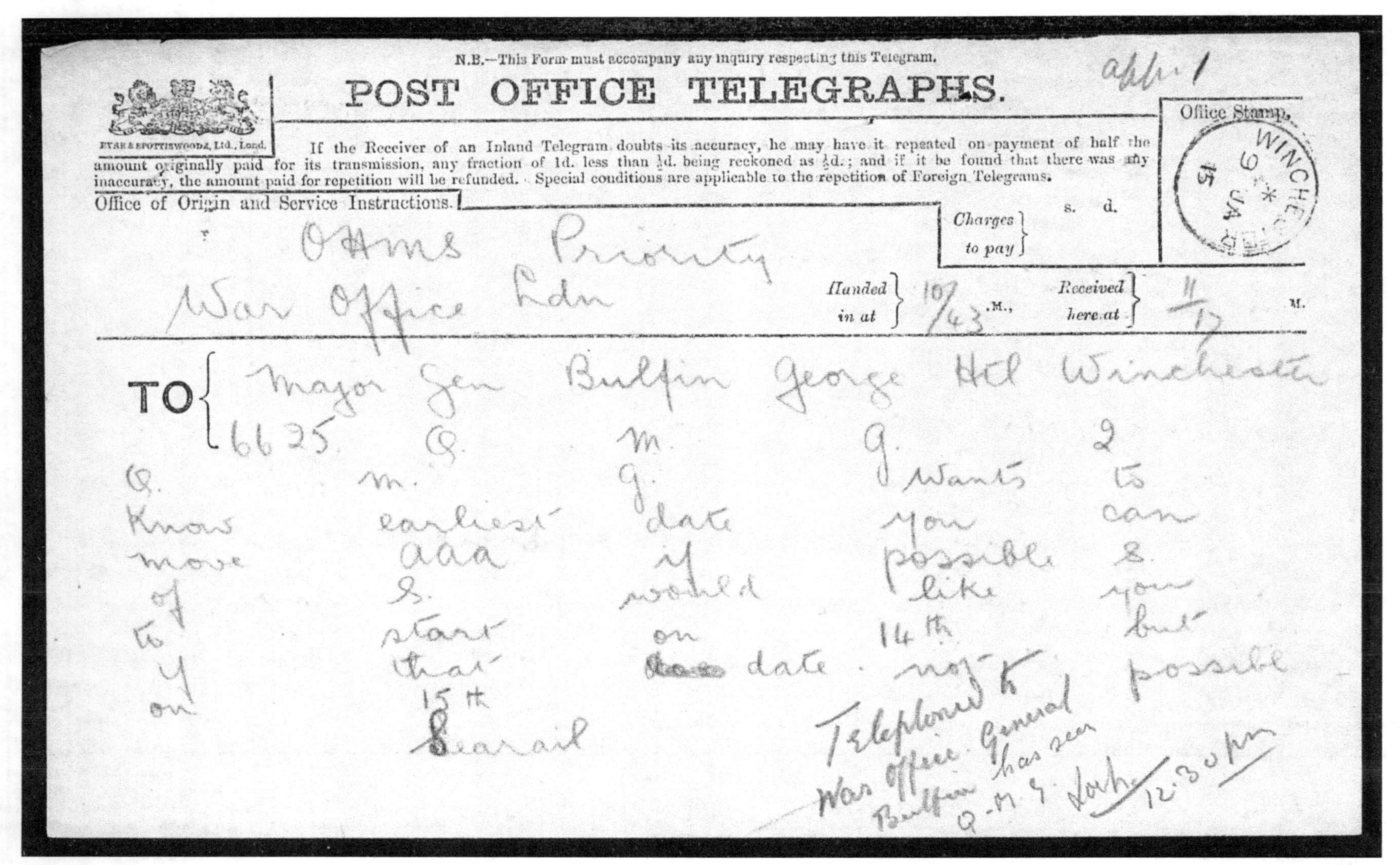

appx 1

N.B.—This Form must accompany any inquiry respecting this Telegram.

POST OFFICE TELEGRAPHS.

EYRE & SPOTTISWOODE, Ltd., Lond.

If the Receiver of an Inland Telegram doubts its accuracy, he may have it repeated on payment of half the amount originally paid for its transmission, any fraction of 1d. less than ½d. being reckoned as ½d.; and if it be found that there was any inaccuracy, the amount paid for repetition will be refunded. Special conditions are applicable to the repetition of Foreign Telegrams.

Office of Origin and Service Instructions.

Charges to pay s. d.

Office Stamp. WINCHESTER 9 JA 15

OHMS Priority

War Office Ldn

Handed in at 10/43 .M., Received here at 11/17 M.

TO { Major Gen Bulfin George Htl Winchester
6625 Q M G 2

Q M G Wants to
Know earliest date you can
move aaa if possible &
of S would like you
to start on 14th but
if that date not possible
on 15th
Searail

Telephoned to War Office General Bulfin has seen Q.M.G. [illegible] 12.30 pm

TO CONFIRM TELEGRAM. app. 2 38

The following is a copy of a Telegram which was sent you this day, and is forwarded in confirmation.

______________ 19

TO { SEARAIL LONDON

QH 95 Jan 10 Your QMG 2
6625 and 6647 dated 9th
and 10th most will be
able to embark majority of
the 28th Division on the 15th

FROM {

(68552). Wt. 17741-58. 2,000. 17/8/14. B., M. & S., Ltd.

TO CONFIRM TELEGRAM. 39

The following is a copy of a Telegram which was sent you this day, and is forwarded in confirmation.

________________19

TO

15th January AAA Still deficient
4 portions of harness Spare
parts machine guns AAA Cycles
Pack Saddlery and Lorry for
Signal Company AAA waggon bodies

FROM

(63552). Wt. 17741-58. 2,000. 17/8/14. B., M. & S., Ltd.

TO CONFIRM TELEGRAM. 40

The following is a copy of a Telegram which was sent you this day, and is forwarded in confirmation.

______________ 19

TO

and limbers for R.A. AAA
The whole Division should be
equipped right through and harness
fitted by 17th January which
is the date I should prefer

FROM General Bulfin

(63552). Wt. 17741-58. 2,000. 17/8/14. B., M. & S., Ltd.

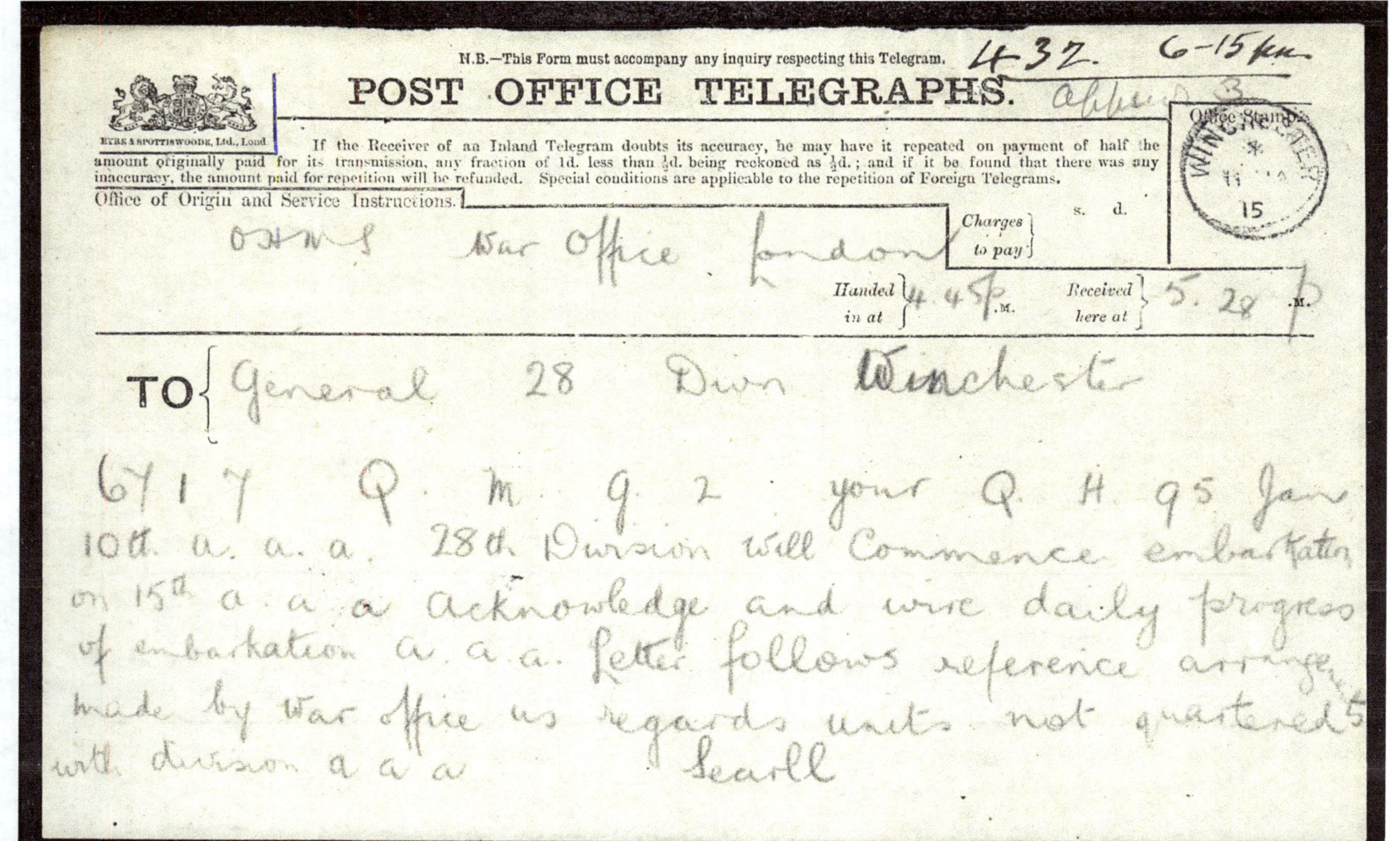

N.B.—This Form must accompany any inquiry respecting this Telegram. 432. 6-15 pm

POST OFFICE TELEGRAPHS.

Appendix 3

Eyre & Spottiswoode, Ltd., Lond.

If the Receiver of an Inland Telegram doubts its accuracy, he may have it repeated on payment of half the amount originally paid for its transmission, any fraction of 1d. less than ½d. being reckoned as ½d.; and if it be found that there was any inaccuracy, the amount paid for repetition will be refunded. Special conditions are applicable to the repetition of Foreign Telegrams.

Office Stamp: WINCHESTER * 11 JA 15

Office of Origin and Service Instructions. OHMS War Office London

Charges to pay s. d.

Handed in at 4.45 P.M. Received here at 5.28 P.M.

TO General 28 Divn Winchester

6717 Q M G 2 your Q H 95 Jan 10th a. a. a. 28th Division will commence embarkation on 15th a a a acknowledge and wire daily progress of embarkation a a a. Letter follows reference arrangements made by War office as regards units not quartered with division a a a Searll

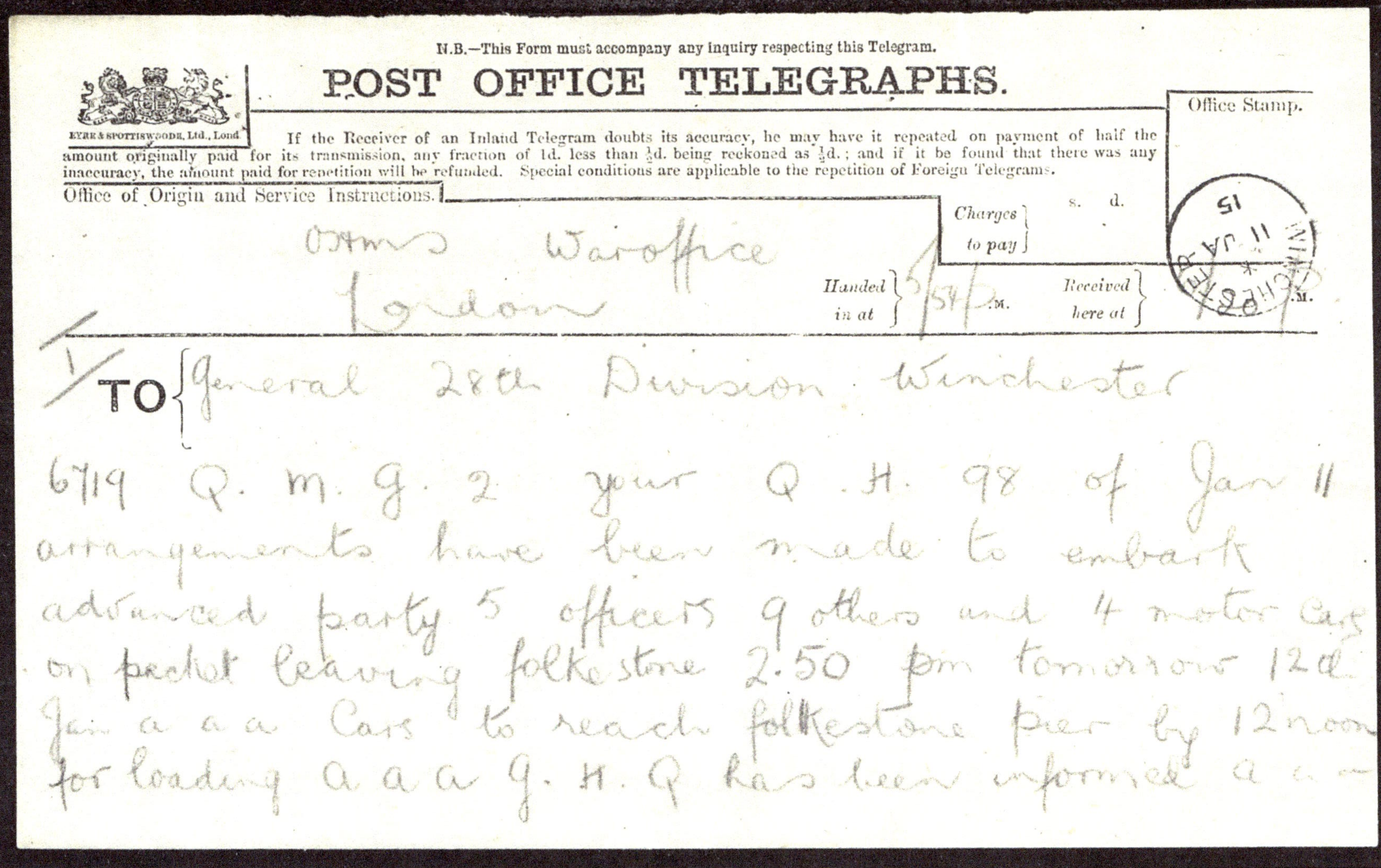

N.B.—This Form must accompany any inquiry respecting this Telegram.

POST OFFICE TELEGRAPHS.

EYRE & SPOTTISWOODE, Ltd., Lond.

If the Receiver of an Inland Telegram doubts its accuracy, he may have it repeated on payment of half the amount originally paid for its transmission, any fraction of 1d. less than ½d. being reckoned as ½d.; and if it be found that there was any inaccuracy, the amount paid for repetition will be refunded. Special conditions are applicable to the repetition of Foreign Telegrams.

Office of Origin and Service Instructions.

OHMS War office
London

Charges to pay s. d.

Handed in at 5/54 P.M.

Received here at

Office Stamp.

WINCHESTER
11 JA 15

1/

TO General 28th Division Winchester

6719 Q. M. G. 2 your Q. H. 98 of Jan 11 arrangements have been made to embark advanced party 5 officers 9 others and 4 motor cars on packet leaving folkestone 2.50 pm tomorrow 12th Jan a a a Cars to reach folkestone pier by 12 noon for loading a a a G. H. Q has been informed a a –

N.B.—This Form must accompany any inquiry respecting this Telegram.

POST OFFICE TELEGRAPHS.

EYRE & SPOTTISWOODE, Ltd., Lond.

If the Receiver of an Inland Telegram doubts its accuracy, he may have it repeated on payment of half the amount originally paid for its transmission, any fraction of 1d. less than ½d. being reckoned as ½d.; and if it be found that there was any inaccuracy, the amount paid for repetition will be refunded. Special conditions are applicable to the repetition of Foreign Telegrams.

Office of Origin and Service Instructions.

Charges to pay s. d.

Office Stamp: WINCHESTER * 11 JA 15

Handed in at .M. Received here at .M.

TO { 11

W.H.

Please wire Searlldate G. O. C and Three staff Officers with Car and servants wish to leave Folkestone a a a

Searll

GM108

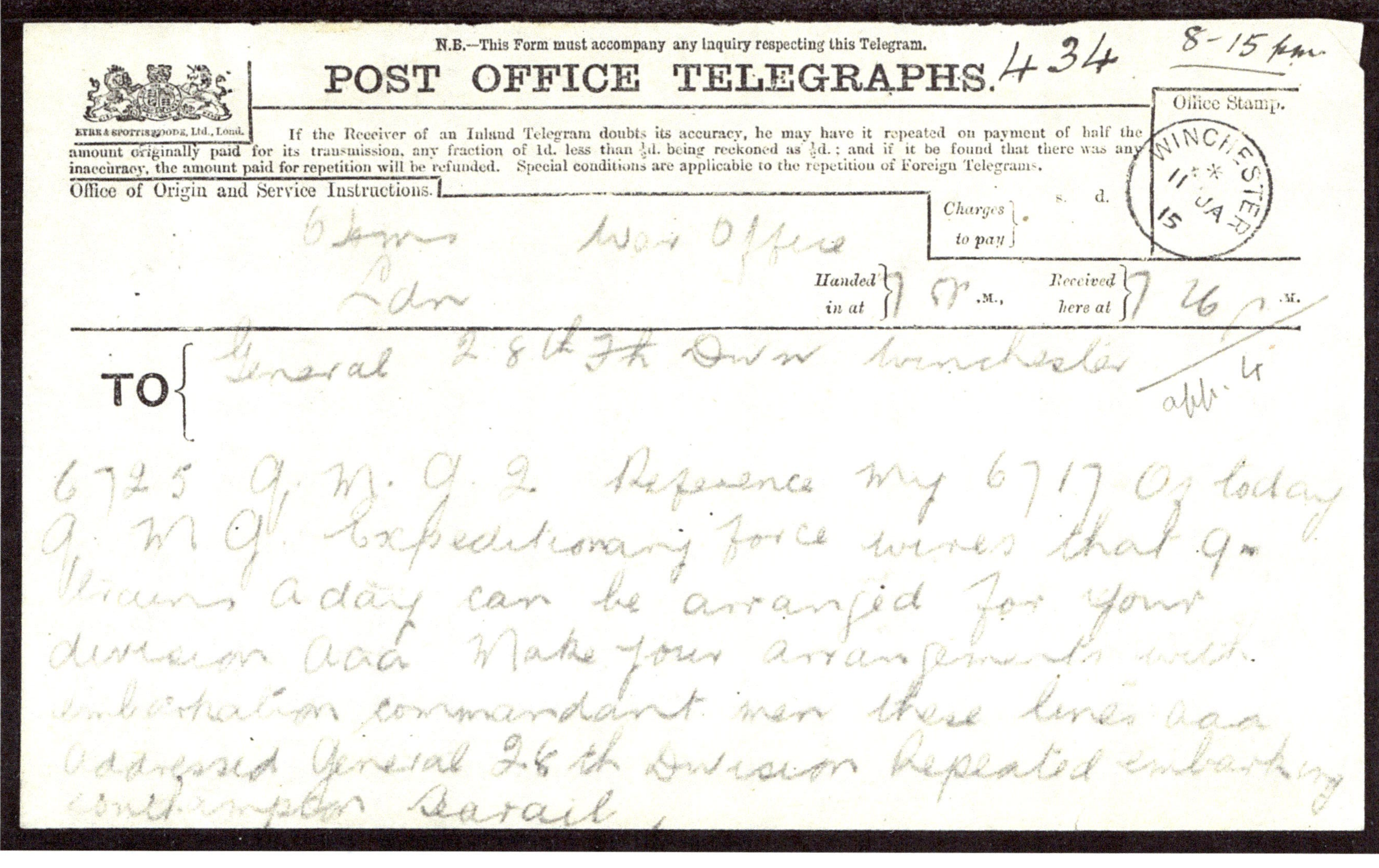

N.B.—This Form must accompany any inquiry respecting this Telegram.

POST OFFICE TELEGRAPHS. 434 8-15 pm

Office Stamp. WINCHESTER 11 JA 15

Eyre & Spottiswoode, Ltd., Lond.

If the Receiver of an Inland Telegram doubts its accuracy, he may have it repeated on payment of half the amount originally paid for its transmission, any fraction of 1d. less than ½d. being reckoned as ½d.; and if it be found that there was any inaccuracy, the amount paid for repetition will be refunded. Special conditions are applicable to the repetition of Foreign Telegrams.

Office of Origin and Service Instructions. 6 Igms War Office Ldn

Charges to pay s. d.

Handed in at 7 5P.M., Received here at 7 26 P.M.

TO General 28th Fh Divn Winchester

App. 4

6725 Q.M.G.2. Reference my 6717 of today Q.M.G. Expeditionary force wires that 9 trains a day can be arranged for your division aaa Make your arrangements with embarkation commandant on these lines aaa Addressed General 28th Division repeated embarking commandant Lavail

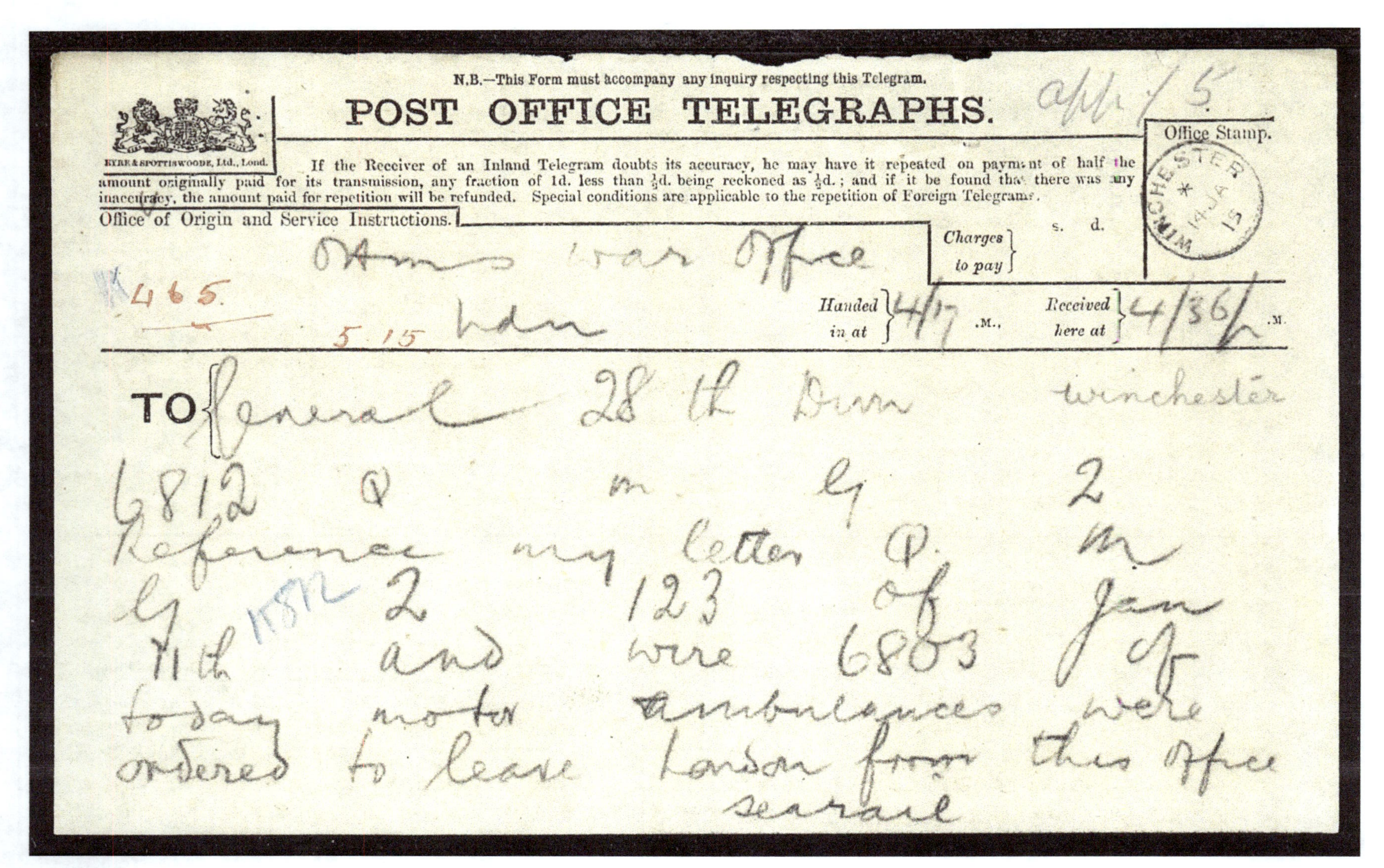

N.B.—This Form must accompany any inquiry respecting this Telegram.

POST OFFICE TELEGRAPHS.

app / 5

EYRE & SPOTTISWOODE, Ltd., Lond.

If the Receiver of an Inland Telegram doubts its accuracy, he may have it repeated on payment of half the amount originally paid for its transmission, any fraction of 1d. less than ½d. being reckoned as ½d.; and if it be found that there was any inaccuracy, the amount paid for repetition will be refunded. Special conditions are applicable to the repetition of Foreign Telegrams.

Office Stamp.

WINCHESTER * 14 JA 15

Office of Origin and Service Instructions.

Charges to pay s. d.

465.

Otams War Office
5 15 Ldn

Handed in at 4/7 .M., Received here at 4/36 p .M.

TO General 28 th Divn Winchester

6812 Q m G 2
Reference my letter Q. M
G 2 123 of Jan
11th and wire 6803 of
today motor ambulances were
ordered to leave London from this Office
searail

11812

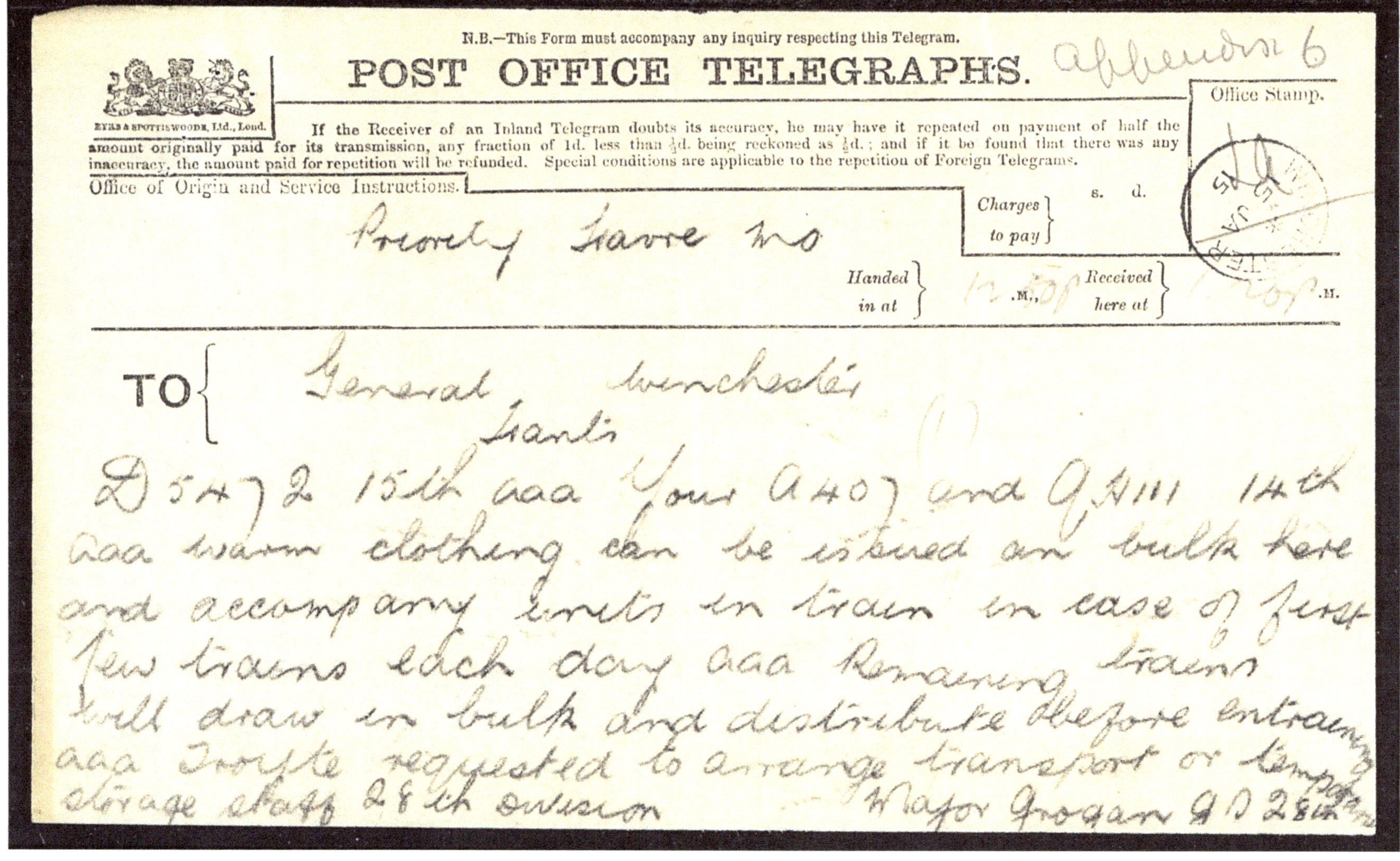

N.B.—This Form must accompany any inquiry respecting this Telegram.

POST OFFICE TELEGRAPHS. Appendix 6

EYRE & SPOTTISWOODE, Ltd., Lond.

If the Receiver of an Inland Telegram doubts its accuracy, he may have it repeated on payment of half the amount originally paid for its transmission, any fraction of 1d. less than ½d. being reckoned as ½d.; and if it be found that there was any inaccuracy, the amount paid for repetition will be refunded. Special conditions are applicable to the repetition of Foreign Telegrams.

Office Stamp.

Office of Origin and Service Instructions.

Priority Havre MO

Charges to pay — s. d.

Handed in at 12.50 P.M., Received here at 1.20 P.M.

TO General Winchester Hants

D 5472 15th aaa Your A407 and QA111 14th aaa warm clothing can be issued in bulk here and accompany units in train in case of first few trains each day aaa Remaining trains will draw in bulk and distribute before entraining aaa Troops requested to arrange transport or temporary storage staff 28th Division Major Grogan GS 28th Div

N.B.—This Form must accompany any inquiry respecting this Telegram.

POST OFFICE TELEGRAPHS.

EYRE & SPOTTISWOODE, Ltd., Lond.

If the Receiver of an Inland Telegram doubts its accuracy, he may have it repeated on payment of half the amount originally paid for its transmission, any fraction of 1d. less than ½d. being reckoned as ½d.; and if it be found that there was any inaccuracy, the amount paid for repetition will be refunded. Special conditions are applicable to the repetition of Foreign Telegrams.

Office Stamp.

WINCHESTER 15 JA 15

Office of Origin and Service Instructions.

Charges to pay s. d.

Handed in at .M., *Received here at* .M.

TO

(2)

Dear Leave 12·30 pm

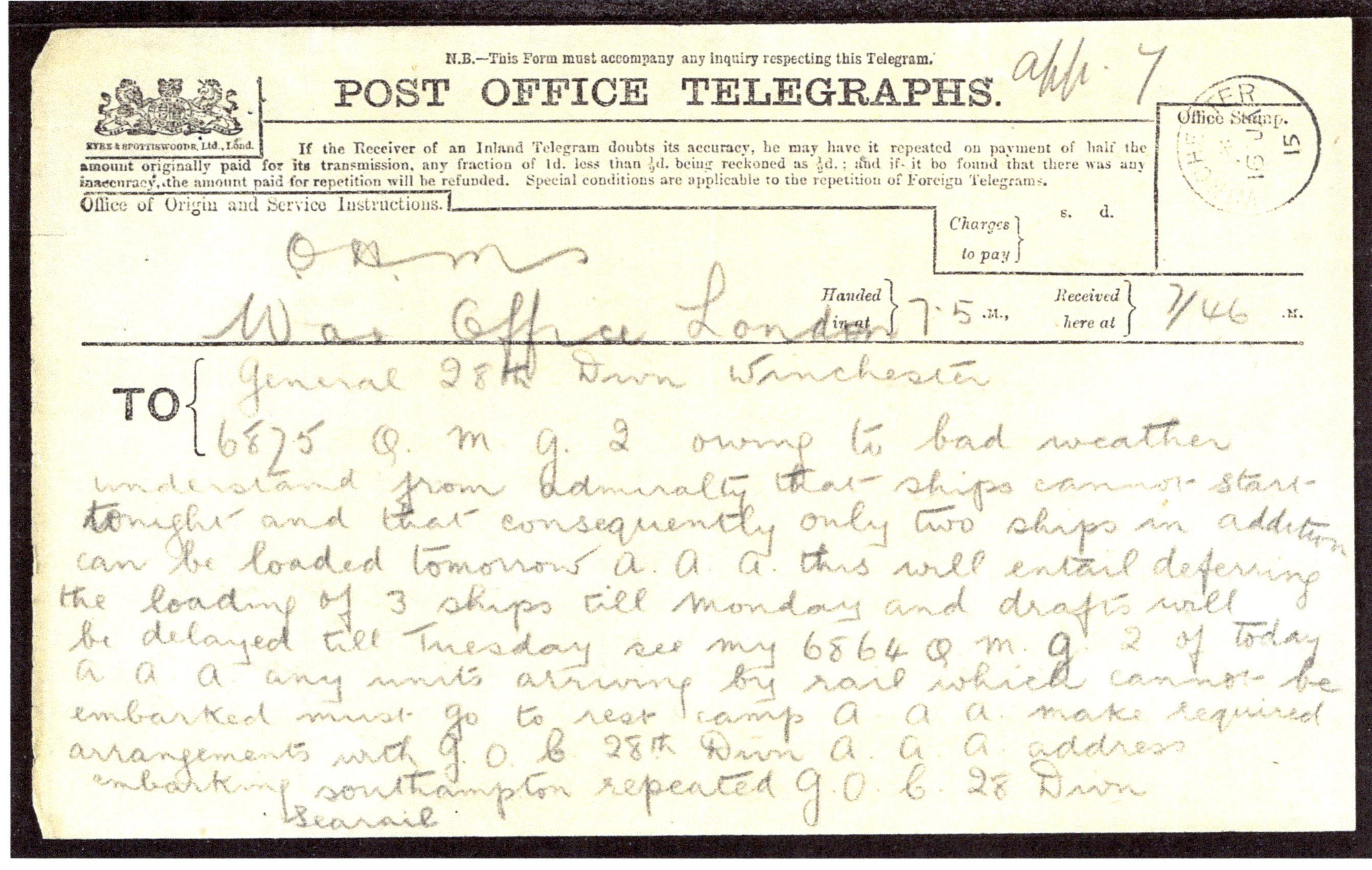

N.B.—This Form must accompany any inquiry respecting this Telegram.

app 7

POST OFFICE TELEGRAPHS.

EYRE & SPOTTISWOODE, Ltd., Lond.

If the Receiver of an Inland Telegram doubts its accuracy, he may have it repeated on payment of half the amount originally paid for its transmission, any fraction of 1d. less than ½d. being reckoned as ½d.; and if it be found that there was any inaccuracy, the amount paid for repetition will be refunded. Special conditions are applicable to the repetition of Foreign Telegrams.

Office Stamp. [stamp: ...CHESTER 16 JA 15]

Office of Origin and Service Instructions. O.H.M.S.

Charges to pay s. d.

War Office London

Handed in at 7.5 .M., Received here at 7/46 .M.

TO { General 28th Divn Winchester

6875 Q. M. G. 2 owing to bad weather understand from Admiralty that ships cannot start tonight and that consequently only two ships in addition can be loaded tomorrow a. a. a. this will entail deferring the loading of 3 ships till Monday and drafts will be delayed till Tuesday see my 6864 Q. M. G. 2 of today a a a any units arriving by rail which cannot be embarked must go to rest camp a a a make required arrangements with G. O. C. 28th Divn a. a. a. address embarking southampton repeated G. O. C. 28 Divn

Bearail

"A" Form. Army Form C. 2121.

MESSAGES AND SIGNALS.

No. of Message

Prefix Code m.	Words	Charge	This message is on a/c of:	Recd. at m.
Office of Origin and Service Instructions.	Sent		Service.	Date
	At m.			From
	To			
	By		(Signature of "Franking Officer.")	By

TO

* Sender's Number	Day of Month	In reply to Number	AAA

85 Bde

Buffs. Ⓔ Rouge Croix.
R Fusiliers Caestre
E. Surrey Road from Caestre to Fletre & FLETRE.
Middlesex Fletre.
75 Battn R.F.A
336 " "
337 " R.F.A
} S of Caestre between railway & Croix Rouge.

Amn Colm.
Field Ambl.
} do

Train near Caestre.

Ph. Scolwell

From
Place
Time

The above may be forwarded as now corrected. (Z)

Censor. Signature of Addressor or person authorised to

* This line should be erased if not required.

158 S. B. Ltd. Wt. W5673/619—50,000. 10/14. Forms C2121/10.

1st Bn. Suffolk Regt.

along MERRIS – STRAZEELE Road.

Name of Farm	Officers	Men
F.15. Delaire.		200.
16. Gerbedoen.	2.	100.
17. Sister Gerbedoen. Bn. Head Qrs.	4.	
18. Dubaele.	4.	50.
19. Hughe.	4.	130.
20. Ganfois.	4.	100.
21. Charlet.	2.	100.
22. Bacquaert.	3.	130
23. Montaigne.	5.	250.
	28	1060

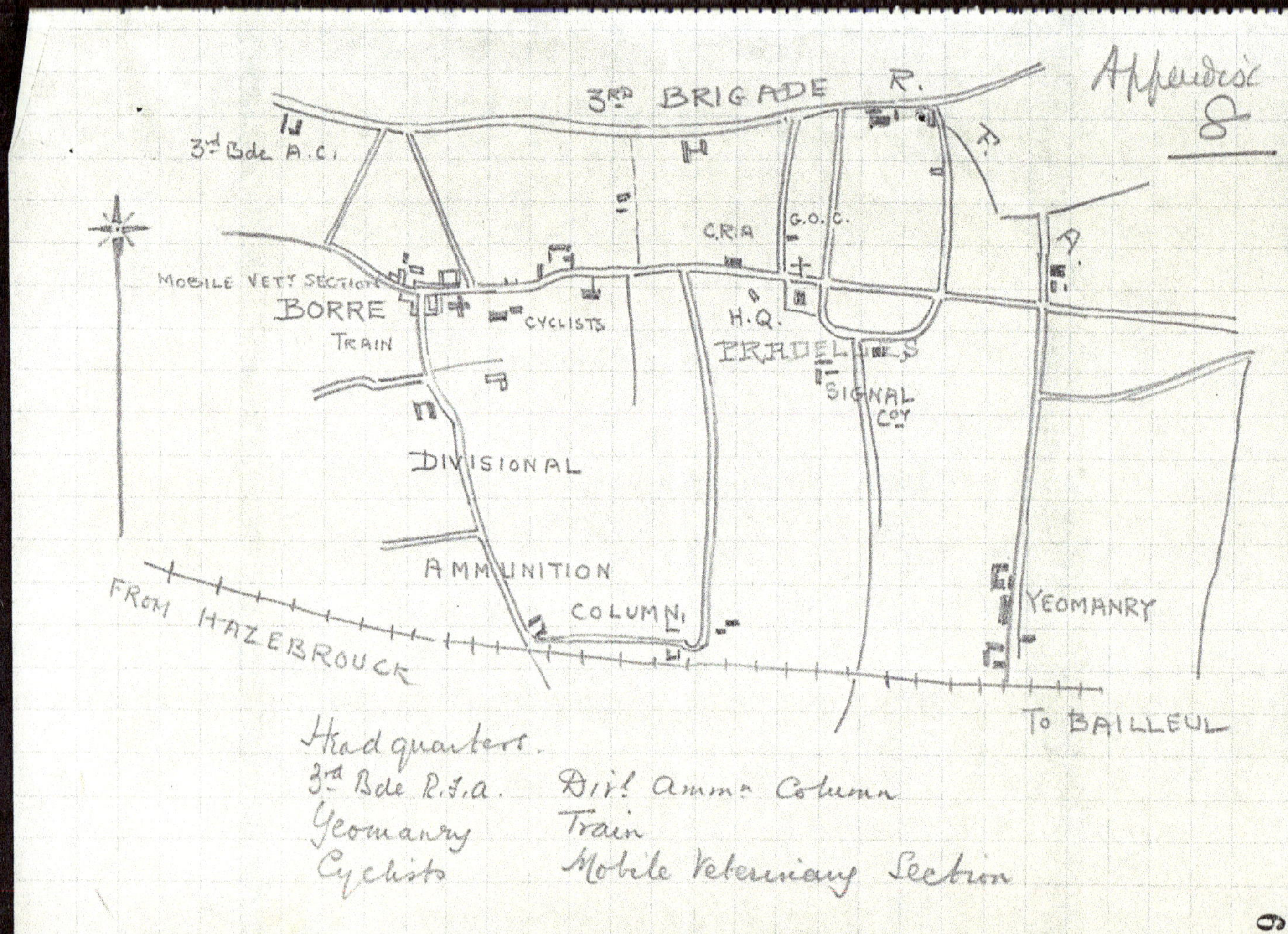
Appendix 8
3RD BRIGADE R. F. A.
3rd Bde A.C.
MOBILE VETY SECTION
BORRE
TRAIN
CYCLISTS
C.R.A
G.O.C.
H.Q.
PRADELLES
SIGNAL COY
DIVISIONAL
AMMUNITION
COLUMN
YEOMANRY
FROM HAZEBROUCK
TO BAILLEUL
Headquarters.
3rd Bde R.F.A.
Yeomanry
Cyclists
Divl Ammn Column
Train
Mobile Veterinary Section

83rd Bde.
Billeting Area

Ref. Map FRANCE St OMER 4. Scale 1/80,000

FROM FLETRE
METEREN
To BAILLEUL
To BAILLEUL
FROM MERRIS
OUTTERSTEENE
Not to Scale.

Bde H.Q.
A Belle Croix Farm Field Ambulance
B R.E. Coy
In OUTTERSTEENE Transport & Supply Coy
" " 1/K.O.Y.L.I.
In METEREN 1/York & Lancaster

E C Gepp Capt
83 Inf Bde

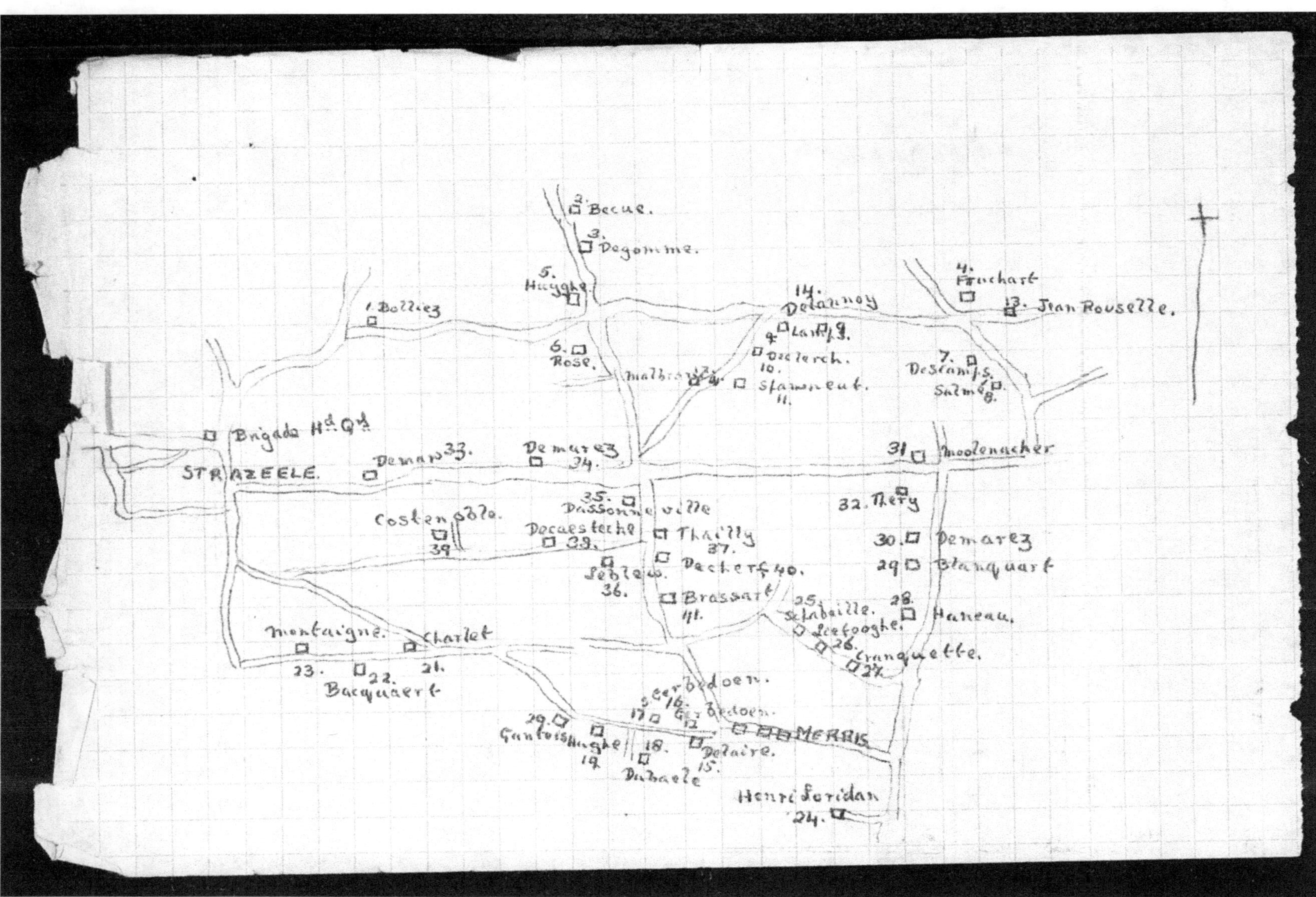

STRAZEELE.
Brigade Hd. Qrs.
1. Bolliez
2. Becue.
3. Degomme.
4. Fruchart
5. Huyghe
6. Rose.
7. Deslamps.
8. Salme
10. Declerck.
11. Stawneut.
13. Jean Rouselle.
14. Delannoy
15. Delaire.
18.
19.
21.
22. Bacquaert
23.
24. Henri Loridan
25. Stabaille.
26.
27.
28. Haneau.
29. Blanquart
30. Demarez
31. Moolenacker
32. Thery
33. Demars
34. Demarez
35. Dassonneville
36. Seblew.
37. Thailly
38. Decaestecker
39. Costenoble.
40. Deckerf
41. Brassart
Montaigne.
Charlet
Merris
Dubaele
Gantois

31st Bde R.F.A.

Name of Farm	Officers	Men.
33. Deman.		100.
34. Demarez.	2.	100.
35. Dassonneville.		20.
36. Leblew. Hd Qrs	3.	100.
37. Thailly.	3.	100.
38. Decaestecke.	2.	80.
39. Costenoble.	2.	80.
40. Decherf.	5.	100.
41. Brassart.	1.	50.
	18.	730

additional Officers in Inn near BRASSART.

1st Bn Welch Regt

In MERRIS.

~~1st~~ 2nd Bn Cheshire Regt.

On MERRIS – METEREN Rd.

Name of Farm	Officers	Men
24. Henri Loridan.	4.	100.
25. Schabaille.	3.	100.
26. Liefooghe.	5.	100.
27. Cranquette.	3.	80.
28. Haneau. Bn Hd Qrs	5.	200.
29. Blanquart.	1.	50.
30. Demarez.	3.	100.
31. Moolenacker.	6.	220.
32. Thery.	1.	50
	31	1000

2nd Northd Fusiliers.

Name of Farm	Officers	men.
1. Bolliez.	1.	50.
2. Becue.		50.
3. Degomme.	2.	50.
4. Frachart.	2.	100.
5. Huyghe (Bn. Hd. Qd.).	4.	150.
6. Rose.	2.	100.
7. Descamps.	2.	100.
8. Salmé.	1.	50.
9. Lamps.	2.	100.
14. Delannoy.	2.	50.
10. Malbrancq.	3.	100.
11. Spanneut.	2.	100.
12. Declerck.	1.	50.
13. Jean Rouselle.	2.	50.
	26	1100

accommodation for extra officers can be found in Inn near Huyghe.

3rd London R. E.
In STRAZEELE.

3 Coy Train.
In STRAZEELE.

3rd London Field Ambulance
In farms around STRAZEELE.

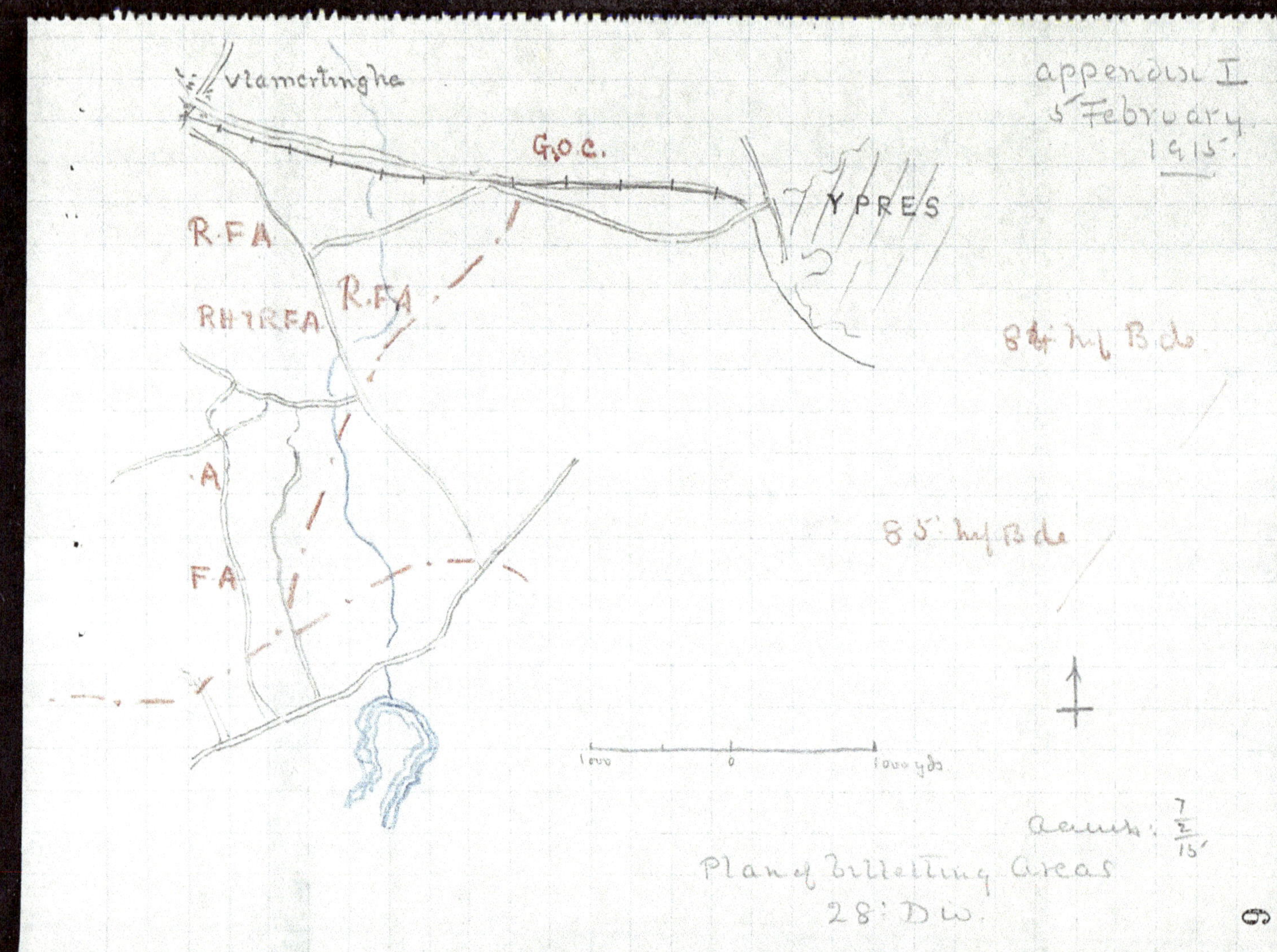
appendix I
5 February
1915
Vlamertinghe
G.O.C.
YPRES
R.F.A
R.F.A
A
F.A
84 Inf Bde
85 Inf Bde
1000 0 1000 yds
7/2/15
Plan of Billetting Areas
28 Div.

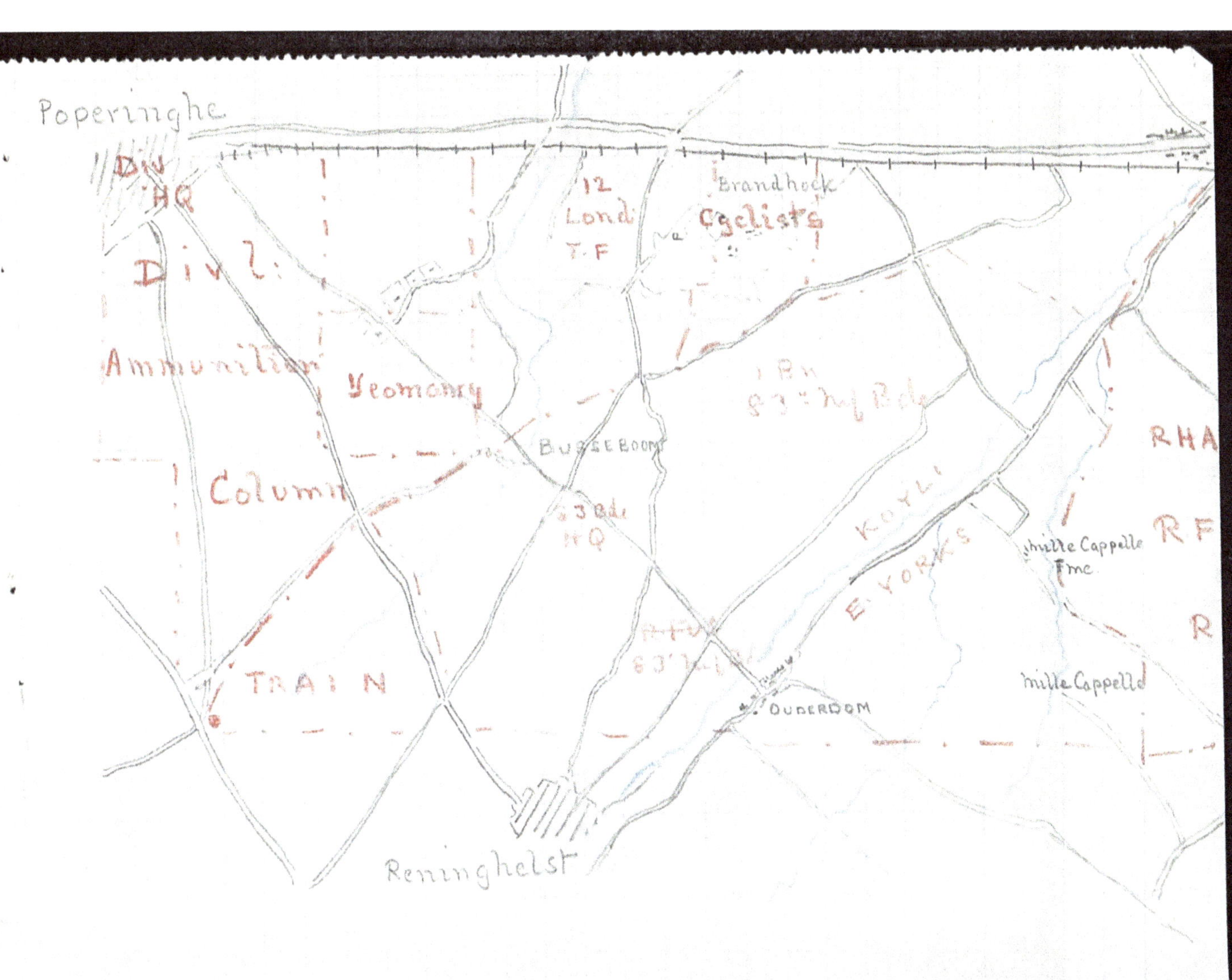

Poperinghe
Div HQ
Div l Ammunition Column
Yeomanry
12 Lond T.F
Brandhoek
Cyclists
BUSSEBOOM
83 Bde HQ
KOYLI
E YORKS
TRAIN
OUDERDOM
Mille Cappelle Fme
Mille Cappelle
RHA
RF
R
Reninghelst

MESSAGES AND SIGNALS. No. of Message 125

Prefix Code m. | Words 24 | Charge

Office of Origin and Service Instructions. Sent At m. To By

This message is on a/c of: 1736 3-50p Service. (Signature of "Franking Officer.")

Recd. at m. Date From By

TO 28th Division

Sender's Number	Day of Month	In reply to Number	AAA
Q.J. 250	12		

Your Senior Supply Officer must arrange that every man who goes into the trenches takes 2 days rations

appx 2

From 5th Corps

Place

Time

The above may be forwarded as now corrected. (Z)

Censor. Signature of Addressor or person authorised to telegraph in his name

McJamesett Col
a.q.m.g.

* This line should be erased if not required.

158 S. B. Ltd. Wt. W5673/619—50,000. 10/14. Forms C2121/10.

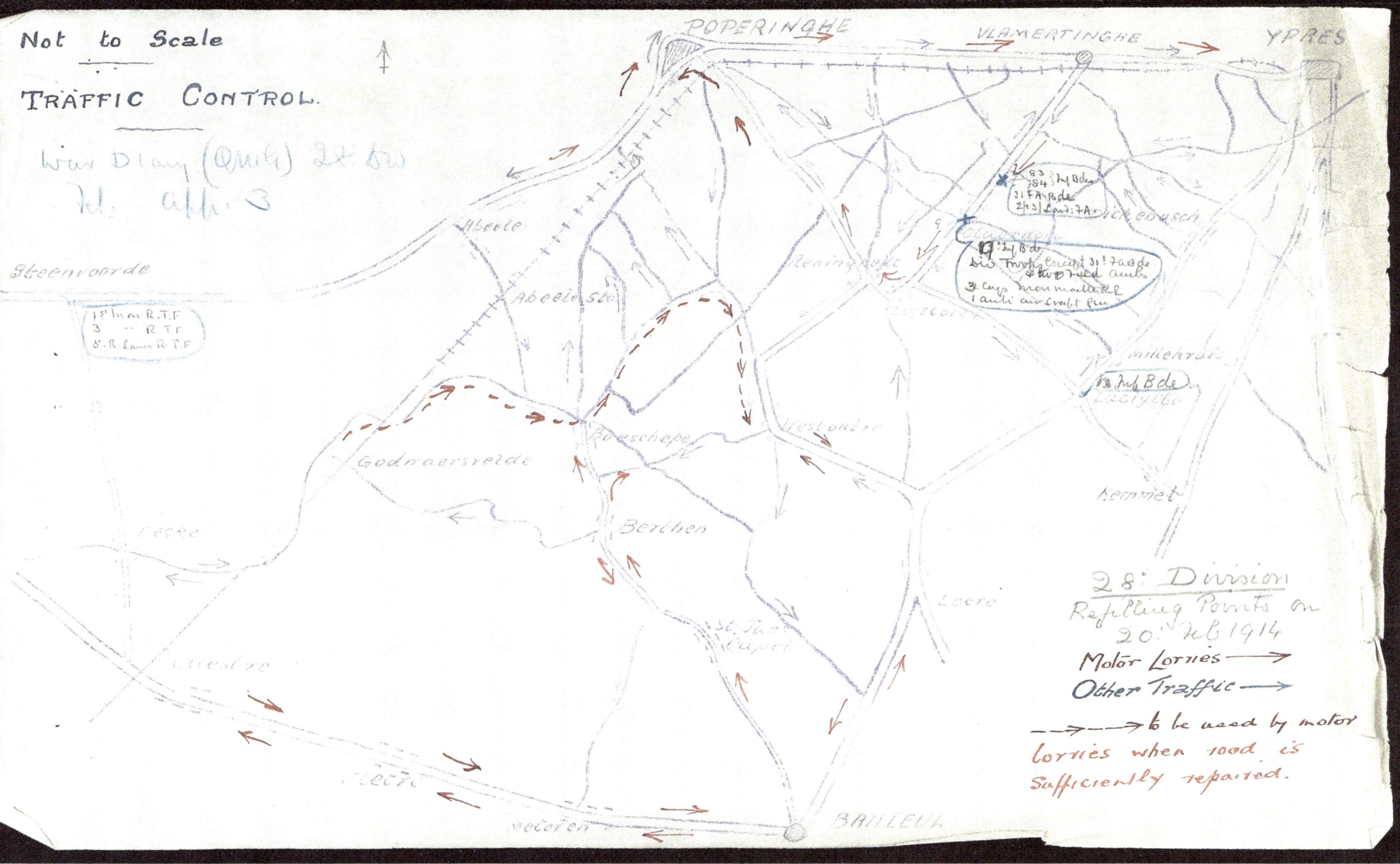
Not to Scale
TRAFFIC CONTROL.
POPERINGHE
VLAMERTINGHE
YPRES
Abeele
Steenvoorde
Abeele Sta
Reninghelst
Godwaersvelde
Boeschepe
Westoutre
Berthen
Kemmel
Locre
St. Jans Cappel
Meteren
BAILLEUL
28th Division
Refilling Points on
20th Feb 1914
Motor Lorries
Other Traffic
to be used by motor
lorries when road is
sufficiently repaired.

Administrative Staff 23/40
Appendix 4
R 3-2-15

Further arrangements for transfer of Brigade Companies of 28th and 5th Divisional Trains.

1. 13th Brigade Company filled up this morning with rations for 83rd Brigade.

2. On 23rd, 84th Brigade will march to BAILLEUL with its Brigade Company baggage section full and supply section empty.

3. On 24th personnel and horses of 84th Brigade Train Company will be exchanged with personnel and horses of 15th Brigade train company.

4. On March 3rd (or when ordered) 83rd Brigade will march to BAILLEUL with 13th Brigade Company Train.

5. On March 3rd (or when ordered) 15th Brigade will march to OUDERDOM (or where ordered) with 84th Brigade Train Company.

6. Requisitioning Officers and Supply details of trains will rejoin their respective divisions as early as possible.

7. Each Brigade Company will retain its own blanket wagons. The Infantry Drivers of 13th Infantry Brigade blanket wagons will drive their wagons on the 3rd to BAILLEUL and will be returned later to their Brigade by 5th Division.

sd/ R. Henvey, Major,
22nd Feb. 1915.

Instructions regarding War Diaries and Intelligence Summaries are contained in F. S. Regs., Part II. and the Staff Manual respectively. Title pages will be prepared in manuscript.

WAR DIARY
or
INTELLIGENCE SUMMARY
(Erase heading not required.)

Army Form C. 2118.

Hour, Date, Place	Summary of Events and Information	Remarks and references to Appendices
11 — 31 . 2 . 15 Bradelle	Following moves took place during day HQ RE (RE) } By road via LOCRE and OUDERDOM to billeting areas RHA & RFA } immediately S of VLAMERTINGHE at 9 a.m. 83rd Inf Bde in 165 Motor Busses – to bivouacs immediately S.W. of VLAMERTINGHE where 1st Line T who had marched previous evening had prepared teas – At 9 pm RA marched to trenches to take over positions held by French Troops at 10.45 pm 83rd Inf Bde " " " " " " " approximately S.E. of the VERBRANDEN MOLEN.	
1 . 2 . 15 Vlamertinghe	At 4 pm Div HQ established as follows. Administrative Staff in BRANDHOEK SCHOOL 3 Kilometres W of VLAMERTINGHE – G.O.C. & G.S. at a farm S of POPERINGHE – YPRES Road 2 K W of YPRES. The mass of accumulated RE Stores for Trenches had been collected by RE at STRAZEELE & moved in rear of the Bus Column to Vlamertinghe where it was offloaded in an RE depot (formed there) – 5 Train Waggons were then loaded up with Stores in a regulated order according to units of 83rd Inf Bde & taken with troops to YPRES, offloaded & a depot formed at PORTE de LILLE. Stores immediately required being carried up by hand.	
9 pm 1 . 2 . 15	Following marched from 84th Inf Bde area for bivouacs & billets S.W. of Vlamertinghe 3/Lond Fd Coy RE – 3/Lond F.A. – 1st Line T 84th Inf Bde; Signal Sec. Weather fine – The Division fired its first rounds in anger 7.5 Hows per gun 12 pm. 5 – 31st Fd Bde. 4 pm 146th Fd Bde.	[signature] Maj [signature]

Instructions regarding War Diaries and Intelligence Summaries are contained in F. S. Regs., Part II. and the Staff Manual respectively. Title pages will be prepared in manuscript.

WAR DIARY
or
INTELLIGENCE SUMMARY

(Erase heading not required.)

Army Form C. 2118.

Hour, Date, Place	Summary of Events and Information	Remarks and references to Appendices
5.20 am 2.2.15 Vlamertinghe	1st Line Transport 84th Inf Bde arrived late in Bivouacs due to Blocked roads.	
	Other moves took place as follows	
9 am "	Remainder of R.H.A. & R.F.A. except Div Amn: Col by Road to billets S [illegible] of Vlamertinghe taking over ~~trenches~~ gun positions from French by night –	
8 am " "	Sqn Surrey Yeomanry – Div cyclists – 1 N'thd Cy R.E. Sig Sec: 12 Lond Regt 2/Nth'd Amb. Divl Train ~~marches~~ and 85th Inf Bde marched to the Vlamertinghe YPRES AREAS	
3 pm " " "	While these were in progress the Div Supply Col which is under Corps Control moving ~~from~~ via Poperinghe – Vlamertinghe to OUDERDOM (Refill. Pt) met the RA & Inf Columns on a narrow road (pavé) with the result that the Supply Col though loaded up at Rail Head on the Evening 1st. Feb did not reach R.P till 9 pm 2nd and Supplies did not reach the Bns of the 83rd Inf Bde till about 5 am 3.2.15 –	
9 pm " "	after teas 84th Inf Bde moving via YPRES relieved the French in the Trenches. The same arrangements were made for 84th Inf Bde regarding RE Stores.	
	Goc had decided that owing to the danger only S.A.A. Carts & M.G. Vehicles were to remain in YPRES (hidden) as representatives of 83 Inf Bde Goc approved of 5 water cart Carts moving up daily	
	V. wet and heavy rain with Easterly wind.	A. Ami [illegible] Maj [illegible]
	Casualties in previous 24 hours 3.	

1247 W 3299 200,000 (E) 8/14 J.B.C. & A. Forms/C. 2118/11.

Instructions regarding War Diaries and Intelligence Summaries are contained in F. S. Regs., Part II. and the Staff Manual respectively. Title pages will be prepared in manuscript.

WAR DIARY
or
INTELLIGENCE SUMMARY
(Erase heading not required.)

Army Form C. 2118.

Hour, Date, Place	Summary of Events and Information	Remarks and references to Appendices
10.45 am 3.2.15 BRANDHOEK	5th Corps notifies that until arrival of Corps HQ at Poperinghe & until railhead of 28th Div is established at ABELE the matter of road control must be arranged between divisions.	
2.55 pm " "	RA notify Ammn R.P at Square H 8(d) on Vlamertinghe–OUTERDOM Road	
7 pm " "	83rd Inf Bde notifies considerable casualties and asks for stretchers & bearers to Chateau LANDHOF	
	Casualties during prev: 24 hours reported 2nd R. Yorks 1 OR wounded – KOYLI 1 OR – 3 killed 34 wounded. 4th [illegible] 1 K 1 W. Total 3 killed 37 wounded	
	arrangements as regards ammunition are that 2 Reps of Bde Ammn Cols Keep touch with Inf Bdes remain at in Infantry Bdes YPRES to weather time. Railhead for Supply GOEDEWAERDE-VELDE: for ammunition ARQUES	
11.35 am 4.2.15 BRANDHOEK	146th Bde RFA having been directed to shell building in Rear of German Trenches ask for expenditure of H.E. Shell not yet received. For Ammn Park at St Sylvestre wired to	[illegible] Maj [illegible]
5.28 pm 4.2.15 "	Owing to counterattack ordered by 83rd Bde to retake Trenches special preparations made for evacuation	
	Following ammunition expended during 24 hours 13 pr 21.5 rounds per gun. 18 pr 4. RHA have sanction from Corps Commander for excessive expenditure of defective shell	
	Casualties during previous 24 hours as follows	

Instructions regarding War Diaries and Intelligence Summaries are contained in F. S. Regs., Part II. and the Staff Manual respectively. Title pages will be prepared in manuscript.

WAR DIARY
or
INTELLIGENCE SUMMARY.
(Erase heading not required.)

Army Form C. 2118.

Hour, Date, Place	Summary of Events and Information	Remarks and references to Appendices
	~~2/180~~ 17 K: 73 W: 5 M: also Lt Mortishead and HEYDEN wounded	
6.15 pm ~~4~~ 4. 2.15 BRANDHOEK	2000 hand or Rifle grenades and all Hales Rifle grenades asked for from Ammn Park.	
	During day quantity of Sandbags & coke sent to Porte de Lille for 84 Inf Bde.	
	GOC arranged for 2 Motor vehicles to be used for carrying rations ammn etc from Porte de Lille forward to Bde HQ to save men carrying – Preparations also made to cover wheels of 1st line T. with sacking to deaden sound.	
	Billets. As shown in appendix	Appendix 1 annex.
	Weather fine	
10.45 am 5. 2.15 BRANDHOEK	Under arrangements of 5th Corps a Section of the Ammunition Park ordered to Poperinghe and later directed to ABEELE also Sec RHA Ammn Park.	
2.30 pm 5. 2.15 "	Supply arrangements worked well Regimental vehicles left R.P before 2.30 pm.	
4. " " Poperinghe	Administrative HQ moved to Poperinghe – G.S. remain near YPRES	
7.43 pm " "	Divisional Ammn Col is to be ordered up under Instructions V Corps	
7.54 pm " "	G.S. report attack on our lines now being made	
8.35 pm " "	2 Bns ~~Res~~ 85 (Res) Brigade ordered to YPRES. Saqué [?] met & billeted as follows 3/R. Fus Inf Bks – 3/Middlesex Cav Bks – ~~[illegible]~~ 400 men 3/Mx proceeded to 83 Bde HQ carry supplies & water to trenches	

Instructions regarding War Diaries and Intelligence Summaries are contained in F. S. Regs., Part II. and the Staff Manual respectively. Title pages will be prepared in manuscript.

WAR DIARY
or
INTELLIGENCE SUMMARY.
(Erase heading not required.)

Army Form C. 2118.

Hour, Date, Place		Summary of Events and Information	Remarks and references to Appendices
		which duty was completed by 2.45am 6.2.15	
		Ammunition Expenditure RHA. 20 Rnds per gun - 18pr 7.75	
11.6 pm	5.2.15 Poperinghe	2/ Army wire through V Corps ordering up 2-6 gun 18pr Batteries to 28th Div. - area billetting area allotted (Batys 22nd & 118th)	
11.25 pm	5.2.15 "	V Corps order all 28th Div units to be clear of old billetting area by noon 8th.	
		Casualty Report for previous 24 hours.	
		83 Inf Bde. Officers killed Lt. O.J. Addyman. Wounded Capt Wilkinson, 2/Lt H J Muller	
		Other ranks 15 killed 44 wounded 61 missing	
		84 Inf Bde 4 killed 18 wounded.	
		Weather Fine.	[signature] Maj
9.45 am	6.2.15 "	5th Corps notifies 22nd & 118 Batteries RFA. are marching on 7th from Hazebrouck for 28th Div billetting area.	
		Postal authorities raise question of locating Div'l Train P.O. as near R.P as possible - arranged for it to be at OUDERDOM this is because this P.O. deals with all letters for Div'l Troops.	
3.15 pm	"	Following movements took place during day.	
		2/Buffs - 2/E. Surrey to YPRES 4pm & billetted in Cav Bks until 8pm when the 85th moved out to relieve 83rd Inf Bde in the trenches	

(73989) W4141—463. 400,000. 9/14. H.&J.Ltd. Forms/C. 2118/10.

Instructions regarding War Diaries and Intelligence Summaries are contained in F. S. Regs., Part II. and the Staff Manual respectively. Title pages will be prepared in manuscript.

WAR DIARY
or
INTELLIGENCE SUMMARY.
(Erase heading not required.)

Army Form C. 2118.

Hour, Date, Place	Summary of Events and Information	Remarks and references to Appendices
	Train Transport ~~and~~ (6 waggons) ~~and~~ to Porte de Lille YPRES, to be in addition to two Motor Lorries – to bring equipment of 83rd Inf Bde out of trenches.	
	Casualties during 24 hours ending 8 am – RA: Lt Richardson wounded. ~~Next~~ 83rd Inf Bde Maj [illegible] K · 2 offrs W – OR 18 K : 84 W : 41 missing. 83 Inf Bde 4 K : 9 W	[illegible] Maj
	Ammunition expended RHA. 7.3 – 18 pr. 32.2 – 4.5" How 1.25 – V. Wet	
3 am. 7.2.15 Poperinghe	83rd Bde now returned from trenches and were located as follows 1 Bn in billeting area near OUDERDOM – 1 Bn in new huts erected by R.E. – 1 Bn in Inf Bks YPRES: 1 in Cav Bks. These latter billeted in YPRES as they were in the front trenches and it was anticipated they could not walk far.	
	Notification was received yesterday that 2 groups (6–4 gun batteries) of Belgian Artillery will join Division on 10th or 11th.	
2 pm " "	22nd & 118th Batteries marched in & billetted at ABEELE also the Amn Col who had some difficulty in shaking down into their new billets.	
	Wastage from sickness for previous 7 days – 14 offrs & 291 OR.	
	During afternoon 84th Infantry Bde holding the left sector of the trenches wired asking for sandbags – a large number have been drawn and deposited in a casemate inside the Porte de Lille YPRES but there has been insufficient supervision over the issue – and the sandbags have been drawn by ~~people~~ troops other than Inf. An Inf Bde takes about 2000 per night	

(73989) W4141—463. 400,000. 9/14. H.&J.Ltd. Forms/C. 2118/10.

Instructions regarding War Diaries and Intelligence Summaries are contained in F. S. Regs., Part II. and the Staff Manual respectively. Title pages will be prepared in manuscript.

WAR DIARY
or
INTELLIGENCE SUMMARY.
(Erase heading not required.)

Army Form C. 2118.

Hour, Date, Place	Summary of Events and Information	Remarks and references to Appendices
	since 4000 bags were collected by RE and used during the night. The large number required is due to the fact that enemy's shrapnel destroy them – Rifle oil was also asked for urgently by 84 Bde and Coke – both these articles were collected and sent to YPRES by midnight.	
	Rounds per gun expended RHA 2·7 – 18Pr · 44.	
8pm. 7·2·15. Poperinghe	5th Corps wires giving authority to purchase any small carts or handcarts for purpose of carrying rations etc towards the trenches in places where ordinary transport cannot be used – investigations as to possibilities commenced by OC Train.	
	Casualty return Capt Crankshaw 3/R. Fus wounded – 3 OR killed – 49 wounded 6 missing.	[illegible]
11·25 am 8·2·15 Poperinghe	House in which were supplies of 84th Inf Bde caught fire from shell & burnt destroying 60 Rifles & sets Equipment – 84th Bde asked for these to be replaced by nightfall. Steps taken as follows – 2/3 London F.A. applied to in case they had not despatched all sets of belonging to casualties – 40 Rifles & sets of Equip. were found & despatched to Porte de Lille YPRES but were not eventually required as Bde found others.	
2·10pm " "	5th Corps notifies ~~that~~ 37th How Batty & 104th Heavy Batty will be transferred to ~~[illegible]~~ V Corps to relieve part of French Artillery.	
	5th Corps notifies that 12th London Regt will form a permanent part of the 84th Inf Bde –	
7·6pm " "	Horsed [illegible] 2nd Army instructs 28 Div to indent for 9 horsed waggons for Belgian artillery (to form their train) – These waggons were eventually ordered to Ouderdom	

Instructions regarding War Diaries and Intelligence Summaries are contained in F. S. Regs., Part II. and the Staff Manual respectively. Title pages will be prepared in manuscript.

WAR DIARY
or
INTELLIGENCE SUMMARY.
(Erase heading not required.)

Army Form C. 2118.

Hour, Date, Place	Summary of Events and Information	Remarks and references to Appendices
7pm 8.2.15 Poperinghe	Lieut Col Sweetman reported on being relieved of Command of 2/C. Yorks	
" "	Casualties during previous 24 hours ~~84~~ 84th Inf Bde K2 W.18. 85th Inf Bde Lt Hammond Buffs wounded. Capt Anderson 3/R. Fus wounded OR 11K – 16W. RE. OR 1W. Rounds ~~per gun~~ expended ~~A~~ RHA ~~86~~. 18pr 11 – 4.5" How ~~Lydd.~~ 15". Shrap 21	
	12 London Regt T.F. moved into Cavalry Bks at YPRES to act as fatigue party in carrying supplies & stores from Bde HQ to the trenches – This work has been found to be ~~as~~ exhausting to men in the trenches as the trench work itself. Weather v. fine and bright.	[illegible]
10am 9.2.15 Poperinghe	2 Groupes i.e. 6–4 gun Batteries of Belgian Artillery are joining 28 Divn on 10th. Their billeting parties reported 10 am and were allotted an area. As regards supply the Belgians have 5 Motor Lorries which will join our Supply Column which we are indenting for 9 horsed waggons to form the supply train	See 7.6 pm 8th Feb
4.45pm 9.2.15 "	V Corps notifies that owing to difficulty of replacing ~~guns~~ 4.7" QF guns which are worn out the 113 Batty will join 28 Divn instead of 114th.	

Army Form C. 2118.

WAR DIARY
or
INTELLIGENCE SUMMARY
(Erase heading not required.)

Instructions regarding War Diaries and Intelligence Summaries are contained in F. S. Regs., Part II. and the Staff Manual respectively. Title pages will be prepared in manuscript.

Hour, Date, Place		Summary of Events and Information	Remarks and references to Appendices
		No of Rounds Expended on 9th 18 pr 46 – How 1 – RHA 46. Casualties. 85th Inf Bde OR 13/9 K – 48 W. Weather v. wet and cold.	[illegible]
12 noon	10.2.15 Poperinghe	Major Sweeney R.Fus. assumed Command of 2/E. Yorks vice Lt Col. Sweetman.	
"	"	B. Genl Sir P. Humphrey Surrey Yeomanry appointed Commdt at YPRES. This was found necessary in order to regulate the collection & disposition of transport of units at YPRES and especially the Infantry Bdes was becoming congested –	
12.53pm	"	V Corps notifies that 37th How & 113th Hy Batteries are accompanied by Section Ammn Cols are marching to join 28 Div on 12th.	
9.43pm	"	83rd Inf Bde raises question as to whether they can draw Rifles from 2/Lond Fd Amb: Reply sent to effect that Fd Ambs are not to collect arms but that any in possession of Fd Ambs at a moment when Brigade requires them will be available	
10.30pm	"	No of rounds Expended 15 pr 94 – 4.5 6 – How 27 RHA 191	
		2 Groupes (6 Batteries) Belgian Artillery marched in during morning. They have with them an M.T. Amn Col.	

1247 W 3299 200,000 (E) 8/14 J.B.C. & A. Forms/C. 2118/11.

Instructions regarding War Diaries and Intelligence Summaries are contained in F. S. Regs., Part II. and the Staff Manual respectively. Title pages will be prepared in manuscript.

WAR DIARY
or
INTELLIGENCE SUMMARY
(Erase heading not required.)

Army Form C. 2118.

Hour, Date, Place	Summary of Events and Information	Remarks and references to Appendices
	1 MT Art Amn Col and a horsed Amn Col. also 5 MT Supply Vehicles and a horsed Baggage train – The 5 Supply Vehicles join our Supply Column and ~~the~~ 9 horsed Train Waggons joined as Supply Train Vehicles	
10.2.15 Poperinghe	Casualties for prev. 24 hours. 84th Inf Bde. 8 K – 16 W – m & Lt Milburn K. 85th " " 19 K – 80 " & Lt Siddel Killed – Maj Hingley Wnded 12th Lon T F 1 31st Fd Bde. 1	
	Weather Fine – Cold During the night the 83rd Bde relieved the 84th in the Trenches	A.A.W.H.
11.2.15 Poperinghe	16 Waggons received by 28th Div Train for Hay Waggons on ~~Dest~~ the Scale of 3 to an Arty Bde 2 to Train etc.	
" "	No of Rounds expended on 11th Feb 18 pr 69 – How Nil – RHA 3 Aircraft 12	
	Railhead changed to ABEELE.	
11.5pm 11.2.15 "	Casualties for last 24 hours 84th Inf Bde 2 K. 9 W: 85th Inf Bde 17 K: 16 W Ra 1 W: Lt Hobbs 3/Mx Wnded. The men in the Trenches are suffering from Standing in the water their feet become affected and swell – approximately ~~5000~~ 500 men are now out of action on this account. 250 prs of gum boots have been issued and we are trying to get more – Weather V. Cold	A.A.W.H.

Instructions regarding War Diaries and Intelligence Summaries are contained in F. S. Regs., Part II. and the Staff Manual respectively. Title pages will be prepared in manuscript.

WAR DIARY
or
INTELLIGENCE SUMMARY
(Erase heading not required.)

Army Form C. 2118.

Hour, Date, Place			Summary of Events and Information	Remarks and references to Appendices
2·21 pm	12·2·15	Poperinghe	83 Inf Bde with a view to avoiding "Swollen feet" cases ask for 1000 pairs of gum boots for the Bde – [illegible] wires to ad 2nd Army. Later in the afternoon DA & QMG of V Corps came over showing a wire from 2nd Army asking if these boots are necessary for 28th Div. Very unsatisfactory.	
"	"	"	37th How Battery and 113th Hy Battery with Amn Col join the Division and billet near BRANDHOEK.	
3 pm	12·2·15	"	The Corps Commander visits ~~Administrative~~ HQ 28 Div and insists that units going into trenches take 2 days supplies. It was pointed out that this is contrary to the System of Supply and contrary to a memorandum received from DA & QMG 2nd Army on 5th – ~~that~~ memorandum stated the normal supply situation at 10 am & 6 pm 6th & asked for confirmation from Divisions which confirmation was duly sent by wire on 6th.	
3·50 pm	12·2·15	"	Wire received from 5th Corps ordering 28th Div to see that Senior Supply Officer arranged that every man who goes into the trenches takes 2 days rations. AQMG wires 5th Corps pointing out that as this is contrary to Regulation arrangements must be made with Regulating Officer to send up the extra Supplies.	Appendix 2
	12·2·15	"	Owing to the numerous difficulties experienced by Belgian artillery arrangements made to attach a Supply Officer to them to assist in all their supply arrangements.	

1247 W 3299 200,000 (E) 8/14 J.B.C. & A. Forms/C. 2118/11.

Instructions regarding War Diaries and Intelligence Summaries are contained in F. S. Regs., Part II. and the Staff Manual respectively. Title pages will be prepared in manuscript.

WAR DIARY
or
INTELLIGENCE SUMMARY
(Erase heading not required.)

Army Form C. 2118.

Hour, Date, Place	Summary of Events and Information	Remarks and references to Appendices
	Considerable difficulty has been experienced in getting the daily issue of 2000 daily newspaper and 1500 weekly newspapers to units – These arrive at the R.P. and are issued to units with rations – but there appear to be difficulties in getting them further	
	a system is being introduced and tried tonight of working all the Bn Pack Animals between Bde HQ and the trenches to save the men – 10 men only per platoon meeting them at Bn HQ to carry the food onwards.	
	Rounds expended 18pr. 256 How ~~tt~~ Shrap 10.	
	Casualties 84 Inf Bde 3K. 8W + Lt Singleton North Fus wounded. 83 " " 1K. 2W 85 " " 8K. 26W 12: London T.F. 3W RE 3K. 5W RFA . 1W Rame . 1W 15 . 46 1	
	Wet & cold. – I	
13. 2. 15 Poperinghe	An 10" shot an 13 hr anti aircraft gun on Ferry [illegible] the town hitting a lot of 30 men & 3 horses.	
	Rounds expended on 13th 18pr 64	
	Casualties 83 Inf Bde 2K – 12W: 85 Inf Bde 5K – 18W – 1M: also Lt Tyrrell 4/Buffs W. Lt Gransmore 3/Mx. W. 4/Lt Tate 3/R. Fus. W.	

Instructions regarding War Diaries and Intelligence Summaries are contained in F. S. Regs., Part II. and the Staff Manual respectively. Title pages will be prepared in manuscript.

WAR DIARY
or
INTELLIGENCE SUMMARY
(Erase heading not required.)

Army Form C. 2118.

Hour, Date, Place	Summary of Events and Information	Remarks and references to Appendices
	number of cases of swollen feet admitted to hospital has suddenly increased enormously. 85 Bde report estimated strengths	
	on 12th Buffs 430 on 13th Buffs 306	
	R. Fus 706 R Fus 476	
	E. Surr 772 E Surr 575	
	Mx 642 Mx 370	
	Considerable investigation made with result that it appears we have lost some 2500 since mobilisation – about 2000 since 1st Feb. 900 of whom are cases of swollen feet – investigation shows that care has been taken to use anti frostbite grease but medical statistics go to show that this delays but does not prevent frostbite – 250 pairs gum boots are undoubtedly in use per Bn but they are too short and the water gets over the tops.	
	V. wet & cold.	[illegible]
10.17 am 14.2.15 Poperinghe	2nd Army informs that no telephones or wire can be spared – this is getting serious as (a) in the trenches wires are repeatedly cut by bullets and (b) the RA especially the recently formed Belgians are short.	
1.26 pm " "	100 additional gum boots allowed per Bn – this makes a total of 350 allowed per Bn.	
6 pm " "	V Corps notifies that following two T.F. Bns join as under – 3/Monmouths 83rd Bde on 16th; 5/R Lancs 83rd Bde on 17th and that they	
	1/ " 84 " " 16	
	will be billeted in the area Steenvoorde – Ryveldt – Terdeghem. To be supplied from ABEELE.	

1247 W 3299 200,000 (E) 8/14 J.B.C. & A. Forms/C. 2118/11.

Instructions regarding War Diaries and Intelligence Summaries are contained in F. S. Regs., Part II. and the Staff Manual respectively. Title pages will be prepared in manuscript.

WAR DIARY
or
INTELLIGENCE SUMMARY
(Erase heading not required.)

Army Form C. 2118.

Hour, Date, Place	Summary of Events and Information	Remarks and references to Appendices
9.5 pm 14.2.15 Poperinghe	Three Batteries are being formed out of the 2 Battys 22 & 118 the new Batty being 22A. Re notify they have been allotted as follows: 22 to 3rd Bde RFA. 22A to 31st Bde RFA – 118th to 146th Bde RFA.	
9.25 pm 14.2.15 "	Lt Col Martin Comdg 2/K.O.R. Lancs reported by 83rd Bde to have broken down under the strain and is being evacuated.	
	Wastage from Sickness during previous ~~24 hours~~ seven days 83rd Inf Bde 5 offrs 470 OR: 84 Inf Bde 2 offs 226 OR: 85th Inf Bde 16 offrs 750 OR 12th Londn TF. 7 OR: RHA 5 OR RFA 19 OR: ASC 11 OR: Yeomany 1 offr 4 OR Div Cyclist 1 OR. AOC 1 OR: RE 14 OR	
	Casualties for last 24 hours 83 Inf Bde 3 K – 17 W: 85 " " 39 K – 101 W: RE " " 2 "	
	The high numbers were due to a German attack on 85 Trench in the morning.	
	Rounds expended during the 14th 18 pr 1291: 4.5" 11 HE & 7 Shrap	
10.10 am 15.2.15 Poperinghe	Vth Corps notifies that 2 Railway Coys will detrain at ABEELE or Poperinghe on 17th or 18th to proceed to YPRES attached 28th Div:	
	number of Rounds expended on 15th Feby 18 pr 951 – HE 110 4.5" 18 HE Shrap 31: 4.7 5	
" " "	1600 pairs of most excellent Socks received from H. M. The Queen	

1247 W 3299 200,000 (E) 8/14 J.B.C. & A. Forms/C. 2118/11.

Instructions regarding War Diaries and Intelligence Summaries are contained in F. S. Regs., Part II. and the Staff Manual respectively. Title pages will be prepared in manuscript.

WAR DIARY
or
INTELLIGENCE SUMMARY
(Erase heading not required.)

Army Form C. 2118.

Hour, Date, Place	Summary of Events and Information	Remarks and references to Appendices
15.2.15	Rounds per gun in front of Railhead at 7 pm. on 14th was 18 pr 347 Shrap: 6 HE — 4.5" How HE 45 — Shrap 131 — 60 pr 280 — 4.7 Shrap 97 — HE 173 — S.a.a 219 3448, Pistol 7328	
15.2.15	[illegible] Coy R.E. joined the Division on 10th at YPRES & is employed in digging assisting with trenches. Capt [illegible]	
15.2.15	Casualty report as far as obtainable. 83rd Bde 2K. 20 W. Lieut Reeves. Lt Parke. Lt Heywood wounded. Buffs 85 Bde 13K. 97 W. 139 M. Capt Reeves 2/Lt Birnie killed. Capt Robinson. Anson. Lt Heales, Swinton, 2/Lt Bratty and other 2/Lt. Surg. wounded RA 2 W. 17 Lancs 2K. 2W. Capt Galloway & 1 OR R. Monmouth RE wounded — 12 London Capt Studd killed, Capt Bransive wounded Weather v. wet – The mud is getting very deep everywhere off the [illegible]	
16.2.15 Poperinghe	5th Corps notifies ~~71st~~ 121st Hy Battery allotted 28 Div.	
10.40 am ~~16.6~~	" " " From today No 28 Ammn Park at STEENVOORDE will have advanced Section at ABEELE and BOESCHEPPE. 27 Amn Park remains as an Emergency Park at S. Sylvestre.	

1247 W 3299 200,000 (E) 8/14 J.B.C. & A. Forms/C. 2118/11.

Instructions regarding War Diaries and Intelligence Summaries are contained in F. S. Regs., Part II. and the Staff Manual respectively. Title pages will be prepared in manuscript.

WAR DIARY
or
INTELLIGENCE SUMMARY
(Erase heading not required.)

Army Form C. 2118.

Hour, Date, Place		Summary of Events and Information	Remarks and references to Appendices
12.25pm	16.2.15 Poperinghe	Great difficulty has been experienced in getting water up to the men in the trenches owing to the mud - darkness & distance - An experiment was tried with painters cans which have proved very successful - to fit out the Bde would ~~take £~~ cost £80 or £90 which ~~[illegible]~~ Supply authority will not approve - We are however trying 100 more cans and authority has been asked for a second water bottle per man.	
2pm	16.2.15 "	Estimate of fighting strength at 2pm as follows 83 Bde - 8̊4 - 2550 84 — 86 - 2900 85 — ? — 1200	
7pm	16.2.15 "	RA reports Belgians have expended up to date 683 Rounds Shrapnel and 702 HE.	
		Question has arisen of how to deal with the surplus arms & amn owing to large numbers of killed & wounded Rifles - Many Rifles &c are now surplus on Corps Regtl charge. Fd ambs cannot get rid of them and have asked DADOS to take it. DADOS has no machinery for this - especially does this apply to amn - not a very suitable store for a motor ambulance - In consequence as a temporary arrangement - Bde Amn Cols directed to draw amn from the 2 Fd ambs in YPRES & try the experiment for a week. ~~Authority asked for a second water~~	
—	16.2.15 —	No of Rounds expended during previous 24 hrs. 18pr 385 - HE 2 RHA 120. — ~~Belgians~~ 2 Mammonth RE Railway Corps arrived and were directed on YPRES.	

1247 W 3299 200,000 (E) 8/14 J.B.C. & A. Forms/C. 2118/11.

Instructions regarding War Diaries and Intelligence Summaries are contained in F. S. Regs., Part II. and the Staff Manual respectively. Title pages will be prepared in manuscript.

WAR DIARY
or
INTELLIGENCE SUMMARY
(Erase heading not required.)

Army Form C. 2118.

Hour, Date, Place	Summary of Events and Information	Remarks and references to Appendices
16-2-15 Poperinghe	121st Hy Battery commenced to arrive 17th	
	Drafts averaging ~~about~~ one officer and 50 men per Bn. commenced to arrive for 28th Divn at ABEELE Railhead.	
	~~Ammunition expended last 24 hours.~~	
	Following names of Casualties were reported.	
	4th R. Susx 2/Lt. Shore killed – wounded Lt Bell Irving & 2/Lt Cober.	
	Weather Showery – Heavy fighting in the trenches at night.	[illegible]
12.30pm 17.2.15 Poperinghe	1/Monmouths Regt T.F. arrived for 28th Divn at CASSEL were met by DAQMG and billetted round RYWELD	
4.30pm 17.2.15 "	71st & 121st Batteries (Heavy) arrived at Poperinghe by rail and were billetted near Brandhoek.	
4.30pm " "	3/Monmouths R.T.F. arrived for 28th Divn at Cassel, Railhead ~~and~~ were met by DAQMG and billetted in CASSEL.	
5.30pm " "	9th Inf Bde arrived at YPRES to reinforce and were billetted in YPRES by DAA & QMG. – Their Refilling point LACLYTE.	
10pm " "	Extra water bottles refused by 2nd Army	See 12.20pm of 16.2.15
17.2.15 "	Rounds expended during past 24 hours 18 Pr Shrap 2547: HE 125. How: HE 26 Shrap 48 – Belgians 253 Shrap 237 HE.	

1247 W 3299 200,000 (E) 8/14 J.B.C. & A. Forms/C. 2118/11.

Instructions regarding War Diaries and Intelligence Summaries are contained in F. S. Regs., Part II. and the Staff Manual respectively. Title pages will be prepared in manuscript.

WAR DIARY
or
INTELLIGENCE SUMMARY
(Erase heading not required.)

Army Form C. 2118.

Hour, Date, Place	Summary of Events and Information	Remarks and references to Appendices
17. 2. 15 Poperinghe	Reinforcements continue to arrive. 113th Fy Batty commences to withdraw.	
	Casualties for 16th as follows. 83rd Inf Bdes O.R. 7K. 10W.	
	" " 17th " " " 1K. 14W.	
	" 16 & 17 " 84 Inf Bdes Officers 9K. 7W O.R. 24K. 109W. – 228 M.	
	~~Killed~~ " Officers Killed Capt Martin, " Harris, Lt Smith, Lt Forbes } 1/Suffolks. Wounded { Capt Cooper, " Campbell, Lt May, " Payne. Missing { Capt Tourtelle(?), Lt Maybery(?), Lt Briggs	
	" { Lt Col Ardenley(?), Capt Aird } 2 North Fus	
	Lt Keating ?. " 2 Lt. Ward. 2/Ches. missing Lt Leah(?)	
	The above casualty reports considered unreliable – weather V. wet.	
6 am 18. 2. 15 Poperinghe	5/K.O.R. Lancs R. arrived Cassel and marched to WINNIZEELE where they billetted. –	
9 am 18. 2. 15 "	3/Monmouthshire moved from CASSEL into billets at STEENVOORDE ?aqua(?) was directed to visit and gather the 3 Bns – This duty was taken in hand.	
18. 2. 15 "	3/Field Squadron joined at YPRES.	
18. 2. 15 "	Following arrangements arrived at during day by the Vth Corps – 85th Inf Bde to move to LOCRE on 19th. – 13th Inf Bde same date to OUDERDOM – Considerable discussion about	

Instructions regarding War Diaries and Intelligence Summaries are contained in F. S. Regs., Part II. and the Staff Manual respectively. Title pages will be prepared in manuscript.

WAR DIARY
or
INTELLIGENCE SUMMARY
(Erase heading not required.)

Army Form C. 2118.

Hour, Date, Place	Summary of Events and Information	Remarks and references to Appendices
	transport matters which resulted in an arrangement of exchange of A.S.C. horses & Personnel – both in the case of the 9th & 13th Inf Bdes – but the number of wires necessitated were considerable and hardly did Camberley Credit – In the long run the 83, 84, 85 Inf Bdes are to be withdrawn and replaced by 9th 13th 15th Inf Bdes.	
	Total number of rounds expended in last 24 hrs. 15pr 80 Shrap – HE 8 – How. 50 HE. 8 Shrap – Belgians Shrap 19 –	
7.45pm 18.2.15 Poperinghe	Water is knee deep in trenches 84th Bde ask for a large supply of Bales which were purchased in Poperinghe & sent out	
	~~3rd Field Squadron joined at YPRES during the day~~ weather wet	
19.2.15 Poperinghe	notification received that ammunition of Belgian Artillery has been transferred from ADINKERCH to ARCQUES –	
	The ~~83~~ 83, 84, & 85 Inf Bdes of the 28th Div have been collecting too many Stores, surplus equipment, trench & regimental in the Infantry Bks at YPRES – This has been in view for some time but it has been found impossible to check as the	

1247 W 3299 200,000 (E) 8/14 J.B.C. & A. Forms/C. 2118/11.

Army Form C. 2118.

Instructions regarding War Diaries and Intelligence Summaries are contained in F. S. Regs., Part II. and the Staff Manual respectively. Title pages will be prepared in manuscript.

WAR DIARY
or
INTELLIGENCE SUMMARY

(Erase heading not required.)

Hour, Date, Place	Summary of Events and Information	Remarks and references to Appendices
	Stores were necessary – now that the 85th Bde is ordered to move today to LOCRES the question of clearing the Stores presents difficulty – during the day 12 waggon loads were moved into Poperinghe and arrangements made for 2 waggon loads to go on 20th with private Regt Stores to LOCRE.	
12 noon 19.2.15 Poperinghe	85th Infantry Bde moves to LOCRE 13th Inf Bde reach OUDERDOM and go into the huts and billets – 13th Inf Bde Supply waggons refill on 20th at LA CLYTTE. – 9th Inf Bde Refills at OUDERDOM.	
19.2.15 "	Number of Rounds expended on 19th Feb 18 pr 119. How 24	
	It has now for some days been arranged that troops going into trenches take with them Supplies for 2 days, as it was found almost impossible to ensure the supply to troops in front trenches. This was effected by L of C sending up ~~a supply~~ an extra day's supply which is stored in YPRES: this arrangement holds good for the new Brigades	
5.25p 19.2.15 Poperinghe	~~Fighting Strength~~ amendments to previous casualty returns notified as follows – 2/E. Yorks – 40 of the 57 missing have rejoined. 2/E. Surry – The 136 missing should be 37	
— 19.2.15 Poperinghe	145 ~~horses~~ Remounts were received for 28 Div at ABEELE & distributed to units.	

Instructions regarding War Diaries and Intelligence Summaries are contained in F. S. Regs., Part II. and the Staff Manual respectively. Title pages will be prepared in manuscript.

WAR DIARY
or
INTELLIGENCE SUMMARY
(Erase heading not required.)

Army Form C. 2118.

Hour, Date, Place	Summary of Events and Information	Remarks and references to Appendices
19·2·15 Poperinghe	Casualties for 24 hours ending 8 am 18th.	
	83 Inf Bde. Offs 4K : 6W Killed Lt Stokes Lt Harford. Lt Hatherway KOR Lanc - Capt G Hill 4/R Fus	
	OR 29K : 65W : 26 m. \ Wounded 1/2 Lt Vake, Maj Bassett, KOR Lancs.	
	2/R York Lt Gunn Lt Kennard, Capt Trimble, Lt Saunders	
	84 Inf Bde Off 5K . 5W . 4m Killed Lt Kealy 2/Ches Suffolks not known.	
	OR 21K 58W . 226m Linkes 2/Lt Ward — Maj 2/Lt Keating.	
	85 Inf Bde. OR 2 . 4 W.	
	RAMC Lt Campbell attd 2/E Yorks killed	
	DWRE OR 1K - 4W.	
	Casualties for 24 hours ending 8 am 19	
	83rd Inf Bde. Offs 1K . 2W Lt Mather Kotted 4 1 L. killed. Lt Lethbridge Y&L Lichfield wounded	
	OR 10K . 24 W.	
	84 " " Offs 1K - 2W Lt Rushbrooke 2/North Fus & Lt Watson 2/Ches wounded	
	OR 7 - 17 W Lt Newson 2/Ches K.	
	Div RE Offs 3K - 1W Killed Capt Bowles, Maj Sewell, Lt Stone	
	OR — 4W wounded 2/Lt Strond.	
	Sup Train OR 1W	
	9th Inf Bde OR. 1K . 8	
	Weather fine — wet later.	[signature]

1247 W 3299 200,000 (E) 8/14 J.B.C. & A. Forms/C. 2118/11.

Instructions regarding War Diaries and Intelligence Summaries are contained in F. S. Regs., Part II. and the Staff Manual respectively. Title pages will be prepared in manuscript.

WAR DIARY
or
INTELLIGENCE SUMMARY

(Erase heading not required.)

Army Form C. 2118.

Hour, Date, Place	Summary of Events and Information	Remarks and references to Appendices
20-2-15 Poperinghe	The new Bdes Inf Bdes 9th & 13th have Travelling Kitchens instead of GS Limbered Cooks Carts – 9th Bde proposes to arrange supply routine as follows – (Supply Col to R.P) – by GS waggon from R.P. to Bn Billet for stores probably between Vlamertinghe & Ouderdom thence by Trav Kitchen to YPRES and as far as it can go beyond Porte de Lille – This is approved –	
	Number of rounds expended 20th 18pr 306. HE 19. How HE 32 Shrap 23. Belgians 38 – HE 4	
	Further reinforcements joined as 1 9th	
11·20 am 20.2.15 "	Investigation shows state of Suffolk officers as follows Killed Capt FW WOOD MARTIN – Wounded Capt F Cooper " R HARRIS " J Campbell Lt. C. Smith Lt. May " D. Forbes " Payne Missing Capt Jourdain Lt. Moysey 2Lt. Biggs State of 1st Middlesex reported missing 21 in Hosp. 3 Returned. 132 missing	
11·20 am " "	5th Corps have called for report on number of miners in the Division and their qualifications.	
	Casualties for 20th 83rd Inf Bde Killed 2Lt S Folker, 70L OR 4. OR K. W. M. wounded 4. 19. 1 84 " " Wounded Capt Phillips, Welsh, 2Lt Saunders " 1. 13 RE " " Dead 1. 9th " " Wounded 2Lt S Mountain 4 R Irish, Capt A Bell 1 R Irish 12 1	
	Weather Heavy Hail Storm with Thunder in middle of day	

1247 W 3299 200,000 (E) 8/14 J.B.C. & A. Forms/C. 2118/11.

Instructions regarding War Diaries and Intelligence Summaries are contained in F. S. Regs., Part II. and the Staff Manual respectively. Title pages will be prepared in manuscript.

WAR DIARY
or
INTELLIGENCE SUMMARY

(Erase heading not required.)

Army Form C. 2118.

Hour, Date, Place	Summary of Events and Information	Remarks and references to Appendices
20.2.15 Poperinghe	Plan showing R.P. in 28th Division attached for 20th Feb	Appendix 3
21.2.15 "	Instructions (through V Corps) from II Army place Col Sir) Hemp(?) Porey Commt Ypres (28th Div) in charge of both Cav and 28 Div areas of YPRES.	
	Rounds Expended 21st 18pr 504. H.E. 9. How Shrap 42 H.E. 74.	
8.15pm 21.2.15 "	Change made in movements of Brigades — as it stands 85th Inf Bde has gone - we have 9th in YPRES — 84th In Trenches 13th In trenches since 8 night 20-21st. 83rd at Ouderdom - Now 84th marches to Bailleul on 23rd being relieved in the trenches by the 13th Bde tonight. This necessitated some considerable detailed arrangements both Supply & Transport because numbers of all Bdes vary considerably - and Bdes of 3rd & 5th Divs; are not similarly organised to 28th Div e.g. 3&5 Divs have 3 Country Carts for blankets driven by Soldiers of the Bdes and called 1st Line. We have 2 G.S. Waggons per Bn considered 2nd Line.	
21.2.15 "	Great difficulty continues to arise in connection with obtaining R.E. Stores and Explosives - especially Sandbags and Rifle grenades - ~~e.g. an ae~~ R.E. indent but don't get the things. Tonight A.Q.M.G. had to go to the R.E. Park ~~for~~ STRAZEELE	

WAR DIARY

or

INTELLIGENCE SUMMARY

(Erase heading not required.)

Army Form C. 2118.

Instructions regarding War Diaries and Intelligence Summaries are contained in F. S. Regs., Part II. and the Staff Manual respectively. Title pages will be prepared in manuscript.

Hour, Date, Place	Summary of Events and Information	Remarks and references to Appendices
	to get some Rifle grenades which happened to be there. Though of course Rifle grenades come up normally in the Ammunition Park – we are trying to carry out this problem.	
21·2·15 Poperinghe	HQ 8th How Bde & 65th How Battery arrived – with 37th this forms 8 How Bde – 86th Battery goes.	
21·2·15 "	Return of Casualties. 83 Inf Bde. 3 off missing Capt Kaulback, Capt Ray, Lt Roche OR K 7 – W 40 – M 27. 84 IB. wounded (Lt Brunker, Lt Legard, Lt Jenkins) Irish Fus. Lt [illegible] 1/Welsh missing Lt A. C. White. OR K 7 – W 82 – M 65. – RE Lt ~~Davis~~ Gedale ~~1 off~~ wounded – OR. K 2 – W 3 9th Inf Bde 1 off. wounded Lt Arnold – OR 4 – 13 W. Weather Showery –	A.A.M.H. –
10·30 am 22·2·15 "	DA&QMG 5th Div visited 28 Div and discussed arrangements regarding change of Brigades – arrangements come to were as shown in Appendix – Wastage from sickness other than wounded during 7 days ending 20th [illegible] amounted to the 1314.	Appendix 4

Instructions regarding War Diaries and Intelligence Summaries are contained in F. S. Regs., Part II. and the Staff Manual respectively. Title pages will be prepared in manuscript.

WAR DIARY
or
INTELLIGENCE SUMMARY
(Erase heading not required.)

Army Form C. 2118.

Hour, Date, Place	Summary of Events and Information	Remarks and references to Appendices
22.2.15. Poperinghe	Casualties during last 24 hours RA ~~W1~~ O.R. W.1 9th Inf Bde 4K. 8 13 " " H. Fyfield 12 Lond: T.F. W. 7 20 Weather Fine – ~~[illegible]~~	
10.10 am 23.2.15 Poperinghe	Notification received that our new battery 22A is to be renumbered 149.	
4.10pm " "	Reinforcements arrived for 1 Gor H and 2/E Yorks.	
	9th Inf Bde ask if supply of amtn boxes could be issued to Bdes each Evening. ~~Orders~~ Authority asked for from Corps and 2 Army as existing orders are to return the boxes –	
10pm 23.2.15 "	authority given & RA & Bdes notified.	
23.2.15 "	Considerable difficulty is being experienced in obtaining Sandbags and ~~Gren~~ Rifle Grenades – The organisation in this Division for drawing RE Trench Stores & explosives is that 3 lorries have been lent by V Corps to 2 Div RE – but Engineer or other ~~Bn~~ RE seem unable to ensure a	

1247 W 3299 200,000 (E) 8/14 J.B.C. & A. Forms/C. 2118/11.

Instructions regarding War Diaries and Intelligence Summaries are contained in F. S. Regs., Part II. and the Staff Manual respectively. Title pages will be prepared in manuscript.

WAR DIARY
or
INTELLIGENCE SUMMARY
(Erase heading not required.)

Army Form C. 2118.

Hour, Date, Place	Summary of Events and Information	Remarks and references to Appendices
	Regular Supply – The whole thing is under close consideration by the Administrative & Gen Staffs —	
– 23.2.15 Poperinghe	Casualties 23 – 9th Inf Bde Lt Wilson 1 Lincolns wounded OR 2K – 17W	
	Weather fine with snow showers at intervals – much colder	Paint —
10.30am 24.2.15 Poperinghe	Belgian Artillery have languished considerably from having being unable to obtain anything from Store e.g. Ankle Boots, Gum Boots, Skin Coats – After much worrying this has at last been authorised and Horse Shoes, Ankle Boots etc are to be issued.	
2 pm 24.2.15 "	226 men of 84th Inf Bde who were unable to march despatched despatched in 12 Motor Busses to Bailleul – Showing the great use of the Motor Busses in all emergencies.	
3.45pm " "	Another failure of Supply of RE Stores. V Corps have up to present lent RE 28 Div 3 Lorries M.T. for work between RE Park STRAZEELE and YPRES. These have just failed us having been taken by 27th Div Ultra Vires:– However V Corps have lent us 2 more but it is not satisfactory.	
" 24.2.15 "	As showing the multitude of different things required 2 several hundred hurdles now asked for from by 83rd Bde (~~the resting~~ to improve the walking in the resting area which is nearly knee deep in mud.	

Instructions regarding War Diaries and Intelligence Summaries are contained in F. S. Regs., Part II. and the Staff Manual respectively. Title pages will be prepared in manuscript.

Army Form C. 2118.

WAR DIARY
or
INTELLIGENCE SUMMARY

(Erase heading not required.)

Hour, Date, Place	Summary of Events and Information	Remarks and references to Appendices
24.2.15 Poperinghe	Opinion of 9th & 13th Bde taken as regards requirements of Rifle Grenades and opinion cut down to 30 or 40 daily – Vth Corps who has taken up this matter tho' their G.S. have told 2nd Army we want 150 daily. Mks	
24.2.15 "	Rounds Expended 24th 18pr 712. How shrap 72 – HE 13 – 4.7 6 Belge 15c1 – Belge HE 15.	
" "	During day large drafts arrived for 9th & 13th Inf Bdes.	
" "	Very quiet during day – weather very bad & snowy and trying for men in the trenches	
24.2.15 "	Casualties as follows. 13th Inf Bde. OR 8k. 5w Mon Fd Coy. ·2 " 9th " " 7k ·37. Lt Maybery killed.	[illegible]
25.2.15 "	Snow fell during night of 24th–25th and was about 3" deep at 8am but a thaw quickly set in.	
4.30pm " "	An additional Section for the Div Sig Company and added to increase facilities for Communication ~~with R~~ between RA & Inf – joined today –	

1247 W 3299 200,000 (E) 8/14 J.B.C. & A. Forms/C. 2118/11.

Instructions regarding War Diaries and Intelligence Summaries are contained in F. S. Regs., Part II. and the Staff Manual respectively. Title pages will be prepared in manuscript.

WAR DIARY
or
INTELLIGENCE SUMMARY
(Erase heading not required.)

Army Form C. 2118.

Hour, Date, Place	Summary of Events and Information	Remarks and references to Appendices
5pm – 25.2.14 Poperinghe	A specially enlisted detachment of 'Kickers' i.e. men who tunnel in sewers and such like – joined and moved to YPRES in strength ~~about~~ 1 offr & 35 OR.	
25.2.14 "	Everything very quiet throughout the Division all day	
"	Casualties RA Killed 2. OR Wounded 1. Officers wounded Major Hope. 13th Bde " 5 " 29. 2/Lt Hess 9 " " 10 " 19 " 2/Lt Cummins (13th) 2/Lt Hord Royal [illegible], Harris RWK	
	Weather heavy falls of snow – at intervals snow did not lie hence much more mud & slush.	[illegible] –
25.2.14 Poperinghe	During the day Capt Couwsmaker RE(T) reported at HQ Div as the agent at HQ for RE the CRE being located in YPRES – By this means it is hoped to ensure coordination between the ~~RE~~ [illegible] the Staff and the RE Depot at YPRES – Capt Couwsmaker being forming thus the missing link.	
4.30pm " "	A motor machine gun Battery of 6 guns with motor cycles and attendant lorries arrived.	
6.30pm " "	Orders received for 1st & 3rd Monmouths & 1/KORL Lancs to march to the 2nd Corps area – on 28th.	
	Casualties RA 2/Lt Simpson wounded – 9th Bde 4K – 15W. 13th Inf Bde 2/Lt Macgregor KOSB. OR 4K – 11W. Weather very fine cold and bright.	[illegible]

Instructions regarding War Diaries and Intelligence Summaries are contained in F. S. Regs., Part II. and the Staff Manual respectively. Title pages will be prepared in manuscript.

WAR DIARY
or
INTELLIGENCE SUMMARY
(Erase heading not required.)

Army Form C. 2118.

Hour, Date, Place	Summary of Events and Information	Remarks and references to Appendices
27-2-15 Poperinghe	V Corps notify following moves 12th London remains until 15th March when it changes with 10th L'pool and 9th London from 2nd Corps. On 2/3 6th L'pool from Bailleul to Vlamertinghe	
10 pm " "	Reinforcements for R Scots Fus arrive Railhead.	
	All very quiet during day. G.O.C. transferred his HQ to YPRES. Casualties during 27th 83 Bde 2 W. 9th Inf Bde 4K. 15 W. 13 " " 4K. 11 W. + Lt Macgregor KOSB K.	
27.2.15 Poperinghe	Ammunition Railhead moved to STRAZEELE. Weather dull and v. cold.	[illegible]
11 am 28.2.15 "	Drafts for 9th and 83rd Brigade arrive	
28.2.15 "	Numbers of Infantry present reported as 83rd Inf Bde 73 offs: 2435 OR: 9th Bde 123 offs. 4919 OR 13th Inf Bde 135 offs: 4998 OR Total 331 offs. 12,352 OR.	
12.15 pm 28.2.15 "	Captain Agg (OC Cyclists) appointed Commandant of the Hutments at Vlamertinghe & his cyclists to form his Staff.	
	Casualties 9th Bde OR. 3K. 31 W: Capt Grantham Killed 2 Lt Bisborne wounded ~~att~~ 1/Lincolns 83rd Bde OR 7K. 22 W	
28.2.15 "	The 1st & 3rd Monmouth Regt T.F. marched from Steenvoorde to join the 5th Div.	
28.2.15 "	During the month of Feb the wastage from ~~all~~ the fighting causes has been - excluding the 9th & 13 Inf Bdes who have only been with us for a short time - Sick 1639: Feet cases 2612: wounded 1543 Total 5794. The 2 Bdes (the 9th & 13th) are ~~477~~ 406: 144: 285 total 835. This does not include killed. Weather v. fine and bright.	[illegible]

121/4804

Head Quarters (A & Q) 28th Division

Vol IV 1 - 31. 3. 15

Confidential

WAR DIARY

of

THE ADMINISTRATIVE STAFF 28th Division

From 1st March 1915 to 31st March 1915

Volume. IV

Instructions regarding War Diaries and Intelligence Summaries are contained in F. S. Regs., Part II. and the Staff Manual respectively. Title pages will be prepared in manuscript.

WAR DIARY
or
INTELLIGENCE SUMMARY.
(Erase heading not required.)

Army Form C. 2118.

Hour, Date, Place	Summary of Events and Information	Remarks and references to Appendices
1 . 3 . 15 Poperinghe	A difficulty has arisen regarding Verys Pistols due to change of Bdes – Circumstances as follows – 15th Bde wired reporting that they had been ordered to hand over all Verys Pistols to 84th Bde – Enquiries elicited the fact that ~~84~~ 15th Bde arrived here with only 4. Further 84th Bde state they left theirs in our trenches on relief by 9th Bde – under orders of G.O.C. There is no sign of the Pistols and no trace of GOC's order – So wire sent to 5th Div notifying them that only those brought with 15th Bde would be available for 15th Bde – Similarly with regard to Braziers – 15th Bde are bringing none – and question arises how far these are 'regimental' or are 'trench' stores.	
1 . 3 . 15 "	Firing of Graze Fuzes by Heavy Guns is again being stopped. This leaves us with only 17 fireable rounds at the moment, – ~~as~~ But D.A. fuzes can be used (exception Emergency)	
3.55pm 1 . 3 . 15 "	5th Corps notifies that 50% of Rifles issued to T.F have been found not to fire Mk VII Cartridges and necessity arises of testing T.F. Rifles at once.	
1 . 3 . 15 "	Casualties 83rd Bde OR. 5K. 16W. 9 " OR. 9K. 45W. Lt Whitter R. Scots Fus wounded. mounted RE 2W.	
1 . 3 . 15 "	Weather v. fine interspersed with Snow & thunder Storm. Violent gale about 3.30pm which did much damage to Telephone & Telegraph and brought down a house in YPRES. 5 KOR Lancs marched to 5th Div area.	G Allhead
1pm 2 . 3 . 15 "	10/L'pool Scottish (T.F) and 6/Liverpool R. arrived and were billeted in the Vlamertinghe Area.	
5pm 2 . 3 . 15 "	Following is entered for purposes of record. Bde HQ of the resting Bde is being transferred from Busseboom to the farm As there is no furniture in latter the Baron Albert de Zuylen de Nyevelt of	

(73989) W4141—463. 400,000. 9/14. H.&J.Ltd. Forms/C. 2118/10.

Instructions regarding War Diaries and Intelligence Summaries are contained in F. S. Regs., Part II. and the Staff Manual respectively. Title pages will be prepared in manuscript.

WAR DIARY
~~or~~
~~INTELLIGENCE~~ SUMMARY.

(*Erase heading not required.*)

Army Form C. 2118.

Hour, Date, Place			Summary of Events and Information	Remarks and references to Appendices
			[illegible] Menin YPRES offered the use of his – The certain furniture was today moved from the Baron's house to the new Bde HQ under supervision of an officer HQ 28 Div: Detailed list of the furniture taken sent to the Baron and another list through Commdt YPRES to the Burgomaster YPRES	
—	2. 3. 15	Poperinghe	Casualties. RA – K OR 4 W 9th Bde 14 . 47 Lt Whittick 12th Lan: wounded 83 " 2 . 4 RE " 1 } 16 . 56	
			Casualties in 9th Bde due to Bombs. Otherwise all quiet. Weather fine. Warmer	[illegible]
—	3. 3. 15	Poperinghe	A very quiet day [illegible] in the administration.	
8.30 am	3. 3. 15	"	The 83rd Inf Bde marched to the 5th Div area. " 15th " " " into OUDERDOM Amount of explosives now collected at the Porte de Lille YPRES is excessive over 7000 lbs gunpowder collected there for G.S. in addition to other things. Casualties Cyclists OR 2 W – RA 1 OR W. 9th Bde 8 K 31 W OR – Lt Goldsmith 12th Lan. K. 13th " 9 K 8 W	
—	3. 3. 15	"	Wet day	[illegible] —
3 pm	4. 3. 15	"	15th Inf Bde report strength including 6 L.posts as 123 off – 4792 OR	
	4. 3. 15	"	Now that Captain A.G.G. has been appointed Commdt of the Huts in the resting area efforts have been increased to improve conditions & [illegible] of the	

(73989) W4141—463. 400,000. 9/14. H.&J.Ltd. Forms/C. 2118/10.

Instructions regarding War Diaries and Intelligence Summaries are contained in F. S. Regs., Part II. and the Staff Manual respectively. Title pages will be prepared in manuscript.

WAR DIARY
or
INTELLIGENCE SUMMARY.
(Erase heading not required.)

Army Form C. 2118.

Hour, Date, Place	Summary of Events and Information	Remarks and references to Appendices
	new huts are very good but the first 2 lots built are bad no floors in same, not waterproof, no washing facilities, and very deep mud – latter cannot be helped but the last remaining Field Company is being taken to Ypres and little can be done – result is loud complaints from 15th and Bde –	
— 4. 3. 15 Poperinghe	Casualties RE. OR K – 5W 13th Inf Bde. OR 1K – 3W. Cyclists 2 RA 2W. 2Lt Strickland & Groome wounded. 9th Bde. 12K – 16W. Capt Piper R. Fus Wnded – 5/Fus Capt Forster & Lieut Radcliffe Slightly wounded. Lt Lancaster R.S. wounded 13th Inf Bde 2 – 6. Total. 15K. 38W.	
5pm – 4.3.15 Poperinghe	15th Bde moved from Ouderdom into right Sector of Trenches relieving 9th Bde who came to Ouderdom. Weather Fine.	Callwell
— 5. 3. 15 Poperinghe	~~hr~~ a new Battery 22A recently named 149 formed out of 22 is mobilising at ABEELE for the 146th Bde – some doubt has existed as to whom this Batty was under IV Corps now notify battery belongs in all respects 146 ~~RA~~ Bde. R.F.A. It is as a matter of fact deficient of 21 draught horses.	
5. 3. 15	Repeated visits of officers of administration 2nd Army are being paid to the resting area to endeavour to get things improved there – what is wanted now is accomodation for officers – washing accomodation for men – Progress The two first are being	

(73989) W4141—463. 400,000. 9/14. H.&J.Ltd. Forms/C. 2118/10.

Instructions regarding War Diaries and Intelligence Summaries are contained in F.S. Regs., Part II. and the Staff Manual respectively. Title pages will be prepared in manuscript.

WAR DIARY
or
INTELLIGENCE SUMMARY.
(*Erase heading not required.*)

Army Form C. 2118.

	Hour, Date, Place	Summary of Events and Information	Remarks and references to Appendices
	5·3·15 Poperinghe	Casualties 9th Bde 4K O.R. – 33W – RL – K·W also Lt White RL 15th " 5K – 22W Lt Rhodes attd 1/Ches wounded 13 " 3K – 7W. Lt. G. Corsham R Lane R.W.	
	5·3·15	Weather Showery. – Very Quiet	A Abbott –
	6·3·15 Poperinghe	Some ablution benches prepared at Ouderdom, braziers, or rather empty grease tins, collected and basins – mud very bad however.	
2·30pm	6·3·15 Poperinghe	Party of Correspondents of 1st newspapers conducted round area under G.H.Q. instructions.	
	6·3·15 "	Casualties 13th Inf Bde OR 3W. RL 1W. 15th " " 45W. 9K. Re " " 1W. 12 Lan " " 5W.	
	6·3·15 "	Weather V. wet. Heavy artillery firing all day	A A McHardy
12·30pm	7·3·15 "	27th Div reports that owing to shell fire road between Millekruiss and DICKEBUSH impossible for transport and requests permission to use the ~~00~~ part of the OUDERDOM Road – This opened up question of changing our R.P from Ouderdom as it practically has fulfilled its objection. A.A & QMG provisionally decided to have 3 R.Ps for Division 1 at hut Camp – 1 at	

(73989) W4141—463. 400,000. 9/14. H.&J.Ltd. Forms/C. 2118/10.

Instructions regarding War Diaries and Intelligence Summaries are contained in F. S. Regs., Part II. and the Staff Manual respectively. Title pages will be prepared in manuscript.

WAR DIARY
or
INTELLIGENCE SUMMARY.
(Erase heading not required.)

Army Form C. 2118.

Hour, Date, Place	Summary of Events and Information	Remarks and references to Appendices
	BUSSEBOOM - 1 for Divisional Troops in artillery are at the Road Junc 1½ miles S.E. of Vlamertinghe.	
5 pm 7 . 3 . 15 Poperinghe	5th Corps notifies that the use of 27 Ammtn Park in case of Emergency is cancelled and that RA will in Emergency draw from No 4 Ammunition Park at ~~STRAZEELE~~ HONDEGHEM.	
	The variety of opinion on forms of grenades is interesting most Bdes dislike the Double Cylinder Bomb - 13 Inf Bde likes them no others do hence it is difficult to regulate the supplies at RE Depot YPRES. Same 1500 odd -	
	There has been a great outcry for Rifle Grenades - we got none yesterday - none today and had it not been for a present from the 1st Cav Div we should have been right out of them - This has been represented but we have been starved in this respect so far	
9 pm 7 . 3 . 15 "	Conference of AA & QMG with ~~travel~~ Supply officers including OC Supply Col regarding new refilling points.	
7 . 3 . 15 "	Casualties 13 Inf Bde O.R. 5K - 16W. Capt Watson KOYLI killed. 15 " " " " 9 32 Belgian RA " " " - 1	
7.15 pm 7 . 3 . 15 "	V Corps notifies that from 9th inst: Hy Gun Ammtn will be drawn at CAESTRE from 27th Ammtn Park. A further correspondence received from V Corps shows that this is to be the Ammtn Park of the Corps Hy Artillery.	
7 . 3 . 15 "	Weather v. wet indeed. Colder.	AA&QMG.

Army Form C. 2118.

Instructions regarding War Diaries and Intelligence Summaries are contained in F. S. Regs., Part II. and the Staff Manual respectively. Title pages will be prepared in manuscript.

WAR DIARY
or
INTELLIGENCE SUMMARY.
(Erase heading not required.)

Hour, Date, Place		Summary of Events and Information	Remarks and references to Appendices
10am.	8.3.15 Poperinghe	As no Rifle grenades have been received ~~lost~~ for two days Ballm G sent to investigate – Report found that none were reaching Army Railhead. Believed to be due to fact that none are arriving in the Country. Report sent to V Corps – without any practical result.	See 9.3.15
2 pm	8.3.15 "	Sir H. Smith Dorrien 2nd Army Commander visited the Rest Camp.	
	8.3.15 "	Casualties RE. OR. 2K – 2W. RA OR ~~6~~ 6W. 15th Bde 7K – 12W & Capt Andrews Bedfords Wounded. 13th " 1 . 5 & 2/Lt Broadway Wounded	
	8.3.15 "	Instruction received during the day to Transfer 12 GS wagons four each to form Am Cols of 116; 115; 121 Heavy Batteries.	
	8.3.15 "	Weather V Cold. Bright Sunshine alternating with Snowstorms.	[illegible]
10.40am	9.3.15 "	V Corps notifies arrival of an 11th of Wilts also Cornwalls Siege Coys Mobile Monmouth Railway Coys.	
—	9.3.15 "	A scheme for ~~Supply~~ pipe supply of drinking water for Rest Encampment ~~at~~ from DICKEBUSCH ~~has~~ is now under consideration.	
	9.3.15 "	In continuation of 10am of 8.3.15. all ~~that~~ that has happened so far on representation of Vth Corps to 2 Army was reply of latter ~~to~~ "You get your share but output is very limited at present".	
7.30pm	9.3.15 "	15th Inf Bde came. Was ~~without~~ only 3 Very Pistols the remainder having been ~~withdrawn~~ withdrawn and	

Instructions regarding War Diaries and Intelligence Summaries are contained in F. S. Regs., Part II. and the Staff Manual respectively. Title pages will be prepared in manuscript.

WAR DIARY
or
INTELLIGENCE SUMMARY.
(*Erase heading not required.*)

Army Form C. 2118.

Hour, Date, Place	Summary of Events and Information	Remarks and references to Appendices
	kept by 5th Div – Crisis had arisen because 9th Bde is due for Trenches on night 10–11 which would have meant that 13th Bde would have handed over ~~line~~ to 15th – and 15th return to 9th – fortunately 18 Pistols – the first we've had for a long time arrived today and saved the situation	
	calculation shows that the number of Courts Martial held in this Division since 18th Jany. is 102	
— 9 3 15 Poperinghe	Casualties up to noon 9th March. 13th Inf Bde 6K – 14W. 15th " 5K – 29W. RA 1W. RE 1W. Lt Wheeler 4 Hussars wounded.	
— 9 . 3 . 15 "	weather v. fine cold.	A.A.
5.37 pm 10 3 15 "	It has been found that ~~in the two~~ great difficulty has been experienced by the Staff of 28 Div detailed to issue Remounts – in classifying the horses received. These horses in bunches of 161 (as on last occasion 3 weeks ago) are bundled out of the train by the Remount officer in charge and handed over to 28th Div – a request has been made that horses may be classified and DDR 2nd Army has promised to do this.	
	our RE depot is at the Porte de Lille Ypres – ~~RE~~ motor lorries specially detailed from Ambt Park bring up RE material	

Instructions regarding War Diaries and Intelligence Summaries are contained in F. S. Regs., Part II. and the Staff Manual respectively. Title pages will be prepared in manuscript.

WAR DIARY
or
INTELLIGENCE SUMMARY.
(Erase heading not required.)

Army Form C. 2118.

Hour, Date, Place	Summary of Events and Information	Remarks and references to Appendices
	from RE Park and certain explosives from Ammunition train right up to the Porte de Lille – we have accumulated a great amount of explosives here now but ~~RE~~ I consider it ~~adv~~ necessary. For instance the Stock today is Hand grenades 1650 – Rifle grenades 75. grenades double Cylinder 1525. Gunpowder Boxes 4, Kegs 4, lbs 6600. Very Pistol Cartridges 1834, Rockets 82, detonators No 8, 3100.	
10.3.15. Poperinghe	During day 10 horse waggon loads and 2–4 ton lorry loads of broken bricks were brought from YPRES and put into the road 1000 yds west of Vlamertinghe the idea originally was to make a R.P. there but owing to the state of the road this will not apparently be possible yet – in any case we are moving the 1st Line Transport of Bdes up to that area.	
10.3.15 "	Casualties up to 12 noon. 10. 13th Inf Bde 2K – 7W. Lt Vance Ches: killed. 15 " " 7. 18. Lt Hagan R.Irs wounded. RA " " 1.W. Major Wickham wounded	
10.3.15 "	weather dull – warmer.	[illegible]
11.3.15 "	All quiet. No events of interest administratively.	
" " "	Casualties 15th Bde 2K 28W. 2Lt Coleman & Bvm Maples Capt Ogden 4/Sussex – Lt Turnbull Lanc } wounded. 9th " 7W. 13 " 3. 7. RA 1.	
" " "	weather dull – warmer.	[illegible]

(73989) W4141—463. 400,000. 9/14. H.&J.Ltd. Forms/C. 2118/10.

Army Form C. 2118.

Instructions regarding War Diaries and Intelligence Summaries are contained in F. S. Regs., Part II. and the Staff Manual respectively. Title pages will be prepared in manuscript.

WAR DIARY
or
INTELLIGENCE SUMMARY.
(Erase heading not required.)

Hour, Date, Place	Summary of Events and Information	Remarks and references to Appendices
9 am. 12 · 3 · 15 Poperinghe	Belgian Artillery have applied for remounts. Instructions received state they must find their own in their own country or in France.	
11 am 12 · 3 · 15 "	Following reinforcements arrived 4/R. Fus 1 Off – 68 OR 1/Suffolks 1 " – 65. 1 R Scots Fus 1 " 61 2/KOSB 1 " 35 2/KOYLI 4 " 20 2/W Rid. 2 " 25 1/W Kent 3 " 87 } Dorsets 2 Offs } Total. } 15 Off 361 OR	
1 12 · 3 · 15 "	During day 84 HD & 58 LD horses were due to arrive. We were warned to expect them at 10·45 – 1 pm – 2 pm – 4·45 pm eventually they arrived at 5·45 pm. It is very irksome for the conducting parties some of whom came 10 miles – It also creates a feeling of unrest at HQ – This rather points to more sympathetic staff work required from Railway Staffs concerned.	
12 · 3 · 15 "	Number of Rounds Expended by RA. 18 pr 679. HE 13 How HE 45. Shrap 10 – 13 pr Aircraft 13 – 4.7 4 – HE 25 – Belgian 181. Casualties 9th Bde 7 K – 11 W. 13th " 3 – 14 RE " — 1	
	~~Vlaam~~ Poperinghe attacked by aeroplane at 2 pm and 4 pm – aeroplane dropped 5 bombs – all exploded except one – Some civilian killed & wounded – Soldiers' [illegible]	

Instructions regarding War Diaries and Intelligence Summaries are contained in F.S. Regs., Part II. and the Staff Manual respectively. Title pages will be prepared in manuscript.

WAR DIARY
or
INTELLIGENCE SUMMARY.
(Erase heading not required.)

Army Form C. 2118.

Hour, Date, Place	Summary of Events and Information	Remarks and references to Appendices
	damaged – 2 motor ambulances smashed and much glass broken in streets.	
12.3.15 Poperinghe	Weather Fine.	[illegible]
11.50am 13.3.15 " "	No Rifle Grenades forthcoming	
" " " "	58 HD and 58 LD horses arrived from Remounts and were distributed at Railhead	
12 noon " "	Drafts averaging 26 arrived for 1/North Fus – W. Ridg and KOSB.	
	Casualties 15 Inf Bde 8K – 14W 2 Lt Moseley 4/ Bedfords Killed. Capt Montgomery & [illegible] wounded. 12 [illegible] – 1 9 Bde 22 – 64 – 17M; RA 1	
2.35pm 13.3.15 "	During day information received that no HE would be issued to or would be used by 9.2 How – 18 pr – 4.5" – 6" How 4.7".	
	Certain administrative arrangements have been confirmed re G. remaking of road 1000x west of Vlamertinghe – building of huts in Rest area – and fitting of latter with braziers, latrine buckets – washing places –	
13.3.15 "	Weather v fine – much warmer.	[illegible]

(73989) W4141—463. 400,000. 9/14. H.&J.Ltd. Forms/C. 2118/10.

Instructions regarding War Diaries and Intelligence Summaries are contained in F. S. Regs., Part II. and the Staff Manual respectively. Title pages will be prepared in manuscript.

WAR DIARY
or
INTELLIGENCE SUMMARY.
(*Erase heading not required.*)

Army Form C. 2118.

Hour, Date, Place	Summary of Events and Information	Remarks and references to Appendices
14.3.15 Poperinghe	9th Brigade again asks for empty ammn boxes of RA – these are normally left at artillery R.Ps. (Vlamertinghe) and have been found very useful for making traverses, seats etc. We are allowed to give them empty S.A.A., 9th – 13; 18 Pr – 415. And is worthy of note for future wars	
10.30am 14.3.15 "	22 LD & 2 mules arrived from Remounts	
12 noon 14.3.15 "	Casualties up to 12 noon 15 Bde 5K – 26 W {Lt. Shears Shrops L I / Lt. Curtis Nth'd Cy} wounded RA Major Curtis wounded RE 1K. 12 Lo 2 W 9th Bde 14K – 37 W {Lt Queen Rifles K / 2Lt. Henley W} Lincolns	
14.3.15 "	Bdes Brigadiers frequently [illegible] are deficient of articles when investigation shows these have either not been indented for or are not in the country. To avoid this D.A.Q.M.G. went to 13th Bde as the first of a series of visits to Bdes to ascertain real requirements – There appears to be 3 arm chairs for Bde HQ	
5pm 14.3.15 "	Very heavy firing towards S. Eloi. Later information showed that Germans were attacking trenches in about S. Eloi &	
8pm 14.3.15 "	by 8pm had gained possession of that place and 9 [illegible] yards of front – It is interesting to note that the D.A.A.Q.M.G. & D.A.Q.M.G. 28 Div watching the flashes 8 miles	

Instructions regarding War Diaries and Intelligence Summaries are contained in F.S. Regs., Part II. and the Staff Manual respectively. Title pages will be prepared in manuscript.

WAR DIARY
or
INTELLIGENCE SUMMARY.
(Erase heading not required.)

Army Form C. 2118.

Hour, Date, Place		Summary of Events and Information	Remarks and references to Appendices
		I heard the Scream of the bits of a German Shell after explosion.	
10 pm	14.3.15 Poperinghe	At 10pm information received that an Inf Bde to support 27th Div would arrive in 28th Div area during night. Arrangements made to receive it about Ouderdom.	
—	14.3.15 "	Sick wastage return for 7 previous days 1 officers 423 O.R.	
	14.3.15 "	Weather V. Fine – warmer	[illegible]
5.45 am	15.3.15 "	The 16th Inf Bde arrived by rail at Vlamertinghe, was met & put into the huts where they remained all day	
10 am	15.3.15 "	A large public funeral was held at Poperinghe to bury 11 victims of the Bomb on 12th. G.O.C. 28 Div was represented by [illegible].	
	15.3.15 "	13th Infantry Brigade lent to 27th Div and moved towards DICKEBUSH.	
3 pm	15.3.15 "	As it became probable that 16th Inf Bde would remain for the night the question of providing rations for consumption on 16th arose - Reference to 6th Div showed that they had not sent any. Arrangements made to fall back on the 4000 Reserve in hands of Railhead Comdt which was	

(73989) W4141—463. 400,000. 9/14. H.&J.Ltd. Forms/C. 2118/10.

Instructions regarding War Diaries and Intelligence Summaries are contained in F. S. Regs., Part II. and the Staff Manual respectively. Title pages will be prepared in manuscript.

WAR DIARY
or
INTELLIGENCE SUMMARY.
(Erase heading not required.)

Army Form C. 2118.

Hour, Date, Place	Summary of Events and Information	Remarks and references to Appendices
	proved their utility – The more one sees of these sudden moves the more apparent it becomes that a Reserve is necessary with the modern system somewhere at Railhead or near it.	
6.30pm ~~6-30~~ 15.3.15 Pope.	2 Bns of 16th Inf Bde entrained for return to Armentières.	
" 15.3.15 "	Instructions received from 27th Div to direct 13 Supply Vehicles of 13th Bde to the Cross Roads 1½ m – S by W of KRUISSTRAAT to be there at 9pm – not easy to arrange – as 13th Bde were out of communication their Transport in process of changing billets & no information on hand as to position of vehicles – The whole spread over a very large area – The situation was saved by sending a Staff Officer in Motor to seek out and direct transport of units to necessary point.	
10. pm 15.3.15 Poperinghe	Orders received to entrain the 2 remaining Bns of 16th Inf Bde at Vlamertinghe. Staff Officer sent to assist – French Rlway authorities kept many trains – The first ~~Bd~~ Bn began entraining at 11.30 and were not finished before 1 am – The second Bn took 1½ hours –	
— 15.3.15 Poperinghe	Weather Fine – drafts arrived during day at Railhead were kept there owing to uncertainty of movements. Casualties 9th Bde. 3K – 22W 15 " 13K – 51W Lt McCurry Ramc K. Lt Griffiths Hay Bowcote W. RE – – 6 – 5m. 13 – not reported –	Aam Ct.

(73989) W4141–463. 400,000. 9/14. H.&J.Ltd. Forms/C. 2118/10.

Instructions regarding War Diaries and Intelligence Summaries are contained in F. S. Regs., Part II and the Staff Manual respectively. Title pages will be prepared in manuscript.

WAR DIARY
or
INTELLIGENCE SUMMARY.
(*Erase heading not required.*)

Army Form C. 2118.

Hour, Date, Place	Summary of Events and Information	Remarks and references to Appendices
16.3.15 Poperinghe	~~A Quiet day~~ on the whole. About 4 pm we decided to relieve the 15th Bde in the trenches by 13th Inf Bde – 12th London R. moved up from Billets S W of Poperinghe to the Hut Camp	
16.3.15 "	Casualties up to 12 noon 16/3 9th Bde 2 K – 8 W " " " " " 13 " 2 – 13. Lt [illegible] K. and on 15th – 10. Lt [illegible] K. Re 1.	
2.30pm 16.3.15 "	Reinforcements arrive including 126 men for 6/Liverpools.	
16.3.15 "	Weather fine. Slightly colder.	[signature]
17.3.15 "	Scale of expenditure of ammunition reduced.	
17.3.15 "	Casualties 9th Bde 3 K – 20 W – Lt [illegible] K. 13 " 2 – 9 15th 4 – 18 Re — 1	
	All quiet. Building proceeding. New hut country is drying up – Re of 1st Line Tr. details back with the transport are building their own ~~[illegible]~~ huts.	
17.3.15	Weather ~~[illegible]~~ dull.	[signature]

(73989) W4141—463. 400,000. 9/14. H.&J.Ltd. Forms/C. 2118/10.

Instructions regarding War Diaries and Intelligence Summaries are contained in F. S. Regs., Part II. and the Staff Manual respectively. Title pages will be prepared in manuscript.

WAR DIARY
or
INTELLIGENCE SUMMARY.
(*Erase heading not required.*)

Army Form C. 2118.

Hour, Date, Place	Summary of Events and Information	Remarks and references to Appendices
— 18.3.15 Poperinghe	A difficult question is arising regarding the disposal of a large number of carcases of horses just in rear of the fighting line. Horses are were originally French or Belgian Artillery horses. We are arranging for the Sanitary Contractor at YPRES to dispose of the carcases nearest that place — giving him quantities of Chloride of Lime — and dealing with the others with ~~quick~~ Chl of lime as we can.	
2.25pm 18.3.15 Poperinghe	As it has been found impossible to cure the numerous cases of cracked heels and debility among horses especially R.A. — they are being taken out of their present muddy standings ~~and~~ into Mob Vet Sec — and evacuated — They will recover no doubt within a month meanwhile it makes a deficiency of some 213 Artillery horses. This is notified to DDR 2nd Army	
	Casualties RE — R — 1 W 13th Bde 3 - 21 9th Bde 4 . 18 Capt Hodgson R. Fus killed.	
18.3.15 "	Weather dull and cold — snow at night	[illegible]
— 19.3.15 Poperinghe	Ground covered with snow in the morning	
1.19pm 19.3.15 "	5th Corps notified that ~~the~~ recently oiling of bores of guns before firing is ~~danger~~ to be discontinued also use of 82 Fuze with Lyddite.	
2 pm 19.3.15 "	Number of Rounds expended to 12 noon March 19th 18pr ~~20~~ 19 — 4.5 H? ·1. No of guns 48 + 12 + 2 + 8 + 24	

Instructions regarding War Diaries and Intelligence Summaries are contained in F. S. Regs., Part II. and the Staff Manual respectively. Title pages will be prepared in manuscript.

WAR DIARY
or
INTELLIGENCE SUMMARY.
(Erase heading not required.)

Army Form C. 2118.

Hour, Date, Place	Summary of Events and Information	Remarks and references to Appendices
19.3.15 Poperinghe	Casualties Rg. K OR W; 13th Bde 6 . 25; 9 " 1 . 8. 2 [illegible] Mounted Rg. W; " Belcher North Fus – W	
19.3.15 "	42 horses and 1 mule arrived from Remounts	
19.3.15 "	Weather very cold & stormy with periods of sunshine – Snow storms on & off all day. Cleared up in Evening	[signature]
1.45pm 20.3.15 "	Following drafts arrived for 9th Bde North Fus 1 off 870; 4/R. Fus 1 " 120; 1/Lincoln 1; " 13 " 9/K.O.S.B. 1 " 105; 2/W. Ridg R 1 " 50	
" 20.3.15 "	Instructions received to take a census of all S.A.A. at 12 noon on 21st. Number of rounds fired up to 12 noon 20th March 18pr 48 : 4.5" 31 4.7" 34. Belgians 14. Casualties Motor Machine Gun K. 1 W; 13th Bde 3 – 13; 9th " 3 – 7 Three cases of accidents with hand grenades have occurred in our trenches during the past week. 2 officers having been killed in the 13th Inf Bde and 1 Motor Machine Gunner wounded as was shown – The first two cases were due to an automatic lighter which they did not know had ~~all~~ already started. ~~[illegible]~~	

(73989) W4141—463. 400,000. 9/14. H.&J.Ltd. Forms/C. 2118/10.

Instructions regarding War Diaries and Intelligence Summaries are contained in F. S. Regs., Part II. and the Staff Manual respectively. Title pages will be prepared in manuscript.

WAR DIARY
or
INTELLIGENCE SUMMARY.
(Erase heading not required.)

Army Form C. 2118.

Hour, Date, Place	Summary of Events and Information	Remarks and references to Appendices
— 20.3.15 Poperinghe.	Much progress is being made in the huts – ~~near~~ Huts have been erected to hold approximately 5 Bns – Officers quarters have been constructed in which to use the hut stoves & camps – Ablution places with benches and pails have been fixed up – and a Sanitary Contractor has been arranged with to ~~be~~ clean latrines as we can get buckets. – a shop is also being fixed up – and ovens for the men.	
	There have been frequent visits of the Corps and Army Commander to the huts.	
10.45 pm 20.3.15 "	Orders issued for the move of the 12 London to move to Bailleul the 9th London coming here same day.	
20.3.15 "	We have only had 20 rounds of 4" Trench How amm since we arrived in France (9 weeks) – Excellent practice has been made with it and though we ask daily for it nothing happens.	Ammn:
20.3.15 "	Weather v. fine	
~~7.30 am 21.3.15~~ "	~~12th London R marched to Bailleul to join 84th Inf Bde~~	
	~~9 — R marched in to YPRES from 5th Division~~.	
10.30 am " "	Ordered to send 6 Travelling Kitchens to 27th Div. These are surplus and with 13th Inf Bde.	
	Lt. Col. Smith 1/Lincolns 9th Bde appointed to command 80th Bde and left for 27th Div:	

Instructions regarding War Diaries and Intelligence Summaries are contained in F. S. Regs., Part II. and the Staff Manual respectively. Title pages will be prepared in manuscript.

WAR DIARY
or
INTELLIGENCE SUMMARY.
(Erase heading not required.)

Army Form C. 2118.

Hour, Date, Place		Summary of Events and Information	Remarks and references to Appendices
12 noon	21.3.15 Poperinghe	In accordance with orders Stock taken of all S.A.A. in Possession of 28th Div at 12 noon – amount found to be. with Machine Guns 295,723 on Soldiers Individually 4.049 584 In Bde Reserves 658 676 " Arty Bde Amn Cols 1495 775 " Div Amn Col 973 850 } Total 7,473588 This return was 2 hours late due to the cutting of the telephone to Infty Bdes in the trenches by Shrapnel.	
—	21.3.15 Poperinghe	Casualties Ra K. – I.W. 9th Bde 4 – 5 13 " 7 – 6	
—	21.3.15 "	V. Quiet day except for the return of S.A.A.	
—	21.3.15 "	Sick wastage for week ending March 20th 9 offrs & 182 OR.	
12 noon	21.3.15 "	Instructions issued that all Hand grenades which have Slides for holding detonators sheared off or which have not RL on base are dangerous	
—	21.3.15 "	Weather v. fine all day.	[illegible]
7.30 am	22.3.15 "	12th Lancers R. marched from YPRES to Bailleul to join 84th Inf Bde.	
—	22.3.15 "	Chloride of Lime is being collected at Porte de Lille and will be issued as a trench Store from the R.E. depot there. In addition C of L will be issued in small quantities at R. Points – In the trenches it will be used for improvement of conditions due to dead bodies and elsewhere	

Instructions regarding War Diaries and Intelligence Summaries are contained in F. S. Regs., Part II. and the Staff Manual respectively. Title pages will be prepared in manuscript.

WAR DIARY
or
INTELLIGENCE SUMMARY.
(Erase heading not required.)

Army Form C. 2118.

Hour, Date, Place	Summary of Events and Information	Remarks and references to Appendices
	[illegible] matters sanitary	
12 noon. 22.3.15 Poperinghe	Casualties up to 12 noon 9th Bde 4K – 22W 13 " 4K – 19W 15th " 2K – 5W RE – 1W	
3 pm " "	9th London R. marched into YPRES to join 13th Bde. Strength 28 offrs – 791 OR. Work on Huts proceeding now satisfactory – Officers quarters much improved –	
— 22.3.15 "	Weather v. fine.	[illegible]
9.30 am 23.3.15 "	Draft arrived for RE.	
" 23.3.15 "	Application for French Howitzer Ammn produced answer none available, supply expected daily	
3 pm 23.3.15 "	Colonel Everett AA&QMG & DA&QMG V Corps & AA&QMG 28 Div had conference regarding area to be occupied by 27 Div. which is about to move.	
— 23.3.15 —	Casualties 15 Inf Bde 5K 5W 13 " " 4K 11 4M.	
4 pm 23.3.15 —	V Corps asked to help us to get more Very Pistols – they are now nearly a month overdue on indent.	

Instructions regarding War Diaries and Intelligence Summaries are contained in F. S. Regs., Part II. and the Staff Manual respectively. Title pages will be prepared in manuscript.

WAR DIARY
or
INTELLIGENCE SUMMARY.
(Erase heading not required.)

Army Form C. 2118.

Hour, Date, Place	Summary of Events and Information	Remarks and references to Appendices
23.3.15 Poperinghe	Weather Fine	
23.3.15 "	A Motor Soup Kitchen capable of giving soup to 550 men per at a time has been handed over to 28 Div. by the Friends Ambulance Unit. It is proposed to station this in the first instance at the Porte de Lille.	AA&QMG
24.3.15 "	Casualties 13 Bde { 1K — 8W. } " " { 2 . 8 } 15 " 2 . 5 RA 1 Belgian. nothing else occurred of administrative interest	
24.3.15	Weather V. wet.	AA&QMG
10.30 am 25.3.15 Pop.	Reinforcements of 8 officers & a few men arrive Vlamertinghe Rly Stn.	
" " 25.3.15 "	Yesterday CE 5 Div notified CRE 28 Div. that daily allowance of Sandbags for 28 Div would be limited to 7000 – GOC Division protested personally to GOC V Corps – Today wire received from 2nd Army that supply would shortly be increased & that endeavours should be made to use other substitutes for revetting. Steps therefore taken to use up the 200 oatsacks which we would otherwise send back to railhead.	
" " 25.3.15 Poperinghe	AA&QMG 2 Army; AA&QMG V Corps and AA&QMG 28 Div held conference on question of reporting casualties	

(73989) W4141—463. 400,000. 9/14. H.&J.Ltd. Forms/C. 2118/10.

Instructions regarding War Diaries and Intelligence Summaries are contained in F. S. Regs., Part II. and the Staff Manual respectively. Title pages will be prepared in manuscript.

WAR DIARY
or
INTELLIGENCE SUMMARY.
(Erase heading not required.)

Army Form C. 2118.

Hour, Date, Place	Summary of Events and Information	Remarks and references to Appendices
	I am notified that in future what was wanted was a rough estimate of casualties as soon after they happened as possible in case of large numbers – with a view to the early despatch of drafts.	
25.3.15 Poperinghe	The 27th Div have been withdrawn from the trenches and the 3rd Div have gone into their area – The general effect is that under V Corps instructions the 27th Div have now taken over bits of our area and remain there e.g. Squares G 9, 10, 15, 20, 21, 26, 27. ~~as~~ but not Squares 21, 27 East of Reninghelst occupied by Belgian Artillery and Square 10 C occupied by Mobile Vety Section. A big piece N.E of Ouderdom has also been handed over for Report centre of the 3rd Div:– (H 26(a) not very satisfactory at the moment – We have also been ordered to move out our Convalescent hospital out of STEENVOORDE within 24 hours which means the dissolution of that hospital.	
25.3.15 "	9 pm. notification received of the move of 2 Bns & 1 Fd Coy 27th Div into YPRES tomorrow.	
25.3.15 "	Casualties 13th Inf Bde. 4K – 20 W 15th " " 14 " also W. Lt Tabor 3/Bedfords.	

(73989) W4141—463. 400,000. 9/14. H.&J.Ltd. Forms/C. 2118/10.

Instructions regarding War Diaries and Intelligence Summaries are contained in F. S. Regs., Part II. and the Staff Manual respectively. Title pages will be prepared in manuscript.

WAR DIARY
or
INTELLIGENCE SUMMARY.
(Erase heading not required.)

Army Form C. 2118.

Hour, Date, Place	Summary of Events and Information	Remarks and references to Appendices
— 25·3·15 Poperinghe	Some remarks on the water of the resting area are attached being of administrative interest as showing the conditions under which the soldiers live.	App. I.
8pm 25·3·15 "	Germans shelled the N. end of the resting area – a piece of shell entering the Cook house of the most Northern huts – no casualties – Out of all 8 fired some fell in Vlamertinghe one of them in a house killing 30 horses & several soldiers.	
— 25·3·15 "	Weather V. wet indeed and cold.	A. A. M. H.
11am 26·3·15 "	9 R. Scots & 9 A & S Highldrs also 1/7 Fd Coy RE ~~&~~ all of 27 Div marched through Ouderdom & Vlamertinghe to billet in YPRES – instructions issued to them to retain only a small portion of their Transport in YPRES remainder is billetted in Rest Area. all quiet	
— 26·3·15 "	Dull and cold	A. A. M. H.

(73989) W4141—463. 400,000. 9/14. H.&J.Ltd. Forms/C. 2118/10.

Instructions regarding War Diaries and Intelligence Summaries are contained in F. S. Regs., Part II. and the Staff Manual respectively. Title pages will be prepared in manuscript.

WAR DIARY
or
INTELLIGENCE SUMMARY.
(Erase heading not required.)

Army Form C. 2118.

Hour, Date, Place	Summary of Events and Information	Remarks and references to Appendices
27.3.15 Poperinghe	The Corps Commander in looking round has taken exception to the state of YPRES Infantry Bks. - It has been very difficult to keep it right. There are about 2 Bns in it Regularly and all the supplies for 2 Bdes at addition to Coal Coke & charcoal go in there - we have had a Belgian Contractor working some time now but the matter is being reorganised as we can no longer leave the welfare of these Bks so much to Bdes.	
27.3.15 " "	Information received from GS that the 2 Army had issued directing Economy in the use of Sandbags and that other Contrivances such as boxes ~~had been to~~ were to be used. Endeavours made at once thro' CRE to secure ½" wood - and make boxes both in RE Sto and Bde Workshops -	
27.3.15 "	Casualties RA - K - 2 W 15 Bde 6 24 9 " 2 "	
27.3.15 "	Weather v fine - Present Strength of Inf 369 Offrs. 14,180 O.R. but very cold.	[signature]

Instructions regarding War Diaries and Intelligence Summaries are contained in F. S. Regs., Part II. and the Staff Manual respectively. Title pages will be prepared in manuscript.

WAR DIARY
or
INTELLIGENCE SUMMARY.
(Erase heading not required.)

Army Form C. 2118.

Hour, Date, Place	Summary of Events and Information	Remarks and references to Appendices
28.3.15 Poperinghe	Instructions have lately been circulated to consider a scheme for the withdrawal of warm clothing and horse rugs and a Scheme has been submitted which contemplated as regards warm clothing – Regimental boards of Survey visited by DADOS who ordered destroyed on spot all unserviceable. The serviceable being despatched forthwith in Supply Supply wagons to AOD Railhead. This to be done in case of Infantry when in resting area – So this having been settled the weather turned bitterly cold and orders have now been issued leaving it to discretion of GOC to withdraw warm clothing – GOC decides to postpone withdrawal until warmer weather sets in	
28.3.15 "	2nd Army order of 27.3.15 as orders that issue of Rum must cease as a regular issue – Today instructions received that this was to be liberally interpreted for present but following point arises in connection with this – the GOC can suddenly make up his mind to issue rum whatever weather may be because the only reserve is about 'one day' – at Railhead and this cannot be circulated in a hurry. We are arranging to draw whatever is there and to issue it tomorrow and next day if possible and base has been asked for more.	

Instructions regarding War Diaries and Intelligence Summaries are contained in F. S. Regs., Part II. and the Staff Manual respectively. Title pages will be prepared in manuscript.

WAR DIARY
or
INTELLIGENCE SUMMARY.
(Erase heading not required.)

Army Form C. 2118.

	Hour, Date, Place	Summary of Events and Information	Remarks and references to Appendices
2.30pm	28.3.15 Poperinghe	Following reinforcements arrived for 9th Bde 1 off + 47 – 13th Bde 2 off + 20 OR 15th " 4 " + 313 OR –	
"	28.3.15 "	Following Remounts arrived and were distributed 51 HD – 27 Riders – Not including this lot we have received since arrival in the country C1, 2 – C2, 31 – Riders 56 – LD 240 – HD 171 – Pack 3 – Mules 5 our normal 3 weekly requirements being about 140 – a week ago we had to indent for 287 to complete This being made up largely of 100 Artillery L.D. Horses which had to be evacuated with bad cracked heels these latter had turned into bad sores: due to standing for weeks nearly up to their belly in mud. We have now been asked if we are prepared to take over some mules for LD for Batteries and have stated we will take 116 out of 145.	
	28.3.15 "	Casualties 15th Bde 2K – 12W 9th " 10 – 17	
	28.3.15 "	Weather v fine but bitterly cold. Some say the coldest day of the winter due to North wind.	A. A. McG. H.

(73989) W4141—463. 400,000. 9/14. H.&J.Ltd. Forms/C. 2118/10.

Instructions regarding War Diaries and Intelligence Summaries are contained in F. S. Regs., Part II. and the Staff Manual respectively. Title pages will be prepared in manuscript.

WAR DIARY
or
INTELLIGENCE SUMMARY.
(Erase heading not required.)

Army Form C. 2118.

Hour, Date, Place	Summary of Events and Information	Remarks and references to Appendices
12 noon 29.3.15 Poperinghe	AA&QMG held a conference ~~on~~ with Transport Officers ~~at~~ ~~the~~ near Vlamertinghe before them to state their troubles with their billets and when moving transport into YPRES.	
29.3.15 "	Sad complaints from 9th & 13th Bdes in the Trenches as to insufficiency of Coke, Charcoal, and Sandbags – As regards the first two – we get up a truck about every two days say 4 tons but units not going into the trenches succeed in drawing and hoarding it – as it stands now there is no charcoal but mainly Coke – a raid on the Qr. Bde Storerooms has it is understood produced 12 or 14 bags –	
	As regards Sandbags ~~an~~ DA&QMG was sent to Dunkirk and earmarked 5000 – also another 13000 which are to come and after that possibly 3000 a day. But it is a terribly hand to mouth existence.	
	We have also today received instructions that Straw ~~Hay~~ is likely to be short soon – ~~and is~~	
	We are already short of Rifle grenades (none) – Coke, Charcoal and Sandbags – and now it is the Straw.	
29.3.15 " "	Otherwise the day was normal.	
29.3.15 " "	Casualties R.E. K 2W also H. Hedges Wounded 15 Bde 1 . 14 . Capt Frost Ad. Cheshires Killed. 9 Bde 2 . 17 .	
29.3.15 " "	Weather very fine but bitterly cold	

(73989) W4141—463. 400,000. 9/14. H.&J.Ltd. Forms/C. 2118/10.

Army Form C. 2118.

Instructions regarding War Diaries and Intelligence Summaries are contained in F. S. Regs., Part II. and the Staff Manual respectively. Title pages will be prepared in manuscript.

WAR DIARY
or
INTELLIGENCE SUMMARY.
(*Erase heading not required.*)

Hour, Date, Place	Summary of Events and Information	Remarks and references to Appendices
30.3.15 Poperinghe	arrangements made to provide a permanent fatigue party of 20 men from each Bde for cleaning the cars & Inf Bks at YPRES. It has been found almost impossible with the coming and going of tired men to keep these Barracks clean. The parties will work under the OC Sanitary Section.	
30.3.15 "	Casualties: Ra K / 15 Bde 4 14 / 9 " 4 10	
30.3.15 "	The cry for coke continued about 12 noon 15th Bde reported there was none – The SSO investigated and found that the supply for 2 days (4 tons) which arrived on 29th was exhausted – The complaints of 15th Bde continued for till evening. The reason of the shortness is that units have been jockeying one another – Coke is intended solely for the trenches because it doesn't smoke and the matter is now being investigated by Div HQ to ascertain who are the offenders.	
Thu 30.3.15 "	Some 5000 sandbags bought from a private source at Dunkirk @ 52 centimes arrived. Weather v. fine but very cold	AAQMG

Instructions regarding War Diaries and Intelligence Summaries are contained in F. S. Regs., Part II. and the Staff Manual respectively. Title pages will be prepared in manuscript.

WAR DIARY
or
INTELLIGENCE SUMMARY.
(Erase heading not required.)

Army Form C. 2118.

Hour, Date, Place		Summary of Events and Information	Remarks and references to Appendices
9am	31.3.15 Poperinghe	Orders received that 85th Bde was to rejoin 28 Div and 9th Bde to rejoin 3rd Div – under following system 2½ Bns of 9th Bde in support to change tonight – on 1st these new 2½ to go into trenches in relief of 9th Bde – on 2nd april remainder of 9th & 85th Bde change – Sequel with ~~DC~~ Train & SSO visited 3rd Div HQ and proposed scheme as follows. 2½ Bns 9th Bde to change tonight with unconsumed portion of rations for 31/3/15 and rations for 1st in Supply Waggons thereafter to be supplied from 3rd Div R.Ps and similarly with 85th Bde from our RPs – because numbers are practically equal as regards Transport we send our horses with the 2½ Bns 9th Bde Train tonight. On 2nd ~~Ar~~ 28 Div horses transfer in 3rd Div area to waggons that ~~Cov~~ are coming with remainder of 85th Bde on 2nd and similarly in case of 85th Bde. This is an excellent method which proved itself on a former occasion and is worthy of notice. 3rd Div agreed.	Appendix 2
1.20pm	" "	Above move postponed for 48 hours	Appendix 3
2.20pm	" "	A shop was opened 10 days ago for the hut Camp and it has been doing a thriving trade. It could probably ~~?~~ turn over 1000 francs a day if we let it. Information now received that it is sold right out – probably a turnover of ~~Rs~~ Fr. 650 – The hut area all round has been enormously improved – The	

(73989) W4141—463. 400,000. 9/14. H.&J.Ltd. Forms/C. 2118/10.

Instructions regarding War Diaries and Intelligence Summaries are contained in F. S. Regs., Part II and the Staff Manual respectively. Title pages will be prepared in manuscript.

WAR DIARY
or
INTELLIGENCE SUMMARY.
(*Erase heading not required.*)

Army Form C. 2118.

Hour, Date, Place	Summary of Events and Information	Remarks and references to Appendices
	R. W. Kents complain they cannot get enough Very Pistols – They have 2 and should have 4. Last time they said Trousers but had omitted to ask for them. Priority wire to V Corps asking them to hasten supply	
31. 3. 15 Poperinghe	a Map showing location of troops 28 Div at 12 noon per today attached.	
31. 3. 15 "	Weather v. Fine and bitterly Cold.	[illegible]

(73989) W4141—463. 400,000. 9/14. H.&J.Ltd. Forms/C. 2118/10.

"A" Form. Army Form C. 2121.

MESSAGES AND SIGNALS.

No. of Message 28 Div

Prefix ____ Code ____ m.	Words	Charge	This message is on a/c of:	Recd. at ____ m
Office of Origin and Service Instructions.			appendix 2	Date
Priority	Sent		Service.	From
	At ____ m.		31.3.15	
	To			
	By		(Signature of "Franking Officer.")	By

TO { 9th Inf Bde
Q For Reference

Sender's Number	Day of Month	In reply to Number	AAA
* GL 360	Thirtieth		

orders	have	been	received	from
Fifth	Corps	that	ninth	and
eighty	fifth	Brigades	are	to
change	places	and	rejoin	their
own	Divisions	AAA	on	the
night	of	thirty first	first the	supporting
Bns of	ninth	Brigade	will change places	
with	the supporting	Bns	of eighty fifth	
Bde AAA	on the	night first	second	these
Bns of	ninth	Bde will	take over	the
trenches	now held	by eighty	fifth Bde	and
vice	versa	AAA	on	night
second	third	the exchange		will
be	completed	AAA	further	details
will	be	sent	tomorrow	

From 28 Div

Place

Time 11.55 pm

The above may be forwarded as now corrected. (Z) Sd. Loch Lt Col G S

Censor. Signature of Addressor or person authorised to telegraph in his name

*This line should be erased if not required.

3662 M. & Co. Ltd. Wt. W929/549—100,000. 6/14. Forms C2121/10

"C" Form (Original).

Army Form C. 2123.

MESSAGES AND SIGNALS. d/3/1 No. of Message

Prefix	Code	Words 37	Received	Sent, or sent out	Office Stamp.
Charges to collect			From	At	
			By	To Staff	
Service Instructions. Administrative War Diary 28 Div				By	

Handed in at Priority Office 1.25 p.m. Received 1.28 p.m.

TO Twentyeighth Division

*Sender's Number	Day of Month	In reply to Number	AAA
G.371	Thirtyfirst		

By order of second army exchange of ninth and eightyfifth Brigades postponed fortyeight hours aaa exchange commences night second third aaa acknowledge

FROM Twentyeighth Division

PLACE & TIME 1.20 pm

* This line should be erased if not required.

Wt. W. 9668—1672. 50,000 Pads. 1584—1/15. S. B. Ltd.—Forms/C.2123.

"Q" War Diary 28 Div
Appendix I
March 1915

Copy.

To,- A.D.M.S. 28th Division (repeated to D.M.S., II Army).

WATER SUPPLY HUTMENTS: Vlamertinghe-Ouderdom Road.

I have already inspected the proposed source of supply in company with Capt.Agg, Camp Commandant of Hutments, and I have personally examined samples of the water.

Both the streams suggested are extremely foul. Their bacteriological content is such that the water requires careful and quiescent storage for long periods before it can be efficiently treated by chlorination.

These two surface streams drain a densely infected typhoid area, in which, in addition, the infantile mortality has been terribly high. This water source should be avoided if humanly possible.

As to quantity, these particular streams are known to dry up, even after a short period of dry weather. They cannot be depended upon as a constant source of supply.

Depp wells may prove more valuable, but a good well is a lucky strike, and much moving sand may be encountered in this neighbourhood. The deeper you dig in this Ypresian formation the greater the amount of salts of soda found in the water,which to those not habituated to their use are liable to give rise to diarrhoea and other bowel disturbance. This matter of salt content is one which has been the subject of special investigation in the Mobile Hygienic Laboratory.

A source of water which I find excellent both in quantity and quality is avilable at l'Etang de Dickebusch. It is derived from Mont Kemmel. It may be brought to the hutment area by a pipe line 3,500 metres in length with the aid of intermediary reservoirs by gravity alone. 5,000 gallons daily of good drinking water requiring no further treatment would then be P.T.O.

available.

I have already submitted an independent survey of the proposed pipe-line and other data to Brigadier General Petrie, R.E. 5th Corps.

Chateau Elisabeth., POPERINGHE 25/3/15.

(s)M.Coplans., Captain, R.A.M.C. Sanitary Office II Army.

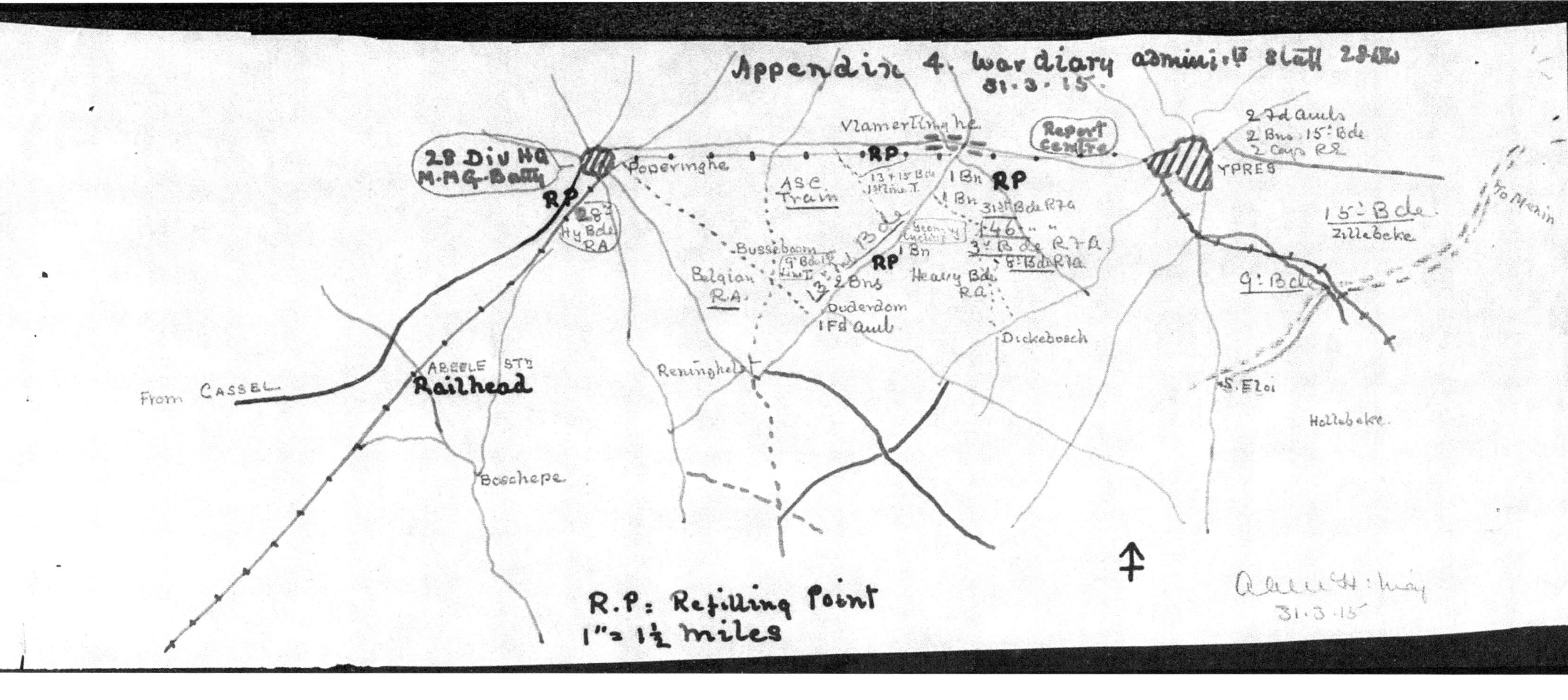

Appendix 4. War diary admin: staff 28 Div
31.3.15.
28 Div HQ
M.M.G. Batty
RP
Poperinghe
Vlamertinghe
RP
Report Centre
YPRES
2 Fd Ambs
2 Bns 15th Bde
2 Coys RE
15th Bde
Zillebeke
To Menin
9th Bde
S. Eloi
Hollebeke
ASC Train
1 Bn
RP
1 Bn
31st Bde RFA
146
3rd Bde RFA
8th Bde RFA
Heavy Bde RA
Dickebusch
Busseboom
Belgian RA
1 Bn
RP
2 Bns
Ouderdom
1 Fd Amb
Reninghelst
28th Hy Bde RA
ABEELE STN
Railhead
From CASSEL
Boeschepe
R.P. = Refilling Point
1" = 1½ miles
31.3.15

Confidential

WAR DIARY

ADMINISTRATIVE STAFF 28 Div:

From 1st April 1915 To 30th APRIL 1915

Volume V

Army Form C. 2118.

Instructions regarding War Diaries and Intelligence Summaries are contained in F. S. Regs., Part II. and the Staff Manual respectively. Title pages will be prepared in manuscript.

WAR DIARY
or
INTELLIGENCE SUMMARY.
(Erase heading not required.)

Hour	Date	Place	Summary of Events and Information	Remarks and references to Appendices
11 am	1.4.15	Poperinghe	Administrative Staff officers 5th Div called in connection with proposed changes of location but as we all know next to nothing & have no areas allotted yet very little could be settled.	
12 noon	1.4.15	"	Notification from Base Remount Depot Dieppe that Remounts for 28 Div had left that place	
	"	"	9th Bde depot having found and buried body of Lt Forbes 1st Suffolks near Trench 24. This officer was killed with 84th Bde early in Feb.	
"	1.4.15	"	Casualties up to 12 noon 1st Belgian Bde K. 2W. 15th Bde · 8W. Col Mcgaw? killed; 13th " · 6W; 9th " 1K · 9W.	
"	1.4.15	"	The grand total of killed, wounded, missing & sickness in this Division for the month of March is as follows.	
"	1.4.15	"	Officers 59 Sick. Nil Frostbite 40 wounded 16 killed + missing ~~The numbers fed in this Division are~~ — Sick To duty 10, Wounded 1 O.R. 2078 – 266 – 1395 – 325 · 27 — 974, 138 Foot cases to duty 116	Appendix I
	1.4.15	"	The numbers fed in this Division on 1st April are as follows. Troops 24,877 of which 975 are Belgian Artillery. Horses 7,220 of which 869 are " "	

Army Form C. 2118.

Instructions regarding War Diaries and Intelligence Summaries are contained in F. S. Regs., Part II. and the Staff Manual respectively. Title pages will be prepared in manuscript.

WAR DIARY
or
INTELLIGENCE SUMMARY.
(Erase heading not required.)

Hour, Date, Place	Summary of Events and Information	Remarks and references to Appendices
3.30pm 1.4.15 Poperinghe	Following Reinforcements arrived 9th Bde 1 off & 51 OR 13 " 9 239 " 15 " 1 " 88 "	
+ 1.4.15 "	During Day portions of 27th Div continued to enter and billet in our area.	
1.4.15 "	Weather v. fine & warm.	AAMG.
6.38 am 2.4.15 "	Wire unexpectedly received at Div HQ with no previous warning that 186 horses & mules had reached Abeele for 28 Div – The last heard of about this train was 12 noon on 1st when it left Dieppe – rather unfair treatment. However the consignment which consisted of 30 Chargers – 41 light draught – 114 mules was distributed by 12 noon.	
10 am 2.4.15 "	AAQMG V Div called on HQ 28 Div: regarding details of billetting in connection with moves but could settle nothing as no definite orders received.	
1.20pm 2.4.15 "	85th Inf Bde notifies his HQ will be Westoutre from 3.45	
2.30pm 2.4.15 "	85th Bde ask for motor lorry to bring Band instruments from La Clyte to Ouderdom – This was arranged.	

(73989) W4141—463. 400,000. 9/14. H.&J.Ltd. Forms/C. 2118/10.

Instructions regarding War Diaries and Intelligence Summaries are contained in F. S. Regs., Part II. and the Staff Manual respectively. Title pages will be prepared in manuscript.

WAR DIARY
or
INTELLIGENCE SUMMARY.
(Erase heading not required.)

Army Form C. 2118.

	Hour, Date, Place		Summary of Events and Information	Remarks and references to Appendices
4pm	2.4.15	Poperinghe	5th Division ask us to clear out of an ASD Store at Ouderdom by 6th reply sent to effect that we can't do that till we know where we are to go.	
—	2.4.15	"	Further conversations and conferences as to new area at HQ V Corps. nothing settled—	
	2.4.15	"	Casualties 9th Bde 9K. 32W 13th " 4 .. 15W. Lt. Carter 9 London wounded. R.E. " 1.	
			Following Bns of 9th Inf Bde (in support) viz R. Fus: Lincolns. ½ 1st Scottish moved to 3rd Div area in relief of following Bns of 85th Inf Bde viz; Buffs: 3 Middlesex: ½ 8 Middlesex R. who rejoined us	
—	2.4.15	"	It is worthy of note that each Bn of the 9th Inf Bde required 3 wagons per Bn full of gifts undistributed to move it.	
—	2.4.15	"	weather v fine & warm then wet.	[signature]
10am	3.4.15	"	AAOAUUG & SAASEUG proceeded on reconnaissance of possibilities of billeting about Vlamertinghe and North of YPRES	
11am	3.4.15	"	Proposed to 5th Div that they should feed 8, 13 & 14 Bdes for 6th & 7th and that we should feed theirs for 8 and vice versa as far as 13 & 15 are concerned to this 5th Div. Tentatively agreed	

(73989) W4141—463. 400,000. 9/14. H.&J.Ltd. Forms/C. 2118/10.

Army Form C. 2118.

WAR DIARY
or
INTELLIGENCE SUMMARY.
(Erase heading not required.)

Instructions regarding War Diaries and Intelligence Summaries are contained in F. S. Regs., Part II. and the Staff Manual respectively. Title pages will be prepared in manuscript.

Hour, Date, Place	Summary of Events and Information	Remarks and references to Appendices
— 3.4.15 Poperinghe	In order that RA taking over new positions may be able to meet attack - 200 Rounds authorised for 18 pr & 4.5 & 100 for Heavy for registration in addition to daily allowance –	
— 3.4.15 Poperinghe	2½ Bns 9th Bde relieved in Trenches by 2½ Bns 85 Inf Bde.	
— 3.4.15 "	Casualties 13 Inf Bde - K. - 10 W. 2/Lt Causton 9th London W. 9 " " - 3 K. - 7 - RA - 1 . - 1 .	
— 3.4.15 "	Very wet all day. - ½ 85 Bde relieved ½ 9th Bde in the Trenches	AAQMG
10am 4.4.15 "	We have received orders to return any surplus ammunition in front of Railhead and have reported to 5th Corps that surplus amm of 18 pr has not been sent to railhead - but is gradually being reduced by daily expenditure and that any surplus will be handed over when the time comes to other Divisions	
2pm 4.4.15 "	AA&QMG 28 Div and DADQMG & CRE V Corps visited area East of Vlamertinghe where it is proposed to erect huts.	
4pm 4.4.15	During the afternoon the area allotted to 28th Div was fairly definitely decided but it is exceedingly limited as regards billeting accommodation —	

Instructions regarding War Diaries and Intelligence Summaries are contained in F. S. Regs., Part II. and the Staff Manual respectively. Title pages will be prepared in manuscript.

WAR DIARY
or
INTELLIGENCE SUMMARY.

(Erase heading not required.)

Army Form C. 2118.

	Hour, Date, Place	Summary of Events and Information	Remarks and references to Appendices
		a good many valuable assets are being taken from us such as our bathing establishment near at Brandhoek. – The Lunatic asylum YPRES which is to be ours for a few days only – our huts – our R.P. points – R.E. Depot and A.O.D. Depot.	
3pm	4.4.15 Poperinghe	During Vlamertinghe and YPRES were shelled – Telephone communicat badly interrupted especially as regards Telephone administrative staff.	
—	4.4.15 "	Casualties reported Ra. K. W. 2/Lt. Renny wounded. 13 Bde. 5. 11. Lewis K.O.S.B. wounded.	
—	4.4.15 "	During the day our R.E. Coy ~~moved~~ 5 Div moved to YPRES and ~~our~~ Northumbrian Fd Coy came out & billetted in H2 The Buffs and East Surreys arrived and the Remainder of 9th Brigade left. A new R.E. Depot has been selected near the entrance to YPRES on the Poperinghe road and the Stores will be moved there tomorrow from the Porte de Lille. Much of the 27 Div and ~~of~~ 5th Div have moved into our area all over in YPRES and otherwise	
—	4.4.15 "	Weather Fine then wet.	A. G. M. H.
—	5.5.15 Poperinghe	During the morning the following reconnaissances were carried out – (a) By a a reconnl, reconnl; & a captain – Billetting area immediately N of Pop^{he} – YPRES Road E of Poperinghe. (b) For Refilling Points at YPRES & Poperinghe	

(73989) W4141—463. 400,000. 9/14. H.&J.Ltd. Forms/C. 2118/10.

Instructions regarding War Diaries and Intelligence Summaries are contained in F. S. Regs., Part II. and the Staff Manual respectively. Title pages will be prepared in manuscript.

WAR DIARY
or
INTELLIGENCE SUMMARY.
(Erase heading not required.)

Army Form C. 2118.

Hour, Date, Place	Summary of Events and Information	Remarks and references to Appendices
	(c) DADOS for AOD Store in YPRES (d) RA for billeting area for Ammunition Cols about S. Jean. (e) ADMS for hospital in YPRES – Reconnaissances satisfactory in each case except in (a) where accomodation is small –	
5.5.13 Poperinghe	arrangements for Infantry generally as follows 85th Inf Bde come out of trenches tonight and go into Vlamertinghe huts ~~as follows~~ – 28th Div are supplying them ~~and~~ with supplies & AOD Stores. 15th Bde ~~& 13~~ moves into trenches we are supplying it ~~for consumption~~ on 8th till we get 84th Bde back ~~until it passes out of 28th Div Command on 6th at 3 pm~~ – 13 Bde is in trenches and passes out of 28th Div Command on 6th we supply it till ~~then~~ 7th incl; ~~no change as regards Artillery etc~~ 83 Bde is at Westoutre and about it; ~~we~~ 5th Div are supplying it with food for consumption on ~~8th~~ 7th. 84 Bde is at Bailleul today. Fed by 84th. No change today as regards RA. as regards RE – 3/London Fd Coy move out of YPRES today billets near Vlamertinghe & leaves for 1st Army tomorrow 1/N Midland leaves 28th Div tomorrow. No change as regards Cyclists or Yeomanry. Train Coy 83rd Bde changes over with Train Coy 85th Bde tomorrow. Northumbrian Field Ambulance moved out of Ouderdom to billets W of Poperinghe	

(73989) W4141—463. 400,000. 9/14. H.&J.Ltd. Forms/C. 2118/10.

WAR DIARY
or
INTELLIGENCE SUMMARY.
(Erase heading not required.)

Hour, Date, Place	Summary of Events and Information	Remarks and references to Appendices
— 5.4.15 Poperinghe	2/London Fd Amb moved out of Rue de Lille YPRES into the Asylum YPRES where is the 3/London.	
5.4.15 "	As regards Ammunition. 83rd Bde drew from 3rd Bde R.F.A. A.C. W of Ouderdom today.	
5pm 5.4.15 "	Notification rec'd that Heavy Batty with this Division would join on 7th.	
5pm 5.4.15 "	Regarding disposal of surplus S.A.A. Ammunition it has transpired that there have been difficulties as regards 27th Division handing loose Ammn over to 3rd Div. Consequently V Corps asked how we should act with loose surplus rounds. V Corps suggest we should endeavour to get 5 Div to take them over. Rounds become loose in many cases because boxes have been used to improve the trenches.	See 10 am 4/4/15
— 5.4.15 "	Casualties 83rd Bde 6K — 15W R.A. 1 — 1 85 " 4 — 6	
— 5.4.15 "	83 & 85th Bdes have commenced to ask for trench stores, at the moment we are pretty well found in these except Rifle grenades and have with R.E. made elaborate arrangements for collecting a good assortment to give us a good start in our new area — for the benefit of	

Instructions regarding War Diaries and Intelligence Summaries are contained in F. S. Regs., Part II. and the Staff Manual respectively. Title pages will be prepared in manuscript.

WAR DIARY
or
INTELLIGENCE SUMMARY.
(Erase heading not required.)

Army Form C. 2118.

Hour, Date, Place	Summary of Events and Information	Remarks and references to Appendices
	future Q Staffs are of the first preparations for taking over a section of trenches is that a large Div RE Park (this is approved in Principle) about 60,000 or 70,000 sandbags are at least required to start with.	
— 5.4.15 Poperinghe	Weather V. wet	
— 6.4.15 "	Transfer of areas proceeding.– ~~1/1 Midland~~ 3/London RE left Div for 2/London Division. Negotiations proceeded during morning regarding allotment of areas – but at the moment some of our troops are in the 27th Div & 5th Div areas and vice versa as regards 27th Div – This also applies to YPRES	
3pm 6.4.15 "	At 3pm GOC 28 Div handed over command of present 28 Div Entrenchment line to 5th Div and left the Report Centre. Head Quarters 28 Div remained at 12 Rue de Boeschepe Poperinghe and arrangements were made to accommodate 5th Div as well ~~at that date~~ but 5th Div went into the Hotel de Ville Pope instead.– The 83rd & 84 Inf Bdes came under 28 Div but not very satisfactorily because their distribution is as follows today 83 Bde HQ and 2 Bns at Westoutre. " 4 " around BOSCHEPE. 84 " HQ. St Jans Capelle. 3 Bns in Dranoutre. 2 " " Bailleul.	

(73989) W4141—463. 400,000. 9/14. H.&J.Ltd. Forms/C. 2118/10.

Instructions regarding War Diaries and Intelligence Summaries are contained in F. S. Regs., Part II. and the Staff Manual respectively. Title pages will be prepared in manuscript.

WAR DIARY
or
INTELLIGENCE SUMMARY.
(Erase heading not required.)

Army Form C. 2118.

Hour, Date, Place	Summary of Events and Information	Remarks and references to Appendices
6.4.15 Pop E	Casualties up to 12 noon 85th Bde. K .3 W 13th " 6 .21 .4 M 15th " 2 .5	
6.4.15 "	The present scheme is for the 85th Bde to move up by bus into trenches [struck through] night 8/9th. For 84th Bde to be moved up closer but there has been much discussion with V Corps as to what area they are to go into – The difficulty being that our future areas still occupied by the French.	
4pm 6.4.15 "	OC Train & Railway selected 2 RP points in the N. end of YPRES – for use by troops (bde) in trenches E of YPRES. Following were points selected; by the abattoir, & in the Cloisters.	
– 6.4.15 "	Weather Fine till evening then wet.	[illegible]
8.20am 7.4.15 "	Information from V Corps that 3E Fd Coy RE will join 28th Div at YPRES on 8th	
– 7.4.15	Following drafts arrived 5 Offrs – 137 OR.	

(73989) W4141—463. 400,000. 9/14. H.&J.Ltd. Forms/C. 2118/10.

Instructions regarding War Diaries and Intelligence Summaries are contained in F. S. Regs., Part II. and the Staff Manual respectively. Title pages will be prepared in manuscript.

Army Form C. 2118.

WAR DIARY
or
INTELLIGENCE SUMMARY.
(Erase heading not required.)

Hour, Date, Place	Summary of Events and Information	Remarks and references to Appendices
7.4.15 Poperinghe	During the day the GOC II Army inspected the 83 & 84 Inf Bdes.–	
	A reconnaissance was made of a place for a new R.P. as the existing one at the Brickworks East of Vlamertinghe ~~to~~ Square H 8(a) will have to be vacated. A suitable side road communicating with main road at both ends in squares G 5 & 6. This will do for the Infantry Baggage & Bdes but will not accommodate the whole of the Artillery supplies.	
	The Surrey Yeomanry moved into the new area –	
	Arrangements which were very difficult to make were eventually made to bring the 83rd Bde ~~up in~~ [illegible] 2¼ hrs up in busses tomorrow evening and ~~the 85th~~ do not relieve the 84th till the 11th or later.	
	Supply difficulty even with all the movement has not so far arisen but within the next two or 3 days when the Artillery & Infantry begin to ~~move~~ change areas and we lose our present R.Ps difficulties will crop up.	
7.4.15 Poperinghe	Following arrangements made for 83rd Bde who move tomorrow. Staff Capt allotted a billet in YPRES – and an orderly from 3rd Cavalry Div [illegible] ~~[illegible]~~ sent to him – new RE Depot near western entrance to YPRES pointed out & list of contents indicated. Probable R.P indicated – also billet for Transport such as is wanted in that place – a farm in Square G 6 West of Vlamertinghe allotted for the remainder.	

(73989) W4141—463. 400,000. 9/14. H.&J.Ltd. Forms/C. 2118/10.

Instructions regarding War Diaries and Intelligence Summaries are contained in F. S. Regs., Part II. and the Staff Manual respectively. Title pages will be prepared in manuscript.

WAR DIARY
or
INTELLIGENCE SUMMARY.
(Erase heading not required.)

Army Form C. 2118.

Hour, Date, Place	Summary of Events and Information	Remarks and references to Appendices
7.4.15 Poperinghe	As regards YPRES the Town Major has made a thorough reconnaissance of our new area – we have allotted a building each for 3 Bns, a place for the transport of each Brigade (such T-port as wanted) billets for RE & we have selected an ASC Store & AOD Store in YPRES. There still remain the bathing establishments to arrange for.	
7.4.15 "	1 N Midland Heavy Battery arrived.	
7.4.15 "	Weather showery & cold with intervals of sunshine. –	
7.4.15 "	Railhead changed to Vlamertinghe	A allen
8.4.15 "	Movements of 27th Div out of and of 28th Div into new area continued –	
	200 tents are now being sent to augment accomodation. Reconnaissance made accordingly for camping grounds for resting Bns till our new huts are ready. But as grazing ground is so much difficult to find at present	
	Further reconnaissance made for R.P.s with some success.	
4 pm 8.4.15 Poperinghe	38 Fd Coy RE joined the Division and billetted in YPRES with its transport (Not required) north of Brandhoek. –	
7.30–9.30 pm 8.4.15 "	Between 7.30 and 9.30 pm 3 Bns of the 83rd Brigade arrived from the Reninghelst area and by bus; detrused in YPRES and marched into the Right Section of the new Trenches – coming under orders of GOC 39th French Division. Their transport had come ahead – and had loaded with RE Stores at the RE Depot – with a second days supplies at the ASC Store at the Depot (Cloisters YPRES) and moved out about 7.30 pm from the Menin Gate. There had been	

(73989) W4141—463. 400,000. 9/14. H.&J.Ltd. Forms/C. 2118/10.

Instructions regarding War Diaries and Intelligence Summaries are contained in F. S. Regs., Part II. and the Staff Manual respectively. Title pages will be prepared in manuscript.

WAR DIARY
or
INTELLIGENCE SUMMARY.
(Erase heading not required.)

Army Form C. 2118.

	Hour, Date, Place	Summary of Events and Information	Remarks and references to Appendices
		a delay of an hour because normally rations are put up by Qr Masters & in a bag and the men take turns to carry it - one Bn had omitted to do this and issued man by man his second days ration - The final result was that the left sector of the trenches received no trench stores because to be safe anything returning had to be back in Verlorenhoek by 4 am.—	
—	8. 4. 15 Poperinghe	3 Coys of another Bn 83rd Bde as working Party arrived & billetted in YPRES. Casualties nil —	
—	8. 4. 15 "	Following alterations were made in arrangements regarding limitation of ammn supply for RA. Supply will now be based on a weekly allowance so that if day is suitable for observation more rounds can be fired. Similarly if guns are out of action they still continue their credit. Consequently ~~there is no~~ authority for the issue of 200 rounds per 18 pr & 100 per Heavy for Registration is withdrawn.	
Th	8. 4. 15 "	At night one section of each of Battery of 18 Pr & 4.5" of 5th Div relieved same of 28 Div but remained on the ground - in readiness.	
7	8. 4. 15 "	Weather Showers & Fine at intervals - Cold.	AAMcH.
11.30am	9. 4. 15 "	Conference at YPRES by AQMG 2 Army with Reps of Divisions regarding prevention of congestion of traffic in and of YPRES	

(73989) W4141—463. 400,000. 9/14. H.&J.Ltd. Forms/C. 2118/10.

Instructions regarding War Diaries and Intelligence Summaries are contained in F. S. Regs., Part II. and the Staff Manual respectively. Title pages will be prepared in manuscript.

WAR DIARY
or
INTELLIGENCE SUMMARY.
(Erase heading not required.)

Army Form C. 2118.

Hour, Date, Place	Summary of Events and Information	Remarks and references to Appendices
9.4.15 Poperinghe	During day movement of CRE & Town Major ~~& Report Centre~~ Office transferred to an area in YPRES – (the Northern portion). Report Centre also opened there.	
9.4.15 "	At Request of General of 89 French Division arrangements made for transport of 83rd Bde (Supplies etc) to leave Menin Gate in rear of French Transport 6.30pm	
9.4.15 "	Casualties 83 Inf Bde 3K – 14W.	
10.30pm 9.4.15 "	Suggested to 85th Bde that following scale be not exceeded) Transport to be kept East of YPRES – Maltese Cart & Water Cart " " " " " " " – Pack Animals, S.A.A. Carts, Machine gun ~~animals~~ vehicles & 2 chargers per Bn Suggestion only made because it is impossible to the Bdrs … they can alone can decide at the moment what is wanted.	
9.4.15	During day following completed. Bearer Division 85 Fd Amb moved to YPRES and hospital opened in the Institut S. Famille YPRES. Where is the whole of 86 Fd Amb. Bde Am Cols moved into new area. Artillery relieved at night by artillery 5th Division. – Further reconnaissance made for accomodation.	
9.4.15 "	Weather Fine.	[signature]

(73989) W4141—463. 400,000. 9/14. H.&J.Ltd. Forms/C. 2118/10.

Army Form C. 2118.

Instructions regarding War Diaries and Intelligence Summaries are contained in F. S. Regs., Part II. and the Staff Manual respectively. Title pages will be prepared in manuscript.

WAR DIARY
or
INTELLIGENCE SUMMARY.
(Erase heading not required.)

Hour, Date, Place	Summary of Events and Information	Remarks and references to Appendices
10.30am 10.4.15 Poperinghe	As 85th Bde was moving out from the huts along Zonnebeke road arrangements made to prevent 27th Div & 83 Div blocking road	
12.30pm 10.4.15 "	2 Bns 85 Bde moved to S. Jean.	
5.30 10.4.15 "	3 Bns of 85 Bde passed Menin Gate moving to trenches in relief of French – 1 hour interval between Bns – a Staff officer 'Q' Staff 28 Div was present to prevent blocking – all went well – units are taking up 2 days into trenches and if they are staying longer are moving up extra days accordingly – The first day of the 2 is packed 8 rations in a sandbag and carried on the men. The second day is picked up at the Cloisters YPRES – Packed on Pack Mules and in GS waggons – RE Stores on GS waggons – with the result that about 8 Pack animals 3 GS Limbered waggons and one GS waggon for outward Stores	
– 10.4.15 Poperinghe	Casualties 83 Bde 11 K – 16 W 85 " 1 W	
– 10.4.15 "	Sunny day Tents to accommodate 1½ Bns pitched about 2 miles NE of Poperinghe.	
– 10.4.15 "	Weather fine.	[illegible]

(73989) W4141—463. 400,000. 9/14. H.&J.Ltd. Forms/C. 2118/10.

Instructions regarding War Diaries and Intelligence Summaries are contained in F. S. Regs., Part II. and the Staff Manual respectively. Title pages will be prepared in manuscript.

WAR DIARY
or
INTELLIGENCE SUMMARY.
(Erase heading not required.)

Army Form C. 2118.

Hour, Date, Place			Summary of Events and Information	Remarks and references to Appendices
2.40pm	10.4.15	Poperinghe	Following reinforcements arrived 5 Offrs 252 OR.	
—	11.4.15	"	Following Casualties up to 12 noon 11th. 19K – 34W.	
—	11.4.15	"	Following were arrangements for night – Part of the trenches (artillery) had to be relieved by an arm. ~~1 Bn of 85th moved from St Jean to trenches in relief of another~~ ~~3 Bns of 83 Bde " " YPRES " " " " " 3 others~~ Trench Stores & Supplies for 83 & 85 Bdes had to be moved up also S.A.A. – 1 Bn 85th in Relief to trenches from St Jean. ~~1 Bn 85 in Relief from St Jean~~. 6 Bns of 27th Div (his) Pack animals had to be fed all through the Menin Gate YPRES – Zonnebeke Road. This has to be arranged from the standpoint that everything on the return journey must be clear of the rise just west of FRAZENBERG by daylight Sunday ~~following ~~ This was satisfactorily completed.	
—	11.4.15	"	Weather Fine – Tent accomodation for 3 Bns 84 Bde (reserve) No 2 Coy Anglesey RE joined Division	a.a.m.w.
12.35pm	12.4.15	"	2 Corps notifies that the Heavy Battery portion of 1/North Midland Div Amn Col & Park will join us – Amn Park moving today to join 27th Park at CAESTRE – as regards Div Amn Col portion ordered to join our Div Amn Col west of Poperinghe town area –	
1pm	12.4.15	"	3 Bns & HQ 84 Inf Bde arrived from ~~Div~~ Bailleul Wieljanbre and were billetted HQ & 2 Bns Vlamertinghe – 1 Bn Poperinghe.	

(73989) W4141—463. 400,000. 9/14. H.&J.Ltd. Forms/C. 2118/10.

Army Form C. 2118.

WAR DIARY
or
INTELLIGENCE SUMMARY.
(Erase heading not required.)

Instructions regarding War Diaries and Intelligence Summaries are contained in F. S. Regs., Part II. and the Staff Manual respectively. Title pages will be prepared in manuscript.

Hour, Date, Place	Summary of Events and Information	Remarks and references to Appendices
12 noon 12. 4. 15 Poperinghe	Following ~~French~~ Casualties OR K. 14 – W. 19. Officers Killed Lt Ramsey 2 Buffs " Wounded Lt Marsh Smith Buffs – Capt Le Fleming E. Surreys (Lt Lethbridge ?)	
4.30pm 12.4.15 "	Head Quarters 28 Div bombed by German aeroplane – one man wounded by glass. Bomb fell in garden & destroyed back part of building – all glass broken – Immediately after another Bomb fell in Rue de l'Hôpital adjoining and caused many casualties chiefly civilians –	
– 12.4.15 "	Tonight was a difficult night for Traffic Control on the Zonnebeke road following had to pass. Out ——— In 1 Bn 85 from S. Jean to trenches in Relief ——— 1 Bn 85 Transport with food & Trench Stores 85 ← Same to Return. Remainder of 28 Div RA ——— French Artillery on relief 3 Bns 85 Bde ——— 3 Bns 83. Transport of 3 Bns 83 Bde ——— ← Same to return. 27 Div food & Trench Stores for 6 Bns ——— ← Same to return Reliefs of 27 Div ——— Relieved to return Time table based on the last unit to be clear of Right of road at Frezenberg by 2.30 am was as follows – It worked out accurately.	

(73989) W4141—463. 400,000. 9/14. H.&J.Ltd. Forms/C. 2118/10.

Instructions regarding War Diaries and Intelligence Summaries are contained in F. S. Regs., Part II. and the Staff Manual respectively. Title pages will be prepared in manuscript.

WAR DIARY
or
INTELLIGENCE SUMMARY.
(Erase heading not required.)

Army Form C. 2118.

Hour, Date, Place	Summary of Events and Information	Remarks and references to Appendices
7.08pm 12.4.15 Poperinghe	1 Bn 85th: leave St Jean – 7.22 arrive Potije Cross Roads	
6.56pm " " "	Transport 85th Bde to leave ~~arrive Potije Cross Roads~~ Menin Gate YPRES	
7.11pm " " "	1 Bn ~~Transport~~ 83 Bde to leave Menin Gate YPRES	
7.26pm " " "	1 Bn 83 Bde to leave " " " "	
7.41pm " " "	1 " " " " " " " "	
7.56pm " " "	4 Secs 146th Bde RFA " " " "	
8.11pm " " "	3 " 31st " " " "	
8.26pm " " "	2 " Hows " " "	
8.41pm " " "	3 " 3rd Bde RFA " " "	
8.56pm " " "	Ration Heavy Bde.	
9.15pm " " "	27 lbs Supplies & Trench Stores for 6 Bns.	
	All the above on a narrow road and in addition to the movements of the ambulances – one cannot leave YPRES much before 7 owing to movements being plainly visible from aeroplanes as we have no anti aircraft guns now.	
12.4.15 "	Army day our new huts NW of YPRES were proceeded with – we are now practically into an ~~area~~ new area less 3 Bns 84th Bde – and Cyclists both of whom were Territorials and the bathing establishment.	
11.58pm 12.4.15	~~Weather & [illegible]~~ a Zeppelin dropped 11 bombs on Kalmt	

(73989) W4141—463. 400,000. 9/14. H.&J.Ltd. Forms/C. 2118/10.

Instructions regarding War Diaries and Intelligence Summaries are contained in F. S. Regs., Part II. and the Staff Manual respectively. Title pages will be prepared in manuscript.

WAR DIARY
or
INTELLIGENCE SUMMARY.
(Erase heading not required.)

Army Form C. 2118.

Hour, Date, Place	Summary of Events and Information	Remarks and references to Appendices
	Vlamertinghe no harm done –	
12 · 4 · 15 Pofm	During the night a new 4-gun French How Batty joined & proceeded to position.	
12 · 4 · 15 Poperinghe	Weather fine	[illegible] –
13 · 4 · 15 "	Authority given from 5th Corps for following additional allowance Ammunition ~~weekly~~ for replenishment to lapse at noon on 17th if not expended 28th Div 18pr 650 Rnds 4.5 Lydd: 40 ~~Shrap~~ Lyddite 80 Shrap.	
13 · 4 · 15 "	Normal arrangements for Ra Supply & Amm Supply are as follows. Batty & Amm Col waggons leave YPRES as implied in following order 3rd Bde – 146 Bde – 31st 8" How – Heavys & march in one Column to Vlamertinghe where the waggons turn off to Batty lines returning by batteries when refilling has taken place Heavy Amm Col & 12 Hy Batty draws direct from advanced Section of the newly formed (27) Hy Amm Park at Abeele – main body of Park is at CAESTRE	
13 · 4 · 15 "	Hy Portion North Midland Div Amm Col arrives to join 28 Div to feed the North Midland Hy Batty	
12 hrs 13 · 4 · 15 " "	Casualties Ra K – 3W ASC – – 1 M.M. Gun – – Major Stewart Wounded 85 Bde. 8 – 45 Lt Leish 1/Buffs · Lt Rogers 3/Mx Wounded 84 " 2 – 3 Lt Collet Browne 1/RO Y&L Killed 83 " – 1 RE – 2	

(73989) W4141—463. 400,000. 9/14. H.&J.Ltd. Forms/C. 2118/10.

Instructions regarding War Diaries and Intelligence Summaries are contained in F. S. Regs., Part II. and the Staff Manual respectively. Title pages will be prepared in manuscript.

WAR DIARY
or
INTELLIGENCE SUMMARY.
(Erase heading not required.)

Army Form C. 2118.

Hour, Date, Place	Summary of Events and Information	Remarks and references to Appendices
6.45 pm 13.4.14 Poperinghe	Units leaving Menin Gate or Zonnebeke Road tonight were 1 Bn 85th Bde – Supplies & Transport for Trench Stores of 85, 83 Bdes & 6 Bns 27th Div – Also reliefs of Batteries and RA Ammtn and Supply wagons 28 Div	
— 13.4.14 "	Weather fine	
— 14.4.14 "	We have been allotted Vlamertinghe Chateau for our new Div HQ. Corps Commander has ordered this to be filled up as well with troops – not very convenient – Result is much thought, consideration and reconnaissance.	
7.30 a 14.4.14 "	102 Remounts arrived for Div: at Railhead – also 180 for 27 Div and same for 5th Corps – As showing how organisation has not stood the test of war – there are at our Railhead. Railhead Comdt under 5th Corps. R.T.O. " I.G.C. Horses for two Divisions arrived in same train V Corps orders Division & Railhead Comdt that 28 Div will not draw horses out until 27th are clear – but R.T.O won't acknowledge this as he has to get his train out of the way.	
12.30 pm 14.4.14 "	2nd Canadian Brigade arrived Vlamertinghe and billeted with 84th Bde till nightfall when it moved	

Instructions regarding War Diaries and Intelligence Summaries are contained in F. S. Regs., Part II. and the Staff Manual respectively. Title pages will be prepared in manuscript.

WAR DIARY
or
INTELLIGENCE SUMMARY.
(Erase heading not required.)

Army Form C. 2118.

Hour, Date, Place	Summary of Events and Information	Remarks and references to Appendices
14.4.14 Poperinghe	to the Trenches – Consequently 3 Divisions are now more or less working on the road into the western entry to YPRES – but there will be no congestion if traffic is controlled from a central authority.	
6.30pm 14.4.14 —	Arrangements for Supply of Infantry Bns in Trenches with RE Stores and Supplies, Sa[a] are generally speaking as follows – Hours are timed so that head of column does not go over the hill W of FRAZENBERG until about 8pm when it is then dark. An order is arranged in which units or Bde Transport a Ra[ilhead] leave Menin Gate – A Bn going to trenches takes 2 days + Iron Ration. These are carried Iron ration & 1 day on man & 1 day on pack animals packed 8 rations in a sandbag 6 to 8 sandbags on a mule remainder in 3 GS limber waggons which together with 1 GS waggon take up RE Trench Stores – Sometimes not so many are required Sometimes Saa is required – A Company as a rule goes up from YPRES as carrying party – The whole go to a point between Frasenberg & Zonnebeke Rly and which it is too narrow for wheeled traffic does not go on account of noise. The pack animals go on and the to Zonnebeke – after the transport stops everything is carried by hand of the Coy which came out for and which returns	
14.4.14	Casualties 43 K. 104 W. 1 M. Lt Webster 4th L wounded – also Capt Hood and Lt Whitelaw ?Buffs — 2/Lt Whitehead 2/S.Surry Killed.	
14.4.14	Weather Wet	

(73989) W4141—463. 400,000. 9/14. H.&J.Ltd. Forms/C. 2118/10.

Instructions regarding War Diaries and Intelligence Summaries are contained in F. S. Regs., Part II. and the Staff Manual respectively. Title pages will be prepared in manuscript.

WAR DIARY
or
INTELLIGENCE SUMMARY.
(Erase heading not required.)

Army Form C. 2118.

Hour, Date, Place	Summary of Events and Information	Remarks and references to Appendices
12 noon 15·4·15 Poperinghe	Casualties up to 12 noon. 14 K – 24 W – Lt Waddell Dudley Kd.	
15·4·15 "	The movements of troops and Transport was upset taught by the confirmed reports of hostile attack following were generally speaking the moves 83 Bde 1 Bn to Trenches the relieved Bn to Polize – 84th Bde 2 Bns from W of YPRES to trenches of 85th & one Bn Poperinghe to Vlamertinghe. 85th Bde 2 Bns from trenches to S. Jean. 1 Bn St Jean to dug outs and Zonnebeke. In addition to this were the feeding supply of trench stores and ammunition to troops in trenches ~~[illegible]~~ including the 6 Bns of the ~~8~~ 27th Division – all worked out pretty well. Road Control ~~to~~ Poperinghe to YPRES is also carried out by Vth Corps to whom we ~~[illegible]~~ now have to report projected moves by 7 pm previous day.	
15·4·15 "	Following changes in allotment Ammunition made 8 Rounds of 4·7" of which 5 may be HE instead of 1.	
15·4·15 "	Weather Fine	A.A.McH.—
5 am 16·4·15 "	Movements continued during the early morning. The Bn 83 moved back from Polize to the huts.– The Bn 85 ~~moves~~ Bde moved one Bn back from Zonnebeke to ~~huts~~ S. Jean – one Bn S. Jean to YPRES one Bn to Vlamertinghe.	

(73989) W4141—463. 400,000. 9/14. H.&J.Ltd. Forms/C. 2118/10.

Instructions regarding War Diaries and Intelligence Summaries are contained in F. S. Regs., Part II. and the Staff Manual respectively. Title pages will be prepared in manuscript.

WAR DIARY
or
INTELLIGENCE SUMMARY.
(*Erase heading not required.*)

Army Form C. 2118.

Hour, Date, Place	Summary of Events and Information	Remarks and references to Appendices
12 noon 16.4.15 Poperinghe	arrangements made for purchase of 8 handcarts for 85th Inf Bde for carrying stores to trenches to supplement existing transport –	
12.30pm " "	3/Canadian Bde ~~cars~~ arrives Vlamertinghe – considerable congestion – Road control to YPRES organised by 5th Corps	
2.30pm " "	Corps commander visits billets in YPRES.	
3-5pm " "	Following moves take place 1 Bn 84th Square G4 to YPRES and Bn 85 ~~Sq~~ YPRES to Square G4	
6.25pm " "	On arrival in this Command 83 Inf Bde drew 970,000 rounds in one day from Bde Amn Col – Enquiries made from HQ in consequence – Bde ~~explains~~ actually took ~~large draw~~ due to taking 220 rounds per man to trenches plus 4 boxes reserve per platoon – SAA carts full. making about 280 rounds per man in trenches alone	
5.30pm 16.4.15 "	Notification received that Trav: Kitchens will arrive tonight complete as turnout as follows – 5 Bns of 85th – 4 each. – 1st Monmouths 84th Bde + 12th London 84th Bde 4 each – This is the first issue.	

(73989) W4141—463. 400,000. 9/14. H.&J.Ltd. Forms/C. 2118/10.

Instructions regarding War Diaries and Intelligence Summaries are contained in F. S. Regs., Part II. and the Staff Manual respectively. Title pages will be prepared in manuscript.

WAR DIARY
or
INTELLIGENCE SUMMARY.
(Erase heading not required.)

Army Form C. 2118.

Hour, Date, Place	Summary of Events and Information	Remarks and references to Appendices
16.4.15 Poperinghe	Casualties R21 – 558W – 1 m. Pte Haydon 'Y.L.' } Killed Pte Tuke [illegible] }	
16.4.15 "	In order to facilitate 5th Corps control of Poperinghe–YPRES road traffic we have to report now by 7pm each day projected moves for following day –	
16.4.15 "	Weather fine – warm.	
16.4.15 "	Plan showing Billeting area – and Refilling Points	~~2 & 3~~ attach: Appendix II
17.4.15 "	Difficulty is again arising regarding supply of Rifle Grenades and Sandbags – we get 5000 per diem up to 20th – after that 10000 – our present requirements are 12000 daily. What makes our Sandbags more than ever necessary is presence of Minen werfer opposite Zonnebeke which throws a shell 30" x 10" and which blows away 140 yds of parapet in one shot. Trenches are so close that artillery fire is in many places impossible and all fighting is done with bombs. Regarding the Sandbags earnest representation has been made to Corps HQ – As also regarding Rifle Grenades	

Army Form C. 2118.

Instructions regarding War Diaries and Intelligence Summaries are contained in F. S. Regs., Part II. and the Staff Manual respectively. Title pages will be prepared in manuscript.

WAR DIARY
or
INTELLIGENCE SUMMARY.
(Erase heading not required.)

Hour, Date, Place	Summary of Events and Information	Remarks and references to Appendices
12 noon 17.4.15 Poperinghe	Casualties to noon 17th 9K - 45W Capt Hart [illegible], Lt Howard [illegible] 5th W	
	During night there was an attack by 5th Div on Hill 60 N of the Canal in our former lines - The Hill was supported by very heavy artillery fire. Yet the Menin Gate easily stood the strain of 2 Divisions traffic of supplies & trench stores for the trenches and a great many ammunition waggons for 2 7" Siege Guns. In fact might there are 3 Divisions feeding from one Railhead Vlamertinghe or rather 2½ as Canadians are not all in there is no difficulty in getting food about - It may be different when the whole of the Canadian Artillery are in. -	
17.4.15 Poperinghe	There have been many changes as to our new HQ. The latest is the town to Vlamertinghe & not the chateau —	
17.4.15 Poperinghe	additional 44 Rounds of 4.5 per diem have been allotted	
17.4.15 "	Weather fine	

(73989) W4141—463. 400,000. 9/14. H.&J.Ltd. Forms/C. 2118/10.

Instructions regarding War Diaries and Intelligence Summaries are contained in F. S. Regs., Part II. and the Staff Manual respectively. Title pages will be prepared in manuscript.

WAR DIARY
or
INTELLIGENCE SUMMARY.
(Erase heading not required.)

Army Form C. 2118.

Hour, Date, Place	Summary of Events and Information	Remarks and references to Appendices
9.10 am. 18.4.15 Poperinghe	5 Division asks for hand and Rifle grenades – unable to spare any.	
10 am. " " "	Meeting between representatives of 28 & 27 Divs to arrange of Road control of YPRES. Bdes notified of arrangements	
18.4.15 "	Supply of 15000 Sandbags per ~~week~~ day authorised for one week.	
18.4.15 "	A new Bathing establishment has been opened in the Asile des Aliénés YPRES.	
	All quiet from an administrative point of view – Bdes were allotted following hours ~~from~~ of departure from Menin Gate ~~and~~ 85: 6.45 pm: 84 7 pm: 83 7.45 pm RA 8.30 pm –. The route to be followed by all except RA & for GS waggons being Elverdinghe St – Boesinghe St: Hout Market – Carlton St – Thourout St – Rd Junc 200 yds N of Asile Aliénés – Menin Rd Junc – This road is narrow and have no good for vehicles – we had to knock down a wall to admit of ~~the~~ a turning a corner – Hence not good enough for GS waggons. Weather Fine –	[illegible]

Instructions regarding War Diaries and Intelligence Summaries are contained in F. S. Regs., Part II. and the Staff Manual respectively. Title pages will be prepared in manuscript.

WAR DIARY
or
INTELLIGENCE SUMMARY.
(Erase heading not required.)

Army Form C. 2118.

Hour, Date, Place			Summary of Events and Information	Remarks and references to Appendices
1.40am	19.4.15	Poperinghe	Urgent appeal for Very Pistol Cartridges and Hand Grenades sent ~~to~~ by 5th Division – Issue of 360 Very Pistol Cartridges & 150 Hand Grenades approved	
9.30am	19.4.15	"	DAAQMG attended meeting at GHQ relative to Suspension of Sentences act.	
—	19.4.15	"	Army Morning YPRES was shelled killing 3 HD horses in the Carts of 85th Bde HQ among other things – These were replaced from Train.	
—	19.4.15	"	GHQ calls for recommendations for despatches.	
2.55pm	19.4.15	"	5th Corps asks if we could spare any Very Pistol Cartridges for 5th Div if required – we replied 500.	
5.50pm	19.4.15	"	5th Corps calls for 500 Very Pistol Cartridges duly sent.	
4.30pm	19.4.15	"	On 17th we received 18 Train Vehicles complete ~~with~~ turnout – on detrainment they went to the Div Train Lines. The ASC drivers who brought them back were ordered to return ~~and~~ this left us with surplus vehicles and no drivers, rather difficult to allow for in a hurry; arrangements made to obtain additional drivers and [illegible] to 5th Corps.	

Instructions regarding War Diaries and Intelligence Summaries are contained in F. S. Regs., Part II. and the Staff Manual respectively. Title pages will be prepared in manuscript.

WAR DIARY
or
INTELLIGENCE SUMMARY.
(Erase heading not required.)

Army Form C. 2118.

Hour, Date, Place	Summary of Events and Information	Remarks and references to Appendices
19.4.15 Poperinghe	Casualties 6K – 44W. also Major Walford Bde Maj 84th Inf Bde.	
10.30p 19.4.15 "	Now decided by 2nd Army that 28 Div HQ billets in Vlamertinghe Chateau and not the Village this is a/c of valuable furniture in the Chateau. ~~Which~~ Army Commander thinks Infantry should in consequence not billet there.	
6.45 – 7.20pm "	While our Transport and reliefs were moving out past Junc. of Menin & YPRES – Zonnebeke road – Germans Shelled that place, consequently for a time Transport had to use the road via S. Jean.	
19.4.15 "	Weather v. fine	Aam G[illegible].
	Capt Fuller [illegible] 28 Div detailed to act as Bde Maj 84th Inf Bde temporarily vice Major Walford killed.	
12.35pm 20.4.15 "	85th Bde Reports 5 horses K & wounded – These were replaced at once by Surplus mules from Suffolk Regt –	
1 am 20.4.15 "	YPRES has been Shelled intermittently ~~for~~ since yesterday they now began to Shell it with 17 inch Shell from S.E. doing great harm to Civilians especially – ~~[illegible]~~ our 3 Bns were ordered out and bivouacked at [illegible] about S. Jean	

(73989) W4141—463. 400,000. 9/14. H.&J.Ltd. Forms/C. 2118/10.

Instructions regarding War Diaries and Intelligence Summaries are contained in F. S. Regs., Part II. and the Staff Manual respectively. Title pages will be prepared in manuscript.

WAR DIARY
or
INTELLIGENCE SUMMARY.
(Erase heading not required.)

Army Form C. 2118.

Hour, Date, Place	Summary of Events and Information	Remarks and references to Appendices
	Fortunately the Tents & Stabs we have been lent have been left in Damise — since the troops returned to YPRES at night [illegible] [illegible] [illegible] to be [illegible] [illegible] — General difficulties are increased by the fact that the Germans are counter attacking hill 60 — and altogether it is not easy to get in or out of YPRES to the East and impossible to stay in the town unless in cellars — our [illegible] and Supply must stay there until we can move them	
5.50 pm 20.4.15 Poperinghe	Canadians give permission to use their road S. Jean Pot. Wieltje to supply wagons of our RFA Bde at S. Jean.	
9 pm 20.4.15 "	We have been ordered to hand over 130 out of our 200 tents to Canadians, leaving us only 70 — [illegible] there are now 3 Bns of tents between Vlamertinghe & YPRES Casualties up to 12 noon — 10 K — 38 W. Lt Swabey 3/Som Lt — Capt Playfair RA killed Lt Berry RHA wounded also Lt. Hughes	
20.4.15 "	Weather V. fine	[illegible]
"		
9 am 21.4.15 "	The 3 Bns turned out of YPRES require shelter as they are in bivouac at St Jean — arrangements accordingly made as follows 50 Tents & Stabs were issued to each Bn there	

Instructions regarding War Diaries and Intelligence Summaries are contained in F. S. Regs., Part II. and the Staff Manual respectively. Title pages will be prepared in manuscript.

WAR DIARY
or
~~INTELLIGENCE SUMMARY.~~
(Erase heading not required.)

Army Form C. 2118.

Hour, Date, Place	Summary of Events and Information	Remarks and references to Appendices
	from AOS YPRES – 40 more per Bn were brought up from Hazebrouck and issued ~~to~~ – RE were directed to get in touch & provide poles ~~etc~~ for Tents d'abri and Timber for dug outs	
11am 21.4.15 Poperinghe	~~Administrative HQ 28 Div moved from Poperinghe to Vlamertinghe Chateau~~ Shelling of YPRES continued throughout the day. ~~The~~ It was impossible to remove the AOS or old stores and as the latter was in the Crypt of the Cloisters it was unnecessary – The RE depot at the Entrance to YPRES from Poperinghe remains there until another site can be arranged for the Explosives – But of course the shelling may stop at any moment – Report Centre closed at YPRES	
21.4.15 ~~Poperinghe~~ Vlamertinghe Chateau	Weather fine	[illegible] –
11am 22.4.15 ~~Poperinghe~~ Vlamertinghe Chateau	Head Quarters 28 Div moved from Poperinghe to the Chateau Vlamertinghe – There is at present no Report Centre in front of this –	
10pm – 3am 21.4.15 – 22.4.15	The YPRES – ZONNEBEKE Road patrolled by a Staff officer 28 Div. to regulate traffic but all was perfectly quiet and regular along the route –	

(73989) W4141—463. 400,000. 9/14. H.&J.Ltd. Forms/C. 2118/10.

Instructions regarding War Diaries and Intelligence Summaries are contained in F. S. Regs., Part II. and the Staff Manual respectively. Title pages will be prepared in manuscript.

WAR DIARY
or
INTELLIGENCE SUMMARY.
(Erase heading not required.)

Army Form C. 2118.

Hour, Date, Place	Summary of Events and Information	Remarks and references to Appendices
10am 22. 4. 15 Vlamertinghe Chateau	Troops in bivouac at S. Jean visited and steps taken to supply wants e.g. straw etc. ~~Shelling of YPRES~~ Further steps taken to clear YPRES where it transpires were still some 1st and 2nd Line Transport of Infantry Bdes	
4pm. 22. 4. 15 Vlamertinghe Chateau	Lieut Col R Hennecy joined as AQMG vice Lt Col Atcherley	
4.30pm 22. 4. 15 "	Shelling of YPRES especially Menin and Dixmude exits recommenced with Heavy Shell & Shrapnel – nearly expending the AAQMG & DAQMG who happened to be there watching traffic – This shelling being carried out evidently with the view of prevention of Transport and reinforcements leaving YPRES.	
~~4.30pm 22.4.15~~		
4.30pm 22.4.15 "	Allies hear very heavy firing also commenced from the North – and N.E.	
6. pm 22.4.15 "	The AA&QMG & DAQMG being forced to move back also out of YPRES owing to shelling – turned back any 2nd ~~Div Train~~ Line Transport they ~~could find~~ met with instructions to turn off the road as soon as they got clear and await instructions for a quieter time to move.	
7.30pm 22.4.15 "	Vlamertinghe – YPRES road now choked with ~~troops~~ soldiers, ~~and~~ Transport and Civilian Traffic	

(73989) W4141—463. 400,000. 9/14. H.&J.Ltd. Forms/C. 2118/10.

Instructions regarding War Diaries and Intelligence Summaries are contained in F. S. Regs., Part II. and the Staff Manual respectively. Title pages will be prepared in manuscript.

WAR DIARY
or
INTELLIGENCE SUMMARY.
(Erase heading not required.)

Army Form C. 2118.

Hour, Date, Place	Summary of Events and Information	Remarks and references to Appendices
	retiring from YPRES — a certain number Div Amm. Col: left YPRES Vautre à Terre — by single waggons or detachments — added to number of Algerian [illegible] the road traffic rapidly ~~became~~ became complicated. Steps were taken to by the Staff officers retiring from YPRES to deal with it.	
	Capt Agg KOYLI the APM (vice Miller temporary Bde Major to 84th Inf Bde) placed such of his police as he could collect at points in the [illegible] about Vlamertinghe where the following arrangements were made — Traffic not to be allowed to move further East than the Vlamertinghe Cross Roads — no ~~west going~~ traffic to stop on any account but ~~to~~ waggons were diverted along the Vlamertinghe — Ouderdom and Ouderdom or Reninghelst — Poperinghe roads others ~~along the~~ [illegible] directed to proceed along Vlamertinghe — Poperinghe Road — ~~28 Div vehicles directed to Collect~~	
	The 5th Corps was ~~asked to~~ telephoned to regarding the situation and requested to sort the traffic at Poperinghe for Capt Agg had directed 28 Div vehicles to Concentrate	

Instructions regarding War Diaries and Intelligence Summaries are contained in F. S. Regs., Part II. and the Staff Manual respectively. Title pages will be prepared in manuscript.

WAR DIARY
or
INTELLIGENCE SUMMARY.
(Erase heading not required.)

Army Form C. 2118.

Hour, Date, Place	Summary of Events and Information	Remarks and references to Appendices
	in Poperinghe and to Canadians to the North of it – 5th Div telephoned that 28 Div vehicles were concentrate about 1 mile East of Poperinghe on the South side of the Road	
8pm 22. 4.15 Vlamertinghe Chateau	Situation was as follows the ~~Fr~~ Germans had let loose asphyxiating gas on the Trenches of the French Division on the Canadian left – (the Canadians are on our left) – and this ~~is~~ being successful followed, ~~and~~ ~~fell~~ up, allegedly falling back to line roughly Gravenstafel – S. Julien then SW for 2 miles then ~~East~~ West to Canal	
	most of the Infantry supplies had already gone up but there remained those of one or two Bns whom the had times and who drifted through to the North of YPRES – and the RA supply waggons which remained parked under all Train and ~~never more~~ did not attempt to go – moreover it was considered that 30 GS waggons turned out add to the block – As a matter of interest it ~~has~~ transpired later that the only ~~Bns~~ troops who did not receive ration were the RA.	

Army Form C. 2118.

Instructions regarding War Diaries and Intelligence Summaries are contained in F. S. Regs., Part II. and the Staff Manual respectively. Title pages will be prepared in manuscript.

WAR DIARY
or
INTELLIGENCE SUMMARY.
(Erase heading not required.)

Hour, Date, Place	Summary of Events and Information	Remarks and references to Appendices
10-12p 22-4-15 Vlamertinghe	During the night 3½ ?? Bns and later another Bn 28 Div were moved up from the new huts just W of YPRES and from S. Jean to fill up the gap between the Canadian left and the French who had retired across the Canal.— The attention of the administration was taken up now (now that the Supply Situation had been dealt with) in keeping the Road clear from YPRES — for the passage of Ammunition.— This was not easy to effect as the Canadian ~~Artillery~~ Division kept halting long columns of Artillery vehicles on the main Road — all other ~~Troops~~ Res keeping their vehicles clear of it. Weather Fine.	
12-30a 23-4-15 Vlamertinghe	GOC ordered everybody of Div HQ and attached who could carry out their work equally efficiently further back to go back at once to Poperinghe — following were left at Chateau of Vlamertinghe of the administrative Staff AA&QMG, DAQMG, APM — of the GS side the 3 GS officers — all horses & Transport were sent	Annex.

Instructions regarding War Diaries and Intelligence Summaries are contained in F. S. Regs., Part II. and the Staff Manual respectively. Title pages will be prepared in manuscript.

WAR DIARY
or
INTELLIGENCE SUMMARY.
(Erase heading not required.)

Army Form C. 2118.

Hour, Date, Place			Summary of Events and Information	Remarks and references to Appendices
2.54 am	23.4.16	Vlamertinghe	5th Corps wires ~~hoping~~ as in any case we have arranged to have Good Supply Centre to be available at daylight and as it may be difficult after daylight to bring anything back all transport required for fighting ~~was~~ can remain forward other transport to be in rear of a North & South line Oosthoek A23 — Busseboom G17 by 6 am.	
			Following instructions issued — Div Train & 1st Line not required for fighting to move ~~west of~~ to fields 1½ m East of Poperinghe South of road where 5th Corps were also directing waggons which had drifted into Poperinghe — Div Cyclists Train waggons to join Train — R.E. Transport To join Yeomanry G 3(a) — Range to Poperinghe with one field Ambulance N. East — This was not completed till about 10 am [Road to YPRES visited by Staff officer who found many Canadian waggons halted along road & these were induced to clear off the road into fields to billet in Poperinghe]	
9.40 am	23.4.11	"	Railhead changed to Caestre by 5th Corps.	
			During the morning repeated visits of Staff officers were made down the road towards YPRES and about Vlamertinghe to watch traffic which is now working well	
12.30 pm	23.4.11	"	York & Durham T.F. Bdes began to arrive — by bus and were put into the new huts N.W. of YPRES. —	
			Casualties to-day reported as officers Killed Capt Arnold Suffolks. 2Lt Fardell 7/R Sussex ~~Killed~~ Wounded 2/Lt Chamberlain Welsh R 2Lt Wilkins Buffs no other names but a total of 2K – 1W – 1M. other ranks 13K. 167W. 1M.	
12 noon	23.4.11	"	Rounds expended to-day 18 pr. 948. 4.5 Shrap 62 & HE 100 4.7" HE 26. Gun number of guns 18 pr. 48. 4.5" 12 — 4.7" 8 — This does not include 146th Bde RFA	

Instructions regarding War Diaries and Intelligence Summaries are contained in F. S. Regs., Part II. and the Staff Manual respectively. Title pages will be prepared in manuscript.

WAR DIARY
or
INTELLIGENCE SUMMARY.
(Erase heading not required.)

Army Form C. 2118.

Hour, Date, Place	Summary of Events and Information	Remarks and references to Appendices
23.4.15 Vlamertinghe	5th Corps asked if we are to feed York & Durham Bde – reply as far as is known at present we feed none of units of Northumbrian Div. Situation has become difficult to handle from an administrative point of view. The 8 Bns of 83 & 85 Inf Bdes are in trenches. 4½ Bns of mixed Bdes are under Col Geddes filling a gap between ~~N of~~ left of Canadians and right of the French – 1 Bn in huts W of YPRES – Remainder about S. Jean & FREZENBERG.	
3.35pm 23.4.15 "	The problem of feeding units in trenches and normal position is normal – as regards units now under Col Geddes who is [illegible] Canadian Division informs that their supply waggons would be at the level crossing 1½ m East of YPRES at 9pm and asks for guides to be sent from Bns to conduct. The 30 [illegible] waggons which were held up last night were sent through early this morning and got through.	
6.30pm 23.4.15 "	Several units have come in this area Eg a Siege Batty – a 9.2" How. and enquiries made from 5th Corps as to whether we feed them or not.	
7.30pm 23.4.15 "	Wire to A.G. GHQ repeating 5th Corps D.2: Any[?] what estimated heavy casualties to men today North Midland Hy Batty [illegible] Buffs over 100	
23.4.15	5th Corps notifies us that RP for Y & D Bde will be near Brielen[?] West of Vlamertinghe tomorrow ~~and D.L.I.~~ at East side of the triangle road and D.L.I. Bde the West End. Bde notified	

(73989) W4141—463. 400,000. 9/14. H.&J.Ltd. Forms/C. 2118/10.

Instructions regarding War Diaries and Intelligence Summaries are contained in F. S. Regs., Part II. and the Staff Manual respectively. Title pages will be prepared in manuscript.

WAR DIARY
or
INTELLIGENCE SUMMARY.
(Erase heading not required.)

Army Form C. 2118.

Hour, Date, Place	Summary of Events and Information	Remarks and references to Appendices
23.4.15 Vlamertinghe	We have by instructions of 5th Corps given up the Divisional RH at the old RH Park East of Vlamertinghe.	
9pm. 23.4.15 "	The Supply Vehicles of Col Geddes Force viz YDL – 1/5 KORL 3/Mx. Buffs. East Yorks. were rendezvoused at level crossing NW of YPRES and awaited supplies. Supply is not altogether simple – YPRES is still being heavily shelled and so are the roads north of it. Later it transpired that everybody received rations except 1/5 KO R Lancs ~~and~~ Fighting continued and heavy shelling continues on the town of YPRES and on the Battle line. Weather v fine.	
12.1 am 24.4.15 Vlamertinghe	Canadian Div wires presuming we are making arrangements to feed Y & Durham Bde – no action is taken on this wire. Instructions issued to Y & D. Bde to send train transport ~~to~~ back to fields 1½ m West of Vlamertinghe.	
1.9 am " " "	5th Corps wires we are not to feed Durham L.I. Bde Notification that train with 125 horses left Base for our new Railhead, Caestre. Number of rounds expended by 146 Bde RFA 12 noon 23/4 720 – 18pr –	

(73989) W4141—463. 400,000. 9/14. H.&J.Ltd. Forms/C. 2118/10.

Instructions regarding War Diaries and Intelligence Summaries are contained in F. S. Regs., Part II. and the Staff Manual respectively. Title pages will be prepared in manuscript.

WAR DIARY
or
INTELLIGENCE SUMMARY.

(Erase heading not required.)

Army Form C. 2118.

Hour, Date, Place			Summary of Events and Information	Remarks and references to Appendices
7 am	24.4.15	Vlamertinghe	5th Corps asked to continue to supply 4th D Brigade with SAA — action already taken, an orderly 146th Bde Amm Col attached & all concerned informed – Lorry with 200000 rounds SAA ordered to point west of Vlamertinghe from Amn Park	
8.30 am	24.4.15	"	5th Corps telephoned that steps should be taken to remove the AOD ASC & RE Stores from YPRES and that lorries would be available but as shelling of YPRES continues it was pointed out that this would be almost impossible to carry out	
11 am	24.4.15	"	Canadians on our left asking for ammn – wire to Canadian Div asking them to arrange own line of supply	
"	"	"	Commence to withdraw RE Park from YPRES to old Head RE Park just west of Poperinghe Vlamertinghe	
1.00 pm	"	"	As stragglers are numerous from Canadians 28th & 27th Div steps taken to block roads leading west from YPRES with police & 5th Div asked to direct 28th & 27th men to Vlamertinghe	
3.15 pm	"	"	Same arrangements made as last night regarding [illegible] rendezvous of supply wagons for units detached for operation with Canadians.	
6.30 pm	"	"	An advanced Dressing Station for the 4 Bns under Col. Geddes is being formed by 28 Div at S. Jean. Canadian Div asked to send guides from Bns to lead stretcher bearers from S. Jean Church to Regimental Aid Posts	

Instructions regarding War Diaries and Intelligence Summaries are contained in F. S. Regs., Part II. and the Staff Manual respectively. Title pages will be prepared in manuscript.

WAR DIARY
or
INTELLIGENCE SUMMARY.

(Erase heading not required.)

Army Form C. 2118.

Hour, Date, Place	Summary of Events and Information	Remarks and references to Appendices
9–12 24·4·15 Vlamertinghe	During last night 13th Infantry Bde moved up from 27th 5th Div area & attached on French Right consequently this increased traffic – The Road through YPRES is very noisy (as indeed is the road North of it) as the 11th Bde were marching through up to S. Jean at day night [illegible] road to be kept clear [illegible] [illegible] from through via North of YPRES to S. Jean only one block – 11th Bde bivouacking about 1½ m – W of YPRES and moving N about 12 mn	
	Casualties have been reported as follows	
	To [illegible] 23rd — 14th Bde 5 W.	
	13th Hy Bde Lt Field K · Lt Sanderman missing & W; OR. 4 W – 21 missing	
	2 [illegible] Officers 4 W; OR 1 K – 12 W	
	To [illegible] 24 — 83 Bde 4 K – 38 W Lt Jenners W.	
	Rawe Lt Wardle · W; Lt Barnsley · W; OR – 1 W	
	3rd Royal Fusiliers — ~~5 Ro Officers K.~~ Capt Carter K – Capt Carter, [illegible], [illegible] – wounded and Lt Evans Capt [illegible] [illegible] [illegible], Lt Kirk. OR about 170 K & W	
	Buffs — Officer Reported Capt Renald K; OR K – 12; wounded Lt Wilkins + ~~58~~ 5 others missing	

(73989) W4141—463. 400,000. 9/14. H.&J.Ltd. Forms/C. 2118/10.

Instructions regarding War Diaries and Intelligence Summaries are contained in F. S. Regs., Part II. and the Staff Manual respectively. Title pages will be prepared in manuscript.

WAR DIARY
or
INTELLIGENCE SUMMARY.

(Erase heading not required.)

Army Form C. 2118.

Hour, Date, Place	Summary of Events and Information	Remarks and references to Appendices
24.4.15 Vlamertinghe	line from 85 Bde [illegible] Middlesex [illegible] Col Hearily [illegible] Col Stephenson killed 84 Bde Capt Baxter, Lt Sweet, Keating, Lord [illegible] wounded OR 8K – 31W. RE 4W ASC – OR 1W.	
24.4.15 "	Very heavy Vlamertinghe shelled and our prospects [illegible] in new HQ at the Town Hall.	
24.4.15 "	Heavy fighting all day north of YPRES Weather fine	[illegible]
25.4.15 Vlamertinghe	Casualty lists are coming in – 85 Bde report [illegible], Capt Hon Hewitt, Jollie; Lts Featherstone killed. Lt Col Ashton & 4 offrs wounded about 60 men killed & wounded 83 Bde OR 3K. 23W. Lt Toms killed Lt [illegible] wounded 84 Bde. OR 16K. 49W. Capt Hext ~~wounded~~ ~~slightly~~ Lt Sweet, Capt Gelling [illegible] wounded, 1 man R Lt Phillips Lt Edwards. 12 Lond: Lt Col Bayliffe Capt Fricker Lt Hoare W. 2/5 Yorks Capt Woodman – [illegible] Lt Hebbert killed. Wounded Lt Col Sweeney Major Berthon Lt Hawkins, 2A Turton SE Callard, De Rigy, Cracroft, Armitage Layton, Carew, Haswell. OR about 400 K, W & M Welsh R report 1 offr K – 7 wounded OR 17K. 83W. 1M.	

(73989) W4141—463. 400,000. 9/14. H.&J.Ltd. Forms/C. 2118/10.

Instructions regarding War Diaries and Intelligence Summaries are contained in F. S. Regs., Part II. and the Staff Manual respectively. Title pages will be prepared in manuscript.

WAR DIARY
or
INTELLIGENCE SUMMARY.
(Erase heading not required.)

Army Form C. 2118.

Hour, Date, Place	Summary of Events and Information	Remarks and references to Appendices
8.5 am 25.4.15 Vlamertinghe	Information received that Rations & Supplies & 1/2 London could not get up actually to troops further than their Local Reserves owing to shell fire – Otherwise all troops were fed. It was later transpired that these were fed also during a lull. But they consumed iron rations	
– 25.4.15 "	Were receiving that 112 horses for 28 Div would reach the railhead at 6.30 am – not very convenient CAESTRE is many miles off – So are Units and the [illegible] HQ Staff – The ADOS had to go and issue in a borrowed motor – altogether a laborious operation.	
10.30 am 25.4.15 "	Total Drafts of 6 off. 251 OR. arrived Caestre [illegible] by Rail bus to Vlamertinghe – Then sent to transport lines to go up with [illegible]	
	Removal of Stores from RE Park YPRES to new site 400 yds W of E of Vlamertinghe continued –	
	Reconnaissance in midst of heavy 12" & 17" shells reported AOS Store shelled – A certain no 650 iron rations were rescued from the Cloisters but remainder were left for present	
3.25 pm 25.4.15 "	108 Hy Battery being sent up and will be today and is to be fed by 28 Div	
– 25.4.15 "	Following movements taking place – 10 Bde passed through yesterday – 11th Bde arrived in Vlamertinghe & huts near huts 6.30 am. Indian Division (Lahore) arrived 11.30 am and halted about Ouderdom.	

(73989) W4141—463. 400,000. 9/14. H.&J.Ltd. Forms/C. 2118/10.

Instructions regarding War Diaries and Intelligence Summaries are contained in F. S. Regs., Part II. and the Staff Manual respectively. Title pages will be prepared in manuscript.

WAR DIARY
or
INTELLIGENCE SUMMARY.
(Erase heading not required.)

Army Form C. 2118.

Hour, Date, Place	Summary of Events and Information	Remarks and references to Appendices
7.4 pm 25.4.15 Vlamertinghe	85th Inf Bde who have had severe fighting have to hand on left wire for 10 000 Sandbags to be sent to point D26 (a) tonight – and bombs. This caused a good deal of difficulty as regards Sandbags a fatigue party of details billeted in Vlamertinghe was ~~sent~~ called out to load Sandbags at the RE dump W of Vlamertinghe – ~~these being sent to~~ a lorry load of Bombs was obtained from V Corps and sent to W End of Ypres where they were ~~taken to~~ transferred to a GS limber & wagons – and the whole convoy under an officer was pushed through to Zonnebeke which it reached about 4 am – a heavy mist in morning favoured movement home –	
	Orders issued to return Empty Jam tins to RE to fill with ammonal as as we are very short of bombs.	
9 pm 25.4.15 "	Same procedure followed regarding ~~to~~ getting supplies to Col Geddes' 5 Bns as hitherto.	
9.15 pm " "	Rounds expended ~~in~~ + 48 hours to 12 noon 2574 18 pr 2132. 18 pr HE 17. 4.5" 522 HE. 233 Shrap 4.7" 38 – HE 4.7 232. Number of guns ~~A40~~ 18 pr 48 4.5 – 12. 4.7 4 ~~Ot~~ This does not include 122 Batty	
10 pm " "	9.2 det attached for administration.	

(73989) W4141—463. 400,000. 9/14. H.&J.Ltd. Forms/C. 2118/10.

Instructions regarding War Diaries and Intelligence Summaries are contained in F. S. Regs., Part II. and the Staff Manual respectively. Title pages will be prepared in manuscript.

WAR DIARY
or
INTELLIGENCE SUMMARY.
(Erase heading not required.)

Army Form C. 2118.

Hour, Date, Place	Summary of Events and Information	Remarks and references to Appendices
10.30pm 25.4.15 Vlamertinghe	5 [illegible] officers from Porte de Lille Bombs of Sorts 228 – Ammunal 500 – But as shelling of YPRES is so severe it was not considered advisable to send vehicles for them.	
11.15pm 25.4.15 Vlamertinghe	~~Number of Rounds Expended day 48 hours~~ As reports of casualties very vague – 1st YOL, 3/Mx, E. Yorks have apparently lost heavily – A.G. GHQ & 5th Corps ~~refs~~ informed accordingly.	
25.4.15 Vlamertinghe	Weather Fine — Dry Every 11th Brigade moved up N E of YPRES – It will be realised that much road control is necessary – So far this has been done by Staff officers, RMCs and APM.	Adams
2.45am 26.4.15 Vlamertinghe	Received information that lorry with bombs and sandbags had ~~got through~~ started for Zonnebeke – One load got through later.	
2.10am 26.4.15 "	estimated casualties to GHQ Sect as 1 Suffolks 4 offrs. 150 OR.	
6.30am 26.4.15 "	Indian (Lahore) Div marching N through Vlamertinghe – road control carried out successfully but Vlamertinghe now v. full of men & vehicles especially ambulance waggons.	
6.45am " "	3/Kings own reports casualties 8 officers 210 OR.	

(73989) W4141—463. 400,000. 9/14. H.&J.Ltd. Forms/C. 2118/10.

WAR DIARY
or
INTELLIGENCE SUMMARY.
(Erase heading not required.)

Army Form C. 2118.

Instructions regarding War Diaries and Intelligence Summaries are contained in F. S. Regs., Part II. and the Staff Manual respectively. Title pages will be prepared in manuscript.

Hour, Date, Place	Summary of Events and Information	Remarks and references to Appendices
10 am 26.4.15 Vlamertinghe	5th Corps telephones 11th Bde – D.L. Inf Bde – Northumbrian Bde – [illegible] Bde are all attached Divs – These telephone conversations on important points are unsatisfactory partly because they are unreliable & partly because the information does not filter in the same way it does as if it was a wire on a file.	
" " "	Visit of A Staff Officer 2nd Army to get casualty lists – These have been almost impossible to get in – a C.O. what with stragglers & cas wounded and killed does not know for some time how he stands –	
11.45 am 26.4.15 "	Wire to 84th Bde directing them to send responsible person such as Qr Mr back with 1st line – unless they do come, it is very difficult to ensure Rations reaching units.	
11–12 26.4.15 "	Visit of Sq ?, SSO, and certain Supply officers Northumbrian Division – This Division is coming up in bits ~~they have~~ consequently their arrangements for Food & Amm. Supply are difficult and as they have only been 4 days in the Country bad also – As regards food they are all right up to point of change between Train & 1st line after which there is not sufficient touch. As regards S.A.A. Section of Bde Amm Cols – little or no steps taken to bring them up to into touch with Bdes – They are now at about Steenvoorde and elsewhere. Written instructions issued to move them up. And whole system thoroughly explained.	
12.15 26.4.15 "	Instructions issued to Northumbrian Bde to what when suffering	

(73989) W4141—463. 400,000. 9/14. H.&J.Ltd. Forms/C. 2118/10.

Instructions regarding War Diaries and Intelligence Summaries are contained in F. S. Regs., Part II. and the Staff Manual respectively. Title pages will be prepared in manuscript.

WAR DIARY
or
INTELLIGENCE SUMMARY.
(Erase heading not required.)

Army Form C. 2118.

Hour, Date, Place	Summary of Events and Information	Remarks and references to Appendices
	Heavy casualties, estimates should be be wired to AG GHQ – 2nd Army, 5th Corps & 28 Div.	
1.20 pm 25.4.15 Vlamertinghe	Very heavy gun fire due to French attack –	
2.30 pm " "	Information received that Park is full of all sorts of Ammunition this is reassuring as there was a rumour that Park was running out. Div Am Col reports it can supply Brigades at three times the rate it has been asked to	
2.30 pm " " "	The first of the Northd Div [illegible] Sections arrived to supply [illegible] Bde [illegible] collected [illegible] 146 Bde 1 m. E. of Vlamertinghe.	
" " "	Owing to heavy shelling night and day the road through YPRES is almost impassable hence traffic goes round North there are now some 3 Divisions on this road. Wire sent to Canadian Division suggesting road circuits by which supply vehicles returning pass through and South of their area on back to Vlamertinghe thus avoiding a very narrow strip of road [illegible]. Eastward route is by road leading N (1 m W of YPRES – road W & E Square A & B – thence S. Jean. Return by Brielen Rd & turning west 3/4 m – SE of Brielen.	
3 pm " " "	Owing to numbers of horses killed & injured by shell – the supply [illegible] passing via N of YPRES and debilitated animals. DDR 2nd Army wired to for 80 Ra LD – 25 RS. 6 Pack.	
3.30 pm " " "	ADMS notifies Dressing Stations with cars at Potyze & S. Jean. Cases cleared from there to Vlamertinghe & Poperinghe	

(73989) W4141—463. 400,000. 9/14. H.&J.Ltd. Forms/C. 2118/10.

Instructions regarding War Diaries and Intelligence Summaries are contained in F. S. Regs., Part II. and the Staff Manual respectively. Title pages will be prepared in manuscript.

WAR DIARY
or
INTELLIGENCE SUMMARY.
(Erase heading not required.)

Army Form C. 2118.

Hour, Date, Place	Summary of Events and Information	Remarks and references to Appendices
4pm 26.4.15 Vlamertinghe	Supply arrangements for Cal feeders made as before –	
4pm 26.4.15 "	Following Reinforcements arrived 8 Yorks 1 off & 50 · KOYLI ·40 · R.I.O. ·80 | 9 H? 209 · 5/Kev 8 · 3/Mon 11	
4pm 26.4.15 "	No 22 French How Batty having finished ammunition orders back tonight in empty Supply Vehicles – to Vlamertinghe.	
" " "	Very Heavy shell fire.	
" 26.4.15 "	In addition to foregoing following drafts also arrived for 84 Inf Bde 1 off – 123 OR. — 85 Inf Bde – 1 O. 57 OR	
	Drafts as they arrive are being sent to train transport to await Bde instructions.	
11.30pm 26.4.15 "	~~2a~~ 11th Bde report 2 Bns 4th D Bde have had no rations for 3 days and are going into trenches tonight – [illegible] interviews ~~away so~~ S.S. Train & Supply Officers who considered this report incorrect – 4 D. Officers could not be found as they were out with rations – 11th Bde asked for 1500 rations to be sent which was of course impossible – also for tools – Northern Division used to ~~and~~ but not ~~[illegible]~~ very much could be done –	

(73989) W4141—463. 400,000. 9/14. H.&J.Ltd. Forms/C. 2118/10.

Army Form C. 2118.

Instructions regarding War Diaries and Intelligence Summaries are contained in F. S. Regs., Part II. and the Staff Manual respectively. Title pages will be prepared in manuscript.

WAR DIARY
or
INTELLIGENCE SUMMARY.
(Erase heading not required.)

	Hour, Date, Place		Summary of Events and Information	Remarks and references to Appendices
—	26·4·15	Vlamertinghe	Casualties reported as 2 Officers killed. 5. W. 2 M. 21 OR " 81 W. 8 M. Includes Lt. Pycott ASC Lt. Verschoyle RE Capt Perry Monmouths Lt Llewellyn Lt Lorie Lt Anderson 2/Lt Jones.	
—	26·4·15	"	Weather Fine.	A.A.
2.30am	27·4·15	"	Regarding report of 11·30 pm last night that 2 Bns 9 & D were short of rations investigation shows that report is false Quarter Master of Bns having handed over supplies regularly to Bns.	
7·20am	27·4·15	"	5th Corps ask for report as to how supplies of food and Ammn now stand. – Reply to 5th Corps Situation normal as regards ~~our own but~~ both Ammn & Supplies.	
"	27·4·15	"	Q.M. & 9 & L Reports arrival of draft of 209 men these are now – as a system directed on the ~~R~~ Transport lines East W. of Pop Vlamertinghe and Bdes notified further orders as to moving up of drafts are issued by them.	
"	27·4·15	"	During the night The various Sections S.A.A. of the Bde Ammn Cols of Northumbrian Div: arrived and were located with 1461 Bde Amm Col and at Brickfields	

(73989) W4141—463. 400,000. 9/14. H.&J.Ltd. Forms/C. 2118/10.

Army Form C. 2118.

Instructions regarding War Diaries and Intelligence Summaries are contained in F. S. Regs., Part II. and the Staff Manual respectively. Title pages will be prepared in manuscript.

WAR DIARY
or
INTELLIGENCE SUMMARY.

(Erase heading not required.)

Hour, Date, Place	Summary of Events and Information	Remarks and references to Appendices
27.4.15 Vlamertinghe	Casualties for 25 & 26 April 11th Bde about 257. Includes Brig Genl Hasler killed and 6 other officers.	
27.4.15 "	From 6.30–7.30 Vlamertinghe was shelled – and evacuated later by most of the inhabitants. Train was moved further East — The Battle raged all day	
28.4.15 "	During the night Genl Hasler Comd 11th Bde was killed. Question arose about successor. Lt Col Hicks 1 Hants was temporary Lt Col for 2½ months before Lt Compton 1 SLI was promoted – shortly after Lt Col Hicks was promoted – without ceasing to hold his temporary rank – the two settled between themselves before decision of GOC that Col Hicks was the senior. The GOC allowed him to command in any case.	
25.4.15 "	Sentences on Le Maitre and Hanson suspended by GOC 2nd Army this being the first case of use of Suspension of Sentences Act	

(73989) W4141—463. 400,000. 9/14. H.&J.Ltd. Forms/C. 2118/10.

Instructions regarding War Diaries and Intelligence Summaries are contained in F. S. Regs., Part II. and the Staff Manual respectively. Title pages will be prepared in manuscript.

WAR DIARY
or
INTELLIGENCE SUMMARY.
(Erase heading not required.)

Army Form C. 2118.

Hour, Date, Place	Summary of Events and Information	Remarks and references to Appendices
	Early Cater lorries were sent to HQ of ~~different~~ Y+D – DLI & Northumbrian Bdes & Representatives of ~~Bdes~~ SAA Sections directed to go out and get in touch.	
27.4.15 Vlamertinghe	Number of Rounds expended to 12 noon 26.4.15 ~~reported~~ 18pr 2688 for 48 guns: 380 – 4.5" HE & 171 Shrap for 12 4.5" Hows: 109 Shrap & 147 HE for 4 – 4.7".	
10.45 am 27.4.15 Vlamertinghe	By 10.45 am one of the SAA Sections Northumbrian Bde was in touch with its Bde	
9.10 am 27.4.15 Vlamertinghe	In response to demand of Corps made 48 hours ago ~~info~~ information received that 3 RA wagons and 1 18pr gun complete with art. would arrive Reninghelst ~~[illegible]~~ tonight – They were directed on Vlamertinghe	
12.40 pm 27.4.15 "	22 French Hawitzer party withdrawn from trenches should have stopped in Vlamertinghe but also went on to Bertren which they should not have done	
11.3 am 27.4.15 "	As we have received ~~some~~ cotton wool respirators soaked in Carbonate of Soda for use in trenches against the asphyxiating gases used by ~~the~~ Germans GHQ are sending flannel instead –	

(73989) W4141—463. 400,000. 9/14. H.&J.Ltd. Forms/C. 2118/10.

Army Form C. 2118.

Instructions regarding War Diaries and Intelligence Summaries are contained in F. S. Regs., Part II. and the Staff Manual respectively. Title pages will be prepared in manuscript.

WAR DIARY
or
INTELLIGENCE SUMMARY.

(Erase heading not required.)

Hour, Date, Place	Summary of Events and Information	Remarks and references to Appendices
	Present Strength returns which are estimated show 83rd Bde. 4180 (6 Bns); 84: 4108; 85, 3050.	
11.45 am 27.4.15 Vlamertinghe	5th Corps notifies arrival of drafts of 276 and 246 for 10th & 11th Bde respectively ~~for~~	
	Poperinghe heavily shelled - found necessary to move B' Echelon HQ to a Chateau $\frac{3}{4}$ m SW of Proven Yeomanry moved near by	
1.45 pm 27.4.15	Wire to 5th Corps notifying good deal of destruction in YPRES especially Menin Gate due to dead horses & men asking if it can be cleared as we can find no labour unless we use Belgian Travailleurs whom we feed	
	Sick Wastage Return for week ending 25th - 129.	
	Normal arrangements made for supply and Vehicles and Stretchers bearers being directed to units	
5.30 - 6.30 pm 27.4.15	Casualties reported to Northumbrian Division H.Q. Bde killed 12. W 66 Missing 15. Wtn 10: 4th Fd 10 8 W 74 M 12. 5th DLI K. 13	
11.45 pm 27.4.15	It transpires there are no bombs in Rd Park urgent representation made to 5th Corps	

(73989) W4141—463. 400,000. 9/14. H.&J.Ltd. Forms/C. 2118/10.

Army Form C. 2118.

WAR DIARY
or
INTELLIGENCE SUMMARY.
(Erase heading not required.)

Instructions regarding War Diaries and Intelligence Summaries are contained in F. S. Regs., Part II. and the Staff Manual respectively. Title pages will be prepared in manuscript.

Hour, Date, Place	Summary of Events and Information	Remarks and references to Appendices
10am 28·4·15 Vlamertinghe	Transport reported returned safe after delivering all rations Number of Rounds expended to 12 noon 27th 18 pr 48 guns {3124 Shrap. / 56 HE; 4.5" 12 guns ~~HE 56~~ HE 342 / Shrap 75; 4.7 Shrap 29 / HE 625 } 32 guns	
12 noon 28·4·15 "	31st [illegible] Bde report loss of 4 vehicles destroyed in fire by shell – 3 Rly wagons 21-18 pr gun ~~[illegible]~~ arrived & were distributed – This within 48 hours of asking.	
10am 28·4·15 "	5th Corps reports in response to appeal for grenades that every available Bomb & hand grenade is being sent. Later on they wired that 2000 Rifle grenades were arriving, only 200 came 100 of which were sent out to the French line at once. –	
3·15pm 28·4·15 "	Steps taken to clear the Poperinghe YPRES road of dead horses by our Yeomanry. Commissary of Police Belgian YPRES asked to clear Grande Place of dead men & horses – and 27th Div beyond that – 5th Corps also communicated with.	
12·20pm 28·4·15 "	Flannel ~~strips~~ pads specially prepared also mask respirators for use against the poisonous gases are being sent up for use by troops in trenches	

Instructions regarding War Diaries and Intelligence Summaries are contained in F. S. Regs., Part II. and the Staff Manual respectively. Title pages will be prepared in manuscript.

WAR DIARY
or
INTELLIGENCE SUMMARY.

(Erase heading not required.)

Army Form C. 2118.

	Hour, Date, Place		Summary of Events and Information	Remarks and references to Appendices
4.0 pm	28.4.15	Vlamertinghe	Following Casualties Reported to 5 Corps Lt Col Burt G.S.O., same regiment 10 other wounded 1 killed. 2 missing. O.R. K 50, W 264 missing uncertain	
			Number of Rounds Expended to 12 noon 27.	
			18 pr 3124, 45 guns; H.E. 56 — 4.5 H.E. 342, Shr. 75 – 12 guns	
			4.7 Shr. 29 – H.E. 625 guns 12.	
4.30 pm	28.4.15	"	It has been found that direct to route through YPRES is the safer nowadays as that town is not so much shelled as the S. Jean route.	
4	28.4.15	"	60000 Sandbags, 200 rolls of barbed wire & [illegible] in R.E. Park to-day. 200 Rifle Grenades were received and 100 sent up to trenches at once this is the biggest issue we have had of Rifle Grenades.	
5.0 pm	28.4.15	"	~~Total~~ 2 officers & 175 OR arrived as reinforcements	
			Following were settled ~~arrived~~ in New huts at night fall 2 Bns 83rd, 1 Bn 85th Bde – 1 Bde Canadians – A & 2 Bns GHQ –	
			Col Geddes 2 Buffs ~~and~~ Commdy Column killed and Captain Crichton his S.O (Acting Bde Maj 84th Bde not joined) ~~Both~~ wounded	
–	28.4.15	"	Ammunition Railhead now at Abeele. But we found it out and were not notified —	
–	28.4.15	"	Casualties to noon 25 K. 64 W. 22 missing not including attached Bdes — 1 officer killed 1 wounded.	

WAR DIARY
or
INTELLIGENCE SUMMARY.
(Erase heading not required.)

Army Form C. 2118.

Instructions regarding War Diaries and Intelligence Summaries are contained in F. S. Regs., Part II. and the Staff Manual respectively. Title pages will be prepared in manuscript.

Hour, Date, Place	Summary of Events and Information	Remarks and references to Appendices
28.4.15 Vlamertinghe	Weather v. fine. Fighting continued all day — Vlamertinghe shelled in evening —	[illegible]
5am 29.4.15 "	Vlamertinghe shelled at 5 am.	
9.45 29.4.15 "	Bdes reminded about arranging to send surplus serviceable arms & equipment back to base. Fatigue parties obtained from [illegible] and endeavours made to clear AOD store — which however proved to be futile — fatigue party sent round to collect empty petrol tins and empty shell boxes and to hand them in to the Park	
	Lt Col Prowse appointed to command 13[illegible] Bde. Capt [illegible] Dillon DSO apptd Bde Major 84th Inf Bde —	
	85 Bde asks urgently for 10000 sandbags to be sent up tonight, 5000 sent up	
— 29.4.15 "	Rounds expended 18pr 940 · 48 guns. 4.5 HE 310 12 guns Shrap 93. 4.7 Shrap 37 HE 45 for 12 guns.	
	[illegible] Arrangements made to reopen washing establishment again tomorrow it has lain dormant for some time now	
2.30pm 29.4.15 "	Conference of [illegible] at Plumer's Force Q as to troops engaged in active operations being now known by that name — Conference was to arrange	

Army Form C. 2118.

WAR DIARY
or
INTELLIGENCE SUMMARY.

(Erase heading not required.)

Instructions regarding War Diaries and Intelligence Summaries are contained in F. S. Regs., Part II. and the Staff Manual respectively. Title pages will be prepared in manuscript.

Hour, Date, Place	Summary of Events and Information	Remarks and references to Appendices
	Billetting areas for troops no[t] required for front line further back W of Poperinghe – Mobile Vety Section moved here [illegible] – Statement of administrative billets attached	appendix 3
29.4.15 Vlamertinghe	121 LD horses 6 Pack 6 HD arrived at Caestre and were distributed by A.D.V.S. Collecting parties were sent from here by buses at 3 am.	
	Rounds expended to 12 noon 29th 18 [pr] 1720 – HE 86, 48 for 4.5" HE 361, Shrap 82 for 12 guns. 4.7" ~~443~~ 243 for 12 guns.	
29.4.15 "	~~Fighting~~ More of a lull in fighting than usual – Vlamertinghe shelled 8–9 during which time S. Lancs arrived for 11th Bde – and again at midnight [illegible] being to catch transport going to [illegible] –	
	Weather v. fine	[illegible]
30.4.15 "	Rations were delivered to units with 1 casualty	
11.5am " " "	Div Amn Col moves to new billets just East of [illegible] and South of road	

(73989) W4141—463. 400,000. 9/14. H.&J.Ltd. Forms/C. 2118/10.

Instructions regarding War Diaries and Intelligence Summaries are contained in F. S. Regs., Part II. and the Staff Manual respectively. Title pages will be prepared in manuscript.

WAR DIARY
or
INTELLIGENCE SUMMARY.
(Erase heading not required.)

Army Form C. 2118.

Hour, Date, Place	Summary of Events and Information	Remarks and references to Appendices
	~~4th Div~~ 10 & 11th Bdes 4th Div will in future be ~~supplied~~ refilled on the Ouderdom Vlamertinghe Road and not at the Brickfields 1 m W of Vlamertinghe	
5pm 30.4.15 Vlamertinghe	Quantities of anti asphyxiating pads being sent up and distributed with rations	
	Rounds Expended to 12 Noon 30th.	
	18pr 1436 – 4.5" 2621; ; 4.7" 319.	
	Casualties to 12 Noon 9 officers W. OR 29 K. 143 W. 8 M.	
	The Battle went on intermittently during the day Shelling was heard about Potije and there were some casualties to transport going forward and back especially coming through Vlamertinghe between 11pm & 1 am – one shell striking this HQ.	
30.4.15 "	Weather V. fine & warm.	ACMcH.

(73989) W4141—463. 400,000. 9/14. H.&J.Ltd. Forms/C. 2118/10.

Appendix I
Administrative Staff
Diary
1st April 1915

Number of Officers and Other Ranks Sick and Wounded admitted to Field Ambulances, Killed, Missing and Returned to Duty during the month of March 1915.

Personnel.	Admitted to Field Ambulances. Sick.	Admitted to Field Ambulances. Feet Cases.	Admitted to Field Ambulances. Wounded.	Killed in action.	Missing.	To Duty. Sick.	To Duty. Wounded.
Officers.	59.	Nil.	40.	16.	Nil.	10.	1.
Other Ranks.	2078.	266.	1395.	325.	27.	974.	138.
						(Feet Cases to Duty) (116)	

Ref Sheet 28 $\frac{1}{40,000}$

Appendix 3
War Diary administrative Staff 28 Div.
28 April 1914

28th DIVISION.

83rd Bde Hd Qrs. D 25 d 3.8
84th Bde Hd Qrs. D 26 C 3.4
85th Bde Hd Qrs. Verlorenhoek
11th Bde Hd Qrs. C 30 C 1.4 (Staff Capt in Vlamertinghe)
4th D Bde Hd Qrs. C Fruits new Camp.
DLI Bde Hd Qrs. C 30 C 2.4

83rd Bde 1st Line Tpt. B Echelon G 4 C 3.9 & G 10 a 8.10 (KOYLI 1E Yorks)
84th Bde 1st Line Tpt. " " G 5 d
85th Bde 1st Line Tpt. G 4 c.
11th Bde 1st line Tpt. " " ~~G 18 a~~ H 15 a. H 1 b
4th D Bde 1st Line Tpt. H 7 b
DLI Bde 1st Line Tpt. " H 7 b ; H 2 d 7.4
Hd Qr Co. Train. G 6 a 3.3
No. 2 Co. Train. G 4 c
No. 3 Co. Train. G 5 d
No. 4 Co. Train. G 4 c 11th Bde Train G 18 A

3rd Bde. Ammn: Column. H 10. A 66
31st Bde Ammn. Column. H 15 b 4.0
146th Bde Ammn Column. H 16 a 3.10
8th Hows. Ammn Column. H 12 a 4.5
13th Heavy Bde Amm Col. G 11 d 12
Divnl Ammn Column. H.Qrs. Junc of Busseboom-abeele } Roads
Poperinghe " }
Advanced Section. G 2 d
Remainder " Vicinity their Hd Qrs
84th Field Ambulance. Poperinghe
85th Field Ambulance. G 4 a C
86th Field Ambulance. G 4 b
Advanced Dressing Station. Potije
" " "
" " "

38th Coy R.E. I 2 d
Transport " " G 9 d

Continued.

2nd Northumbrian Fd Co R.E. I 3 c

Transport " " " G 9 d

Anglesey R.E. " " " I 3 b

Transport " " " " Lorries Poperinghe

other R.E. attached.

171 Tunnellers" H 9 b

Wilts & Fortress RE ?

Cornwall Fortress RE.

R.E. Park —— H 9 b

Surrey Yeomanry. H 1 a

" " "

Cyclists. Vlamertinghe Chateau

" " "

Attached Troops.

3 Motor Machine Gun Coy ?

9.2 Set " A 24

108 Hy ~~Batty~~ Gun Col. B 20 d 7 9

2/ London Heavy on Watou Road W of Poperinghe

" " "

North Midland

" " "

" "

Supply Railhead. Caestre

Ammunition Railhead. Abeele.

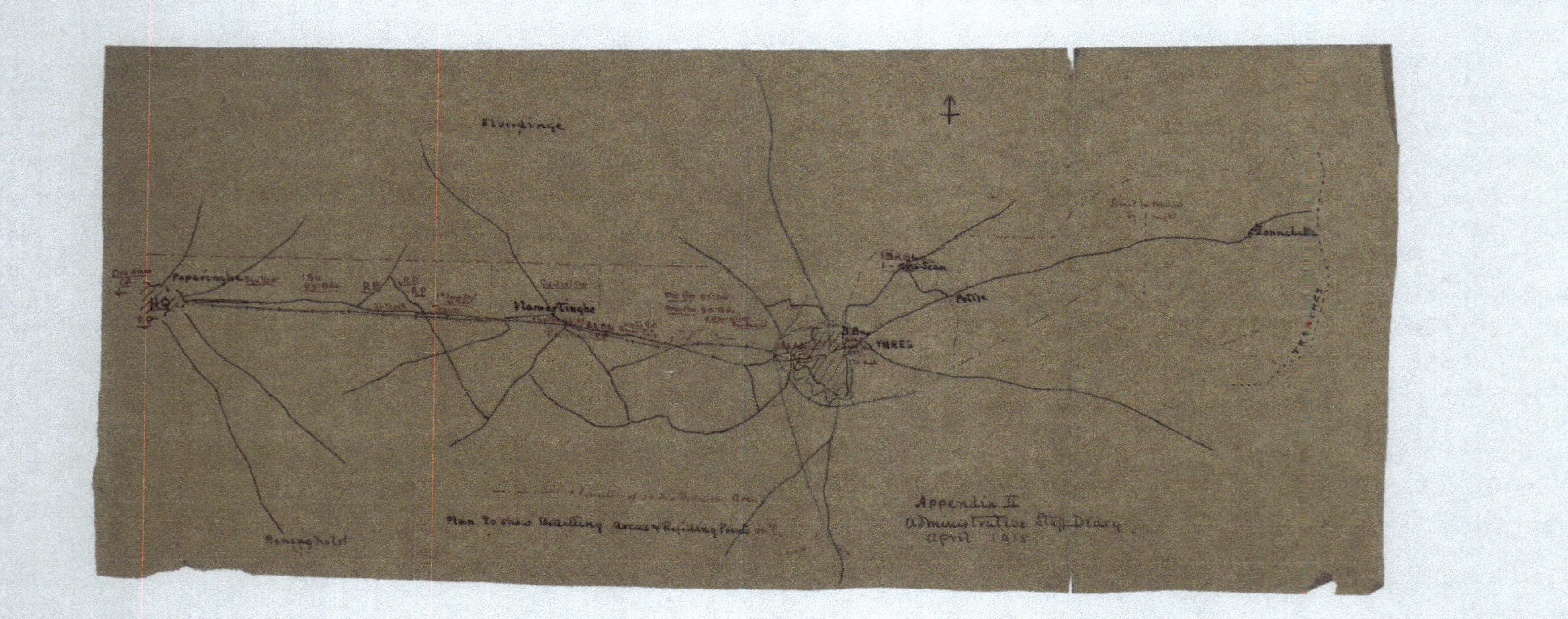
Appendix II
Administrative Staff Diary
April 1915
Plan to show Billeting Areas & Refilling Points
Poperinghe
HQ
R.P.
Vlamertinghe
YPRES
Potijze
Zonnebeke
Elverdinge

28th Division

Confidential

Administrative War Diary

Head Quarter Staff 28th Division

B. E. F.

121/5555

From 1st May 1915

To 31st May 1915

Volume VI

Instructions regarding War Diaries and Intelligence Summaries are contained in F. S. Regs., Part II. and the Staff Manual respectively. Title pages will be prepared in manuscript.

WAR DIARY
or
INTELLIGENCE SUMMARY.
(*Erase heading not required.*)

Army Form C. 2118.

	Hour, Date, Place		Summary of Events and Information	Remarks and references to Appendices
9 am	1.5.14	Vlamertinghe	As the Chateau in which this HQ was situated was hit last night GOC decided that Administrative HQ should move further back.	
9.40 am	1.5.14	"	Brigadier [illegible] reports 1st line Transport near Poperinghe(?) being heavily shelled & asks for it to be allowed to move back — Investigation shows it refers to vehicles required for fighting — Later they were informed they must remain.	
—	1.5.14	"	OC Train reports units fed during night with following Casualties to Transport from Shrapnel fire. 1 man [illegible] 4 horses wounded — 2 killed — 2 limbers smashed.	
—	1.5.14	"	Rations issued 30.4.15 — British 21,993, Belgian 100 Horses [illegible] 1417 · LD 4506 Mules 295 Cobs 86	
11 am	1.5.14	"	Arrangements made to replace Casualties in Transport as far as we can by absorbing GS limbered wagons rendered surplus [illegible] Cookers. as Transport is [illegible] to HQ Div Train — OC Div Train directed to see to this.	
11.15 am	1.5.14	"	Reinforcements arrive for 83, 84, 85 Bdes.	
11.30 am	"	"	Indent for Horses submitted and added to several times Total indent 130 — added small surplus to replace Transport Casualties and 80 LD reported required by RA.	

Instructions regarding War Diaries and Intelligence Summaries are contained in F. S. Regs., Part II. and the Staff Manual respectively. Title pages will be prepared in manuscript.

WAR DIARY
or
INTELLIGENCE SUMMARY.
(Erase heading not required.)

Army Form C. 2118.

Hour, Date, Place		Summary of Events and Information	Remarks and references to Appendices
1.5.15	Vlamertinghe	Canadian Div: requests Administrative HQ to clear out of Chateau Couthove near Provens	
4.45pm 1.5.15	Vlamertinghe	5th Corps Q reports many dead horses in and about YPRES we are to demand [illegible] of lime & burn them – [illegible] 85th Bde reply to message asking them to do same S. of YPRES – to effect that they have disembowelled all – fires not caused well lit & ask for Paraffin	
1.5.15	"	Rounds expended to 12 noon 1.5.15 – 18pr 1126 – 4.5" 162 ~~190~~ 4.7" ~~300~~ 190 – 60pr 219 – 9.2" 77.	
9-0pm 1.5.15	"	Owing to sudden movements various road controls were instituted – one in Vlamertinghe – 1 at Menin Gate – 1 at Potije all went well	
11.55pm 1.5.15	"	Administrative HQ moves to Chateau Couthove near Proven where Echelon B of the Administrative HQ has been stationed already some days.	
11.5 1.5.15	"	Weather fine & warm	A. Allen
2.5.15	"	Though the HQ unit of 28 Div is at Chateau Couthove the administrative staff are working at the Report Centre at Chateau Vlamertinghe.	
2.45am "	"	In continuation of reallotment of billeting areas – Train commenced to move west of Poperinghe last night – 1st line of	

Instructions regarding War Diaries and Intelligence Summaries are contained in F. S. Regs., Part II. and the Staff Manual respectively. Title pages will be prepared in manuscript.

WAR DIARY
or
INTELLIGENCE SUMMARY.
(Erase heading not required.)

Army Form C. 2118.

Hour, Date, Place			Summary of Events and Information	Remarks and references to Appendices
—	2.5.15	Vlamertinghe	Infantry Units moved to Map 28 Square 4 a.c — Ammunition Columns of 2a Bdes working back to space occupied ~~by~~ recently by Train. Div Amn Col has moved nearer Poperinghe — New Refilling point opened 1 mile West of Poperinghe —	
9.30 am	2.5.15	"	Train reports all units fed last night no casualties —	
9. am	"	"	Anti Aircraft Section previously withdrawn rejoins.	
"	"	"	Mobile Vety Section moves from 1 m East of Poperinghe to 3 miles S.W. between Boeschepe and Poperinghe.	
12.20 pm	"		Question of clearing dead horses in Ypres and in area beyond having become acute — Div Cav detailed to clear YPRES which they do.	
	"	"	Tonight commenced the withdrawal to new line — There was of course necessarily much movement on Roads East of YPRES. ~~Representatives of Admin~~ ½ Artillery had to be withdrawn to new positions and whole of Durham L.I. Bde to the Huts where they ceased to be under 28th Div Command. In addition to normal feeding arrangements, ammunition supply and requirements for digging ~~here~~ and strengthening new line — Representative of Q Staff (Scammell) was present on the Roads ~~&~~ East of YPRES throughout the night till all was clear —	

(73989) W4141—463. 400,000. 9/14. H.&J.Ltd. Forms/C. 2118/10.

WAR DIARY
or
INTELLIGENCE SUMMARY.
(Erase heading not required.)

Instructions regarding War Diaries and Intelligence Summaries are contained in F. S. Regs., Part II. and the Staff Manual respectively. Title pages will be prepared in manuscript.

Army Form C. 2118.

Hour, Date, Place	Summary of Events and Information	Remarks and references to Appendices
2-5-15 Vlamertinghe	order that the difficulties of supply of food, ammn & trench stores may be realised hereafter. It must be understood that the Germans ~~shelled~~ with the object of impeding supply shelled the roads during the hours at which they seemed to know transport went and returned. Poperinghe & Vlamertinghe and the neighbourhood of Div HQ there were shelled usually about 7.30p – 8.30p – 12 mn – 1.30 am and about 5 am – The Road between Vlamertinghe and Ypres was shrapnelled at intervals – The Roads round the North of YPRES – the entrances to and exits from Ypres especially the Porte de DIXMUDE (North) and the Menin Gate (East) ~~were shelled with~~ and the town itself were plastered with shrapnel, 8", 12" & 17" HE shell unceasingly – In addition to the inconvenience and casualties in men horses and vehicles – the 8" & 12" shell made huge crater like holes in the middle of the YPRES – Zonnebeke and YPRES – WIELTJE Roads into which motor ambulances and other vehicles frequently drove and stuck. – These two main thoroughfares ~~were also~~ to the East were also incessantly swept by shrapnel. ~~from~~ This night was one of the worst ~~and~~ all supplies reached units ~~but only~~ due to the heroism of the 1st Line & Train Transport. About midnight a terrific block occurred between ~~the~~	

Instructions regarding War Diaries and Intelligence Summaries are contained in F. S. Regs., Part II. and the Staff Manual respectively. Title pages will be prepared in manuscript.

WAR DIARY
or
INTELLIGENCE SUMMARY.
(Erase heading not required.)

Army Form C. 2118.

Hour, Date, Place	Summary of Events and Information	Remarks and references to Appendices
	Potijze and the North End of the Cross Road ½ m West of S. Jean an Infantry Bde, Rev, ~~and~~ Train and Motor ambulances all moving on the same part of the road at the same time and specially due to the fact of Motor ambulances trying to pass slower moving GS waggons & then while doing so meeting other traffic – and to the fact of Rev leaving ammn waggons on the narrow Road while the Battery occupied a new position – This block took nearly 2½ hours to clear. Nobody's fault because the nights are very short and everything has to get through at the same time – The policy therefore is one of give and take, and common sense on the Road.	
2.5.15 Vlamertinghe	Weather V. Fine – moonlight night.	[illegible initials]
9.15am 3.5.15 "	Rumours of straggling and looting in YPRES but it is highly improbable.	
8.30am 3.5.15 "	As line is being shortened tonight all civilians who wished otherwise to be left in farms ordered to be cleared i.e. all inhabitants inside our lines East of a North & South line thro' a point midway between Potijze and Verloren Hoek.	
3.5.15 "	DADOS is now at Caestre (Railhead). We have done away with an ADS advanced store so to	

Instructions regarding War Diaries and Intelligence Summaries are contained in F. S. Regs., Part II. and the Staff Manual respectively. Title pages will be prepared in manuscript.

WAR DIARY
or
INTELLIGENCE SUMMARY.
(Erase heading not required.)

Army Form C. 2118.

Hour, Date, Place	Summary of Events and Information	Remarks and references to Appendices
	about 100 wounded of 11th Bde.	
	number of Rounds expended 48 hours ending noon 3/5/15	
	18pr 2627 for 48 guns: 1022 rounds 4.5", 12 guns; 1000 Rounds for 8: 60pr; 708 Rounds for 4.7", 8 guns – 9.2" – 97 Rounds 1 gun.	
— 3.5.15 Vlamertinghe	Weather v. Fine – night v dark until moon Rose	[illegible]
10.15am 4.5.15 Chateau Coutove	HQ 83 Bde from their new HQ in YPRES reports 3 casualties from Shell fire including M. G. officer and Staff Capt & that they are moving.	
" " "	arrangements made to send 140 bivouac shelters to 3 85th Bde Bns who are bivouacking in rest area East of Poperinghe.	
	Total Rounds expended to 12 noon 4th: 18pr ~~409~~ 2120 48 guns – 4.5", ~~78~~ 191, 60pr 162, 4.7 215, 9.2" 1. Last gun mentioned Sheared some pins.	
— " " "	Ammunition in front of Railhead at 12 noon 2nd may perhaps 18pr 487. 4.5" 212, 60pr 112; 4.7, 148, 9.2" 153.	
— " " "	Collecting Station has ~~had~~ been ~~[illegible]~~ by reason of Shelling moved to Lunatic Asylum YPRES from Potijze.	
1pm 4.5.15 "	Following reinforcements were met by Staff officer at GODWAERSVELDE and conducted sent to 1st Line Transport S of Poperinghe Viz 83 Bde OR 484 — 85 Inf Bde 4 officers 211 OR — 84 Bde 3 officers	

(73989) W4141—463. 400,000. 9/14. H.&J.Ltd. Forms/C. 2118/10.

Army Form C. 2118.

WAR DIARY
or
INTELLIGENCE SUMMARY.
(Erase heading not required.)

Instructions regarding War Diaries and Intelligence Summaries are contained in F. S. Regs., Part II. and the Staff Manual respectively. Title pages will be prepared in manuscript.

Hour, Date, Place			Summary of Events and Information	Remarks and references to Appendices
3.15pm	4.5.15	Chateau Couthove	as shelling may interfere with passage of rations to troops 5th Corps orders 2 days rations in addition to next day's Iron ration to be maintained by all troops E of YPRES – These additional rations to be completed by in course of 48 hours or so – Great scarcity of Bombs and Hand grenades	
5pm	4.5.15	"	Whole of administration move permanently to Chateau Couthove – Report Centre moves out of Vlamertinghe Chateau – which has been shelled – to a point S.E of Brandhoek	
6.30p	4.5.15	"	84th Bde Wires asking for many things to be sent up to Bns in Trenches – This is sent on to Qr Masters who manage it but the only sound plan is for Bde Staff to see to it themselves.	
–	4.5.15	"	Casualties (approximate) for last 3 days as shown in appendix 1	Appendix 1
–	4.5.15	"	Weather Fine then Wet –	A.A.W. Hant[illegible]
6.45am	5.5.15	"	260 Remounts arrive GODESWAERDE and are detrained by DDR 2nd Army and brought by Yorks Hussars on to a field 1m S.E Poperinghe where they are distributed by DAQMG about 2 pm.	

Instructions regarding War Diaries and Intelligence Summaries are contained in F. S. Regs., Part II. and the Staff Manual respectively. Title pages will be prepared in manuscript.

WAR DIARY
or
INTELLIGENCE SUMMARY.

(*Erase heading not required.*)

Army Form C. 2118.

Hour, Date, Place	Summary of Events and Information	Remarks and references to Appendices
	Speak and send it up same time as supplies withdrawing therefrom again if not issued. Formerly we had a small store in which we collected stuff not issued at R.P.	
— 5.5.15 Vlamertinghe	Supplies of anti asphyxiating gas pads continue to be issued.	
3.30pm " "	11th Bde heavily attacked ask for assistance to remove casualties tonight – ADMS collects stretcher bearers from other Divns and motor ambulances from 6th Corps – This is highly important as final retirement to new position takes place tonight.	
— " " "	Reinforcements of 4 officers & 244 other ranks arrive. Arrangements being made to receive 260 remounts due 5th May, not v. convenient under existing conditions some 16 or 17 miles away.	
7pm " " "	3rd Cav Division arrive as supports during withdrawal and are [illegible] visited Road Centres East of YPRES saw RA pass with clear Road – 4th Bde Bns marched back to huts and left 28 Div. 2 Bns each of 83 & 84 Bde marched to huts – H 5 d 85 Bde back to area G. 4, 5, 6. –	
12 M " " "	All went exceptionally well during retirement except that it was found impossible to evacuate	

(73989) W4141—463. 400,000. 9/14. H.&J.Ltd. Forms/C. 2118/10.

Army Form C. 2118.

Instructions regarding War Diaries and Intelligence Summaries are contained in F. S. Regs., Part II. and the Staff Manual respectively. Title pages will be prepared in manuscript.

WAR DIARY
or
INTELLIGENCE SUMMARY.
(Erase heading not required.)

Hour, Date, Place	Summary of Events and Information	Remarks and references to Appendices
11.10 am 5.5.15 Château Couthove	AA & QMG wires 84th Bde Belfast that he cannot be channel of communication between them & the Qr Masters – 84th Bde have lately been wiring calling for all sorts of articles at short notice.	
12 noon 5.5.15 "	Bombs and hand grenades very short at RE Park only 14 unserviceable in hand	
6.45 pm 5.5.15 "	85th Infantry Bde report being short of Rifles and equipment as a temporary measure arrangements made to draw on field ambulances.	
7.15 pm 5.5.15 "	The big shells have made enormous craters in the ~~YPRES~~ road North East of YPRES – AA & QMG asks for help from 5th Corps to fill these in and sends party of the Surrey Yeomanry to see what can be done to fill it up – Party report it will require 30 waggon loads bricks to fill it up	
7.30 pm 5.5.15 "	To meet sudden calls for GS waggons to take trench stores arranged that Blanket waggons remain with ~~tra~~ 1st line Transport –	
— 5.5.15 "	Rounds expended to 12 noon 5th 18 pr. 2267, – 4.5" 391, 60 pr 157 number of guns unchanged	
5.5.15 "	Weather v fine & warm.	AAH ?

(73989) W4141—463. 400,000. 9/14. H.&J.Ltd. Forms/C. 2118/10.

Instructions regarding War Diaries and Intelligence Summaries are contained in F. S. Regs., Part II. and the Staff Manual respectively. Title pages will be prepared in manuscript.

WAR DIARY
or
INTELLIGENCE SUMMARY.
(Erase heading not required.)

Army Form C. 2118.

Hour, Date, Place		Summary of Events and Information	Remarks and references to Appendices
6.5.15	Chateau Couthove	Billeting accommodation is being augmented with Bivouac Shelters we were originally issued 270 but lost all except 20 at S. Jean during the fighting & shelling. Since then we have been issued 240 and so far have issued 150 to Insty Bde, 15 to Sig Coy.	
9.30am 6.5.15	"	5th Corps have issued instruction that in addition to current day and Iron Ration ~~att~~ – 2 days Res rations must be maintained for troops. This has almost been completed. 5th Corps now calls for ~~daily~~ report each morning as to whether Sd Supply Situation normal or otherwise	Appendix 2
9.35am "	"	4th Northumberland ~~Div~~ Howitzer Bde suddenly attached and as showing how little supply situation is realised, that Div wire "will you ration 4th North How Bde whilst attached to you", being then S.W.D. find out date from when – Strength and whether vehicles for Supply Col and Train have been detached.	
6.5.15	"	Train reports following casualties due to supplying troops 5 G.S. waggons 1 water Cart	
3.30pm 6.5.15	"	Notification received of additional Chaplain posted to Division (leaving Senior Chaplain in Div free to be posted to Div HQ if necessary as an administrator.)	
4.15pm 6.5.15	"	24th Bde complains (9.15am) transport moved up 4 day in daylight & was heavily shelled – fire being directed by German Observation Balloon – message received 4.15 pm	

Instructions regarding War Diaries and Intelligence Summaries are contained in F. S. Regs., Part II. and the Staff Manual respectively. Title pages will be prepared in manuscript.

WAR DIARY
or
INTELLIGENCE SUMMARY.
(Erase heading not required.)

Army Form C. 2118.

Hour, Date, Place	Summary of Events and Information	Remarks and references to Appendices
	because despatch rider killed. necessary action taken [illegible] Transport –	
4 pm 6.5.15 Chateau Couthove	Reports of looting in YPRES especially by French Soldiers received. APM who is still at Vlamertinghe duly notified.	
4.30 pm 6.5.15 "	Reports received that the 85 Bde [illegible] Kitchens recently issued are of shoddy make and unsatisfactory – Reports called for from other 2 Bdes.	
4.50 pm " "	Issue of Anti asphyxiating respirators is becoming a big matter arrangement made that they are to be considered a medical Store and sent up in Motor Ambulances or if thought advance issued ~~with~~ through Supply echelons –	
5.30 pm " "	5th Corps bring to notice fact that water supply likely to be short and ~~[illegible]~~ for directs consideration of question –	
	Famine of Hand Grenades and Bombs continues – very light new added. ~~Bombs [illegible] to them~~ Casualties to 12 noon OR 31 K. 110 W: officers Lt Townsend 1 Mon. 2/Lt Stanton Suffolk Capt Royle [illegible] killed – wounded 10 officers.	
6.5.15 "	Situation quieter – less ~~heavy~~ shelling but Poperinghe suffered badly at night –	
	[illegible] Bde [illegible], Visited Report centre, RE, [illegible] 146: Bde & HQ 85 Inf Bde.	
6.5.15 "	Weather v. fine – ~~Casualties to 12 noon~~	[signature illegible]

(73989) W4141—463. 400,000. 9/14. H.&J.Ltd. Forms/C. 2118/10.

Instructions regarding War Diaries and Intelligence Summaries are contained in F. S. Regs., Part II. and the Staff Manual respectively. Title pages will be prepared in manuscript.

WAR DIARY
or
INTELLIGENCE SUMMARY.
(Erase heading not required.)

Army Form C. 2118.

Hour, Date, Place		Summary of Events and Information	Remarks and references to Appendices
—	7.5.15 Chateau Coutlrove	Report received that all rations have been delivered and an limber axle broken during process.	
—	7.5.15 "	Several further devices being issued today for use against asphyxiating gas viz. 40 Spraying machines with 7 cwt Theosulphate of Soda — 3 Miners Masks for trial by machine gunners — also 1000 respirators made up by ADMS ~~and~~ all issued to 84th Bde as signs of gas preparation reported in front of that Bde — also 1000 Mufflers from AOD which are prepared with the solution issued ~~[illegible]~~ to 85th Bde —	
1.5pm	7.5.15 "	North'n Div again wires asking if arrangements are complete for rationing Howitzer Bde	
		Numerous complaints about Travelling Kitchens continue	
—	7.5.15 "	[illegible] proceeds round each Billeting area to ascertain if any are [illegible] vice versa.	
1pm	7.5.15 "	12 officers 159 OR ~~500~~ reinforcements arrive Caestre and are sent on to 1st Line	
—	7.5.15 "	83rd Inf Bde are short of 11 Machine guns damaged by Shell	
5pm	7.5.15 "	Officer of Administrative Staff visited 1st Line Transport and discussed means of getting food to units. ~~and~~ So far scheme is in not in any case crystallised general plan is to take R.E. stores and rations up in Limbers — For rations 2 Limbers sufficient with small Bns — These are dumped at Potijze and mostly carrying parties from Supports who take them to Trenches — Some units use Pack Mules but these are not popular because	

(73989) W4141—463. 400,000. 9/14. H.&J.Ltd. Forms/C. 2118/10.

Instructions regarding War Diaries and Intelligence Summaries are contained in F. S. Regs., Part II. and the Staff Manual respectively. Title pages will be prepared in manuscript.

WAR DIARY
or
INTELLIGENCE SUMMARY.
(Erase heading not required.)

Army Form C. 2118.

Hour, Date, Place	Summary of Events and Information	Remarks and references to Appendices
	units like to get their Transport out of the Shell swept area quickly as possible and Mules are slow – However the Staff principle we follow is to allow freedom of initiative and under the circumstances not to tie down units ~~to a scheme~~ ~~an unsuitable~~ scheme to ~~~~ unsuitable to them – because they are the people who have to do the job – not the Staff –	
	R.E. Park also visited to [illegible] at present especially in explosives – Very Pistol Cartridges –	
	[illegible] brought back to A HQ, from which place he can go forward daily.	
— 7. 5. 15 Chateau Couthove	Quiet day – weather v. fine.	[illegible]
	Casualties reported as Officers K { 2nd Lt A Tuke 2/North Fus R; W { 2nd Lt A Kennedy RE, 2nd Lt [illegible] 2/KO, " R V Taylor 2/North Fus, Capt N Wells 2/Ches	
	OR. 63 K. 195 W. 37 M.	
6.45 am 8. 5. 15 "	Rations safely delivered and Transport returned	
10.20 am 8. 5. 15 "	RA now report requirements in Horses as follows [illegible] 260 making approximately 540 animals required during last 3 weeks – These have mainly been expended by Shell fire in the YPRES Salient.	
	Russians having offered a percentage of decorations for gallantry Names of NCOs & men are being selected	
	S. George's Cross 3 & 4 Class (3 = Victoria Cross) = 42	
	medals of S. George 4 Classes = 73	

(73989) W4141—463. 400,000. 9/14. H.&J.Ltd. Forms/C. 2118/10.

Instructions regarding War Diaries and Intelligence Summaries are contained in F. S. Regs., Part II. and the Staff Manual respectively. Title pages will be prepared in manuscript.

WAR DIARY
or
INTELLIGENCE SUMMARY.
(Erase heading not required.)

Army Form C. 2118.

Hour, Date, Place	Summary of Events and Information	Remarks and references to Appendices
11.45pm 9.5.15 Chateau Couthove	Instructions to RE to create a Reserve of Bombs, Hand grenades & Very lights.	
12.15pm 8.5.15 "	5th Corps appealed to to assist in obtaining Shirts & Socks	
8.5.15 "	~~Heavy~~ an attack on 83rd ~~[illegible]~~ Bde continued with heavy artillery fire commenced about 7 am this morning. In order to keep touch with adv 28th Div are acting as Liaison officers in turn. It then became apparent that attack was serious and at 2 pm an administrative SO (Bagwell) ~~[illegible]~~ visited 1st Line T formations & was informed — 2nd Buffs 1st Line having been shelled ~~and~~ 2 horses being killed & 1 man wounded — Intermittent shells of the High Velocity type dropped near once or twice while ~~a 12~~ an occasional 12" ~~[illegible]~~ possibly aimed at the observation balloon 300 yards dp added to the ~~[illegible]~~ uneasiness. Moreover stragglers from the battle brought in bad tales of the situation as they always do and Qr Masters were uncertain as to how to get rations to units who were becoming badly mixed in the Battle line — wires being cut continually it was impossible to furnish accurate any information of positions and Qr Master decided to move transport to the farm (Vlamertinghe) one mile W of YPRES and having done so to endeavour to gain ~~information~~ touch — This was done later ~~[illegible]~~ as heavy casualties were expected Inf. Bde Supply vehicles returning were instructed to call at the	
2pm " " "		
6pm " " "		

(73989) W4141—463. 400,000. 9/14. H.&J.Ltd. Forms/C. 2118/10.

Instructions regarding War Diaries and Intelligence Summaries are contained in F. S. Regs., Part II. and the Staff Manual respectively. Title pages will be prepared in manuscript.

WAR DIARY
or
INTELLIGENCE SUMMARY.
(Erase heading not required.)

Army Form C. 2118.

Hour, Date, Place	Summary of Events and Information	Remarks and references to Appendices
	dressing Station at YPRES. and later wounded to the Field amb reopened in Rue Bassern Poperinghe —	
7 h 8.5.15 Chateau Couthove	From 7–9 pm ambulances & wagons were on the main Road controlling traffic — Blocks being rather numerous owing to movement of troops	
8.45 pm " "	83 Bde reports fighting Strength as 900.	
11 9.5.15 "	Casualties of ~~83~~ to noon 8th Officers K. Ra. H. J. Gamble & Equiton (not all in) OR. 10K. 877W. W. H. J. [illegible] R.2. H. L. [illegible]	
	Number of Rounds expended to noon 8th. 18pr 4532 for 48 guns — 4.5" 777 for 12 guns - 60 pr 398 - guns 9.2 4 for 1 gun —	
" 8.5.15 "	Weather V. Fine, High N. westerly wind.	
	It has been laid down regarding the 2 days Reserve of rations held by units East of YPRES that they will hand over these to relieving units — If numbers of troops are increased units will notify Supply Officers if decreased Reserve ration will be utilised for daily use & so reduced — It is feared that in the Battle much may have become lost	Remarks — Appendix III
11 8.5.15 "		

Instructions regarding War Diaries and Intelligence Summaries are contained in F. S. Regs., Part II. and the Staff Manual respectively. Title pages will be prepared in manuscript.

WAR DIARY
or
INTELLIGENCE SUMMARY
(Erase heading not required.)

Army Form C. 2118.

Hour, Date, Place	Summary of Events and Information	Remarks and references to Appendices
— 9.5.15 Chateau Couthove	We have been notified that certain units are attached 28 Div	App: IV
— 9.5.15 "	Ration situation has become v complicated – The Division has been much depleted 1/Suffolks & 12/London have almost ceased to exist as regiments – and all have suffered heavily consequently the rations as indented for by units are far too many. Moreover it is not known yet whether the 2 days Reserve has been lost or not – The SSO is arranging all this question with QrMrs and the Stock East of YPRES is being rapidly reduced	
2.30am 9.5.15 "	Wire received from 84 Bde asking for 1000 Shovels at POTIJZE at once – These were got through in a lorry from RE Park but in spite of haste did not start before 5 am –	
8.45am " "	83 Bde reports strengths of units as 2/KO, 100; 2/E York 200; KOYLI 100; 5 Kings own 200, 3 Mon 100. The RP at North of Brandhoek closed today – New refilling point will be 3/4 mile S of Poperinghe on Poperinghe–Westoutre road.	
10.0am " " "	Estimated Casualties 85 Bde 3/Mx 500, E Surrey 200, Rfus 150 RE 2 officers killed 1 wounded OR 10 K – 10 W.	
— " "	Informed that 2 Transport horses were killed last night no casualties to ~~horses~~ personnel.	
11 am " "	84 Bde reports Strength Welsh R. 16 offs 270 OR. Ches 3, 170 OR 1/Mon 1 off 10 OR, 12 London 30 OR. No news of Suffolks yet 83 Bde reports 2KO. 3 offs 200 OR, E Yorks 4 offs 270 OR, KOYLI 3 offrs 300 OR, Y&L 2 offs 260 OR, 5/KO. 7 offs 220, 3/Mon 5 offs 185 OR 83 Bde Reports names of officers killed and wounded.	

Instructions regarding War Diaries and Intelligence Summaries are contained in F. S. Regs., Part II. and the Staff Manual respectively. Title pages will be prepared in manuscript.

Army Form C. 2118.

WAR DIARY
or
INTELLIGENCE SUMMARY
(Erase heading not required.)

Hour, Date, Place			Summary of Events and Information	Remarks and references to Appendices
—	9.5.15	Chateau Couthove	Killed and wounded which include 3 Lt Cols 3 Majors 1 Capt 1 [illegible]	
1pm	9.5.15	"	First Line Transport moved from its position where it was shelled yesterday to safer farms immediately N of Brandhoek	
—	9.5.15	"	RE report requirements in horses as 260 – Indent by wire to DDR 2 Army.	
—	9.5.15	"	Brig Genl Gay Gorse relieved and has ordered home. Brig Genl (Lt Col) Arbuthnot taking over.	
4pm	9.5.15	"	Reinforcements of 45 officers and 1329 OR arrived. Rounds expended to 12 noon 18pr 4033, 4.5" 884, 60pr 203	
10pm	9.5.15	"	GOC ordered all Stragglers now with 1st Line Transport to be equipped and sent up tomorrow, Following Staffs taken. DADMS ordered to Hazebrouck tomorrow morning to search clearing hospitals, DADOS ordered to report here –	
—	9.5.15	"	Weather v fine but cold.	[illegible]
6.22am	10.5.15	"	OC Train reports Rations delivered and transport returned except 4 of 21 [illegible] – no casualties.	
7.15am	"	"	2 Electric lights with waggon left Railhead to [illegible]	

1247 W 3299 200,000 (E) 8/14 J.B.C. & A. Forms/C. 2118/11.

Instructions regarding War Diaries and Intelligence Summaries are contained in F. S. Regs., Part II. and the Staff Manual respectively. Title pages will be prepared in manuscript.

WAR DIARY
or
INTELLIGENCE SUMMARY

(Erase heading not required.)

Army Form C. 2118.

	Hour, Date, Place		Summary of Events and Information	Remarks and references to Appendices
9am	10.5.15	Chateau Couthove	In response to 12.15 pm of 8/5. 2000 Shirts, 3000 Socks, 2000 Towels despatched from base.	
10am	"	"	DADOS returns from search of Clearing Hospitals Hazebrouck having earmarked some 450 sets Equipment & Rifles – DADOS visits 28 Div Fd Amb at Hoogen Graaff – SE Poperinghe earmarks 20 sets there and meets lorry returning to base with 60 sets also earmarked. DADOS to Bailleul.	
11.25 / 12-30 pm	"	"	2 guns 18 Pr – 2 – 5" – 3 Ammn Waggons arrived Railhead.	
1pm	"	"	5th Corps orders daily report by 9 am of estimated fighting strength of Inf Bns made up to 6.30 am – this will be done of course but is impossible to get and has to be made up by guess work in this office – while units still remain mixed it is impossible for even Bde Commanders to know what they have –	
	10.5	"	500 more respirators being sent to 85 Bde tonight – Bdes asked if every man now has respirators.	
3pm	10.5.15	"	DADOS visits 1st Line of all units and investigates requirements in Rifles & Ammn – very few required because any stragglers seem to have come back with rifle equipt complete and have now gone up again, but comes on with the collected arms ammn at the old Refilling point at 4 pm and issued to any one who wanted them –	
6pm	10.5.15	"	DAQMG 5th Corps visited HQ 28 Div ~~and~~ regarding immediate provision of one Respirator per man – is arranging to send up stuff and get 3000 made tonight and tomorrow – we have already issued 5000 respirators of sorts – These made will be sent to Lunatic Asylum YPRES whence Bdes can get them –	

Army Form C. 2118.

Instructions regarding War Diaries and Intelligence Summaries are contained in F. S. Regs., Part II. and the Staff Manual respectively. Title pages will be prepared in manuscript.

WAR DIARY
or
INTELLIGENCE SUMMARY

(Erase heading not required.)

Hour, Date, Place	Summary of Events and Information	Remarks and references to Appendices
10.5.15 Chateau Coulheure	Total number rounds expended to 12 noon 10th May 18pr 5862 for 48 guns – 4.5" 289 for 12 guns, 60pr 261 for 6 guns 9.2" 4 for 1 gun.	
	Fairly quiet day on 28 Div line except on extreme right administrative situation busy but ~~more~~ fairly clear – no attempt being made to thoroughly organise until more peaceful time.	
10.5.15 "	Weather v fine – No authentic reports of units can yet be obtained regarding casualties – approximate fighting strength of Infantry of the Division 6200. Assuming average strength on 7th May was 700 per Bn casualties on 8th approximate 7000.	Gau 4H
6.30am 11.5.15 "	DA&QMG personal visit requires details of disappearance of Suffolk. Also demands that every man has a respirator.	
6.40am 11.5.15 "	Returns delivered no casualties last night – ~~action~~ ~~taken~~ ~~accordingly~~.	
9.5am 11.5.15	Fighting Strength reported to 5th Corps as 141 officers – OR 6114 Infantry only.	
— "	83 & 84 Bdes ~~having~~ come out of trenches tonight	
— "	We have been issued 70 sprayers for clearing trenches	

Instructions regarding War Diaries and Intelligence Summaries are contained in F. S. Regs., Part II. and the Staff Manual respectively. Title pages will be prepared in manuscript.

WAR DIARY
or
INTELLIGENCE SUMMARY
(Erase heading not required.)

Army Form C. 2118.

Hour, Date, Place			Summary of Events and Information	Remarks and references to Appendices
			of gases – There were sent to Bdes who cannot understand them – matter of preparation & instruction being taken in hand by ADMS –	
11 am	11.5.15	Chateau Couthove	5th Corps call for administrative report on fighting round YPRES. 22nd – 10th.	
11.15	11.5.15	"	2nd Army Q notifies 1200 Respirators & 1000 Smoke helmets are to be sent for ~~at~~ from at S. Omer – Impossible to send – we have 4 ASC lorries who are fully occupied with current demands. Later 5th Corps called up saying we had not fetched them – they must be done tomorrow – ~~[illegible]~~ a very poor example of Staff work on someone's part –	
—	11.5.15	"	ADR notifies departure ~~[illegible]~~ of 252 ~~173~~ horses for RA from Boulogne tomorrow –	
	11.5.15	"	More ingredients, respirators & Sprayers continue to arrive from 5th Corps – These are being collected at the dressing station at YPRES and units informed to draw from there. 1st Cav Div which relieves 83 & 84 ~~brigades~~ is allotted 2000.	
9 pm	11.5.15	"	In view of the withdrawal of 83, 84 Bdes ~~brigades~~ 550 rations more ready and changes load of lorries from Pres to fresh meat.	

1247 W 3299 200,000 (E) 8/14 J.B.C. & A. Forms/C. 2118/11.

Instructions regarding War Diaries and Intelligence Summaries are contained in F. S. Regs., Part II. and the Staff Manual respectively. Title pages will be prepared in manuscript.

WAR DIARY
or
INTELLIGENCE SUMMARY
(Erase heading not required.)

Army Form C. 2118.

	Hour, Date, Place	Summary of Events and Information	Remarks and references to Appendices
—	11.5.15 Chateau Coulhove	Situation of the 48 hours [illegible] held by troops East of YPRES is shown in appendix - the balance is being handed over to the relieving Cavalry.	Appendix 5
—	11.5.15 "	Reinforcements arrived 13 offs 332 OR.	
		Casualties officers k.1 - W.5. OR K6 - W 33	
		24 hours ending 12 noon 11th - Totals added to previous list of Casualties 8th to 11th officers K 5 offs - W 18 - M 26. W O R [illegible]	
—	11.5.15 "	Weather fine	Remarks
—	12.5.15 "	During the night 83 & 85 Bdes came out of trenches and billeted between Vlamertinghe and Poperinghe.	
12.25pm	12.5.15 "	Instructions that men recovered from asphyxiating gas will not be sent back at once but kept for a few days.	
3pm	12.5.15 "	Arrangements made to clear battlefield - working parties found by cyclists - weapons by train - Quantities of equipment lying abandoned about N of Ridge. [illegible] - 1st Cav Div - are helping.	
—	12.5.15 "	Question of Command of Inf Bns is difficult at present - all senior officers killed or wounded, adjutants practically all gone in 83, 84th Bdes. and in many cases some of Reserve too —	

1247 W 3299 200,000 (E) 8/14 J.B.C. & A. Forms/C. 2118/11.

Army Form C. 2118.

WAR DIARY
or
INTELLIGENCE SUMMARY
(Erase heading not required.)

Instructions regarding War Diaries and Intelligence Summaries are contained in F. S. Regs., Part II. and the Staff Manual respectively. Title pages will be prepared in manuscript.

Hour, Date, Place	Summary of Events and Information	Remarks and references to Appendices
12.5.15 Chateau Couthove	Col Jerome CRE has gone home on 3 weeks leave worn out —	
6.40pm " " "	Godwaersvelde reports arrival of 173 mules & horses. This is the first intimation.	
12 noon [?] " "	Rounds expended up to 12 noon has dropped to 459 · 18pr other types in proportion.	
	Reinforcements of 3 offrs & 886 OR arrived	
	Casualties to 12 noon 1 offr wounded. OR 8k – 69 w.	
	~~weather~~ water Reconnaissance of 28 Div area carried out during afternoon —	
	weather ~~fine~~ dull – colder.	[illegible]
3am 13.5.15 "	85 Inf Bde came out of the trenches – The 84th had been moved to area immediately West of Poperinghe and 83 closed up to immediately East of Poperinghe. Artillery are still in the trenches and detachments of R.E.	
[illegible]am 13.5.15 "	5th Corps now states medical authorities doubtful if khaki masks any good against asphyxiating gases & considers them to be well soaked in solution — not very clearing [?] so — Not notified to Bdes	

Army Form C. 2118.

Instructions regarding War Diaries and Intelligence Summaries are contained in F. S. Regs., Part II. and the Staff Manual respectively. Title pages will be prepared in manuscript.

WAR DIARY
or
INTELLIGENCE SUMMARY
(Erase heading not required.)

Hour, Date, Place			Summary of Events and Information	Remarks and references to Appendices
11.35 am	13.5.15	Chateau Coulhove	Wire recd that 28 Div less RE & RA ~~with~~ pass to Army Reserve [illegible] & to rest 3 days in afternoon - This was done & areas allotted as follows - Div HQ Chateau Coulhove near Proven - 83rd Bde WINNIZEELE - 84th Bde HERZEELE - 85th Bde WATOU, HOUTKERQUE Genl Boyle 83rd Bde Sick (worn out) - Lt Col Marden 1/Welsh succeeds him.	
6 pm	13.5.15	"	83 horses & mules for artillery arrived Godwaersvelde. As we are withdrawing to ~~Rest~~ Army Reserve - all RE Stores and anti asphyxiating pads placed at disposal of 1st Cav Division who relieve us - we are trying to build up a reserve but with all the various calls on us it is very difficult	
9 pm	13.5.15	"	Orders issued for move of troops to rest areas attached While this was in progress of distribution orders issued by the Corps Army to form a Composite Bde - which was done as follows Brig Genl Bols & 84 Bde Staff 2/North Fus, 1/Y&L 2/Ches, 1/Welsh 2/Buffs, 85 Field Amb, No 3 Coy Train To be collected in an area west of Vlamertinghe	Appendix VI

1247 W 3299 200,000 (E) 8/14 J.B.C. & A. Forms/C. 2118/11.

Instructions regarding War Diaries and Intelligence Summaries are contained in F. S. Regs., Part II. and the Staff Manual respectively. Title pages will be prepared in manuscript.

WAR DIARY
or
INTELLIGENCE SUMMARY
(Erase heading not required.)

Army Form C. 2118.

Hour, Date, Place	Summary of Events and Information	Remarks and references to Appendices
	during night:	
	The Composite Bde was duly collected in Squares G6 - H1 H7. - all units were warned including of Train. who had a complicated problem to solve - Refilling Points for Supply present no difficulty for Trains - no special arrangements necessary for S.A.A. as Bde Amm Cols are not moving!	
	Capt Miller APM was sent to Staff the Remnants of the 84th Bde.	
— 13.5.15 Chateau Coutiliere	Copy of Report on recent operations attached Appendix VII	Append VII
	Weather Fine cold.	[illegible]
	Casualties W.? 2 [illegible] officers K2 W2 M1 OR K 9. W 25, M[illegible]	
	Rounds expended [illegible] 12 [illegible] 13 - 18 pr. 4122 for 48 [illegible] etc.	
10 am 14.5.15 "	27th Div call urgently for Very Pistols & Very lights - we reply that any Composite Bde are taking all we have but if any over will send - getting practically no Very lights or Pistols now.	
10.45 14.5.15 "	Fitting out Composite Bde with Shelters drawn from other Bdes —	

1247 W 3299 200,000 (E) 8/14 J.B.C. & A. Forms/C. 2118/11.

Instructions regarding War Diaries and Intelligence Summaries are contained in F. S. Regs., Part II. and the Staff Manual respectively. Title pages will be prepared in manuscript.

WAR DIARY
or
INTELLIGENCE SUMMARY
(Erase heading not required.)

Army Form C. 2118.

Hour, Date, Place	Summary of Events and Information	Remarks and references to Appendices
14.5.15 Chateau Coutiere	were respirators coming.	
	Corps Commander reopens leave – Composite Bde excepted – GOC decides 5 days leave giving 3 clear days in England – 1/3 of officers to go	
	are condemned 60 per destroyed by Premature at 18?	
7 pm 14.5.15 "	Wires sent out to collect all empty Jam tins and bully beef tins at RE Park wherewith to make Bombs	
	as supply RE report 26 sets of Running out Springs deficient.	
	~~Casualties~~ RE. OR 1 K 3 W.	
— 14.5.15 "	Weather wet – Country muddy at once	[illegible] —
— 14.5.15 "	Troops except Comp Bde moved into rest areas –	
9.15 am 16.5.15 "	GOC orders that every Bde be instructed in the use of Sprayers – ~~arrangements~~ these being [to] clean trenches & dug outs of asphyxiating gases – arrangements made with ADMS to train Bdes at Fd Ambulances except Composite Bde which will be taught in Poperinghe –	

1247 W 3299 200,000 (E) 8/14 J.B.C. & A. Forms/C. 2118/11.

Army Form C. 2118.

Instructions regarding War Diaries and Intelligence Summaries are contained in F. S. Regs., Part II. and the Staff Manual respectively. Title pages will be prepared in manuscript.

WAR DIARY
or
INTELLIGENCE SUMMARY
(Erase heading not required.)

Hour, Date, Place			Summary of Events and Information	Remarks and references to Appendices
9.45am	15.5.15	Chateau Coultere	Captain Miller recalled from 84th Inf Bde.	
"	"	"	Re report being short of 26, 18 pr mining at ships. Altogether we have lost 4 guns 'crumped', 1 'A' tube shifted 26 ships done in – during the last 10 days	
11 am.	15.5.15	"	AA & QMG visited Composite, 83, 85 Bdes to find out & supply their wants — Stores are being taken to open baths at the 3 Bde areas.	
6.30pm	15.5.15	"	Following reinforcements arrived 18 officers 1374 OR.	
—	15.5.15	"	weather dull – cold.	[illegible]
—	16.5.15	"	no events of administrative interest weather dull.	[illegible] –
12.20pm	17.5.15	"	Indisputable evidence notified by 5th Cahs that Germans have poisoned with arsenic the stream which runs between S.ELOI and VERMEZEELE into the YPRES moat – all notified. Swimming Baths at YPRES reported not fouled –	

1247 W 3299 200,000 (E) 8/14 J.B.C. & A. Forms/C. 2118/11.

Army Form C. 2118.

Instructions regarding War Diaries and Intelligence Summaries are contained in F. S. Regs., Part II. and the Staff Manual respectively. Title pages will be prepared in manuscript.

WAR DIARY
or
INTELLIGENCE SUMMARY

(Erase heading not required.)

Hour, Date, Place		Summary of Events and Information	Remarks and references to Appendices
9.15 pm	17.5.15 Chateau Courhove	Brig Gen Pereira assumed command of 85 Inf Bde. vice Brig Genl Chapman to England.	
—	17.5.15 "	Reinforcements of 2 Offrs & 32 OR arrived.	
—	17.5.15 "	Weather ~~Fine~~ Wet.	A.A. & Q.M.G. H —
12 noon	18.5.15 "	Rounds expended to noon today only amount to 18 pr. 100 for 48 guns. 4.5 64 for 12 guns. 15" ~~78~~ etc.	
1.5 pm	18.5.15 "	1 Offr & 60 OR arrived to reinforce Anglesey RE.	
	18.5.15 "	For future guidance it is noted here that arrangements were made ~~for~~ for omnibuses to pick up officers going on leave and take them to Boulogne & bring them back	
6.30 pm	18.5.15 "	Arrangements regarding change of clothing have now to be altered owing to paucity of stock – change cannot be guaranteed at baths so troops must bring change with them –	
—	18.5.15 "	Weather ~~Fine~~ Wet & Stormy, Cold.	A.A. & Q.M.G. H.
—	19.5.15 "	Following moves taking place this morning. 85th Bde in toto relieves Composite Bde at Brandhoek — Composite Bde breaks up	

1247 W 3299 200,000 (E) 8/14 J.B.C. & A. Forms/C. 2118/11.

Army Form C. 2118.

WAR DIARY
or
INTELLIGENCE SUMMARY

(Erase heading not required.)

Instructions regarding War Diaries and Intelligence Summaries are contained in F. S. Regs., Part II. and the Staff Manual respectively. Title pages will be prepared in manuscript.

Hour	Date	Place	Summary of Events and Information	Remarks and references to Appendices
			and becomes 84th Bde at HERZEELE.	
3.30pm	19.5.15	Chateau Couthove	1st and 2nd Line Transport ~~83 Inf~~ 12 London arrived at STAPLES en route for TAITINGHEM nr S. OMER where 12th London R. proceeds on withdrawal to GHQ Troops. This is necessary owing to fact of that T.F. Bns can get no reinforcements and the 12th London is much depleted – being 7 Offrs & 212 OR.	
—	19.5.15	"	Casualties during last 24 hours. Ra – 1 OR wounded.	
—	19.5.15	"	Lieut Col. R. Ravenshaw arrived to assume command of 83rd Inf Bde	
—	19.5.15	"	Weather v. hot. Mud again v. deep	A A McH.
—	19.5.15	"	Following alterations in expenditure of Amm. per diem. 18 pr – 3. 4.5. 30 (1 HE) – 4.7 8 (of which 5 may be HE)	ditto
—	20.5.15	"	C in C visits 83rd Inf Bde.	
2pm	"	2pm	12th London Regt move to TAITINGHEM to join GHQ Troops.	
	"	"	Leave of 83 & 85 Bde officers cancelled as Bdes move to trenches 21st/22nd.	
	"	"	Reinforcements of some 23 officers arrived	
	"	"	A batch of 30 Remounts was expected at Coestre	

1247 W 3299 200,000 (E) 8/14 J.B.C. & A. Forms/C. 2118/11.

Army Form C. 2118.

Instructions regarding War Diaries and Intelligence Summaries are contained in F. S. Regs., Part II, and the Staff Manual respectively. Title pages will be prepared in manuscript.

WAR DIARY
or
INTELLIGENCE SUMMARY

(Erase heading not required.)

Hour, Date, Place			Summary of Events and Information	Remarks and references to Appendices
5.45 pm	20.5.15	Chateau Couthove	and a party was sent to that place – We were then warned that a they would arrive at 6.30 (1 hr 45") at GODWAERSWELDE and another party was sent. Later we received a wire that 2 of the horses had gone to ARNEKE W of S. OMER. Eventually the horses were detrained at Caestre. Staff arrangements as above make things very difficult	
			Orders received that the 1st & 3rd Monmouths & 2nd Monmouth from 4th Div were to be amalgamated and join 84th Inf Bde. This is because of the difficulty experienced in obtaining reinforcements. The Preliminary Steps were taken but it being represented that this will spoil esprit de Corps of the 3 Bns & T.F. recruiting will necessarily suffer matters were not hastily pushed	
—	20.5.15	"	Casualties in the Division from 22nd April to 13th May incl. work out at 343 officers 9908 OR.	Appendix VIII
			Present Strength of Infantry } Officers 232. OR 9831	
—	20.5.15	"	Weather fine	[illegible]
8.10 am	21.5.15	"	Capt R Follett [illegible] Rifle Bde appointed Bde Major 83rd Bde vice Major Mumby returns to duty	

Instructions regarding War Diaries and Intelligence Summaries are contained in F. S. Regs., Part II. and the Staff Manual respectively. Title pages will be prepared in manuscript.

WAR DIARY
or
INTELLIGENCE SUMMARY

(Erase heading not required.)

Army Form C. 2118.

Hour, Date, Place	Summary of Events and Information	Remarks and references to Appendices
12 noon 21.5.15 Chateau Coutthove	C in C inspects 84th Inf Bde.	
4 pm 21.5.15 "	Following drafts arrive 18 officers 1097 OR for Infantry & 2 officers and 187 for RA. The Infantry drafts were originally ordered to detrain at Caestre & move forward by bus – none of latter being available 83, 85 & RA were ~~moved to~~ detrained at Caestre and 84 at Abeele whence they marched to Herzeele.	
— 21.5.15 "	A most unfortunate epidemic of cars is occurring out of five cars 1 ~~both~~ is with GOC at Boulogne, 1 with ADOS at Caestre ~~and~~ 2 are broken down leaving 1 at HQ – The cause of breakages chiefly springs as the roads are very bumpy now due to MT traffic.	
— 21.5.15 "	During the afternoon the 83rd Bde less 3 Mon moved to Brandhoek Area relieving 85th Bde who move into trenches tonight – Gradually we are resuming areas occupied before we moved to rest but not very easy as 4th Div, Belgian Artly & Cavalry are occupying many of our farms. 85th Bde moved in with 2 days rations plus emergency and iron ration – ~~Post~~ Bde Post offices will collect to & from Refilling point which from tomorrow inclusive will be at the former site 1 mile S E Poperinghe. that for Div Troops will be still on the Pop? – ~~Reninghelst~~ Westoutre Road. Weather fine	AAW H

1247 W 3299 200,000 (E) 8/14 J.B.C. & A. Forms/C. 2118/11.

Instructions regarding War Diaries and Intelligence Summaries are contained in F. S. Regs., Part II. and the Staff Manual respectively. Title pages will be prepared in manuscript.

WAR DIARY
or
INTELLIGENCE SUMMARY
(Erase heading not required.)

Army Form C. 2118.

Hour, Date, Place	Summary of Events and Information	Remarks and references to Appendices
2pm. 22. 5. 15 Chateau Couthove	During afternoon 84th Inf Bde moved up to Brandhoek relieving 83rd Bde who go into trenches tonight under Cavalry Corps. The RA 28 Div came under our orders at 6am today at which hour GOC 28 Div assumed command of the line held by 85th Bde – we still labour under the difficulty of getting strangers out of our area – we find our RN Div Section (Kites) in Q 5 b 6 who have to be billetted by us.	
12 noon 22. 5. 15 "	Casualties up to 12 noon Capt Brigham 5/R Lancs K. 4 OR W.	
	Scale of Ammn expended: altered for 6" How to read Lyddite 3 Shrapnel Nil	
	QMG Supplies States still going into question of situation & treatment of tents & bivouacs they want bivouacs used in forward area, tents behind them & so on – not easy to arrange – as dug outs are the only safe things forward.	
12 " 22. 5. 15 "	Rounds fired up to 12 noon have been 18 pr. 51 for 48 guns, 4.5" How Nil – 13 pr AA 32 – 15 pr BLC 25 for 12 guns, Belgians 41 for 12 guns	
	Weather fine & warm	A[illegible]

1247 W 3299 200,000 (E) 8/14 J.B.C. & A. Forms/C. 2118/11.

Instructions regarding War Diaries and Intelligence Summaries are contained in F. S. Regs., Part II. and the Staff Manual respectively. Title pages will be prepared in manuscript.

WAR DIARY
or
INTELLIGENCE SUMMARY
(Erase heading not required.)

Army Form C. 2118.

Hour, Date, Place	Summary of Events and Information	Remarks and references to Appendices
— 2B.5.15 Chateau Couthove	5' Corps notifies that a weekly running a/c can be kept for Canteen closing 12 noon each Sunday.	
1.45pm " "	31 men who had been left at WINNIZEELE brought back and linked with 84th Inf Bde	
5pm " "	Following reinforcements arrive 15 Offrs 337 OR.	
6pm " "	As regards Sprayers for Cleaning Trenches of Anti Asphyxiating Gas we ~~had on~~ handed over to Cavalry on 13th May 57 – They have given back 16. 5' Corps asked for more	
— 2B.5.15 "	5' Corps orders reserve supply of Antigas mixture to be kept ~~and~~ under arrangements of SSO & DADOS – 28' Div Scheme as follows – Respirators are issued thro' DADOS now – To Sanitary Sec. at Place Berthen Pop? who dip them & transfer to 85 the adv Dressing Station at YPRES – we had about 8000 Reserve at 5pm on 24/5. Anti Gas mixture supplied by S.S.O. and issued to Place Berthen who mixes it & in Petrol tins sends it to the adv Dressing Station whence some of it goes to Bde Hd Qrs – 500 Res respirators are to be issued by DADOS to each Inf Bn as well & ADMS is making & keeping a reserve at Place Berthen	

Instructions regarding War Diaries and Intelligence Summaries are contained in F. S. Regs., Part II. and the Staff Manual respectively. Title pages will be prepared in manuscript.

WAR DIARY
or
INTELLIGENCE SUMMARY
(Erase heading not required.)

Army Form C. 2118.

Hour, Date, Place	Summary of Events and Information	Remarks and references to Appendices
23.5.15 Chateau Coutliano	At 10 am [illegible] estimates we were issued with brown bivouac shelters in 2 lots which were like a sort of [illegible] Store — we lost 270 when S Jean was shelled, were given 240 more and to try to keep check of them with the constant chopping and changing this is almost impossible. 100 tents have been given us.	
	Rounds expended to 12 noon	
	5B 18 h. for 48 guns 26 - 4.5" for 12 guns. ed.	
	Casualties Offrs nil OR K 13 . W 67	
" "	M.M.G Coy moved from Hergeele to NE Pop^e	
" "	Instructions issued during day for 1st line T & S ^ 83 & 85" Bde to sort themselves as laid down and line cleanly in farm G 4 a C 84 Bde 1st line to move to their billets	
23.5.15 "	Weather V fine & warm	[illegible]
1 am 24.5.15 "	Enemy commenced to gas our trenches.	
3.30 am 24.5.15 "	" use gas shells followed by attack	
5.55 am " " "	85 Bde asks for ambulance to remove gassed cases when taken	

1247 W 3299 200,000 (E) 8/14 J.B.C. & A. Forms/C. 2118/11.

Instructions regarding War Diaries and Intelligence Summaries are contained in F. S. Regs., Part II. and the Staff Manual respectively. Title pages will be prepared in manuscript.

WAR DIARY
or
INTELLIGENCE SUMMARY

(Erase heading not required.)

Army Form C. 2118.

Hour, Date, Place			Summary of Events and Information	Remarks and references to Appendices
6.30 am	26.5.15	Chateau [illegible]	Heavy Arty firing continues – 4th Div ask for 13 pr AA Ammn 200 rounds Sent from RHA Am Col by arr CRA.	
6.54 am	26.5.15	"	In anticipation of orders 84th Bde ask for more respirators (as they reported 5000 in possession they should have been complete	
7.30 am	"	"	RA ask for issue of 4.5" & 15 Pr Ammn to be reopened at Park – 5th Corps asked – Park report had no 4.5" – 2nd Army Q invoked. as RA informed.	
9.15 am	"	"	In anticipation of requirements 5th Corps asked for more Sprayers.	
10.15 am	"	"	ADMS & DADMS collect 1000 Respirators in motor move towards YPRES issue to form. units requiring them. depositing balance in Asylum YPRES	
12.36 pm	"	"	4th Div ask for a further 200 Rnds A.A.	
2 pm	"	"	ADMS commences enquiry into gas from Patients arriving at Asylum YPRES and at 85th Fd Am.	
2.5 pm	"	"	84th Bde call for Pres meat ration as they are moving up – This was obtained from Railhead – on arrival 84th Bde said they preferred fresh meat cooked – Such are the trials of 'Q'.	

Instructions regarding War Diaries and Intelligence Summaries are contained in F. S. Regs., Part II. and the Staff Manual respectively. Title pages will be prepared in manuscript.

WAR DIARY
or
INTELLIGENCE SUMMARY
(Erase heading not required.)

Army Form C. 2118.

Hour, Date, Place		Summary of Events and Information	Remarks and references to Appendices
2 pm	26.5.15 Chateau Couthove	~~Further~~ efforts made to obtain Sprayers from 5th Corps & 2 Army	
—	26.5.15 "	Casualties up to 12 noon given to 6 · OR K 5 W 62 M 1	
2.15	" "	Heavy Casualties expected in 2/Buffs & 3/R Fus.	
—	" "	We are getting short of Copper Sprays for 18 prs — 6 more Gas guns today 2nd Army tries 2nd Corps no result so far	
3 pm	" "	Counter attack of 84th Bde and 80th Bde Commences. Rounds expended to 12 noon. 18 Pr 5979; 48 guns — 4.5" 758 for 12 guns — Q 1912 for 12 guns — Belgian 1900 for 12 guns — 13 pr AA 1380.	
—	" "	Weather v fine & warm —	[signature]
—	25.5.15 Chateau Couthove	The Counter attack progressed for a bit but ~~but~~ did not get far — after which matters settled down — In going out to the action on 26th the 84th Bde lost in Transport 4 horses & GW. 1 missing. 1 man killed 1 missing — 1 vehicle broken —	

1247 W 3299 200,000 (E) 8/14 J.B.C. & A. Forms/C. 2118/11.

Instructions regarding War Diaries and Intelligence Summaries are contained in F. S. Regs., Part II. and the Staff Manual respectively. Title pages will be prepared in manuscript.

WAR DIARY
or
INTELLIGENCE SUMMARY
(Erase heading not required.)

Army Form C. 2118.

Hour, Date, Place			Summary of Events and Information	Remarks and references to Appendices
3 pm	26.5.15	Chateau Coutliere	14 LD horses arrived.	
5.45 pm	"		5th Corps wire saying that men of 85 Bde state they have never seen sprayers in their front line trenches and call for report – Report of 85 negatives completely this statement gives numbers in front trench of each unit & states they proved most useful.	
	"	"	Rounds expended to [illegible] 18 pr 4558 for 48 pr 4.5" – 905 for 12 guns – Belgians 2570 for 12 guns – 13 pr ~~[illegible]~~ 1486 for 12 guns	
–	"	"	Following reinforcements arrived 6 off. 350 OR	
"	"	"	Boes in trenches are clamouring for water carrying receptacles – The point being that water carts go up a certain distance ~~after which~~ to a point where carrying parties meet them and it is up from the carts that receptacles are required – Petrol tins are the best but if we use them then it means shortage of these tins at the base – vermorel sprayers are short – 5th Corps has not yet sent us any but instead asks us tonight if we want any more in addition or replacement	
			~~Present fighting Strength of Division – Infantry 292 offs.~~	
			Estimated Casualties 2/N. Mid. Fus 10 offs – 350 OR; 1/Suff. 8 – 300; 2/Ches 9 – 300; 1/Welsh 12 – 600 } 39 – 1550	

1247 W 3299 200,000 (E) 8/14 J.B.C. & A. Forms/C. 2118/11.

Instructions regarding War Diaries and Intelligence Summaries are contained in F. S. Regs., Part II. and the Staff Manual respectively. Title pages will be prepared in manuscript.

WAR DIARY
or
INTELLIGENCE SUMMARY.
(Erase heading not required.)

Army Form C. 2118.

Hour, Date, Place	Summary of Events and Information	Remarks and references to Appendices
— 25·5·15 Chateau Couthove	During the past 36 hours fighting and owing to gas Stragglers have been numerous – practically they are East of YPRES and indeed some W of it have been passed some more some less – They all say they are suffering – and discrimination is difficult – we now put police posts on all roads leading out to W – S & N of YPRES – Collect Stragglers into them to a rendezvous and move them back in Trucks to 1st Line Transport –	
— " " "	Estimated Cas 85th Bde. 2/Buffs 4 Off – 340 OR. 3/R Fus 1 – 500 (CO); 2/E Surr – 250; 3/Mx – 200; 8/Mx – 150 (adj K.) — 54 · 1440 OR	
10 pm " " "	4th Div asked to send 2 Men to join 28 Div on 27th –	
— " " "	Weather v fine & hot. Guns out of action on 24th were 14 – chiefly firing at Strips –	Annex —
10.40 am 26 " "	area WATOU – HOUTKERQUE – HERZEELE – WINNIZEELE given for when 28 Div becomes Army Reserve –	
12.15 pm 26 " "	8th Bde who have been supporting us report no Vermorel Sprayers & require 64 – 5th Corps informed	

Instructions regarding War Diaries and Intelligence Summaries are contained in F. S. Regs., Part II. and the Staff Manual respectively. Title pages will be prepared in manuscript.

WAR DIARY
or
INTELLIGENCE SUMMARY.
(Erase heading not required.)

Army Form C. 2118.

Hour, Date, Place			Summary of Events and Information	Remarks and references to Appendices
3.30pm	26.5.15	Chateau [illegible]	Re apply for Sprayers.	
—	26.5.15	"	During morning administrative staff inspect Govt drinking pond in H1a and take steps to keep it pure – Sanitary Section post established	
4.40pm	"	"	83 Bde apply for Sprayers.	
5pm	"	"	Specialist Squad of respirator fixers instruct 84th Bde –	
—	"	"	Rounds expended to 12 noon 18pr 561 – 4.5" 80 rds	
8.30am	"	"	Estimated Strength of Division Infantry 220 offrs. 7625 OR	
—	"	"	Casualties to 12 noon OR K 20. W 65. M 22.	
—	"	"	Genl Pereira 85th Bde wounded.	
11pm	"	"	Message received that Adv Dress Station were unable to supply 8th Bde with 1400 Respirators as arranged during day – Lorry despatched to collect them and take them up to Bienfaisance – which was done — Weather v Fine. v Hot.	[illegible]

(73989) W4141—463. 400,000. 9/14. H.&J.Ltd. Forms/C. 2118/10.

Instructions regarding War Diaries and Intelligence Summaries are contained in F. S. Regs., Part II. and the Staff Manual respectively. Title pages will be prepared in manuscript.

WAR DIARY
or
INTELLIGENCE SUMMARY.
(Erase heading not required.)

Army Form C. 2118.

Hour, Date, Place	Summary of Events and Information	Remarks and references to Appendices
2am 27.5.15 Chateau Couthove	84 Bde comes out of trenches and billets W of Vlamertinghe + East of Poperinghe – Capt Leverill BM 85 Bde temporarily Comd 85th Bde with temporary rank of Lieut Col – as Lt Col Dudgeon coming up to Command temporarily.	
– 27.5.15 "	We are getting up a lot of respirators in waste Paper – when damp, waste paper adheres to respirators & prevents them being redamped. This fact reported to 5th Corps.	
3pm " " "	Following reinforcements arrived 9 Offrs – 637 OR. 2nd Mon from 4th Div joins 84th Bde and amalgamation of 1st 2nd 3rd Mons commenced under Major Bridge as none of the Bns have a Lieut Col:	
– " " "	Instructions received that we are to go into 2nd Army Reserve – no Tents or bivouacs to be taken W of Poperinghe –	
27.5.15 "	Casualties Offr. 1K – 1W – 1M : OR. K43. 271 W. M403. These include corrections of 21 Chest & 5 Fus to previous reports	
– " " –		
– 27.5.15 –	Weather dull & cold.	a.a.m.c.H.
– 27.5.15 –	Col R.H. Hare RA DSO assumed duties of GSO(1) vice Lt Col Lord Loch to 6th Corps	

Instructions regarding War Diaries and Intelligence Summaries are contained in F. S. Regs., Part II. and the Staff Manual respectively. Title pages will be prepared in manuscript.

WAR DIARY
or
INTELLIGENCE SUMMARY.
(Erase heading not required.)

Army Form C. 2118.

Hour	Date	Place	Summary of Events and Information	Remarks and references to Appendices
11 am.	28.5.15	Chateau Coutbove	84th Inf Bde moves to HERZEELE area.	
3 pm	28.5.15	"	We have been notified of the issue of some new 'Gas Bombs' before receiving any we have been asked to Return them ~~to railhead~~.	
—	"	"	Arrangements made by DADMG for a small store of fresh Stores in the reserve ~~rest~~ area so that if Bdes are suddenly flung into the line they will not go forward in the destitute condition Bdes have always come out.	
	28.5.15	"	Casualties 1 officer gassed OR 1K. 7W. 1 gassed.	
	"	"	Reinforcements 4 off. 409 OR.	
—	"	"	Weather dull & Cold —	[illegible signature] —
9.30 am	29.5.15	"	Instructions received that 50% blankets may be retained while in Army Reserve —	
—			Approximately 2300 Pres Rations returned by 9th Bde from Potijze to S.S.O. 1.5. 1 days ration —	
—	29.5.15	"	Every morning units and Transport of 6th Div began [illegible] in the area E of Poperinghe and W of YPRES which is now becoming v. crowded.	

(73989) W4141–463. 400,000. 9/14. H.&J.Ltd. Forms/C. 2118/10.

Instructions regarding War Diaries and Intelligence Summaries are contained in F. S. Regs., Part II. and the Staff Manual respectively. Title pages will be prepared in manuscript.

WAR DIARY
or
INTELLIGENCE SUMMARY.
(Erase heading not required.)

Army Form C. 2118.

Hour, Date, Place	Summary of Events and Information	Remarks and references to Appendices
— 29.5.15 Chateau Couthove	31st Fa Bde gradually withdrawn & replaced by 2nd Fa Bde	
7.25 pm " " "	5th Corps avers tents & shelters to be struck and handed into Cassel — Pointed out that these they are still occupied. MT Transport asked for & refused.	
9.30 pm " "	8th Bde asks for Hop Poles & Timber, directed on RE Park.	
	Lt Col Compton assumes Command of 85th Inf Bde on 29th vice Capt (Temp L Col) Deverill.	
4 pm " "	Inf Bdes warned to hold a reserve of respirators of 500.	
— 29.5.15 "	Reinforcements arrived 19 Offrs — 400 OR.	
— " "	Casualties to 12 Noon 29/5. Total 33	
— 29.5.15 "	Weather dull & cold — Railhead to ARNEKE	Aam 4H —
— 30.5.15 "	18th Bde arrives early and is billetted S.E of Poperinghe	
— 30 "	There has been considerable trouble the last 2 days about Shortage of 4.5" Amtn probably the reflection of the Political trouble in England. Last night Shortage of 4.5" was in DAC was 132 rounds ~~govt all~~ 45 rounds ~~Short of~~ per gun	

Army Form C. 2118.

WAR DIARY
or
INTELLIGENCE SUMMARY.
(Erase heading not required.)

Instructions regarding War Diaries and Intelligence Summaries are contained in F. S. Regs., Part II. and the Staff Manual respectively. Title pages will be prepared in manuscript.

Hour, Date, Place	Summary of Events and Information	Remarks and references to Appendices
30 30.5.15 Chateau Couthove	Following units move during the day to rest area — (Watou) ~~38 3d Coy~~ ~~84, 86~~ & Cyclists, — Yeomen, M. Machine Gun —	
11.25 am " "	8th Bde asks for 500 Hales Grenades, 1000 Tonite. 500 hand — This is of course excessive and this fact was indicated to the Bde.	
2.25 pm " "	DADOS office moved to Railhead ARNEKE	
2.45 pm " "	85th Bde calls for Sprayers — ~~Action~~ 5th Corps asked.	
30.5.15	Shortage of Amtn in DAC at 12 mn 132 Rnds of 4.5" Shrap	
3. pm " "	Arrangements made for buses to convey 18th ~~#~~ Bde officers to trenches for reconnaissance —	
7.7 pm " "	GHQ anxious to send expert to examine 3 unexploded asphyxiating Shell lying near Polliffe Chateau — after investigation Shell earmarked	
" " "	amalgamation of 1, 2, 3 Monmouths taking place today	
— " "	Information received that 11 Northumbrian Bdy RFA will go to Northumbrian Division.	
— " "	as regards Respirators figures go to show that about 10,500 have been got through in about 5 days though	

(73989) W4141—463. 400,000. 9/14. H.&J.Ltd. Forms/C. 2118/10.

Army Form C. 2118.

Instructions regarding War Diaries and Intelligence Summaries are contained in F. S. Regs., Part II. and the Staff Manual respectively. Title pages will be prepared in manuscript.

WAR DIARY
or
INTELLIGENCE SUMMARY.
(Erase heading not required.)

Hour, Date, Place	Summary of Events and Information	Remarks and references to Appendices
	all units have been supplied with them before – reason is that they get many issued covered wrapped in wax paper which sticks to the Respirator after it has been damped and you can't re damp them, so men ~~throw~~ throw them away	
30.5.15 Chateau Coulliere	Weather Fine —	
	Casualties. Officers 1 W — OR 5K. 33 W —	
	~~Reinforcements.~~ —	Ram H.
10 am. 31.5.15 "	Div Amm Col 2 & Div marches to Winnizeele and with it in error marches How. Section which is recalled because we are leaving 8th How. Bde behind & according to principle its quota of Div A.C. remains too – This section ordered back.	
12.0 pm ~~Midnight~~ 31.5.15 "	As 27th Bde has come into area – Arranged that 18th Inf Bde going into Trenches tonight in relief of 9th Bde in left Section draws S.A.A. from it.	
— " " " "	Order received to withdraw all smoke helmets fitted with mica windows and to refit them with ACETOID transparent windows.	
3.10 pm " " " "	5th Corps orders area immediately S of S. Jean to be cleared which was done during the day	

(73989) W4141—463. 400,000. 9/14. H.&J.Ltd. Forms/C. 2118/10.

Instructions regarding War Diaries and Intelligence Summaries are contained in F. S. Regs., Part II. and the Staff Manual respectively. Title pages will be prepared in manuscript.

WAR DIARY
or
INTELLIGENCE SUMMARY.
(Erase heading not required.)

Army Form C. 2118.

Hour, Date, Place	Summary of Events and Information	Remarks and references to Appendices
11 am 31.5.15 Chateau Couthove	85th Bde raises a cry against the method adopted by certain Bde regarding Sprayers which have been found most efficacious and considered trench stores. 9th Bde for instance brought 12 per unit with them and they are afraid that when they go to the trenches they may be let in for they are going to 2nd Corps area – & 5th Corps informed and asked to acquaint 2nd Corps which they do.	
10.45 pm " "	Specialists notify their arrival at Poperinghe 1.30 pm to examine the asphyxiating shell lying there – action taken	
11 pm " "	6th Div commence to arrive at Chateau Couthove	
1.23 pm " "	Shortage of Shrapnel Ammn 4.5" in D.A.C. reported as 212 Rounds	
— " " "	Considerable doubt arising as to what Corps we shall be under if any when we go to Army Reserve at midnight – we are being told several and it is constantly being changed on the telephone anyhow it is 5th or 6th –	

(73989) W4141—463. 400,000. 9/14. H.&J.Ltd. Forms/C. 2118/10.

Army Form C. 2118.

Instructions regarding War Diaries and Intelligence Summaries are contained in F.S. Regs., Part II. and the Staff Manual respectively. Title pages will be prepared in manuscript.

WAR DIARY
or
INTELLIGENCE SUMMARY.
(Erase heading not required.)

Hour, Date, Place	Summary of Events and Information	Remarks and references to Appendices
1.50pm 31.5.15 Chateau Couthove	All smoke helmets to be withdrawn and replaced by with Acetoid windows —	
4 pm " "	GOC inspects 85th Bde. 151st Bde raise [illegible] that they might be inspected as well	
— " "	Instructions received that 1/1 Northumbrian Field Coy are to leave us — and later that Anglesey RE will too.	
	Arty 48 Rnds 18 pr — 46 Belgian Arty & 5 Rnds 15 pr fired up to noon today	
10.55pm " "	No 3 Motor Machine Gun Batty transferred to 3rd Div when we pass to 6th Corps which we understand we do at midnight	
9.30pm " "	Belgian Arty transferred to 3rd Div.	
— " "	Handing over from 28th Div to 6th & 3rd Div gradually nearing completion — 3rd Div are working the medical arrangements & have taken over —	
— " " —	Casualties up to 12 noon OR K 2. W 45.	

Instructions regarding War Diaries and Intelligence Summaries are contained in F. S. Regs., Part II. and the Staff Manual respectively. Title pages will be prepared in manuscript.

WAR DIARY
or
INTELLIGENCE SUMMARY.
(Erase heading not required.)

Army Form C. 2118.

Hour, Date, Place			Summary of Events and Information	Remarks and references to Appendices
12 hrs	31.5.16	Chateau Couthove	Handing over to 6th Div completed — 28 Div Passes to 5th Corps & Army Reserve —	
			HQ 28 Div moves to WATOU	
			" RE also RA —	
"	"		During day 146th Fd Bde & 3rd Fd Bde move to WATOU & WINNIZEELE.	
"	"		Weather fine. 28 officers arrived.	[illegible] —
			1/6/15 [signature]	Maj
			D.A.Q.M.G.	28 Div

	K	W	M	K	W	M
May 2 —	1	3	2	86	215	395
May 3 —	1	10	–	21	113	—
" 4		5	–	7	34	12
	2	18	2	114	362	407
	K	W	M	K	W	M

War Diary administrative Staff 28 Div app I. May 1915

These figures do not include an estimate of 200 Casualties of the 2nd E. Kents on May 4, also estimate of 150 of the 3rd R. Fusiliers of the same date.

Killed. Lt. J. H. Brough 8th Middlesex
" Lt. C. H. G. Martin 3rd Monmouth Regt
Wounded 2nd Lt. F. J. Foy 2nd Kings Own
2nd Lt. Thompson 2nd E. Surrey
Lt R. F. M. Buller 8th M'sex
Lt. F. G. Pritchard } 2nd E. Yorks
Lt. R. Chrystall }
Lt. C. N. Crawford 3rd Monmouth.
2nd Lt. T. H. Williams }
2nd Lt. T. S. Bowen } 1st Welsh
Capt. E. L. Wilcox }
2nd Lt. E. McCawley }
Lt. R. C. Neil (R.A.M.C.) - 8th M'sex
Capt. L. Corbally. 65th Battery R.A.
Major Wilson. No 2 Siege Co R.A.R.E.
(Capt. R. Wallace, E. Yorks) 83rd Bde Hdqtrs
2nd Lt. C. Saer 5th Kings Own
(Capt. G. R. F. Leverson, North Lancashire) 84th Bde Hdqtrs
(Lt. T. S. Emery, the Buffs) 84th Bde Hdqtrs
(Lt Col. H. E. T. Kelly R.F.A.) 31st Bde Hdqtrs
Missing Maj A. C. Ruston }
Lt P. Mynton } 8th Middlesex

1496

Appendix 2
6.5.15
Administrative War Diary 28 Div

To A. A. & Q. M. G.
28th Division

All Units of this Division have received their supplies for consumption today.

Units East of YPRES composed as under are in possession of current days ration, Iron Ration, and two unauthorised days as a reserve.

		Strength MEN	HORSES
Divl Troops	3rd Bde R.F.A.	130	
	31st "	130	
	65th (How) Bty	60	
	38th Fld Co R.E.	150	11
	1st North'n R.E.	40	
	Motor Mach Gun Sec	68	
	6 Sec. AA Bde R.M.A.	53	
83rd Inf Bde	83rd Bde Headquarters	141	
	2 East Yorks	750	
	1st York & Lancs	1000	
	2nd K.O.R. Lancs	900	(900)
	3rd Monmouth	750	
	K.O.Y.L.I.	700	
84th Inf Bde	84th Bde Headquarters	88	
	1st Suffolks	averaged at 750	
	1st Welch		
	2nd Cheshires		
	12th C of London		
85th Inf Bde	No 2 Siege Co. R.A. R.E.	220	
	171 Coy. R.E.	30	

K Kearne
Major A.S.C.
S.S.O.
28th Division.

In the Field.
6.5.15.

Administrative War Diary
28 Div.
Appendix III
9 - 5 - 15

SECRET.

It is intended that all Units EAST of YPRES should be in possession of the following rations:-

Current days ration:

Iron Ration:

Two days Reserve Ration,

so that, in the event of transport being unable to get through, troops will be self contained for four days.

When reliefs by Brigades or Battalions are effected, the Unit relieved will hand over their two days reserve tothe relieving units.

In the event of additional units proceeding EAST of YPRES they will immediately notify their Brigade Supply Officers, so that arrangements may be made to issue two days reserve as speedily as possible. Similarly should the troops EAST of YPRES be reduced, Brigade Supply Officers will be notified; the reserve rations will then be reduced by the Supply Officer sending up no daily ration until the adjustment is effected.

Quartermasters or representatives of all Units EAST of YPRES will notify their Supply Officers each day by 6 a.m. that their unit has received the current day's ration, or not, as the case may be. This is most important.

R. HERVEY.,
Lieut Colonel,
A.A. & Q.M.G. 28th Division.

7/5/1915.

Sir
You asked for a copy for Diary

Administrative War Diary 7.8.1520
Appendix IV
May 1915

Y.A.129/5th Corps.

28th Division.,

The following Corps and Army Units are attached to Divisions as shown, for administration:-

Xl Heavy Brigade R.G.A.	27th Divn.
Xlll ditto.	4th do.
21st Heavy Battery (1 section) R.G.A...	4th do.
do. ditto. (1 section) do......	28th Divn.
108th/Heavy Battery R.G.A.....................	28th do.
1/1 N.Riding Heavy Battery R.G.A.......	4th do.
1/4 Northumbrian (How) Brigade R.F.A...	28th do.
2 Sects.No.12 Siege Howitzer Battery R.G.A.	do.do.
No.9 A.A. Section	4th.do.
Sub-section No.10 A.A.Section	27th.do.
No.20 A.A. Section	28th do.
"C" Anti-aircraft Battery R.M.A........	28th do.
No.22 Trench Howitzer Battery	4th do.
No.2 Bridging Train R.E................	4th do.
4th R.Monmouth Siege Co R.E............	28th do.
2nd R.Anglesey Siege Co R.E............	28th do.
Advanced Park Company Wilts Fortress R.E.	28th do.
No.2 Advanced Park Co.Cornwall Fortress	28th do.
171st Mining Company R.E...............	27th do.

(s) W.K.Legge., Major.,

7/5/15. D.A.A. & Q.M.G. 5th Corps.

Appendix V
Administrative War Diary – May 1915

List of Reserve Rations issued to Units of 28th Division.

UNIT		No	INTACT	LOST	REMARKS.
Divl Troops	3rd Bde R.F.A.	260	Yes		
	31st Bde R.F.A.	260	Yes		
	65 (How) Bty	120	Yes		
	38 Fld Co R.E.	300	Yes		
	1st Northn R.E.	80	Yes		
	Motor Machine Gun Sec	136	Yes		
	C Bty (A.A. Sec) R.M.A.	106	Yes		
	4th North Bde R.F.A.	200		Yes	Abandoned.
83rd Inf Bde	Bde Hd Qrs	282	Yes		
	1st Y. & Lancs	2000		Yes	Deposited in Battalion Hd Qrs, Building now in enemy's hands
	5th K.O.R.L.	1500		Yes	Dug out in which rations were stored, destroyed by shell fire.
	2 K.O.R.L.	1800		Yes	Deposited in farm off YPRES–ZONNEBEKE RD. Building burnt and rations destroyed.
	K.O.Y.L.I.	1400		Yes	Deposited in Battalion Hd Qrs. Building now in enemy's hands
	1/3 Monmouth	1500		Yes	Deposited in Battalion Hd Qrs. Building shelled, fired and razed to the ground
84th Inf Bde	Bde Hd Qrs	176	Yes		
	1st Suffolks	1300	Yes		
	Cheshire Rgt	1800	Yes*		* Part of Grocery Rations missing
	Welch Rgt	1550	Yes		
	12th City of London	1200			Uncertain.
	2nd North Fus.	1100	Yes		
85th Inf Bde	No 2 Siege Co. R.A.E.	320	Yes		

[illegible]
Major [illegible]
S.S.O.
28th Division

11/5/15

App. VII
Administrative War Diary
May 1915

Copy No.

28th DIVISIONAL ORDER No.1.

13th May 1915.

1. 28th Division, less R.A. and R.E. will move to-morrow as follows,-

(a) 83rd Inf.Bde group	83rd Inf Bde X 84th Fd Amb No.2 Coy.Div Train Sqn.Surrey Yeomy.	To. WINNIZEELE.
(b) 84th Inf Bde group.	84th Inf Bde. ⊗ ~~85th Fd Amb~~ No.3 Coy Div Train	To HERZEELE
(c) 85th Inf Bde group	85th Inf Bde X 86th Fd Amb No.4 Coy Div Train Div Cyclists Co.	To WATOU & HOUTKERQUE.

March table attached.

2. With a view to the prevention of blocking of Traffic, gaps will be left at convenient intervals in columns.

3. Supply Sections of Train will march under special instructions issued to O.C., Divisional Train.

4. Boundaries of billetting areas have been allotted to Staff Captains of Infantry Brigades. Billetting parties will report to Staff Captain as under:-

(a) 84th Field Ambulance No.2 Coy Divl Train Sqn Surrey Yeomanry	Under special instructions.
(b) ~~85th Field Ambulance~~ No.3 Coy.Divl Train	HERZEELE 10 a.m.
(c) 86th Field Ambulance No.4 Coy.Divl Train Divl Cyclists Coy	"MAIRIE" WATOU 11 a.m.

5. Divisional Headquarters will remain at CHATEAU COUTHOVE, near PROVEN.

X less 1/York & Lancs
⊗ less Welch, Cheshires 5th Fusiliers and Bde Hd Qrs
X less Buffs

R.HENVEY.,
Lieut Colonel.,
A.A. & Q.M.G. 28th Division.

Unit.	March Table Route.	Time of start.
Infantry of 83rd Brigade.	By Bus from POPERINGHE. Head of Bus Column will be at junction of Rue de Boeschepe, and Rue de l'Hopital.	8.30 a.m.
83rd Brigade 1st Line Transport, and Baggage Section Divisional Train.	Via HIPSHOEK, and WATOU.	To be clear of POPERINGHE by 8 a.m.
Infantry of 84th Brigade.	By Bus from POPERINGHE. Head of Bus Column will be at Road Junction in L.4.b. Sheet 47.	2 p.m.
84th Brigade 1st Line Transport, and Baggage Section Divisional Train.	ABEELE and WATOU.	3 p.m.
85th Infantry Brigade, and Baggage Section Divl Train.	POPERINGHE and HIPSHOEK.	Head to pass POPERINGHE at 10 a.m.

(2).

Unit.	March Table Route.	Time of start.
84th Field Ambulance.	ABEELE and STEENWOORDE.	10 a.m.
85th Field Ambulance	POPERINGHE, HIPSHOEK, HOUTHKERQUE	12 noon.
86th Field Ambulance.	ABEELE.	11 a.m.
Divisional Cyclists Co.	POPERINGHE.	9 a.m.
Surrey Yeomanry.	POPERINGHE, ABEELE, STEENVOORDE.	3 p.m.

Administrative war diary 28 Div
Appendix VII
20 · 5 · 15

28th DIVISION.

~~Casualties 24 hours ending 12 noon May 1915.~~

Casualties April 22 to May 13. 1915.

Unit.	Officers.			Other ranks.			Officers	O.R.	
	K.	W.	M.	K.	W.	M.			
83rd Infantry Brigade.									
2nd K.O.R.Lancs.	4	10	8	69	220	766	22	1055	
2nd E.Yorks.	4	20	2	92	456	67	26	615	
1st K.O.Y.L.I.	5	5	2	71	207	273	12	551	
1st York & Lancs.	5	12	1	67	365	301	18	733	83rd Bde
5th Kings Own R.Lancs.	3	18	-	48	228	22	21	298	Officers 117.
3rd Monmouths.	7	9	2	40	162	274	18	476	O.R. 3.728.
84th Infantry Brigade.									
2nd Northld Fus.	4	11	8	24	108	385	23	517	
1st Suffolks.	3	13	10	27	158	499	26	684	
2nd Cheshires.	-	11	8	31	165	449	19	645	
1st Welsh.	-	13	-	58	288	9	13	355	84th Bde
12th London.	-	13	7	42	276	122	20	440	Officers 129
1st Monmouths.	6	11	11	63	104	411	28	578	O.R. 3.219.
85th Infantry Brigade.									
2nd The Buffs.	5	10	5	76	348	379	20	803	
3rd R.Fusiliers.	8	15	1	122	377	95	24	594	
2nd E.Surrey Rgt.	7	11	-	174	392	158	18	724	85th Bde
3rd Middlesexs.	6	13	-	68	332	196	19	596	Officers 97
8th Middlesexs.	6	8	2	54	155	35	16	244	O.R. 2.961.
	73	203	67	1126	4341	4441	343	9908	

Officers 343. O.R. 9908.

Major General.,
Commanding 28th Division.

121/5871

28th Division

Head Quarters (A & Q) 28th Division

Vol VIII 1 – 30. 6. 15.

Original

Confidential.

War Diary

of

Administrative Staff 28th Division

from 1st June 1915 to 30th June 1915.

~~Duplicate~~ Original

Instructions regarding War Diaries and Intelligence Summaries are contained in F. S. Regs., Part II. and the Staff Manual respectively. Title pages will be prepared in manuscript.

WAR DIARY
or
INTELLIGENCE SUMMARY.
(Erase heading not required.)

Army Form C. 2118.

1

Hour, Date, Place	Summary of Events and Information	Remarks and references to Appendices
1.6.15 WATOU	Order received from 5th Corps that Stick Bombs are not to be used till further orders	
1.6.15 "	Considerable interest in Sprayers which are Trench Stores and should not be moved – we handed over 57 to our Corps & got back 16 – and 83rd Bde with one here. 5th Corps now insist that 85th must not take any away	
— 1.6.15 "	amalgamation of Mammalls R. practically completed. Surplus transport reported to 6th Corps for detail instructions	
12 noon " "	Arriving & drawing ~~report~~ visit HQ 2nd Army and ascertain that we are under 6th Corps, we were not certain as we being Army Reserve we gathered we might be under 2nd Army –	
2pm 1.6.15 "	Also visit Arneke and arrange with ~~the~~ RTO regarding disposal of parties of Reinforcements of men & horses who may arrive –	
7.15pm 1.6.15 "	14th Div asked if when 85th Bde moves into their area we may leave its Train Coy in its present Billets (1 mile S by E Poperinghe) & feed Bde from there.	
	All Division is now in Rest area except 85th Bde at Brandhoek about to be loaned to 3rd Div and 83 Bde still in trenches –	

Army Form C. 2118.

Instructions regarding War Diaries and Intelligence Summaries are contained in F. S. Regs., Part II. and the Staff Manual respectively. Title pages will be prepared in manuscript.

WAR DIARY
or
INTELLIGENCE SUMMARY.
(Erase heading not required.)

Hour, Date, Place	Summary of Events and Information	Remarks and references to Appendices
1.6.15 WATOU	To show supply work that is being completed with list of units fed & Refilling point attached	Appendix 1
1.6.15 WATOU	Casualties 17 OR. Weather v fine.	Allen Hurd
10.45 am 2.6.15 WATOU	Problem of Sprayers for 83rd Bde when they go to 14th Div. continues. 2nd Corps now wires that the 85th will only take over ½ the normal of number because 84th took over none which is very arr because 83rd Bde took over bits of trenches from 80th 84th & 85th so to speak in the middle of a Battery.	
2.6.15 "	6th Corps orders us to fill up all echelons of Gun Amm. Ammunition. — Yesterday we sent the How Sec of DAC to work with 6th Div DAC but they only kept 4 GS waggons — and thus we are of course now refilling the remainder which seems anomalous.	
2.6.15 "	We are opening baths at each of our centres WINNIZEELE, WATOU, HERZEELE – HOUTKERQUE but keeping on our old depot for baths at the Place Berthen Poperinghe.	

3

Army Form C. 2118.

Instructions regarding War Diaries and Intelligence Summaries are contained in F. S. Regs., Part II. and the Staff Manual respectively. Title pages will be prepared in manuscript.

WAR DIARY
or
INTELLIGENCE SUMMARY.
(Erase heading not required.)

Hour, Date, Place	Summary of Events and Information	Remarks and references to Appendices
— 2.6.15 WATOU	Reports having been received that there are a number of 28 Div Stragglers lying up steps taken to find out numbers – only 2 can be traced Ouderdom way.	
3.30pm 2.6.15 "	Orders issued for Ceremonial parades. Terms under arrangements of Brigadiers & units on the occasion of HM the King's Birthday	
— 2.6.15 "	much detail work administratively but no big measures in hand Casualties Weather v fine & warm.	
— 2.6.15 "		
9am 3.6.15 "	The Problem of attachments is clearing up – 6th Div acknowledge 37 Batty – 65 Batty (8 How Bde) – Monmouth R?.	
— 3.6.15 "	The day was largely occupied in ensuring that 85th Bde proceeding into trenches tonight near Vierstraat was ~~completely~~ arranged for in SAA supply – medical arrangements – Sprayers – anti asphyxiation mixture – & food. ~~Regarding~~ 85 ~~This~~ Bde was going to tender messes of 14th Div a new Kitchener Army Division just arrived who need not	RAMH.

4

Army Form C. 2118.

Instructions regarding War Diaries and Intelligence Summaries are contained in F. S. Regs., Part II. and the Staff Manual respectively. Title pages will be prepared in manuscript.

WAR DIARY
or
INTELLIGENCE SUMMARY.
(Erase heading not required.)

Hour, Date, Place	Summary of Events and Information	Remarks and references to Appendices
	answer wires - as regards Ambs, eventually arranged with 14: Div that a Bde Am Col of 14 Div Supplies SAA - we continue to feed Moving train Coy into 2: Corps area. This necessitated a visit to 14 Div HQ at Westoutre when it was found that they were not a working Div but a Div under instruction - They had made no medical arrangements which necessitated an ADMS going down to them to organise it - They refused to supply anti asphyxiating mixture which necessitated an arranging to send down same with supplies tomorrow. Divisions new to this country do require watching - Somehow in spite of all training Staffs are not au fait and that was an own experience.	
3.6.15 WATOU	28: Div Transferred to 2: Corps.	
3.6.15 —	Casualties. OR 25 Kow.	
3.6.15 —	83 Bde was relieved by 9: Bde - Came out to Ouderdom reached full afternoon & marched to WINNIZEELE - Straggling bad - but a tiring and dusty march -	
3.6.15 —	85: Bde to 14: Div Trenches weather dull - fine	Aam[illegible] -

5

Army Form C. 2118.

Instructions regarding War Diaries and Intelligence Summaries are contained in F. S. Regs., Part II. and the Staff Manual respectively. Title pages will be prepared in manuscript.

WAR DIARY
or
INTELLIGENCE SUMMARY.

(Erase heading not required.)

Hour, Date, Place	Summary of Events and Information	Remarks and references to Appendices
9 am ~~4~~5. 6. 15 WATOU	2nd Corps asks if we wish ~~them~~ 14th Div to feed 85th Bde and asks position of Supply Col & Ammn Park – we tell them we are feeding 85th –	
" " "	6th Div is pressing us ~~for~~ to hand over Lorries from Supply Col to feed the attached units we have ~~sent to~~ transferred – but we received no Lorries for the Supply Column moreover the odd part of it all is that we dont control the Supply Col – However we do not hand over Lorries needless to state.	
" " "	Represented to Second Corps ~~Army Q~~ that the supply of Smoke Helmets is coming in very slowly – 2nd Corps promise to expedite	
" " "	AA&QMG and DAAQMG paid an administrative visit to 85th Bde at DICKEBUSH because we had scruples that they might be starved in the matter of bombs and other Trench Stores and they were being so apparently eventually they found some Sandbags and wire – They collected some grenades – we sent them 240 Very lights ~~and~~ 6 Sprayers & 2 Syringes. by Motor Car	

(73989) W4141–463. 400,000. 9/14. H.&J.Ltd. Forms/C. 2118/10.

Army Form C. 2118.

6

Instructions regarding War Diaries and Intelligence Summaries are contained in F. S. Regs., Part II. and the Staff Manual respectively. Title pages will be prepared in manuscript.

WAR DIARY
or
INTELLIGENCE SUMMARY.
(Erase heading not required.)

Hour, Date, Place	Summary of Events and Information	Remarks and references to Appendices
— 4/5 . 6 . 15 WATOU	Following Reinforcements arrived 3 off 1362 OR. and detrained at Poperinghe. Casualties 2 OR. K in 85 Bde. Weather fine	[illegible]
12.20 pm 5 6 . 15 "	Instruction received appointing Major McHardy [illegible] the AA & QMG 9th Div and to be succeeded by Major Hope R.F.A.	
	Above engaged in small outbreak of Enteric 146th Bde R.F.A. believed to have been caused by a 'Carrier'	
5.53 pm 5 6 . 15 "	A historic message received from 14th Div states it is reported that some of 28 Div viz Mac, E. Surreys & ASC have encroached on 14th Div billet area – This is specially comic because the units consist of 85th Bde & Supply Sections which are holding part of 14th Div line under 14th Div orders & constitute for the moment a part of their Division	

(73989) W4141—463. 400,000. 9/14. H.&J.Ltd. Forms/C. 2118/10.

Instructions regarding War Diaries and Intelligence Summaries are contained in F. S. Regs., Part II. and the Staff Manual respectively. Title pages will be prepared in manuscript.

WAR DIARY
or
INTELLIGENCE SUMMARY.
(Erase heading not required.)

Army Form C. 2118.

7

Hour, Date, Place	Summary of Events and Information	Remarks and references to Appendices
5. 6. 15 WATOU	Casualties ending 12 noon 5th OR 2K 6W Weather fine.	AleMcH
6. 6. 15. WATOU.	Major J. W. HOPE R.F.A took over duties of DAQMG from Major McHardy. Casualties ending 12 noon 6th Lieut. H. L. KIRBY 3/Royal Fusilrs. wounded. OR 2K 2W. Reinforcements arrived 28 Offrs 229 OR. Weather fine	JWH.
7. 6. 15 WATOU	Casualties other ranks O.R. W. 4 M.W. 1 Weather fine	JJH.
8. 6. 15. WATOU	AA & QMG attended conference at 5th Corps H.Q. to arrange demonstration to show effectiveness of respirators and helmets Sent to THIENNES 20 miles for 28 remounts Drafts 17 Offrs O.R. 37 Casualties Off. wounded 2 O.R. K 1 W. 18 85th Bde rejoined Division and billetted in HOUTKERQUE area leading Battalion got in about 8.30 p.m.	JJH.
8 Jun	Weather hot, thunderstorm.	

(73989) W4141—463. 400,000. 9/14. H.&J.Ltd. Forms/C. 2118/10.

8

Army Form C. 2118.

Instructions regarding War Diaries and Intelligence Summaries are contained in F. S. Regs., Part II. and the Staff Manual respectively. Title pages will be prepared in manuscript.

WAR DIARY
or
INTELLIGENCE SUMMARY.
(Erase heading not required.)

Hour, Date, Place	Summary of Events and Information	Remarks and references to Appendices
9. 6.15. WATOU	Demonstration at BRANDHOEK to show efficacy of masks and respirators against gas	[illegible]
	95 remounts arrived GODEWAERSVELDE late at night	
10.6.15 WATOU	Remounts detrained and issued at WATOU. Quite a good lot	
	Reinforcements 1 officer 101 men arrived GODEWAERSVELDE	
	Brig General PEREIRA rejoined from hospital	
	Orders to keep 25 per cent of blankets received	
	84th Bde ordered to move to 14th Division area. 14th Division allot. billets to units without consulting Bde or Division	[illegible]
~~1.6.15. WATOU.~~	Bde Major 84th Bde goes sick. Capt. MILLER takes over his duties and Lt COLEMAN assumes duties of ADC temporarily	
11. 6.15. WATOU	Capt A.G.G. takes over duties of Staff Capt 84th Bde temporarily as Capt LEVERSON is sick	
	Capt R.A. CRAUFORD Royal Scots Fusiliers appointed Bde Major 84th Bde	
	Surplus transport [illegible] sent off to advanced horse transport depot	
	5 officers 840 other ranks reinforcements arrived	

9

Army Form C. 2118.

Instructions regarding War Diaries and Intelligence Summaries are contained in F. S. Regs., Part II. and the Staff Manual respectively. Title pages will be prepared in manuscript.

WAR DIARY
or
INTELLIGENCE SUMMARY.
(Erase heading not required.)

Hour, Date, Place	Summary of Events and Information	Remarks and references to Appendices
WATOU 11.6.15.	1 man killed and 16 wounded in 1st K.O.Y.L.I. by bomb explosion. Court of Enquiry being held	8315.
WATOU 12.6.15.	3 men North. Fus. wounded by bomb explosion. Court of enquiry held. List of units fed and refilling points attached. Weather fine. 84th Inf Bde moved into trenches attached 14th Division. HQ Map square H.32, b.5.9 (Sheet 28).	Appendix II
WATOU. 13.6.15.	Casualties Killed O.R. one, wounded O.R. five. Weather fine. Orders received for move ~~HQ Div.~~ ~~HQ and~~ one Inf Brigade to ZEVENKOTEN as Corps reserve, Divl HQ. to WESTOUTRE GOC. 28th Divn to take over command area from GOC. 14th Divn on 14th June. DAA + QMG arranged billeting areas for above. ~~[illegible]~~ Difficulty in obtaining authorised quantity of smoke	

(73989) W4141—463. 400,000. 9/14. H.&J.Ltd. Forms/C. 2118/10.

Army Form C. 2118.

Instructions regarding War Diaries and Intelligence Summaries are contained in F. S. Regs., Part II. and the Staff Manual respectively. Title pages will be prepared in manuscript.

WAR DIARY
or
INTELLIGENCE SUMMARY.
(*Erase heading not required.*)

Hour, Date, Place	Summary of Events and Information	Remarks and references to Appendices
	helmets.	
WESTOUTRE. 14. 6. 15.	Weather fine. Reinforcements O, 3 OR, 7. Casualties OR, 11 wounded. 83rd Inf Bde marched via Poperinghe to area LA CLYTE as Corps Reserve. ~~at~~ 28th Divnl HQ to WESTOUTRE, Command of area taken over from 6 PM by GOC 28th Divn from GOC 14th Divn. Infantry mostly billeted in huts + shelters. Artillery ~~[illegible]~~ and 85th Inf Bde left in rest billets in HOUTKERQUE – HERZEELE area. S.A Ammn supply of 84th Inf Bde temporarily maintained by Ammn Columns of 14th Division.	
WESTOUTRE 15. 6. 15.	Weather fine. Reinforcements:- Artillery OR. 14. Casualties:- Killed OR one, wounded officers one Lieut. H. R. BARKWORTH, 2nd Northumberland Fusiliers, OR:-10. ~~[illegible]~~. Arranged for 48th F.A. Bde. Ammn Colm to temporarily supply 83rd and 84th Inf Bdes with S.A. Ammn if required.	

(73989) W4141—463. 400,000. 9/14. H.&J.Ltd. Forms/C. 2118/10.

Army Form C. 2118.

Instructions regarding War Diaries and Intelligence Summaries are contained in F. S. Regs., Part II. and the Staff Manual respectively. Title pages will be prepared in manuscript.

WAR DIARY
or
INTELLIGENCE SUMMARY.
(Erase heading not required.)

Hour, Date, Place	Summary of Events and Information	Remarks and references to Appendices
	Brigades asking for extra issue chloride of lime especially 84th Inf Bde whose trenches very insanitary. Wired to 2nd Corps for authority to draw extra.	
WESTOUTRE. 16.6.15.	Weather fine. Casualties Kld OR 2 Wdd OR 5. Draft of 50 OR arrived two hours before they were due at BAILLEUL station, and, owing to error on part of R.T.O, were sent back to HAZEBROUCK. DAA+QMG arranged for them to billeted at HAZEBROUCK and sent on to BAILLEUL tomorrow. Administrative visit to DICKEBUSCH, LA CLYTTE and RENINGHELST arranging watersupply and baths. ~~5th Div. at~~ Arranged with 5th Divn to use baths at RENINGHELST administered by them in exchange for baths at DICKEBUSCH administered by us on three days per week. Received ~~[illegible]~~ memorandum from HQ urging strictest economy gun ammunition.	

(73989) W4141—463. 400,000. 9/14. H.&J.Ltd. Forms/C. 2118/10.

12

Instructions regarding War Diaries and Intelligence Summaries are contained in F.S. Regs., Part II. and the Staff Manual respectively. Title pages will be prepared in manuscript.

WAR DIARY
or
INTELLIGENCE SUMMARY.

(Erase heading not required.)

Army Form C. 2118.

Hour, Date, Place	Summary of Events and Information	Remarks and references to Appendices
WESTOUTRE. 17.6.15.	Weather fine. Reinforcements 2 officers 50 OR. Casualties OR Kld 2 wdd 4. Arranged water supply LA CLYTTE to be improved. Orders received for 85th Bde. to move up into area tomorrow at disposal G.O.C. 28th Divnl Arty moved one section of each battery up during night relieving sections of 14th Divnl Arty.	Refilling Points and Units fed Appendix II.
WESTOUTRE. 18.6.15	Weather fine. Reinforcements 5 officers, 425 OR. Casualties Kld OR 8 wounded Offrs one Lieut J. COWAN RAMC. OR 35 CRA urged ~~[illegible]~~ improvement water supply for horses ~~[illegible]~~ in LA CLYTTE area. At present water for animals from small stream ROSENHILLBEEK, etc. and shallow wells. Arranged with CRE for wells to be deepened, pumps supplied, etc. Urgent demand by ~~[illegible]~~ Infantry for sandbags could not be met by R.E. park, and ~~[illegible]~~ demand was temporarily met by borrowing from 5th Divnl RE Park at DICKEBUSCH. R.E. Park also could not supply sufficient rifle grenades. DAQMG went to SAN SILVESTRE CAPELLE to draw 50 rifle grenades from 28th Divnl Park ~~[illegible]~~ there which he took	

13

Instructions regarding War Diaries and Intelligence Summaries are contained in F. S. Regs., Part II. and the Staff Manual respectively. Title pages will be prepared in manuscript.

WAR DIARY
or
INTELLIGENCE SUMMARY.
(Erase heading not required.)

Army Form C. 2118.

Hour, Date, Place	Summary of Events and Information	Remarks and references to Appendices
	to 84th Inf Bde HQ. himself at 10 P.M.	
WESTOUTRE. 19.6.15.	Weather cold but fine. Casualties ~~[illegible]~~ Kld OR 2 Wdd OR 8.	
	Orders received contracting area available for billetting this Division ~~[illegible]~~ giving up some area to 5th Div.	
	No 25 Trench Howitzer Battery arrived with no ammunition.	
WESTOUTRE. 20.6.15.	~~Re[illegible]~~ Weather fine. Reinforcements 11 Officers 75 OR. Casualties Kld OR 3 Wdd O. 2 Lieut. J. G. C. JONES 3rd Wilts and Lieut J. R. TROUP 38th Fd. Coy R.E. OR 5.	
	70 Remounts chiefly for Artillery arrived at BAILLEUL and taken over by Divl Ammn Coln.	
	Wire received from 2nd ~~[illegible]~~ Army that ~~1st Line~~ Cookers, watercarts + surplus transport of 8th Middlesex to be left behind for disposal later.	
	85th Inf Bde moved from ~~[illegible]~~ HOUTKERQUE to	

(73989) W4141—463. 400,000. 9/14. H.&J.Ltd. Forms/C. 2118/10.

14

Army Form C. 2118.

Instructions regarding War Diaries and Intelligence Summaries are contained in F. S. Regs., Part II. and the Staff Manual respectively. Title pages will be prepared in manuscript.

WAR DIARY
or
INTELLIGENCE SUMMARY.

(Erase heading not required.)

Hour, Date, Place	Summary of Events and Information	Remarks and references to Appendices
	Billets in LA CLYTTE area vacated by 83rd Inf Bde who moved into trenches + billets in KEMMEL area. (2 Battns in Trenches, 1 billeted in KEMMEL and 2 LOCRE) 8th Middlesex Regt left behind at HOUTKERQUE ordered out of ~~xxx xx~~ Division to amalgamate with 7th Middlesex	
WESTOUTRE. 21. 6. 15.	~~Fine~~ weather fine. Casualties OR Kld 7 (4 by trench howitzers) wdd OR 22 (12 by trench howitzers). Arranged for supply of Grenades and rockets for infantry to be by R.A. Ammn Coln instead of R.E. the Divl Ammn Coln to retain emergency reserve of 10 per cent.	
WESTOUTRE. 21. 6. 15.	weather fine. Reinforcements 3 officers 47 OR. Casualties Kld Os 1, Lieut C. J. COKER, 1/Welsh. OR. 2. ~~Wdd~~ wdd. OR 7. R. Naval Kite Balloon Section arrived. Orders received altering distribution Infantry tomorrow night. Administrative visit to 84th Bde re Trench Stores + disinfectants for trenches. Brig-Genl RYCROFT DA + QMG 2nd Army + Brig-Genl. Sheckleton ~~for~~ 2nd Corps paid	

15

Army Form C. 2118.

Instructions regarding War Diaries and Intelligence Summaries are contained in F. S. Regs., Part II. and the Staff Manual respectively. Title pages will be prepared in manuscript.

WAR DIARY
or
INTELLIGENCE SUMMARY.
(*Erase heading not required.*)

Hour, Date, Place	Summary of Events and Information	Remarks and references to Appendices
	administrative visit during afternoon.	
*WESTOUTRE. 23. 6. 15.	Weather fine with occasional showers in the evening. Casualties OR. Kld. 3 Wdd. 10. 83rd Bde moved one Battalion to Canada Huts + shifted Bde HQ from LA CLYTTE to a point N.W. of DICKEBUSCH, preparatory to putting one Battn in the trenches.	J.H.
WESTOUTRE. 24. 6. 15.	Weather fine. Casualties Kld. Officers one Captn G. A. ANSTEY 1st Devons (attd 2/Cheshires). Wdd. OR. 14. Steps taken to improve the comfort and sanitation of the various hutments in area, very little having been done by previous occupants. Measures undertaken to provide furniture for officers and offices, latrines, cookhouses etc. erected. Supply of Smokehelmets very slow.	J.H.
WESTOUTRE 25. 6. 15.	A good deal of rain + mist. Reinforcements 3 officers and 291 men; train very late arriving BAILLEUL.	

(73989) W4141—463. 400,000. 9/14. H.&J.Ltd. Forms/C. 2118/10.

16

Army Form C. 2118.

WAR DIARY
or
INTELLIGENCE SUMMARY.
(Erase heading not required.)

Instructions regarding War Diaries and Intelligence Summaries are contained in F. S. Regs., Part II. and the Staff Manual respectively. Title pages will be prepared in manuscript.

Hour, Date, Place	Summary of Events and Information	Remarks and references to Appendices
	Casualties Kld. OR 4 Wdd. 6.	
WESTOUTRE 26.6.15.	Weather fine. Reinforcements 10 Officers 61 OR. Casualties OR Kld 3 Wdd 14. Arranged with Administrative Staff 50th Division to obtain furniture from KEMMEL village for Officers' huts, the local gendarmerie collecting & handing over the furniture. ~~Offi~~ Captain Bursley ~~—~~ arrived ~~to~~ from HQ 2nd Army to enquire into system & give advice on use of Smoke Helmets.	
WESTOUTRE. 27.6.15.	Weather fine with a few showers. Casualties Kld OR 2 Wdd. Officers one, 2nd Lt T. PACKARD 1st Suffolks, OR 11. AA&QMG and DAQMG paid a visit to ARMENTIERES workshops to see latest patterns grenades & other stores being manufactured there.	
WESTOUTRE. 28.1.15.	Wth cloudy & showery. Reinforcements OR 13. Casualties Kld One Officer, Lieut. G.E LOCKET 3rd Bn Suffolks OR 1 Wdd. OR 17.	

(73989) W4141—463. 400,000. 9/14. H.&J.Ltd. Forms/C. 2118/10.

17

Instructions regarding War Diaries and Intelligence Summaries are contained in F. S. Regs., Part II. and the Staff Manual respectively. Title pages will be prepared in manuscript.

WAR DIARY
or
INTELLIGENCE SUMMARY.
(Erase heading not required.)

Army Form C. 2118.

Hour, Date, Place	Summary of Events and Information	Remarks and references to Appendices
WESTOUTRE. 29.6.15.	Weather cloudy with some rain. ~~Reinforcements 2 Officers 22 OR.~~ Casualties ~~Kld 2~~ Kld OR 2 Wdd Officers 2 Lieut. S. LONG-INNES 2/KO R. Lancs. and Lieut F.C. NAPER 2/K.O. R. Lancs. OR 17.	
WESTOUTRE. 30.6.15.	Weather cloudy with some rain. Reinforcements 2 Officers, 22 OR. Casualties Kld. OR 3. Wdd. Officers 2, Lieut. L.D. WHITEHEAD, Monmouths and Lieut T.H. MASON 3/Middlesex. OR 19. The ~~proposal for~~ arrangements for collection of furniture from empty houses in shelled areas fell through owing to difficulties with inhabitants. Received orders that 1200 Cavalry arriving tomorrow to dig trenches. Arranged to camp them near CANADA and ROSENHILL Huts, Tents being issued for this purpose by 2nd Corps.	J.W. Hope Major DAQMG ~~1st~~ 28th Div. 30/6/15

(73989) W4141—463. 400,000. 9/14. H.&J.Ltd. Forms/C. 2118/10.

Appendix I.
Administrative War Diary
28 Div June 1915

List of Refilling Points and Units
Refilled 2/6/1915.

App. I

Refilling Point.	Units refilled.
Cross roads K.1.a (sheet 27).	**Divisional Troops.** Divisional Headquarters. Royal Artillery ditto. Royal Engineers ditto. Divl Train ditto. 3rd Brigade, R.F.A. 31st ditto. 146th ditto. Surrey Yeomanry. Divl Cyclists Co. Signal Co. 38th Field Co R.E. H.Q.Co Divl Train. Sanitary Section. Military Police.
J.10.d. (sheet 27).	Divl Ammn Column.
L.17.D.	**83rd Infantry Brigade.** Brigade Headquarters. 1st K.O.Y.L.I. 2nd East Yorks. 1st York & Lancs. 2nd K.O.R.Lancs. 5th K.O.R.Lancs. 8th How Bde R.F.A. C Section Anti-Aircraft. 20th ditto. A.O.D. No.2 Coy Divl Train.
HERZEELE.	**84th Infantry Brigade.** Brigade Headquarters. 2nd Northumberland Fus. 2nd Cheshire Rgt. 1st Welsh Rgt. 1st Suffolk Rgt. Monmouth Regt. No.3 M.M.Gun Battery. No.3 Coy Divl Train. 84th.Field Ambulance. 85th Field Ambulance. 86th Field Ambulance.

(2).

Refilling Point.	Units Refilled.
L.17.D.	**85th Infantry Brigade.**
	Brigade Headquarters.
	2nd The Buffs.
	2nd East Surrey Rgt.
	3rd Middlesex Rgt.
	8th Middlesex Rgt.
	3rd Royal Fusiliers.
	Cornwall R.E.
	Anglesey R.E.
	Monmouth R.E.
	No.4 Coy Divl Train.
	Mobile Veterinary Section.
	Field Amb Workshop.

I

Appendix II
Administrative War Diary 28th Divn.
June 1915.

Refilling Points - 17th June 1915.

App. II

Divisional Troops. Map Square K 1 a. Sheet 27.	R.A. Headquarters. 3rd Brigade R.F.A. 31st Brigade R.F.A. 146th Brigade R.F.A. Hd.Qrs.Coy. Divl. Train. Sanitary Section. Postal Section. Mobile Veterinary Section.
Map Square J 24 c.	28th Divl. Ammunition Column.
83rd Brigade. Map Square M 11 c. Sheet 28.	Headquarters, 83rd Brigade. 2nd Bn. King's Own. 2nd Bn. East Yorks. 1st York & Lances. 1st Bn. K.O.Y.L.I. 5th Bn. King's Own. 2nd Coy. Divl. Train. 84th Field Ambulance. 38th Field Coy. R.E. A.O.D. Section. Surrey Yeomanry. Cyclist Corps.
84th Brigade. Map Square M 6 d. Sheet 28.	Headquarters, 84th Brigade. 2nd Bn. Northumberland Fusiliers. 2nd Cheshire Regt. 1st Welsh Regt. 1st Suffolk Regt. Composite Monmouths. 3rd Coy. Divl. Train. 2/1st North Midland Fd. Co. R.E. Divisional Headquarters. R.E. Headquarters. Signal Coy. R.E. Train Headquarters. Military Police. 85th Field Ambulance.
85th Brigade. HOUTKERQUE.	Headquarters, 85th Brigade. 2nd Bn. The Buffs. 2nd Bn. East Surreys. 3rd Bn. Middlesex Regt. 8th Bn. Middlesex Regt. 3rd Bn. Royal Fusiliers. 28th Fd. Ambulance Workshop. 4th Coy. Divl. Train. 86th Field Ambulance.

28th Division

181/6196

Head Quarters (A & Q), 28th Division

Vol VIII. 1 – 31.7.15.

Original

Confidential

War Diary.

of

Administrative Staff 28th Division

from 1st July 1915 to 31st July 1915.

Volume No 8

Instructions regarding War Diaries and Intelligence Summaries are contained in F. S. Regs., Part II. and the Staff Manual respectively. Title pages will be prepared in manuscript.

WAR DIARY
or
INTELLIGENCE SUMMARY.
(*Erase heading not required.*)

Army Form C. 2118.

1

Hour, Date, Place	Summary of Events and Information	Remarks and references to Appendices
WESTOUTRE 1.7.15.	Weather cloudy with slight rain occasionally. Casualties Wdd. O.R. 10. Staff of 4th & 5th Cavalry Brigades came up to arrange for camps. The 4th Cav. Bde camp pitched by the reserve Infantry near LA CLYTTE and that of 5th Cav Bde near CANADA Huts. These places were selected by the Staff of IInd Corps. The camp near CANADA Huts rather close to front line. Wired for colouring material to render these less conspicuous. Cavalry being fed by their own Supply Columns. The Cavalry themselves arrived during night, sending their horses back. The Infantry are demanding more periscopes and telescopic ~~rifles~~ sighted rifles. DADOS failed to get the former at ARMENTIERES owing to scarcity of mirror glass. He then went to DUNKIRK, purchased some to make up into periscopes. Telescopic sighted rifles very difficult to obtain.	
WESTOUTRE 2.7.15.	Weather fine. Reinforcements Officers 4 OR 511. Casualties Kld OR 5 Wdd Officers 1 Lieut E. H. BOX 1st Suffolks OR 21.	

Instructions regarding War Diaries and Intelligence Summaries are contained in F. S. Regs., Part II. and the Staff Manual respectively. Title pages will be prepared in manuscript.

WAR DIARY
or
INTELLIGENCE SUMMARY.
(Erase heading not required.)

Army Form C. 2118.

2

Hour, Date, Place	Summary of Events and Information	Remarks and references to Appendices
WESTOUTRE. 3.7.15.	Weather fine. Casualties Kld OR 3 Wdd Officers 3 Lieut. C.E.H. RECKITT and 2nd Lieut. D.D. ANDERSON 2nd/E. Yorks, and 2nd Lieut. T.J. NEWELL 3/Cheshires. OR 9. Some difficulty experienced in getting materials wood, waterproof canvas, etc. for temporary huts & shelters latrines etc. but some progress made. The chief difficulty as regards wood is the lack of Transport. Steps are now being taken to buy canvas for shelters from ~~Boulogne~~ Dunkirk & Paris, but sanction from higher authorities has first to be obtained, which takes time.	
WESTOUTRE. 4.7.15.	Weather sultry. Reinforcements 1 Officer 81 OR. Casualties Kld Officers 1 Lieut. G.H. HIGHFIELD 1/York & Lancs. OR 3, Wdd OR 16. Water supply difficulties, pipe leading through filterbed KEMMELBEEK stream near LA CLYTTE too small and water flows through so slowly that it takes about 1 hour to fill one watercart. Trying to get R.E. to put another pipe in	

(73989) W4141—463. 400,000. 9/14. H.&J.Ltd. Forms/C. 2118/10.

Instructions regarding War Diaries and Intelligence Summaries are contained in F. S. Regs., Part II. and the Staff Manual respectively. Title pages will be prepared in manuscript.

WAR DIARY
or
INTELLIGENCE SUMMARY.
(*Erase heading not required.*)

Army Form C. 2118.

3

Hour, Date, Place	Summary of Events and Information	Remarks and references to Appendices
	but all these watersupply questions have to be referred to 2nd Corps who are arranging for the work.	
WESTOUTRE. 5.7.15.	Weather fine. Casualties Kld OR 1 Wdd OR 21. 2nd Lieut. NEWELL 2nd Cheshires reported wounded on 3rd now died of wounds. The 1/6 Welsh Regt. arrived in the morning and bivouacked between CANADA and LA CLYTTE Huts. Difficulty in obtaining shelter for them overcome by taking tents + shelters from other units (including a Field Ambulance), by which means sufficient to shelter about 500 men was obtained.	
WESTOUTRE 6.7.15.	Weather fine, but some rain in evening. ~~Reinforcements~~ + Casualties Kld ~~Officers~~ OR 2 Wdd. Officers 1 Lieut A.J. HOPKINSON (S. at D.) OR 15. Remounts received 50. Some difficulty being experienced as regards watersupply; wells + streams drying up.	

Instructions regarding War Diaries and Intelligence Summaries are contained in F. S. Regs., Part II. and the Staff Manual respectively. Title pages will be prepared in manuscript.

WAR DIARY
or
INTELLIGENCE SUMMARY.
(Erase heading not required.)

Army Form C. 2118.

4

Hour, Date, Place	Summary of Events and Information	Remarks and references to Appendices
WESTOUTRE. 7.7.15.	Weather gusty with some heavy showers. Casualties Kld ~~Officers~~ OR 3 Wdd Officers 1 Lieut A.J. HOPKINSON 2/North Fus. previously reported wdd slightly now admitted to hospital. OR 12. Water supply difficulty still continues; arranging to have time tables to relieve congestion of watercarts. No Very's lights have been received for a week.	
WESTOUTRE. 8.7.15.	Weather stormy + rain. Reinforcements 1 Officer + 30 OR. Casualties Kld. OR 2 Wdd Officers 1 2nd Lieut W.D. BENTALL, 1st K.O.Y.L.I. OR. 20. Commenced preparations for moving second line units, Divl A.C., ~~[illegible]~~ Train, etc. further back so as to utilise depth of area to the full and relieve congestion in front.	
WESTOUTRE 9.7.15.	Weather stormy, with some rain. Reinforcements 10 Officers + 172 OR. Casualties Kld. OR 7 Wdd. OR 18. Supply of Grenades, Bombs, Very's lights very limited. DADMG visited Park to ascertain cause of delay, but no	

(73989) W4141—463. 400,000. 9/14. H.&J.Ltd. Forms/C. 2118/10.

Instructions regarding War Diaries and Intelligence Summaries are contained in F. S. Regs., Part II. and the Staff Manual respectively. Title pages will be prepared in manuscript.

WAR DIARY
or
INTELLIGENCE SUMMARY.
(Erase heading not required.)

Army Form C. 2118.

5

Hour, Date, Place	Summary of Events and Information	Remarks and references to Appendices
	explanation could be given as to why they are not arriving at Railhead.	
WESTOUTRE. 10. 7. 15.	Fine day. Reinforcements 24 machine gunners arrived. Casualties Kld. OR 2 Wdd. Officers 1 2nd Lt. J. ROSEIGH 2/Cheshires (accidentally) OR 21. 2/1 North Midland Fd Coy R.E. left Division and replaced by 2/1 Northumbrian Fd Coy R.E. Heavy fatigue of heavy draught horses and G.S. wagons required all day and night daily in connection with roadmaking and trench digging by Belgians under supervision of R.E. These details supplied by Divl Train and Divl Ammn Column.	
WESTOUTRE. 11. 7. 15.	Cold, stormy day. Casualties Kld. Officers 1, 2nd Lieut J. C WATMOUGH, 3rd Bn North Fus. OR 4. Wdd Officers 2 2nd Lieut J. WALTON and Lieut C. CRAIG, 3rd Bn North. Fus. (accidentally by bomb). OR. 27. Units refilled + refilling points, table attached	Appendix A.

(73989) W4141—463. 400,000. 9/14. H.&J.Ltd. Forms/C. 2118/10.

Instructions regarding War Diaries and Intelligence Summaries are contained in F. S. Regs., Part II. and the Staff Manual respectively. Title pages will be prepared in manuscript.

WAR DIARY
or
INTELLIGENCE SUMMARY.
(Erase heading not required.)

Army Form C. 2118.

6

Hour, Date, Place	Summary of Events and Information	Remarks and references to Appendices
WESTOUTRE 12.7.15.	~~Fi~~ Weather fine. Casualties Kld OR 1. Wdd OR 17. Making preparations for moving Divl Ammn Colm, Train & Bde Ammn Colms further west to make more room in front & utilise the depth of the area to the full.	
WESTOUTRE. 13.7.15.	~~Fine~~ Weather fine. Casualties Kld. Officers 1, 2nd Lieut. J. M. T. KINLOCH. R.E. OR. 7. Wdd. Officers 2. 2nd Lieut. R. G. MILLS, The Buffs, and 2 Lieut. F. L. CARTER 2nd E Surreys. OR 23. Preparations made for moving 85th & ~~[illegible]~~ 84th Inf Bdes to the right of the 83rd Inf Bde, the 9 Brigade to come in on the left in relief. Orders received for Capt. ACLAND-TROYTE appointed DAA & QMG. 7th Corps to proceed to GHQ. tomorrow to take up appointment.	
WESTOUTRE 14.7.15.	Weather cloudy and rain. Casualties Kld O. Wdd. Officers 1 2nd Lieut H. G. DICKENS, 2/E Yorks. OR 27. Arrangements completed for move of 84th & 85th	

Instructions regarding War Diaries and Intelligence Summaries are contained in F. S. Regs., Part II. and the Staff Manual respectively. Title pages will be prepared in manuscript.

WAR DIARY
or
INTELLIGENCE SUMMARY.
(Erase heading not required.)

Army Form C. 2118.

7

Hour, Date, Place	Summary of Events and Information	Remarks and references to Appendices
	Inf. Bdes into new area. Movement commenced during the night. 84th Bde move 1½ Battns to CANADA Huts, 3 Battns to area round WESTOUTRE, Bde HQ to LOCRE. 85th Bde move 1 Battn to LOCRE, 2 to ROZENHILL and 1 to neighbourhood LA CLYTTE. Some difficulty in obtaining shelter in new area owing to no definition of new boundaries, but difficulties overcome by judicious transfer of shelters, moving Battns into back area temporarily etc. ~~Units~~ Refilling points + units refilled, table attached	Appendix B
WESTOUTRE 15.7.15.	Weather fine. Reinforcements 1 Officer 120 OR. Casualties Kld OR 4 Wdd Offrs 3, 2nd Lieut. W. H. GREET 2/E Yorks, Lieut R. H. COWING, 5/K. O. R. Lancs, 2nd Lieut C. MEAD, 2/E. Surreys, OR. 34 Missing OR 9. Most of casualties due to explosion German mine. Movement into new positions continued. 84th Bde moved into trenches (2 battns), 1 Battn in KEMMEL Shelters. 85th Bde.	

Instructions regarding War Diaries and Intelligence Summaries are contained in F. S. Regs., Part II. and the Staff Manual respectively. Title pages will be prepared in manuscript.

WAR DIARY
or
INTELLIGENCE SUMMARY.
(Erase heading not required.)

Army Form C. 2118.

8

Hour, Date, Place	Summary of Events and Information	Remarks and references to Appendices
	2 Battns into back area near BERTHEN, 2 Battns to LOCRE.	
	New area defined, we lose LA CLYTTE, except that 83rd Bde HQ permitted to stay there.	
WESTOUTRE 16.7.15.	Weather raining. Casualties Kld OR 3. Wdd OR 5.	
	Movement into new positions continued. 85th moved 2 Battalions into trenches and 2 to DRANOUTRE.	
	Arranged to billet 2½ battalions 84th Bde. in LOCRE, and left room there for 1 Battn 83rd Bde from LA CLYTTE but at present 5th Corps do not require LA CLYTTE accommodation so 83rd Bde remaining there.	
WESTOUTRE 17.7.15.	Cold stormy weather with rain. Casualties Kld OR. 2 Wdd OR 8. One battalion of the 83rd Bde ordered to be attached to 85th Bde and to go into trenches on night 18th/19th. This caused great congestion in DRANOUTRE and all available shelters and tents were sent over to help them. The water supply at DRANOUTRE not very	

9

Army Form C. 2118.

Instructions regarding War Diaries and Intelligence Summaries are contained in F. S. Regs., Part II. and the Staff Manual respectively. Title pages will be prepared in manuscript.

WAR DIARY
or
INTELLIGENCE SUMMARY.
(Erase heading not required.)

Hour, Date, Place	Summary of Events and Information	Remarks and references to Appendices
	satisfactory; the C.R.E. urged to go into this with 2nd Corps and 50th Division.	
WESTOUTRE. 18.7.15	Weather fine. Casualties Kld OR 3 Wdd OR 16. 2nd Royal Irish attached to us for rations from today; they have been attached to 50th Division, resting in back area. The supply of grenades, Very's lights etc. getting a bit better. Casualties for six months ending today table attached	Appendix C.
WESTOUTRE. 19.7.15.	Weather fine. Casualties Kld OR 5. Wdd. Officers 2. Capt. J. A. JERVOIS 1/KOYLI. (slightly) 2nd Lt. H. S. COOLEY. RFA. OR. 32. Difficulties about water supply at DRANOUTRE and LOCRE, wells going dry. Sanitary conditions LOCRE, bad, town at LOCRE in a very dirty condition.	
WESTOUTRE 20.7.15.	Weather fine. Casualties Kld OR 3 Wdd Officers 1 2nd Lieut R. KING-SMITH 2/Cheshires (slight) OR 7. Orders issued dividing Divisional Areas into ~~Bri~~ 3 Brigade	

(73989) W4141—463. 400,000. 9/14. H.&J.Ltd. Forms/C. 2118/10.

Instructions regarding War Diaries and Intelligence Summaries are contained in F. S. Regs., Part II. and the Staff Manual respectively. Title pages will be prepared in manuscript.

WAR DIARY
or
INTELLIGENCE SUMMARY.
(Erase heading not required.)

Army Form C. 2118.

10

Hour, Date, Place	Summary of Events and Information	Remarks and references to Appendices
	Areas and a Back area ~~intended for~~ administered by O.C. Divl Ammn Colm. Sanitary Committees for LOCRE and DRANOUTRE to be appointed.	
	Orders received that Monmouths to be divided again 2nd/Monmouths to go to 4th Division.	Appendix D.
	Refilling points and units refilled, table attached	
WESTOUTRE 21.7.15.	Weather fine. Reinforcements 4 Officers and 360 OR. Casualties Kld OR 3 Wdd Officers 2 Lieut W.P. BRADLEY-WILLIAMS 1/KOYLI, and Lieut G.G.N. LODGE 2/C Surreys, OR 9. Completing scheme required by 2nd Army giving proposals for huts ~~etc.~~ & other accommodation required for winter. Area cut down by taking BOESCHEPE area away. 2nd/R. Irish Regt. left to join 4th Div. during night.	
WESTOUTRE 22.7.15.	Weather raining. Reinforcements OR 16. Casualties Kld. OR 4. Wdd. Officers 2 Lieut H.A. WILKINSON. Yorks L.I., 2nd Lieut W. S. WILLIAMS, 6/Welsh.	

(73989) W4141—463. 400,000. 9/14. H.&J.Ltd. Forms/C. 2118/10.

Army Form C. 2118.

Instructions regarding War Diaries and Intelligence Summaries are contained in F. S. Regs., Part II. and the Staff Manual respectively. Title pages will be prepared in manuscript.

WAR DIARY
or
INTELLIGENCE SUMMARY.

(Erase heading not required.)

Hour, Date, Place	Summary of Events and Information	Remarks and references to Appendices
	~~Wdd~~ OR. 5. 17th Division Troops arrived suddenly at LA CLYTTE and we were forced at very short notice to clear remaining battalion of 83rd Brigade out of the huts there, as well as the Sixth Field Ambce. Former accommodated in bivouack shelters near SCHERPENBERG, latter at WESTOUTRE.	
WESTOUTRE. 23.7.15.	Weather fine. ~~Reinforcements~~ Casualties Kld OR 3, Wdd OR 6. Received 800 (2-man) shelter tents from 2nd Corps Ordnance Stores. Supply of Grenades & Very's lights improving, but rifle grenades still very short. RA Hd Qrs shifted to chateau on LOCRE-BAILLEUL Road (M.28)	
WESTOUTRE 24.7.15	Weather fine. Reinforcements 4 Officers and 284 OR. Casualties Kld. Officers 1 Lieut K.R. FORDE, 2nd/Buffs ~~OR Wdd~~ OR 6 Wdd OR 17. 2/Monmouths, having been divorced from the amalgamated regiment entrained at GODESWAERVELDE ~~[illegible]~~ to join 4th Division.	

Instructions regarding War Diaries and Intelligence Summaries are contained in F. S. Regs., Part II. and the Staff Manual respectively. Title pages will be prepared in manuscript.

WAR DIARY
or
INTELLIGENCE SUMMARY.
(Erase heading not required.)

Army Form C. 2118.

12

Hour, Date, Place	Summary of Events and Information	Remarks and references to Appendices
WESTOUTRE. 25.7.15.	Weather fine. Casualties ~~Kld~~ Wdd OR 18. Received letter from 2nd Corps ~~[illegible]~~ directing steps to be taken to distribute Small Arm Ammn in proper proportion between various echelons, and reduce surplus without delay AAA Divl Ammn Coln now quite empty of S.A. Ammn. G.O.C. directs that certain quantity is to be kept in Trenches, etc. and Divl Ammn Colts remain practically empty.	
WESTOUTRE. 26.7.15.	Weather fine. Reinforcements 11 Officers, 101 OR. Casualties Kld OR. 4 Wdd. OR 20.	
WESTOUTRE. 27.7.15.	Weather fine. Casualties Kld OR 4 Wdd Offrs. 1 Lieut C. F. MARSH-ROBERTS, 33rd Trench How. Bty. OR 13. Great demand for Trench How Ammn. 200 Rds of 4 Pr Trench Mortar Ammn not fixed for issue; also demand for grenades which are reported not obtainable; 2nd Corps recommends asking Canadian Divn if they can supply.	

(73989) W4141—463. 400,000. 9/14. H.&J.Ltd. Forms/C. 2118/10.

Instructions regarding War Diaries and Intelligence Summaries are contained in F. S. Regs., Part II. and the Staff Manual respectively. Title pages will be prepared in manuscript.

WAR DIARY
or
INTELLIGENCE SUMMARY.
(Erase heading not required.)

Army Form C. 2118.

13

Hour, Date, Place	Summary of Events and Information	Remarks and references to Appendices
WESTOUTRE 28.7.15	Weather fine. Casualties Kld OR 4 Wdd Offrs 1 2nd Lieut H. R. WATERMAN 3/Middlesex, OR 30. Settled S.A. Ammn question, returning surplus 100,000 rounds to Railhead, consigned to ROUEN, and arranging for certain small quantities to be kept in Bde & Divl Ammn Colns, and average up in trenches of 350 rounds per rifle.	
WESTOUTRE. 29.7.15.	Weather fine. Casualties Kld OR 1. Wdd OR 18. Administrative visit to the trenches of 84th Brigade. Periscopes & grenades chief deficiencies noticed.	
WESTOUTRE. 30.7.15.	Weather fine. Reinforcements OR. 144. Casualties Kld OR 2 Wdd OR 19. Great demand for Rifle Grenades which are very scarce. A considerable amount of S.A. Ammn found & collected in rear	

(73989) W4141—463. 400,000. 9/14. H.&J.Ltd. Forms/C. 2118/10.

Instructions regarding War Diaries and Intelligence Summaries are contained in F. S. Regs., Part II. and the Staff Manual respectively. Title pages will be prepared in manuscript.

WAR DIARY
or
INTELLIGENCE SUMMARY.
(Erase heading not required.)

Army Form C. 2118.

14

Hour, Date, Place	Summary of Events and Information	Remarks and references to Appendices
	trenches, left behind by troops of Divisions which preceded us.	
WESTOUTRE. 31.7.15.	Weather fine. Casualties Kld OR 6 Wdd Officers 2, Lieut A.V. WHITEHEAD ~~of~~ 4th South Staffords ~~attached~~ and 2nd Lieut J.A. HART, both attached E Surreys OR 35. Good water supply found at Chateau DOUVE, requires pipe line laid down. Orders received cancelling move southwards & 83rd Bde to go back to LACLYTE, other bdes moving a little south again.	
	WESTOUTRE 31-7-15	J.H. [illegible] Major DAQMG

(73989) W4141—463. 400,000. 9/14. H.&J.Ltd. Forms/C. 2118/10.

3rd Middx

Report on Area

Brigade Order S/820

Tracing of sheet 28 S.W. $\frac{1}{20000}$ 19.7.15

(a) The majority of the houses in Squares 32 & 33 are occupied by R.F.A. There are guns distributed in all parts of this area & it is very unsuitable for billeting troops. There are fire & communication trenches dug also masses of barbed wire entanglements

N 32 a & b Area marked red on tracing is suitable for erection of huts. The farm houses adjacent are suitable & would accommodate

92

about 200 men The farm N 32 b 5.0 is already occupied by 3 Officers of the R.F.A.

N 33 a Red line indicates dug-outs occupied by R.F.A.

Farm N 33 a. 5.4, occupied by 20 men R.F.A

Area marked [cross-hatching] in squares N 33 and 34, T 3 and 4 is under observation by the enemy

Farm T 3 b 9.7 is occupied by Genl. Seeley's Mounted Brigade Bomb-throwing School

There's no area in T 4 a suitable for billeting troops or building huts

Houses & Farm in vicinity of road junction T3 b 3.4 will accommodate 200 men and are occupied by R.F.A.

Farm T3 b 4.7 will accommodate 180 men and is at present unoccupied

Farm N32 b 6.5 is occupied by R.F.A. Anti Aircraft Gun is here

Report on Area

East of a line running N & S thro' N31 and 32

Northern boundary DRANOUTRE — LINDENHOEK pavé road.

Southern The DOUVE brook

Reference to small figures on map

1 farm right section 116th Heavy Battery 38 men.

2 small cottage, with small toolhouse only empty. 5 by 7 yds.
5 inhabitants of cottage.

3 farm, formerly brigade HQ, RA, 60th Division, now vacant, but wd barely accommodate ½ Coy.

4 line of dugouts in disrepair.

4

5 dugouts of 149th Field Battery RFA

6. farm, in occupation of 149th Battery RFA

7. section 118th Battery RFA in farm.

10, 11, houses, shelled occasionally : some occupied by RFA officers.

12 small farm accomodation for 3 officers outhouses would hold 2 platoons, but are in an insanitary condition

13. Bus Farm, vacant now, but troops expected. formerly in occupation of Canadians

14 small estaminets

15 blacksmith's shop, which might hold ½ company

16 artillery officers' billets 75th Battery RFA

17. now vacant, but artillery officers have generally billeted here, :– not much accomodation for troops.

18 cottage only servant's quarters for RFA officers who stay at farm, South of the brook.

The best places for ~~new~~ new huts or shelters are lettered, though none are very suitable lest they should betray our artillery positions to hostile aircraft.

A. hedge in a valley. B. lines of tall poplars giving some cover from aircraft. C sheltered meadow. D. line of willows. E abandoned dug-outs.

85 Bde area ref sheet 28 $\frac{1}{40000}$.

Southern Boundary.

Point where Locre - Bailleul Rd crosses River Douve
M. 34 a 7.7 Eastwards along river Douve to
Wulverghem.

Northern Boundary.

M 34 a 7.7 to M 30 d 0.0 thence along road
to N 25 d. 20 thence due East along red
line.

Tracing to be taken from map 28 $\frac{1}{20.000}$.

Information required by 4 pm 19/7/15 at the latest

(a). Number of farms huts etc with description
of each type with accomodation available.

(b). Names & positions of any units occupying
Farms houses huts etc in area

(c) any sites suitable for erecting new huts.

O.C. Buffs will detail one ~~officer~~ or more officers to report on area from West boundary to line running N + S between squares N 31 . 32 + T 1 + 2.

O.C. Middlesex will detail one or more officers to report on the area E of this line to line running N + S thro' N34 a.b.

TRACING from map 28 $\frac{1}{20000}$

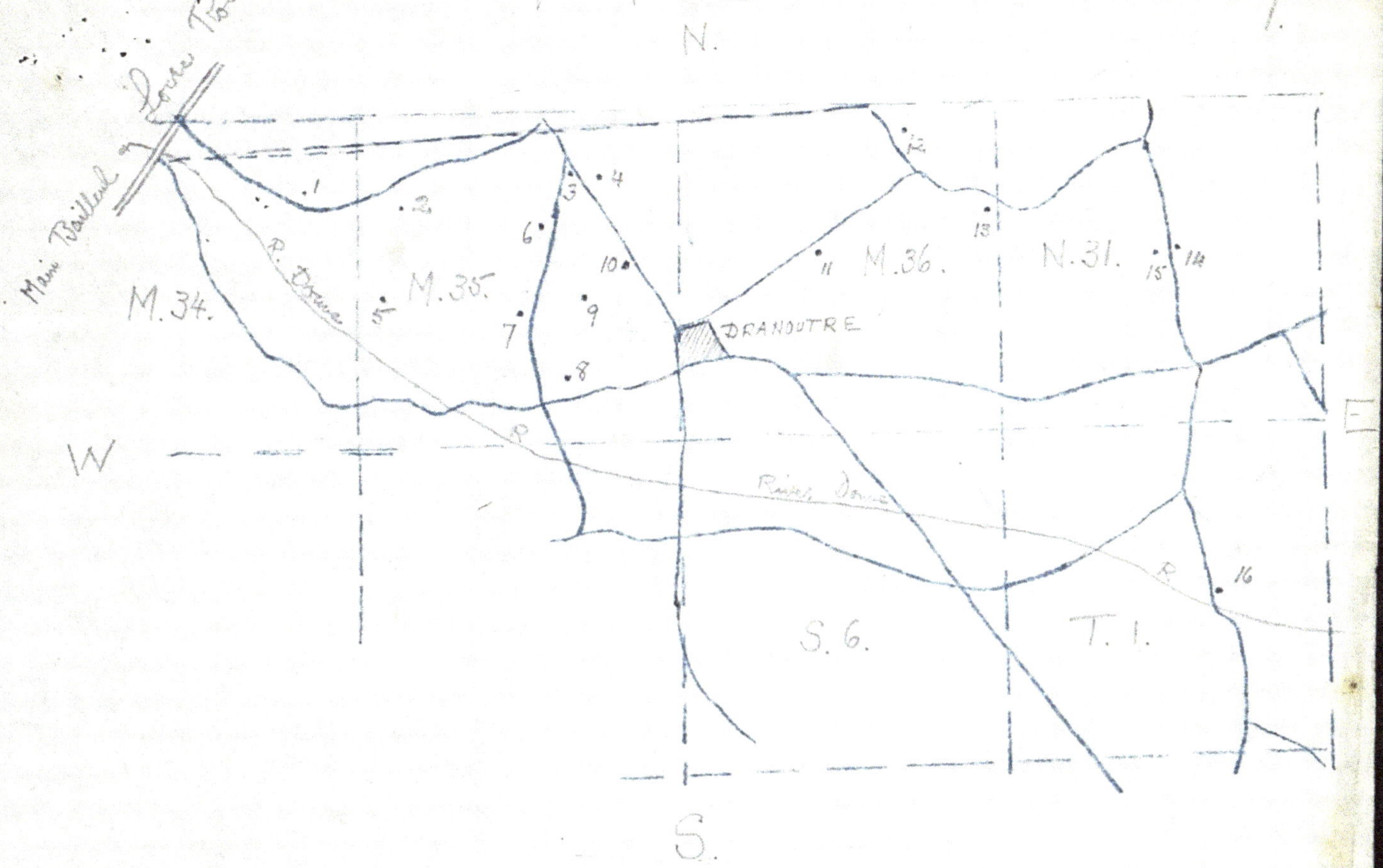

1.

N.

Main Bailleul Locre Road

M.34.

M.35.

M.36.

N.31.

DRANOUTRE

R. Douve

River Douve

W

E

S.6.

T.1.

S.

19th July /15

Reference of Tracing.

	Position	No. of farms	Description	Accomodation	Units previously in occupation: + [illegible]: °	Remarks
1	M34b	1	Small	40 men	none	no good
2	M35a	1	+ Large good meadow	30 men	2/Northumbrian F. Amb. +	water
3	M35b	13 Huts	9 for men (30 in each) 2 for stores, 1 for officers + 1 kitchen.		1st Wilts R.E.°	61 men 3 off no water
4	M35b	1	Small	30 men	none	not good
5	M35a	Splendid site for large camp in wood, plenty of water.				
6	M35b	Large meadow				
7	M35d	Large meadow				
8	M35d	Large meadow				
9	M35b	1	Excellent	Occupied by 84th Field Ambulance (83rd Brigade.)		
10	M35b	Empty 14 huts for men (30 in each) 1 store hut, 1 large officer's hut, 1 servant's hut + kitchen, 1 guard room + 1 orderly room.				
11	M36a	1 (4 buildings) + Large meadows		500 men	2/Buffs °	water
12	M36b	1	+ good meadow	60 men (in farm)	East Yorks +	water
13	M36b	4 huts	being used by officers only (100 men)		3/Middlesex °	good
14	N31b	1	+ good meadow	100 men	artillery +	in view of enemy
15	N31a	Large meadow		good water		in view of enemy
16	P1d	1	Large. Officers 3 rooms (large) + Large meadow.	260 men	4th Northumbrian Howitz Bde. Headquarters +	good water

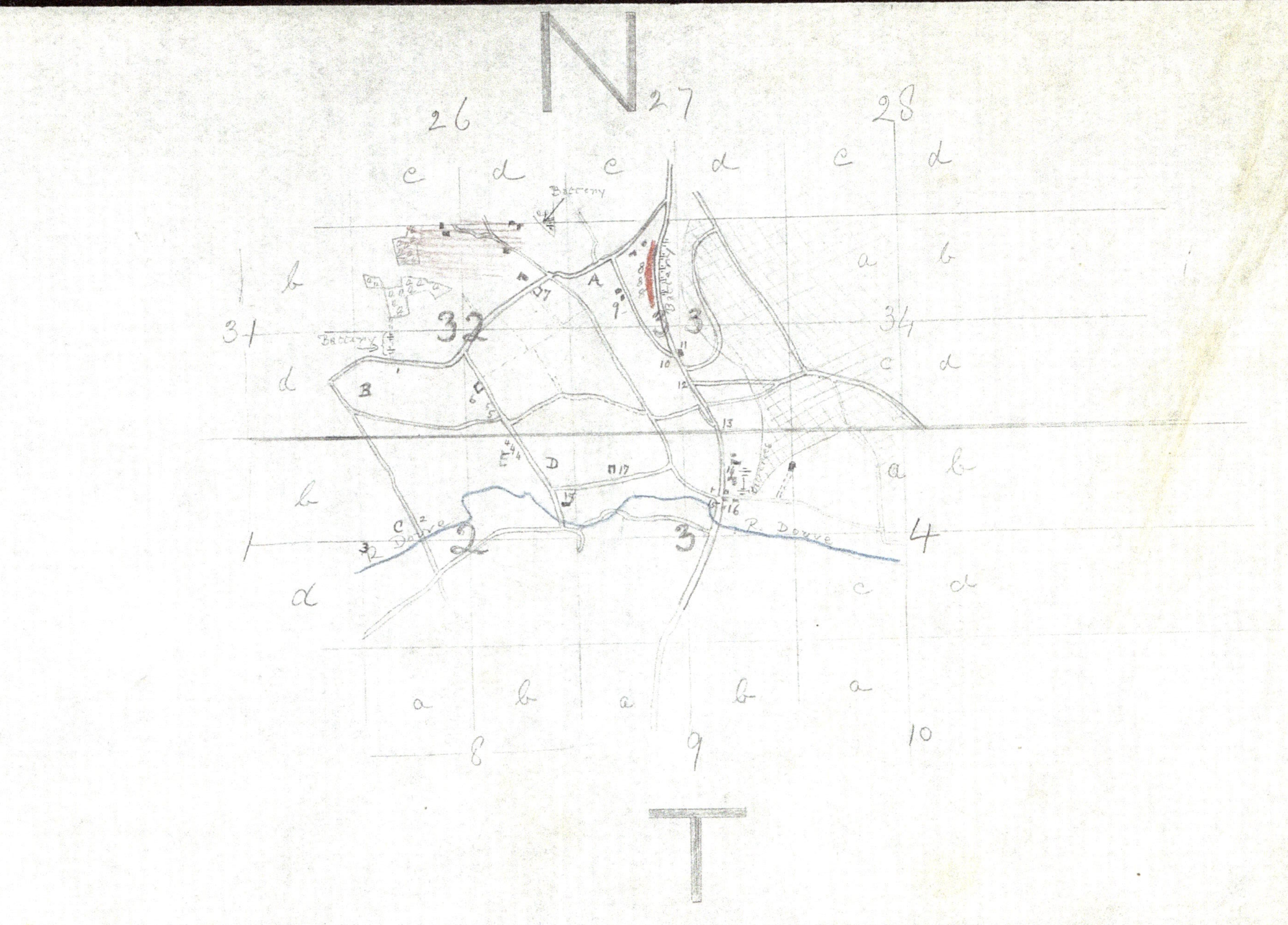

N
26
27
28
Battery
A
B
D
32
33
34
31
Battery
R. Douve
4
1
2
3
8
9
10
T

85th Infy Brigade.

With reference to attached instructions, Brigades will furnish a weekly return (made up to 12 noon Sundays) by 12 noon Mondays showing the Small Arm Ammunition in Excess of War Establishments held at the trenches in accordance with the attached pro-forma.

2. The daily Expenditure of Small Arm Ammunition up to 12 noon will be reported to this office with the casualty report.

3. Units will keep records of their daily expenditure for future reference.

4. Units will keep a record of S.A.A. taken or handed over in the trenches on relief.

Lt.Colonel.

26/7/1915. S/1065 A.A.& Q.M.G., 28th Division.

All units 85th B'de

2 With ref to para 2 of letter No. 2148 d/26/7/15 daily expenditure of S.A.A. up to 12 noon will be forwarded with casualty report.

1. Ref para 1. return will be rendered by 6pm Sunday.

3/ For compliance

4 For compliance. Amount will be shown on trench report.

Infantry Brigade.

Return showing Ammunition allowed by, and in excess of, War Establishment held at Trenches

Battalion.	Trench Strength No. of M.Guns.	In front Trenches				At Supporting points.				Held at Battn Hd Qrs.
		On Man	Excess	With M.Gun (According to W.Estab.	Excess.	On Man.	Excess.	With M.Gun According to W.Estab.	Excess.	

/ / 1915.

17,000

880
18
7040
880
15,840

85th Infantry Brigade

Return showing ammunition allowed by, and in excess of, War Establishment, held at Trenches.

Battalion	Trench Strength	No. of M. Guns	In front Trenches				At supporting points				Held at Battn Hd. Qrs
			On Men	Excess	With M. Guns (according to W. Estab)	Excess	On Men	Excess	With M. Guns (according to W. Estab)	Excess	
3/R. Fusiliers	837	5	75240	117360	10500	6000	25200	58800	12000	1500	16 boxes
2/E. Surreys	806	4	93720	140580	10500	Nil	3150	6840	6000	—	— " —
2/Kings Own	657	4	70800	124000	14000	12000	8760	27000	—	6000	— " —

475,500 at Brigade Stores, withdrawn from units & salvaged. Awaiting instructions.

2/8/15

5/1168

P.G. Scarlett Capt.
for Brig. Gen. Comdg, 85th Inf. Bde.

"A" Form. Army Form

MESSAGES AND SIGNALS.

No. of Message

Prefix ...... Code ...... m.	Words	Charge	This message is on a/c of:	Recd. at ...... m.
Office of Origin and Service Instructions.	Sent		...... Service.	Date
	At ...... m.			From
	To			
	By		(Signature of "Franking Officer.")	By

TO 28th Div.

* Sender's Number.	Day of Month.	In reply to Number	AAA
S 1201/11	3		

reference amended ammunition return rendered this morning aaa add East Yorks to column in rear etc. 1000 strong 14 machine guns rounds 135000 aaa regimental reserve 129000

From 83rd Inf Bde.

Place

Time

The above may be forwarded as now corrected. (Z)

Censor. Signature of Addresser or person authorised to telegraph in his name.

* This line should be erased if not required.

(32264) Wt.W. 14142-641. 16,000. 4-15. H G.& S., Ltd.

Appendix A

Refilling Points and Units refilled
July 11th 1915.

DIVISIONAL TROOPS.	R.A. Headquarters.
	3rd Bde R.F.A.
	31st do.
N.1.c. 24.	146th do.
	Headquarter Co Divl Train.
Sheet 28.	Sanitary Sect.
	Postal ..
	Mobile Veterinary Sect.
	"A" Bty 49th Bde R.F.A.
	49th Bde Amm Column.
	25 Trench How Bty.
	33 ..
	No.2 Kite Balloon Sect.R.N.A.S.
	"B" Sub Sect.Anti-Aircraft Sect.
	171 Tunnelling Co R.E.
Map Sq R.18.a.Sheet 28 on WESTOUTRE-BOESCHEPE Rd.	28th Divl Ammn Column.
	Headquarters 83rd Bde.
83rd Bde.	2nd K.O.R.L.
	2nd East Yorks.
M.9.d.	1st Y & Lancs.
	1st K.O.Y.L.I.
Sheet 28.	5th K.O.R.L.
	2 Coy Divl Train.
	84th Fd Amb.
	38th Fd Co R.E.
	A.O.C.Sect.
	Surrey Yeomanry.
	Cyclist Coy.
84th Bde.	Headquarters 84th Bde.
	2nd Northumberland Fus.
M.6.d.	2nd Cheshires.
	1st Welsh.
Sheet 28.	1/6 Welsh.
	1st Suffolks.
	Composite Monmouths.
	3 Coy Divl Train.
	2/1 Northumbrian Fd Co R.E.
	Divl Headquarters.
	Train ..
	R.E. ..
	Military Police.
	85th Fd Amb.
	Signal Co R.E.
85th Bde.	Headquarters 85th Bde.
	2nd Buffs.
M.17.c.4.7.	2nd E.Surrey.
Sheet 28.	3rd Middlesex.
	3rd Royal Fus.
	Divl Fd Amb Workshop.
	4 Coy Divl Train.
	86th Fd Amb.

10

Appendix B

Refilling points & Units refilled.
July 14th/15.

DIVISIONAL TROOPS.	R.A.Headquarters. 3rd Bde R.F.A. 31st ditto. 146th ditto.
M.9.c.0.3. Sheet 28.	Headquarter Coy.Divl Train. Sanitary Section. Postal do. Mobile Vetinary Section. "A" B'y 49th Bde R.F.A. 25 Trench How.Battery. 33 do. No.2 Kite Balloon Sect R.N.A.S. "B" Sub Sect Anti-Aircraft Sect. 171 Tunnelling Co,R.E.
R.28.d. Sheet 27.	28th Divl Ammn Column.
83rd Bde. R.17.b. Sheet 27.	Headquarters 83rd Bde. 2nd K.O.R.L. 2nd E.Yorks. 1st Y & Lancs. 1st K.O.Y.L.I. 5th K.O.R.L. 2 Coy.Divl Train. 84th Fd Amb. 38 Fd.Coy R.E. A.O.C.Section. Surrey Yeomanry. Cyclist Co. 83rd Bde Mining Sect.
84th Bde. R.18.a.Sheet 27.	Headquarters 84th Bde. 2nd Northumberland Fus. 2nd Cheshires. 1st Welsh. 1/6 Welsh. 1st Suffolks. Composite Monmouths. 3 Coy Divl Train. 2/1 Northumbrian Fd Co R.E. Divl H.Qs. R.E. .. Train .. Military Police. 85th Fd Amb. Signal Co R.E.
85th Bde. R.18.a. Sheet 27.	Headquarters 85th Bde. 2nd Buffs. 2nd E.Surrey. 3rd Middlesex. 3rd Royal Fus. Divl Fd Amb Workshop. 4 Coy.Divl Train. 86th Fd Amb.

I. Appendix C

Consolidated Casualty Return Feb 2 to July 18 1915

Unit	Date	Officers			O. Ranks			Officers			O. Ranks		
		K.	W.	M.	K.	W.	M.	K.	W.	M.	K.	W.	M.
83rd Bde.	Feb 2 Mch 2	8	17	-	216	718	118						
84th "	" 4 Feb 22	11	18	4	130	417	263	31	61	5	493	1676	747
85th "	" 6th " 19th	12	26	1	147	541	366		97			2916	
9th "	Mch 4 - Ap 4	5	15	-	185	732	20						
13th "	Feb 21 " 6	10	14		139	476	15	20	46	-	428	1705	35
15th "	Mch 5 " 6	5	17		104	477	-		66			2168	
83rd "	Ap 9 July 18	33	96	15	556	2283	1728						
84th "	" 13 " 18	28	122	54	383	1850	2640	101	306	84	1648	6725	6175
85th "	" 4 " 18	40	88	15	709	2592	1807		491			14,548	
R. A.	Feb 2 July 18	5	37	6	49	253	30						
R. E.	"	6	13	2	24	158	26						
Surrey Yeo	"				1	1	-						
Div Cyclists	"					8	-	11	56	10	78	448	59
Signal Co	"		2			8			77			585	
Div Train	"		2	2		7							
R.A.M.C.	"		2	-	4	13	3						
Total Casualties Feb 2 to July 18.		163	469	99	2647	10,554	7,016						
			731			20,217.							

Extract from above figures. Period April 22 to June 5.

Unit	Date	Officers			O. Ranks			Officers			O. Ranks		
		K.	W.	M.	K.	W.	M.	K.	W.	M.	K.	W.	M.
83rd 84th 85th Bdes	April 22 to June 5.	89	255	84	1325	5499	5766		428			12,590	
R.A. & R.E.		7	36	9	58	305	36		52			399	
		96	291	93	1383	5804	5802		480			12,989.	
			480			12,989							

28th Division Expeditionary Force.

Return showing Wastage of Officers and Other Ranks for the period January 24th to July 18th, inclusive.

Month.	Officers.	Other Ranks.	Remarks.
1st to 24th January.	6.	322.	(a) Includes 23 Feet cases.
February.	76. (a)	3631. (b)	(b) Includes 639 Feet cases.
March.	42.	1345. (c)	(c) Includes 311 Feet cases.
April.	19.	434.	
May.	36.	1114.	
June.	14.	234.	
1st to 18th July.	3.	195.	
Totals.	196.	7273. (6 written over final 3)	Total Feet cases. O. 23, O.R. 950.

Lieut-Colonel,
D. A. D. M. S., for
A. D. M. S., 28th Division.

July 19th 1915.

Appendix D

Refilling Points and Units refilled.

July 20th.

DIVISIONAL TROOPS. M.9.c. D.3. Sheet 28.	R.A.Headquarters. 3rd Brigade R.F.A. 31st ditto. 146th ditto. Headquarter Co Divl Train. Sanitary Section. Postal ditto. Mobile Veterinary Sect. "A" Battery 49 Bde,R.F.A. 49 Brigade Ammn Column. 25 Trench How Battery. 33 ditto. No.2 Kite Balloon Sect. No.4 .. .. 10th Anti Aircraft Sect. 171 Tunnelling Co R.E. 10 Heavy Brigade R.G.A. Battery Headquarters.
R.28.b.centre sheet 27.	28th Divl Ammn Column.
83rd Brigade. R.17.b. Sheet 27.	Headquarters 83rd Brigade. 2nd K.O.R.L. 2nd E.Yorks. 1 K.O.Y.L.I. 1 Y & Lancs. 5th K.O.R.L. No.2 Coy Divl Train. 84 Field Amb. 38 Field Co R.E. A.O.C.Section. Surrey Yeomanry. Cyclist Co. 53 Cie Belge Travailleurs.
84th Brigade. R.18.a. sheet 27.	Headquarters 84th Brigade. 2nd Northumberland Fus. 2nd Cheshires. 1st Welsh. 1/6 Welsh. 1st Suffolks. Composite Monmouths. No.3 Company Divl Train. Divl Headquarters. R.E. .. Train .. Military Police. 85 Field Amb. Signal Co R.E. 2/1 Northumbrian Fd Co R.E. 2nd Bn Royal Irish Rgt.
85th Brigade. R.18.a. Sheet 27.	Headquarters 85th Brigade. 2nd Buffs. No.4 Coy Divl Train. 2nd E.Surrey. 86 Field Ambulance. 3rd Middlesex. 3rd Royal Fus. 28th Divm Fd Amb Workshop.

~~83rd Brigade.~~
~~84th Brigade.~~
85th Brigade.

The following amount of Small Arm Ammunition will be kept with Battalions :-

"A".	<u>In trenches.</u>	On the man.	120	rounds.
	For each man in the firing and support trenches (kept in S.A.A. boxes) in addition.		180	rounds.
	For each machine gun		3,500	do.
	<u>Supporting points.</u>	On the man.	120	do.
	For each man of garrison (kept in S.A.A. boxes) in addition.		280	do.
	For each machine gun.		6,000	do.
	<u>Elsewhere.</u>	On the man.	120	do.

16 boxes of ammunition will be kept as a reserve at Battalion Headquarters.

The regimental reserve (1st Line Transport) will be kept full at all times.

The excess rounds held at the trenches and supporting points both for man and machine gun will be considered as "Trench Stores".

[signature]

Lt. Colonel,

26th July 1915. A.A. & Q.M.G., 28th Division.

28th Div.
G. 322.

~~83rd Infantry Brigade.~~
~~84th Infantry Brigade.~~
85th Infantry Brigade.

With reference to No. 2148 dated 26th instant, it is to be understood that ammunition in excess of the 120 rounds carried on the man is not to be carried in bandoliers but to be kept in S.A.A. boxes until required for issue.

The 16 boxes kept in reserve at Battalion Headquarters will be available for such an emergency as the occupation of Switch or Subsidiary Lines.

R. H. Hare

Lieut-Colonel,

26th July, 1915. General Staff, 28th Division.

AUGUST 1915

Confidential.

War Diary

of

28th Division, Administrative Staff.

from 1st Aug 1915 to 31st Aug 1915

Volume 9.

1

Army Form C. 2118.

Instructions regarding War Diaries and Intelligence Summaries are contained in F. S. Regs., Part II. and the Staff Manual respectively. Title pages will be prepared in manuscript.

WAR DIARY
or
INTELLIGENCE SUMMARY.
(Erase heading not required.)

Hour, Date, Place	Summary of Events and Information	Remarks and references to Appendices
WESTOUTRE. 1. 8. 15.	Weather fine. Reinforcements 2 Officers and 165 OR. Casualties Kld OR 3 Wdd Officers 1 2nd Lieut G. H. MILLS 6/Welsh OR 17.	
WESTOUTRE 2. 8. 15.	Weather fine with a few showers. Casualties Kld Officers 1 Capt. W. W. WILSON 3/Monmouths ~~OR Wdd OR~~ OR 3 Wdd OR 15. Nearly ½ million rounds S.A. Ammn collected by 85th Bde from subsidiary trenches taken over from other divisions.	||
WESTOUTRE. 3. 8. 15.	Weather stormy with rain. Casualties Kld OR 2 Wdd 4. Arrangements being made to send Bread & meat rations direct from Railhead to Supply sections so as to save a day and deliver them to troops fresher. Some difficulty anticipated in this as our supply	

(73989) W4141—463. 400,000. 9/14. H.&J.Ltd. Forms/C. 2118/10.

Army Form C. 2118.

Instructions regarding War Diaries and Intelligence Summaries are contained in F. S. Regs., Part II. and the Staff Manual respectively. Title pages will be prepared in manuscript.

WAR DIARY
or
INTELLIGENCE SUMMARY.
(Erase heading not required.)

Hour, Date, Place	Summary of Events and Information	Remarks and references to Appendices
	farm does not deliver to supply lorries until about midday and ~~could~~ these lorries with bread + meat would not reach refilling points until about 1.30 PM, whereas supply sections load up at refilling points at about 9 AM.	
WESTOUTRE 4.8.15	Weather: showery. Casualties: killed Lt S. LONG INNES, 2nd Kings own Regt, 4 other ranks. Wounded 20 other ranks, including 1 accidentally, and one slightly, at duty. Missing 6 other ranks. Of these casualties, 1 killed, 12 wounded and 6 missing, all of the 1st Bn Welch regt, were due to the explosion of a mine.	
WESTOUTRE 5.8.15	Weather: fine generally. Casualties – other ranks wounded 12. Of the six men of the 1st Bn Welch regt reported missing yesterday, 5 are now reported killed and 1 wounded. Drafts arrived – 3 officers, 186 other ranks	
WESTOUTRE 6.8.15	Weather: fine generally. Casualties – killed Capt E. G. VENNING 3rd Suffolk Regt (attached 1st Suffolk Regt) and 1 other ranks. Wounded 13 other ranks. Drafts arrived – 6 officers 377 other ranks. Orders received that Monmouth regiment was to be reconstituted as 1st and 3rd Battalions. 1st Battalion to remain in 84th Brigade, 3rd Battalion to go to 83rd Brigade. Orders issued accordingly: 1st Bn to keep all 1st line transport and material of battalion headquarters.	

Army Form C. 2118.

WAR DIARY
or
INTELLIGENCE SUMMARY.

(*Erase heading not required.*)

Instructions regarding War Diaries and Intelligence Summaries are contained in F. S. Regs., Part II. and the Staff Manual respectively. Title pages will be prepared in manuscript.

Hour, Date, Place	Summary of Events and Information	Remarks and references to Appendices
WESTOUTRE 7.8.15	Weather fine. Casualties – Killed other ranks 3; wounded other ranks 5. Drafts arrived – 1 officer, 55 other ranks. Staff Captains of 110th and 112th Brigades arrived to see camping grounds for units of their brigades. B (Howitzer) battery 89th Bde. arrived from Indian Corps.	
WESTOUTRE 8.8.15	Weather fine. Casualties – Killed other ranks 4; wounded other ranks 5. Drafts arrived – 1 officer, 13 other ranks. 110th Infantry Brigade, 37th Division, arrived about 3 p.m., and were accommodated in fields, 1 battalion in 83rd Bde area 1 battalion in 84th Bde area, 2 battalions in 85th Bde area, Bde H.Q. at LOCRE HOF farm. 158 tents were drawn from II Corps Ordnance for accommodation of this brigade. A. (Howitzer) Battery, 73rd Bde R.F.A. arrived from Indian Corps.	
WESTOUTRE 9.8.15	Weather dull and close. Casualties – Killed other ranks 6; wounded Lt E. BELFIELD 3rd Bn Middlesex, other ranks 23, including one slightly at duty.	

(73989) W4141—463. 400,000. 9/14. H.&J.Ltd. Forms/C. 2118/10.

4

Instructions regarding War Diaries and Intelligence Summaries are contained in F. S. Regs., Part II. and the Staff Manual respectively. Title pages will be prepared in manuscript.

WAR DIARY
or
INTELLIGENCE SUMMARY.
(Erase heading not required.)

Army Form C. 2118.

Hour, Date, Place	Summary of Events and Information	Remarks and references to Appendices
WESTOUTRE 10. 8. 15.	Weather fine. Casualties ~~Officers~~ Kld Officers 1 Lieut. E. H. CRAMER - ROBERTS 2/Buffs. OR 5. Wdd. OR 23. Water supply getting rather short, R.E. expediting preparation of pipe + tank at Chateau DOUVE. D.A.Q.M.G. 22nd Division attached for instruction. Refilling Points and units refilled	Vide Appendix A
WESTOUTRE. 11. 8. 15.	Weather fine. Casualties Kld OR. 2 Wdd. OR. 11. Arrangements completed for new watersupply for 85th Brigade area by pipe laid from pond at Chateau DOUVE to ~~[illegible]~~ LOCRE - BAILLEUL Road; capable of supplying 20,000 gallons daily.	
WESTOUTRE 12. 8. 15	Fine day. Casualties Kld OR 2, Wdd OR 17. Major F. C. GEPP, Staff Captain 83rd Brigade appointed Brigade Major 84th Brigade. Capt. J. BOYCE 2/K. own appointed Staff Captain 83rd Bde. Captain TAPLEY, ADVS. left for England on ~~[illegible]~~ transfer to KHARTOUM, Captain	

5

Army Form C. 2118.

Instructions regarding War Diaries and Intelligence Summaries are contained in F. S. Regs., Part II. and the Staff Manual respectively. Title pages will be prepared in manuscript.

WAR DIARY
or
INTELLIGENCE SUMMARY.
(Erase heading not required.)

Hour, Date, Place	Summary of Events and Information	Remarks and references to Appendices
	R. W. MELLARD A.V.C joined as ADVS.	
	Major H. S DE ARETT. D.S.O. left to take up appointment G.S.O. (1) 3rd Division, Major H. NEEDHAM, Gloucestershire Regt. joined as G.S.O. (2).	
WESTOUTRE 13·8·15	Weather – showery. Casualties – wounded Captain G. D'A. ELLIOTT-COOPER, 3rd Bn Royal Fusiliers, 11 other ranks including one slightly, at duty; 6th Bn Leicester Regt attached, 1 other rank wounded.	
	Drafts arrived – 2nd Bn Kings Own 20 other ranks, 1st Bn York Lancaster 6 other ranks, 2nd Bn Northumberland Fusiliers 6 other ranks, 2nd Bn East Surrey 40 other ranks.	
WESTOUTRE 14·8·15	Weather – fine. Casualties – wounded 2nd Lt N. M. MELLOR 3rd Bn Royal Fusiliers and 11 other ranks, including 3 of 110th Brigade. Major HOPE D.A.Q.M.G. went sick and his place was filled temporarily by Capt AGG K.O.Y.L.I. commanding Divisional Cyclist Co	
WESTOUTRE 15·8·15	Weather – showery in morning, fine in afternoon. –	
	Casualties – Killed O.R. 3 – wounded O.R. 11 including one slightly at duty: 6th Leicester Regt attached. 2. O.R. wounded. 8th Leicester Regt. attached 1. O.R. wounded –	

6

Instructions regarding War Diaries and Intelligence Summaries are contained in F. S. Regs., Part II. and the Staff Manual respectively. Title pages will be prepared in manuscript.

WAR DIARY
or
INTELLIGENCE SUMMARY.
(Erase heading not required.)

Army Form C. 2118.

Hour, Date, Place	Summary of Events and Information	Remarks and references to Appendices
WESTOUTRE 15.8.15 Ctd.	Drafts arrived - 2nd Cheshire Regt. 105. O.R. A.S.C. - - 6. O.R.	
WESTOUTRE 16-8-15	Weather fine - Casualties ~~Kld OR 2 Wdd OR 48~~ ~~including [illegible]~~ Kld OR 2. Wdd Officers 1 2/Lieut. C.E.N. LOGAN, 9th Leicesters OR 11. New instructions issued regarding new pattern of "P" Smoke helmet, also a special Tube pattern for Officers N.C.Os & a few specialists. General Bulfin departed on 7 days leave, Br. Genl. Pereira assumed command.	
WESTOUTRE. 17.8.15.	Weather rainy. Casualties Kld OR 3 Wdd OR 48, including 1 Kld & 16 Wdd by accidental explosion of bomb.	
WESTOUTRE 18.8.15.	Weather fine. Casualties Kld OR 3 Wdd Officers 1 2Lt. R.J. DAVIDSON 2/Buffs, OR 10. Lord Kitchener and M. Millerand visited the Scherpenberg and	

(73989) W4141—463. 400,000. 9/14. H.&J.Ltd. Forms/C. 2118/10.

Instructions regarding War Diaries and Intelligence Summaries are contained in F. S. Regs., Part II. and the Staff Manual respectively. Title pages will be prepared in manuscript.

WAR DIARY
or
INTELLIGENCE SUMMARY.
(Erase heading not required.)

Army Form C. 2118.

Hour, Date, Place	Summary of Events and Information	Remarks and references to Appendices
	and inspected two Battalions and some Artillery there.	
WESTOUTRE. 19. 8. 15.	~~Fine~~ Weather fine. Casualties Kld. OR 2 Wdd OR. 8. Divisional Ammun Column being re-horsed with L.D. horses instead of Heavy Draught.	
WESTOUTRE. 20. 8. 15.	Weather fine. Reinforcements 2 officers 191 OR. Casualties Kld OR 5 Wdd OR. 13.	
WESTOUTRE. 21. 8. 15.	Weather stormy with rain. Casualties Wdd OR 5	
WESTOUTRE 22. 8. 15.	Weather fine. Casualties Kld OR 3. Wdd. ~~4~~ OR 1[illegible].	
WESTOUTRE 23. 8. 15.	Weather fine. Reinforcements 1 officer 147 OR. Casualties. Kld OR 4. Wdd. Officers 2, Lieut C. E. HAMILTON	

(73989) W4141—463. 400,000. 9/14. H.&J.Ltd. Forms/C. 2118/10.

8

Army Form C. 2118.

Instructions regarding War Diaries and Intelligence Summaries are contained in F. S. Regs., Part II. and the Staff Manual respectively. Title pages will be prepared in manuscript.

WAR DIARY
or
INTELLIGENCE SUMMARY.

(Erase heading not required.)

Hour, Date, Place	Summary of Events and Information	Remarks and references to Appendices
	2/North Fus, 2/Lieut. V. L. MILLER-HALLETT, 3/R. Fus. OR 11.	
WESTOUTRE. 24. 8. 15.	Weather fine. Casualties Kld OR 3. Wdd Officers 1 2/Lieut. J. F. PULLEN 1/Welsh Regt. OR 28. Digging parties 2000 men of 112th Bde 37th Divn left our area today entraining at GODEWAERSVELDE.	
WESTOUTRE. 25. 8. 15.	Weather fine. Reinforcements 4 Officers 15 OR. Casualties Kld OR 2 Wdd OR 14. Hd Qrs Coy of Divl Train shifted to Cx de POPERINGUE.	
WESTOUTRE. 26. 8. 15.	Weather fine. Reinforcements 11 Officers 30 OR. Casualties Kld OR 3 Wdd Officers Lieut G. L. CHEONY 2nd Lieut. I. R. BLAIN. 2/K.O.R.L. Regt. OR. 19. G.O.C. inspected Divl Amm Colm and Divl Train.	

9

Army Form C. 2118.

WAR DIARY
or
INTELLIGENCE SUMMARY.
(Erase heading not required.)

Instructions regarding War Diaries and Intelligence Summaries are contained in F. S. Regs., Part II. and the Staff Manual respectively. Title pages will be prepared in manuscript.

Hour, Date, Place	Summary of Events and Information	Remarks and references to Appendices
WESTOUTRE. 27.8.15.	Weather fine. Casualties Kld OR 1 Wdd Officers 1 Lieut G. R. WALKER 2/North Fd Coy RE. OR 7 arrangements have now been completed for Supply Column Lorries to supply direct to 1st Line Transport lines of Infantry Brigades, thus releasing Supply Sections of Train ~~situated~~ refilling points and Units refilled.	Appendix B.
WESTOUTRE. 28.8.15.	Weather fine. Casualties ~~Kld OR~~ Wdd Officers 1 Lieut W E BECKETT 3/Cheshires OR 6. A great deal of correspondence in administrative office reports required on Rations, ammunition expenditure, Bombs, etc.	
WESTOUTRE 29.8.15.	Weather misty & raining. Casualties Kld OR 3 Wdd Officers 1 Lieut M. VAUGHAN-LEWES, OR 9	

10

Instructions regarding War Diaries and Intelligence Summaries are contained in F. S. Regs., Part II. and the Staff Manual respectively. Title pages will be prepared in manuscript.

WAR DIARY
or
INTELLIGENCE SUMMARY.
(Erase heading not required.)

Army Form C. 2118.

Hour, Date, Place	Summary of Events and Information	Remarks and references to Appendices
WESTOUTRE. 30.8.15.	Weather cold but fine on the whole. Casualties Kld OR 2 Wdd OR 12. G.O.C. 2nd Army inspected one Battalion from each Brigade which paraded in their rest areas.	
WESTOUTRE 31.8.15.	Weather cold but fairly fine. Casualties Kld OR 5 Wdd OR 11. G.O.C. 2nd Army inspected 2nd K.O.R. Lanc Regt. of 83rd Brigade.	
	In the Field. 31st August 1915. J. Hope Major D.A.Q.M.G. 28th Division	

85th Infantry Brigade

Number of rounds S.A.A. on charge at 12 noon Sunday 1.8.15.

Unit	In trenches: Strength	In trenches: No. of M. Guns	In trenches: Total rounds at 300 per rifle and 3500 per M. Gun	In supporting points: Strength	In supporting points: No. of M. Guns	In supporting points: Total rounds at 400 per rifle and 6000 per M. Gun	In rear, reserve or resting out of trenches: Strength	In rear, reserve or resting out of trenches: No. of M. Guns	In rear, reserve or resting out of trenches: Total rounds at 120 per rifle + 3500 per M. Gun	At Battn. Hd. Qrs.	Regimental Reserve 100 rounds per rifle + 8000 per M. Gun	Surplus on charge	Grand Total	Remarks
3/R. Fusiliers	627 ~~837~~	3	198600	210	2	96000	251	-	30120	16000	137000		477720	
2/E. Surreys	732	4	233600	38	-	15200	239	-	26680	16000	129000		422480	
2/King's Own	584	4	189200	73	-	29200	242	-	29040	16000	129000	14400	406840	
2/Buffs							975	4	131000	-	129000	7620	267620	
3/Middx.							822	4	112640	-	129000		241640	
Total	1943	11	621400			140400			331480	48000	653000	22020	1816300	

512500. at Bde. Hd. Qrs. (Stores) withdrawn from units + salvaged.

4/8/15.

R. T. Scarth[?], Capt.

for Brig. Gen., Comdg. 85th Inf. Bde.

85th Brigade.

As the information regarding Small Arms Ammunition on charge of Brigades arrived at by the attached return is not quite clear, it is regretted that it will be necessary to alter the pro.forma and to ask for this information as regards rounds on charge on Sunday, 1st August, to be entered thereon and the return re submitted as soon as possible.

The new pro.forma will be used for returns submitted in future instead of the old one.

Major.

August 3rd. 1915. D.A.~~A.&~~ Q.M.G. 28th Division.

Appendix A

REFILLING POINTS, AND UNITS REFILLED, AUGUST 10th.1915.

Divisional Troops. M.0.c. 0 3 Sheet 28.	R.A.Headquarters. 3rd Brigade R.F.A. 31st Brigade R.F.A. 146th Brigade R.F.A. "A" Bty. 49th Bde.R.F.A. "B" Bty. 89th Bde.R.F.A. "A" Bty. 73rd Bde.R.F.A. 33rd Trench Howitzer Bty. 172nd Tunnelling Co. R.E. 9th Anti-Aircraft Section. 20th Anti-Aircraft Section. No.2 Kite Balloon Sec.R.N.A.S. Trench Howitzer School.	Headquarters Divl. Train. Mobile Veterinary Section. Postal Section. 15th Sanitary Section.
R.28.b.centre. Sheet 27.	28th Divisional Ammunition Col.	
83rd Brigade. R.17.b.Sheet 27.	Headquarters 83rd Bde. 2nd K.O.R.L. 2nd East Yorks. 1st K.O.Y.L.I. 1st Yorks & Lancs. 5th K.O.R.L. Surrey Yeomanry. 2 Coy.Divisional Train.	12th Anti-Aircraft Section. 38th Field Coy. R.E. Cyclist Company. 84th Field Ambulance. A.O.D.
84th Brigade. R.18.a.Sheet 27.	Headquarters 84th Bde. 2nd Northd.Fusiliers. 2nd Cheshires. 1st Welch. 1/6th Welch. 1st Suffolks. 1st & 3rd Monmouths. 28th Divl. Signal Co. R.E.	Divisional Headquarters. Train Headquarters. R.E. Headquarters. 3 Coy. Divisional Train. 2/1st Northn.Field Coy. 85th Field Ambulance. Military Police.
85th Brigade. R.18.a.Sheet 27.	Headquarters 85th Bde. 2nd The Buffs. 2nd East Surreys. 3rd Middlesex. 3rd Ryl.Fusiliers. 25th Trench How.Bde.	4 Coy.Divisional Train. 86th Field Ambulance. 28th Field Amb.Workshop.

Appendix B.

REFILLING POINTS AND UNITS REFILLED, AUGUST 27th.15.

Divisional Troops. Croix de Poperinghe. M.33.d. Sheet 28.	R.A.Headquarters. 3rd Brigade R.F.A. 31st Brigade R.F.A. 146th Brigade R.F.A. "A"Bty, 49th Bde. R.F.A. "B"Bty, 89th Bde. R.F.A. "A"Bty, 73rd Bde. R.F.A. Trench Howitzer Bde. 130th Howitzer Brigade. 9th Anti-Aircraft Section. No.2 Kite Balloon Sec.R.N.A.S.	Divisional Headquarters. R.E.Headquarters. Headqtrs.Coy.Divl. Train. 15th Sanitary Section. Postal Section. Mobile Veterinary Section.
R.28.b.centre. Sheet 27.	28th Divisional Ammunition Col.	
83rd Brigade. M.17.c.Sheet 28.	Headquarters 83rd Bde. 1st York & Lancs. 2nd K.O.R.L. 2nd East Yorks. 1st K.O.Y.L.I. 5th K.O.R.L. 1/3rd Monmouths. 33rd Trench How.Battery. Surrey Yeomanry. 38th Field Coy. R.E.	28th Divl.Signal Coy.R.E. Train Headquarters. 12th Anti-Aircraft Section. 2 Coy. Divisional Train. 84th Field Ambulance. Cyclist Company. Military Police. A.O.D.Section.
84th Brigade. LOCRE.	Headquarters 84th Bde. 2nd Northd.Fusiliers. 2nd Cheshires. 1st Welch. 1/6th Welch. 1st Suffolks. 1st Monmouths.	2/1 Northn.Field Coy. 3 Coy.Divisional Train. 85th Field Ambulance.
85th Brigade. S.5.b.Sheet 28.	Headquarters 85th Bde. 2nd The Buffs. 2nd East Surreys. 3rd Middlesex. 3rd Ryl.Fusiliers. 25th Trench How.Batty.	4 Coy.Divisional Train. 86th Field Ambulance. 28th Field Amb.Workshop. 51st Belgian Travailleurs.

Number of rounds of S. A. A. on charge of .... Regiment, at noon, Sunday ...... August

---000---

	In Trenches.			In supporting points			In rear, reserve or resting out of Trenches			At Battn. H. Q.	Regimental Reserve		
UNIT.	Strength.	No. of M.G.	Total Rounds at 200 per rifle and 3500 per M.G	Strength.	No. of M.G.	Total Rounds at [illegible] per rifle and 6000 per M.G.	Strength	No. of M.G.	Total Rounds at 120 per rifle and 3500 per M.G		100 rounds per rifle and 5000 per M.G	Surplus on Charge	Grand Total Rounds on Charge
												Total.	

To all units under No. 5/1139 d/- 5.8-15

Specimen

Number of Rounds of Small Arms Ammunition on charge of —— Brigade, at 12 noon, Sunday —— August

Brigade of 5 Battalions, each of strength 1000 rifles and 20 Machine Guns.

Three Battalions in Trenches, and two resting.

-o0o-

UNIT.	In Trenches.			For Supporting points.			In rear, reserve or resting out of Trenches			At Battn. H. Q.	Regimental Reserve.	Surplus on Charge.	Grand Total. Rounds on charge.
	Strength.	No. of M.G's	Total Rounds at 300 per rifle and 3500 per M.G.	Strength.	No. of M.G's	Total Rounds at 400 per rifle and 5000 per M.G.	Strength.	No. of M.G's	Total Rounds at 120 per rifle and 3500 per M.G.		100 rounds per rifle and 8000 per M.Gun.		
2/Bn.	900	4	284,000	40	nil	16,000	60	nil	7200	16,000	132,000	—	455,200
3/Bn.	800	2	247,000	100	2	52,000	100	nil	12,000	16,000	132,000	—	459,000
1/Bn.	-	-	—	-	-	—	1000	4	134,000	—	132,000	—	266,000
3/Bn.	700	3	220,500	60	1	30,000	240	-	28,800	16,000	132,000	—	427,300
1/Bn.	-	-	—	-	-	—	1000	4	134.000	—	132,000	—	266,000
												Total.	1,873,500.

28th Division

121/7049

Head Quarters (A & Q) 28th Division

Vol X

Sep 1. 15

"Confidential"

War Diary (Original)

of

Administrative Staff

28th Division

from Sep 1st to Sep 30th 1915

Volume X

1

Instructions regarding War Diaries and Intelligence Summaries are contained in F. S. Regs., Part II. and the Staff Manual respectively. Title pages will be prepared in manuscript.

WAR DIARY
or
INTELLIGENCE SUMMARY.
(Erase heading not required.)

Army Form C. 2118.

Hour, Date, Place	Summary of Events and Information	Remarks and references to Appendices
WESTOUTRE. 1.9.15.	Weather cold + stormy with rain. Casualties Kld Officers 2 2Lieut. E. H. NOWELL 1/Suffolks and 2Lieut. O. P. PULVERMAN 2/Cheshires. ~~Kld~~ OR 1 Wdd OR 17. Administrative visit to BERTHEN Trench Howitzer Brigade to ascertain exact situation as to how far they come under our administration.	
WESTOUTRE. 2.9.15.	Weather cold + stormy with rain. Casualties Kld OR 4 Wdd Officers 1 2Lieut P. SHUTTLEWOOD 6/Welsh. OR 15. Orders received for ~~[illegible]~~ transfer of 1st and 3rd Monmouths to 46th and 49th Divisions respectively as Pioneer Battalions. G.O.C. saw the Officers of both Battalions to say goodbye.	
WESTOUTRE. 3.9.15.	Weather cold + stormy with much rain. Casualties Kld. OR 2 Wdd OR 5. 1st + 3rd Monmouths marched off at 9 AM to join their new Divisions.	
WESTOUTRE. 4.9.15.	Weather cold + stormy with rain. ~~[illegible]~~ Reinforcements 2 Officers, 141 OR. Casualties Kld ~~Officers~~ OR 1 Wdd Officers 1 2Lieut C. G. BEWICKE 1/Welsh, a record ~~[illegible]~~ minimum casualty list. HdQrs and 2 Companies Labour Battalion arrived + camped near LOCRE	

(73989) W4141—463. 400,000. 9/14. H.&J.Ltd. Forms/C. 2118/10.

2

Army Form C. 2118.

Instructions regarding War Diaries and Intelligence Summaries are contained in F. S. Regs., Part II. and the Staff Manual respectively. Title pages will be prepared in manuscript.

WAR DIARY
or
INTELLIGENCE SUMMARY.
(Erase heading not required.)

Hour, Date, Place	Summary of Events and Information	Remarks and references to Appendices
WESTOUTRE 5.9.15	Weather finer, but still cold with some rain. Casualties wdd Officers 1 Lieut A.G. LYNCH 1/York & Lancs. OR. 8. Diggers 2nd Cavalry Division departed leaving us their tents & some wood work for workhouses etc.	
WESTOUTRE 6.9.15.	Weather fine. Casualties Kld OR 4 Wdd OR 15 (5 RFA accidentally by playing with unexploded enemy shell)	
WESTOUTRE 7.9.15.	Weather fine. Casualties Kld OR 2 Wdd OR 9. Reinforcements OR 36. ~~B~~ One blanket per man now ~~to~~ nearly completed issue.	
WESTOUTRE. 8.9.15.	Weather fine. Reinforcements Officers 4 OR. 58. Casualties: Kld OR 1 Wdd OR 9.	
WESTOUTRE. 9.9.15.	Weather fine. Casualties ~~Kld~~ Wdd OR 10 missing 1 (wounded). G.O.C. 2nd Army inspected three resting	

(73989) W4141—463. 400,000. 9/14. H.&J.Ltd. Forms/C. 2118/10.

3

Army Form C. 2118.

Instructions regarding War Diaries and Intelligence Summaries are contained in F. S. Regs., Part II. and the Staff Manual respectively. Title pages will be prepared in manuscript.

WAR DIARY
or
INTELLIGENCE SUMMARY.
(Erase heading not required.)

Hour, Date, Place	Summary of Events and Information	Remarks and references to Appendices
	battalions, 1 from each Brigade.	
WESTOUTRE. 10.9.15.	Weather fine. Casualties Kld OR 3 Wdd OR 8.	
WESTOUTRE 11.9.15.	~~Fine~~ Weather fine. Casualties Kld ~~OR 1 Wdd OR 8~~ ~~Officers~~ OR 2 Wdd OR 7 Missing Officers 1 Lieut W. P. KEY 1/KOYLI.	
WESTOUTRE 12.9.15.	Weather fine. Casualties Kld OR 1 Wdd OR 8 64 Remounts arrived to replace casualties.	
WESTOUTRE. 13.9.15.	Weather fine. Casualties Kld OR 2 Wdd Officers 1 Lieut F. H. PEARMAN 1/York & Lancs. OR. 12.	
WESTOUTRE. 14.9.15.	Weather dull & raining. Casualties Kld OR 4 Wdd Officers 1 Lt. P. F. C. CAMPBELL-JOHNSTON 130th Bde RFA. OR 12. G.O.C. 2nd Army inspected 1/KOYLI. 1/North. Fus. and 3/R Fus. Notice given to expect a Brigade of Canadians and some artillery in a few days for instructional purposes.	

4

Instructions regarding War Diaries and Intelligence Summaries are contained in F. S. Regs., Part II. and the Staff Manual respectively. Title pages will be prepared in manuscript.

WAR DIARY
or
INTELLIGENCE SUMMARY.
(Erase heading not required.)

Army Form C. 2118.

Hour, Date, Place	Summary of Events and Information	Remarks and references to Appendices
WESTOUTRE 15.9.15.	Weather fine. Reinforcements 264 OR. Casualties: Kld OR 1 Wdd OR 14. 21 Officers of 21st Division arrived & were attached 7 to each brigade to spend 24 hours in trenches.	
WESTOUTRE 16.9.15.	Weather ~~f~~ dull & hazy. Casualties: Kld OR 4 Wdd Officers 1 2Lieut A.H. ROBERTS 3/Middlesex. OR 15.	
WESTOUTRE 17.9.15.	Weather fine. Preparations being made for relief of Division by 2 Brigades of 2 Canadian Division and 1 Brigade of ~~A~~ 1st Canadian Division in near future. Casualties Kld OR 2 Wdd Officers 2 Lt. E.A.M. WILLIAMS and 2nd Lt. A.H. CLINE, 3/Middlesex. OR 19	

(73989) W4141—463. 400,000. 9/14. H.&J.Ltd. Forms/C. 2118/10.

5

Army Form C. 2118.

Instructions regarding War Diaries and Intelligence Summaries are contained in F. S. Regs., Part II. and the Staff Manual respectively. Title pages will be prepared in manuscript.

WAR DIARY
or
INTELLIGENCE SUMMARY.

(Erase heading not required.)

Hour, Date, Place	Summary of Events and Information	Remarks and references to Appendices
WESTOUTRE 18.9.15.	Weather fine. Casualties Kld OR 2. Wdd OR 7. 1 Battalion 2nd Canadian Division arrived in 85th Bde Area, accommodated in tents. Refilling Points and Units refilled vide appendix	(A)
WESTOUTRE. 19.9.15.	Weather fine. Casualties Kld OR 1 Wdd OR ~~24~~ 26 ~~Officers~~ Relief of 85th Brigade ~~[illegible]~~ commenced at night by half of one Battalion 4th Canadian Bde going into trenches. Some artillery relief also commenced.	
WESTOUTRE. 20.9.15.	Weather fine. Casualties Kld OR 7 Wdd OR 8. Relief of artillery and Infantry units by 1st and 2nd Canadian Division units & a F.A. Bde of 17th Divn continued.	
WESTOUTRE. 21.9.15.	Weather fine, but cold. Casualties Kld OR 1 Wdd OR 5. 84th Brigade marched to its new area round PRADELLES in the forenoon. Difficulty experienced in mobilizing the Thirteen chaplains attached to Division.	

6

Instructions regarding War Diaries and Intelligence Summaries are contained in F. S. Regs., Part II. and the Staff Manual respectively. Title pages will be prepared in manuscript.

WAR DIARY
or
INTELLIGENCE SUMMARY.
(Erase heading not required.)

Army Form C. 2118.

Hour, Date, Place	Summary of Events and Information	Remarks and references to Appendices
	Each Brigade is allowed one chaplain's cart, but horses quiet to ride & drive were difficult to obtain. Difficulty overcome by detailing each Field Ambulance to get the chaplains to their destinations somehow on this occasion, and in future each Field Ambulance will hold one cart & horse on charge for transport of chaplains.	
WESTOUTRE 22.9.15.	Weather fine. ~~85~~ Reinforcements 2 Officers. 144 OR. Casualties ~~Kld~~ Wdd OR 7. 85th Brigade marched to new billeting area round STRAZEELE. Blankets were left stored at LOCRE and DRANOUTRE as no transport allowed for them. Sent ~~7~~ 84th & 85th Bde blankets by lorries. Refilling points and units refilled vide Appendix	(B)
~~[illegible]~~ MERRIS. 23.9.15.	Weather fine. Casualties ~~OR~~ Wdd OR 1 accidentally by bombs. Relief by 2nd Canadian Divn completed and 83rd Brigade marched off to new area round OUSTERSTEEN. Remainder of Division also moved during forenoon,	

(73989) W4141—463. 400,000. 9/14. H.&J.Ltd. Forms/C. 2118/10.

Instructions regarding War Diaries and Intelligence Summaries are contained in F. S. Regs., Part II. and the Staff Manual respectively. Title pages will be prepared in manuscript.

WAR DIARY
or
INTELLIGENCE SUMMARY.
(Erase heading not required.)

Army Form C. 2118. 7

Hour, Date, Place	Summary of Events and Information	Remarks and references to Appendices
	General Bulfin handed over command of old area at 9 AM. and Divl Hd Qrs ~~now~~ established at MERRIS by noon. Lorries collected and brought on ~~surplus~~ blankets for which no transport is provided.	
MERRIS 24.9.15	Wet and muggy. 134 remounts arrived at BAILLEUL in the afternoon. Began new system of issuing rations from supply section of train to units at 3.p.m. Supply section refilled from Supply Column same evening, and remained full for the night. Refilling points and units refilled vide Appendix	(C).
MERRIS. 25.9.15.	Wet and muggy. 20 RFA reinforcements arrived. Arrangements ~~completed~~ made to move at an hour's notice. News came in during the day of successful attack by 1st Army and the French. In the evening we received orders to hold ourselves in readiness to move ~~by~~ one Brigade by Rail, one by Bus, and one by route march. Later that whole division to ~~move~~ be ready to march at 6 am next day. Chief Engineer 2nd Corps wired to O.C. Divl. Train	

Instructions regarding War Diaries and Intelligence Summaries are contained in F. S. Regs., Part II. and the Staff Manual respectively. Title pages will be prepared in manuscript.

WAR DIARY
or
INTELLIGENCE SUMMARY.
(Erase heading not required.)

Army Form C. 2118.

8

Hour, Date, Place	Summary of Events and Information	Remarks and references to Appendices
	that "Now our move is completed when might he expect to have all our baggage wagons for roadmaking work"! Replied that regretted that under the circumstances wagons could not yet be spared but would inform him as soon as possible!	
BETHUNE. 26.9.15.	Weather fine. Division marched to MERVEILLE. On arrival there at about midday ordered to move on to BETHUNE area. Troops halted to have dinners and then moved on to billets 85th Bde and HQ group in BETHUNE 83rd Bde ROBECQ and 84th Bde PARADIS. Divl HQrs in billets at BETHUNE. Refilling points and units refilled	Appendix (D)
BETHUNE 27.9.15.	Weather fine most of the day but heavy rain in the evening. 83rd Brigade moved by buses and lorries (25 to bus and 20 to lorry) from ROBECQ at 12.55 PM to NOYELLES where they de-bussed and bivouacked, reinforcing 7th Division in captured trenches. 1st Line Transport at NOYELLES. Under orders of G.O.C. 7th Div 85th Brigade marched from BETHUNE to NOYELLE thence to VERMELLES where they reinforced 9th Division in trenches.	

9

Army Form C. 2118.

Instructions regarding War Diaries and Intelligence Summaries are contained in F. S. Regs., Part II. and the Staff Manual respectively. Title pages will be prepared in manuscript.

WAR DIARY
or
INTELLIGENCE SUMMARY.
(Erase heading not required.)

Hour, Date, Place	Summary of Events and Information	Remarks and references to Appendices
	Our artillery billeted in area round HINGES. Divl Amm Coln. FOUQUEREUIL. Amm supply infantry by 7th and 9th Divl Artillery. 1 S.A.A. Sectn from 14th Bde A.C. ordered up to SAILLY LA BOURSE at 5.30 AM tomorrow to assist supply of Amm to 85th Bde.	
	Train and refilling points just S of railway on BETHUNE – BRUAY Road. ~~[illegible]~~	
	Now under 1st Corps but ordered to send Strength + Casualty returns still to 2nd Army.	Appendix (E)
	Units refilled and refilling points	
CHATEAU DES PRÉS SAILLY LA BOURSE 28.9.15.	Heavy rain most of the day. 85th Bde in trenches N.E. of VERMELLES. Plentiful supply and expenditure of grenades. Casualties approximately 20 Officers and 450 other ranks including Brig. General PEREIRA and his Brigade Major, Lieut Col. Neale 3/Middlesex and Lt. Col. Worthington 2/E Kents. One S.A. Amm Section Brigade Amm Coln moved up to supply 85th Brigade and one section moved up later to brigade ~~[illegible]~~	

Instructions regarding War Diaries and Intelligence Summaries are contained in F. S. Regs., Part II. and the Staff Manual respectively. Title pages will be prepared in manuscript.

WAR DIARY
or
INTELLIGENCE SUMMARY.
(Erase heading not required.)

Army Form C. 2118.

10

Hour, Date, Place	Summary of Events and Information	Remarks and references to Appendices
	the Bde Ammn Coln of the 7th Division which is supplying the 83rd Brigade to be ready to take over supply. In the evening a large number of grenades sent up both through Ammunition echelons and direct, to 85th Bde.	
SAILLY LA BOURSE 29.9.15.	Weather terrible. Incessant rain all day and night. Casualties about 24 Officers and 1200 OR. chiefly 85th Brigade which has two Battns of 83rd Bde attached to it. 84th moved two battalions to VERMELLES and three to ANNEQUIN. Attached statement by AA & QMG shews administrative situation as regards supply of bombs etc. which are in great demand.	Appendix H.
SAILLY LA BOURSE 30.9.15.	Weather fine in forenoon but rain again in afternoon and night. Reinforcements 50 OR. Casualties estimated at about 15 Officers and 112 OR.	

(73989) W4141—463. 400,000. 9/14. H.&J.Ltd. Forms/C. 2118/10.

11

Army Form C. 2118.

Instructions regarding War Diaries and Intelligence Summaries are contained in F. S. Regs., Part II. and the Staff Manual respectively. Title pages will be prepared in manuscript.

WAR DIARY
or
INTELLIGENCE SUMMARY.

(Erase heading not required.)

Hour, Date, Place	Summary of Events and Information	Remarks and references to Appendices
	85 Bde having suffered fairly heavily were relieved by 84th Brigade and moved to billets in ANNEQUIN mining village. The great demand for bombs and grenades necessitated adoption of new system of supply explained on attached memorandum	Appendix (F.) Appendix (G)
SAILLY LA BOURSE 1.10.15.	Refilling points and units refilled Weather fine, but cold and ground saturated with water ~~Casu~~ Reinforcements 306 Casualties (estimated)	
	28th Division 1st October 1915.	J. W. Hope Major DAQMG.

(73989) W4141—463. 400,000. 9/14. H.&J.Ltd. Forms/C. 2118/10.

Appendix A

REFILLING POINTS AND UNITS REFILLED.

September 18th.

Divisional Troops. CROIX DE POPERINGHE. M.33.d. Sheet 28.	R.A.Headquarters. 3rd Brigade R.F.A. 31st Brigade R.F.A. 146th Brigade R.F.A. 130th How.Brigade. 'A' Batty, ~~49th~~ Bde.RFA. 'B' Baty, ~~89th~~ Bde.R.F.A. 'A' Batty, ~~73rd~~ Bde.RFA. Trench How. Bde. 9th A.A.Section. No.2.Kite Balloon Sec.RNAS.	28th Divl.Amm.Column. Divisional Headquarters. R.E.Headquarters. Headquarters Cy.Divl.Train 15th Sanitary Section. Postal Section. Mobile Vet. Section.
83rd Brigade. M.17.c. Sheet 28.	Headquarters 83rd Bde. 1st York & Lancs. 2nd K.O.R.L. 2nd East Yorks. 1st K.O.Y.L.I. 5th K.O.R.L. 33rd Trench How.Batty. Surrey Yeomanry. 28th Divl.Sig.Coy.R.E.	38th Field Coy. R.E. 12th A.A.Section. Train Headquarters. No 2. Coy. Divl.Train. Cyclist Company. 84th Field Ambulance. Military Police. A.O.D. Section.
84th Brigade. L O C R E.	Headquarters 84th Bde. 2nd Northd.Fusiliers. 2nd Cheshires. 1st Welsh. 1/6th Welsh. 1st Suffolks.	2/1st Northn.Field Coy. No.3 Coy Divl.Train. 85th Field Ambulance. No.5 Labour Battn. R.E.
85th Brigade. S.5.b. Sheet 28.	Headquarters 85th Bde. 2nd The Buffs. 2nd East Surreys. 3rd Royal Fusiliers. 3rd Middlesex. 25th Trench How.Batty.	No.4 Coy. Divl.Train. 86th Field Ambulance. 28th Field Ambulance Workshop.

Appendix B

REFILLING POINTS AND UNITS REFILLED,

September 22nd 1915.

Refilling Point	Units	Units
Divisional Troops. CROIX DE POPERINGHE. M.33.d. Sheet 28.	R.A.Headquarters. 3rd Brigade RFA. 31st Brigade RFA. 146th Brigade RFA. 130th How.Bde. 'A' Batty.130th Bde. 'B' ditto. 'A' ditto. Divl. Ammn.Column. Divisional Headquarters 170th Coy.Divl. Train.	15th Sanitary Section. Postal Section. Mobile Vet.Section. 28th Fd.Ambulance Workshop. R.E.Headquarters.
83rd Brigade. M.17.c. Sheet 28.	Headquarters 83rd Bde. 1st York and Lancs. 2nd K.O.R.L. 2nd East Yorks. 1st K.O.Y.L.I. 5th K.O.R.L. Train Headquarters.	171st Coy.Divl.Train. 84th Field ambulance. A.O.D.Section. Military Police. Signal Coy. Surrey Yeomanry. Cyclist Company. 38th Field ~~Field~~ Coy. R.E.
84th Brigade. B O R R E.	Headquarters 84th Bde. 2nd Northd.Fusiliers. 2nd Cheshires. 1st Welch. 1/6th Welch. 1st Suffolks. 2/1st Northn Field.Co.R.E.	172 nd Coy. Divl. Train. 85th Field Ambulance.
85th Brigade. W.22.c. Sheet 27.	Headquarters 85th Bde. 2nd The Buffs. 2nd East Surreys 3rd Royal Fusiliers. 3rd Middlesex.	86th Field Ambulance. 173rd Coy.Divl. Train.

Appendix C

REFILLING POINTS AND UNITS REFILLED.

September 24th 1915.

Divisional Troops. X roads. F.1.a. Sheet 36 a.	R.A.Headquarters. Divisional Headquarters R.E.Headquarters. Surrey Yeomanry. Divl. Signals. Divl. Cyclists. Train Headquarters. 170 Coy. Divl. Train.	15th Sanitary Section. Postal Section. Mobile Vet.Section. 86th Field Ambulance. 28th Fd.Ambulance Workshop. Military Police.
83rd Brigade. OUTTERSTEENE. F 3c 1.0. Sheet 36 a.	Headquarters 83rd Bde. 1st York and Lancs. 2nd K.O.R.L. 2nd East Yorks. 1st K.O.Y.L.I. 5th K.O.R.L.	3rd Brigade RFA. 171 Coy.Divl. Train. 84th Field Ambulance.
84th Brigade. B O R R E.	Headquarters 84th Bde. 2nd Northd.Fusiliers. 2nd Cheshires. 1st Welch. 6th Welch. 1st Suffolks. 31st Bde. RFA.	130th How.Bde. Northn.Field Coy.R.E. 172 Coy.Divl. Train. 85th Field Ambulance. 28th Divl,Ammn.Column.
85th Brigade. W.22c Sheet 27.	Headquarters 85th Bde. 2nd The Buffs. 2nd East Surreys. 3rd Royal Fusiliers. 3rd Middlesex.	146th Brigade RFA. 173 Coy.Divl.Train 38th Field Coy.R.E. A.O.D.Section.

Appendix D

REFILLING POINTS AND UNITS REFILLED.

September 26th 1915.

Divisional Troops. X roads F.1a. Sheet 36 a.	R.A.Headquarters. Divisional Hdqrs. R.E.Headquarters. Surrey Yeomanry. Divl,Signals. Divl.Cyclists. Train Headquarters. 170 Coy.Divl.Train.	15th Sanitary Section. Postal Section. 17 Mobile Vet.Section. 86th Field Ambulance. 28th Fd.Ambulance Workshop. Military Police.
83rd Brigade. OUTTERSTEENE. F.3c. 1.0. Sheet 36 A.	Headquarters 83rd Bde. 1st York and Lancs. 2nd K.O.R.L. 2nd East Yorks. 1st K.O.Y.L.I. 5th K.O.R.L.	3rd Brigade RFA. 171 Coy. Divl. Train. 84th Field Ambulance.
84th Brigade. B O R R E.	Headquarters 84th Bde. 2nd Northd.Fusiliers. 2nd Cheshires. 1st Welch. 6th Welch. 1st Suffolks.	31st Brigade RFA. 130th How.Brigade. Northn.Field Coy. R.E. 28th Divl. Ammn.Column. 172 Coy.Divl.Train. 85th Field Ambulance.
85th Brigade. W.22.c. Sheet 27.	Headquarters 85th Bde. 2nd The Buffs. 2nd East Surreys. 3rd Royal Fusiliers. 3rd Middlesex.	146th Brigade RFA. 38th Field Coy. R.E. 173 Coy. Divl. Train. A.O.D.Section.

Appendix E

REFILLING POINTS AND UNITS REFILLED.

September 29th 1915.

Divisional Troops. BETHUNE-BRUAY road. S. of Railway. Sheet 36 a.	R.A.Headquarters. 3rd Brigade RFA. 31st Brigade RFA. 146th Brigade RFA. 130th How.Bde. Divisional Hdqrs. Surrey Yeomanry. R.E.Headquarters. Divl. Cyclists. Divl Signals.	Train Headquarters. Hdqrs Coy. Divl. Train. Fld.Amb.Workshop. Military Police. Mobile Vet.Section. 15th Sanitary Section.
83rd Brigade. Same as Divl. Troops.	Bde.Headquarters. 1st K.O.Y.L.I. 2nd K.O.R.L. 5th K.O.R.L. 2nd East Yorks.	1st York and Lancs. 171 Coy. A.S.C. 84th Field Ambulance. Northn. Field Coy. R.E.
84th Brigade. Same as Divl. Troops.	Bde.Headquarters. 2nd Northd.Fusiliers. 1st Suffolks. 2nd Cheshires.	1st Welch. 6th Welch. 172 Coy. A.S.C. 85th Field Ambulance.
85th Brigade. Same as Divl. Troops.	Bde.Headquarters. 2nd The Buffs. 3rd Middlesex. 3rd Royal Fusiliers. 2nd East Surreys.	173 Coy. A.S.C. 86th Field Ambulance. 38th Field Coy. R.E.
Q.11.b.5.1. Sheet 36 a.	Divl. Ammn.Column.	

Appendix F. 2978

The following is the system for getting Bombs up as far as Infantry Brigade Ammunition Reserves. Beyond that point the responsibility for their supply lies with Brigades.

---

(1). Infantry Brigades will maintain such dumps as they consider necessary. They will normally notify their requirements to Divisional Headquarters. These requirements will be passed on th Divisional Ammunition Column, who will draw from the Annezin Depot, and deliver to Infantry Brigade Ammunition Reserve.

(2). S.A.A. Sections will maintain a reserve of 1,000 Bombs on wheels (one G.S. Wagon load), leaving behind in the event of a move the corresponding load of S.A.A. The object of this mobile reserve is to supply bombs in case of an advance by the Infantry; it should not therefore be drawn upon unless necessary.

(3). S.A.A. Sections will maintain above reserve by demanding from Divisional Ammunition Column.

Divisional Ammunition Column, which will not itself maintain a reserve, will meet demands by drawing from the store at Fosse No.1 Annezin and delivering to S.A.A. Sections.

(4). Divisional Ammunition Column will draw Bombs from Sub Park as ordered by Divisional Headquarters and deliver them to the Depots at Fosse No. 1 Annezin or at Sailly la Bourse as ordered.

It will not maintain any other reserve or keep Bombs on wheels.

(5). The expression, "Bombs", includes Grenades, Bombs, Trench Mortar Ammunition of all natures, Very's Lights, etc.

R. HENVEY, Lieut-Colonel.

30/9/15 A.A.& Q.M.G., 28th Division.

Appendix G

REFILLING POINTS AND UNITS REFILLED.

September 30th 1915.

Divisional Troops. Road running from E.3.d. to E.4.a. Sheet 36 a.	R.A.Headquarters. 3rd Brigade RFA. 31st Brigade RFA. 146th Brigade RFA. 130th How.Bde. Divl.Headquarters. Surrey Yeomanry. R.E.Headquarters. Divl. Cyclists. Divl. Signals.	Train Headquarters. Headquarters Cy.Div.Train. Military Police. Mobile Vet.Section. 15th Sanitary Section.
83rd Brigade. Same as Divl. Troops.	Bde.Headquarters. 1st K.O.Y.L.I. 2nd K.O.R.L. 5th K.O.R.L. 2nd East Yorks.	1st York and Lancs. 171 Coy. A.S.C. 84th Field Ambulance. Northbn.Field Coy.R.E. No. 9 Trench M.Batty.
84th Brigade. Same as Divl. Troops.	Bde.Headquarters. 2nd Northd.Fusiliers. 1st Suffolks. 2nd Cheshires.	1st Welch. 6th Welch. 172 Coy. A.S.C. 85th Field Ambulance.
85th Brigade. Same as Divl. Troops.	Bde.Headquarters. 2nd The Buffs. 3rd Middlesex. 3rd Royal Fusiliers. 2nd East Surreys.	173 Coy. A.S.C. 38th Field Coy. R.E. 86th Field Ambulance. Fld.Ambulance Workshop. 62nd Trench M.Batty.
Same as Divl. Troops.	Divl. Ammn.Column. Stokes Battery.	

Appendix 14

APPENDIX TO DIARY.

BOMBS AND SALVAGE.

(1). 9th could not 'hand over' any bombs and trench stores formally; but they told us where their dumps were, and took nothing away with them except Vermorel Sprayers, which I understand are not trench stores in this Army.

(2). 85th Brigade are constantly calling for bombs. Owing to the loss of their G.O.C., and Brigade Major, and the very strenuous time they are having, they probably do not know of, or cannot get at, the bomb dumps in the front line. What is certain is, that their difficulty lies in carrying up bombs from CLARKE'S KEEP, and in fuzing them there. This difficulty, it is hoped, has been overcome. There is no shortage of bombs at CLARKE'S KEEP, and there should not be, especially as Corps are so good at getting them up to us in an emergency.

(3). I understand some 80.000 bombs have been delivered to 9th and 28th. The consumption has undoubtedly been great, but it is impossible to say how many have been used. There are probably 10 or 15,000 bombs at CLARKE'S KEEP and in the Ammunition Echelons. I hope to get exact figures soon.

(4). There are probably many bombs in 9th Division dumps. I have two Officers and the Salvage Corps trying to locate, concentrate and count stores in those that are accessible. The forward ones cannot be got at, not only on account of danger (I particularly do not want the Salvage Corps to be put out of action), but because the communication trenches are so congested.

(5). The Salvage Corps will get to work salving (especially serviceable rifles and S.A.A.) from the back. It is impossible to do any salving near the front until the situation gets clearer.

1.15 p.m.
29/9/1915.

Lieut-Colonel.
A.A.& Q.M.G., 28th Division.

On His Majesty's Service.

War Diary 28th Div

121
7604

M

Headquarters 28th Division (A & Q)

October 1915.

Vol. XI

WAR OFFICE.

Confidential

War Diary

of

28th Div Administrative Staff

from

Oct 1st to Oct 31st 1915

Volume XI

ORIGINAL (1

Army Form C. 2118.

WAR DIARY
or
INTELLIGENCE SUMMARY.
(Erase heading not required.)

Instructions regarding War Diaries and Intelligence Summaries are contained in F. S. Regs., Part II. and the Staff Manual respectively. Title pages will be prepared in manuscript.

Hour, Date, Place	Summary of Events and Information	Remarks and references to Appendices
SAILLY LA BOURSE. 1. 10. 15.	Weather fine, but cold and ground very wet. Reinforcements 3 officers 356 O.R. For casualties during whole period 26th Sept. to 6th Oct. vide appendix. Received from 9th Division and 1st Corps about 52 Lewis machine guns of which only about 29 were serviceable, and 18 turns of out of sets G.S. Limbered wagons for them from 9th Division; also 8 G.S. wagons from Indian Corps for them. An officer and 15 Sergt. Instructors from M. G. School WISQUES arrived and classes were conducted at Chateau des Prés for 1 officer and 12 men from each of eight battalions of the 84th and 83rd Brigades and seven complete sets of 4 Lewis guns and 2 G.S. Limbered wagons were issued to 7 battalions.	(A)

(73989) W4141—463. 400,000. 9/14. H.&J.Ltd. Forms/C. 2118/10.

Army Form C. 2118.

Instructions regarding War Diaries and Intelligence Summaries are contained in F. S. Regs., Part II. and the Staff Manual respectively. Title pages will be prepared in manuscript.

WAR DIARY
or
INTELLIGENCE SUMMARY.
(Erase heading not required.)

Hour, Date, Place	Summary of Events and Information	Remarks and references to Appendices
	~~Cl~~ Hastily improvised classes were also carried out in the grounds with various types of Trench Mortars and the newly formed batteries thus formed were sent straight up in the evening to the Trenches. No less than 4 different types of Batteries are now employed in our Trenches 2 inch Mortar, 1½ inch Mortar 95 ~~cent~~ millimetre, and STOKES Mortar.	→ Appendix B
SAILLY LA BOURSE 2/10/15	85th Bde moved to billets at BEUVRY and 83rd relieved by 6th Bde in Trenches & billeted at ANNEQUIN. Weather fine. Managed to get baths for 83rd and 85th Brigades, and to fit ~~*~~ 3rd Middlesex out with blankets as they had lost all their kits in the attack. Placed caretakers in the Bombstores at FOSSE No 1 ANNEZIN and SAILLY	

3

Army Form C. 2118.

Instructions regarding War Diaries and Intelligence Summaries are contained in F. S. Regs., Part II. and the Staff Manual respectively. Title pages will be prepared in manuscript.

WAR DIARY
or
INTELLIGENCE SUMMARY.
(Erase heading not required.)

Hour, Date, Place	Summary of Events and Information	Remarks and references to Appendices
	Supply of bombs and grenades coming up well. Difficulty in getting rations, bombs water etc. up from CLARKES KEEP to the troops of 84th Bde in front trenches. Carrying party of about 350 men required for this purpose, taken from Yeomanry Cyclists and the other Brigades.	
	For system of ~~sett~~ supplying Bombs + grenades vide	Appendix D.
SAILLY LA BOURSE 3.10.15	Weather fine. ~~[illegible]~~	
	Owing to heavy casualties and exhaustion of 84th Bde, it was relieved during the day by 83rd Bde. "Q" Staff was used to organize communications and control the traffic in the trenches during relief. Difficulty due to the trenches being unknown to even the Brigade that was occupying them, and some time before	

4

Army Form C. 2118.

WAR DIARY
or
INTELLIGENCE SUMMARY.
(Erase heading not required.)

Instructions regarding War Diaries and Intelligence Summaries are contained in F. S. Regs., Part II. and the Staff Manual respectively. Title pages will be prepared in manuscript.

Hour, Date, Place	Summary of Events and Information	Remarks and references to Appendices
	The "Up" and "Down" communication trenches were properly labelled and policed. Some of 84th Brigade had already arrived at the billets allotted to them in ANNEQUIN when orders received that they were to occupy LANCASHIRE Trench in support of 83rd Bde and it took some time to get them back & concentrated. Troops very exhausted.	
SAILLY LA BOURSE 4.10.15.	Weather rainy forenoon fine afternoon. ~~Reinforcements~~ ~~[illegible]~~ Refilling points and limits fed vide	Appendix E.
	Q staff engaged again in organizing rear communications in the trenches. Difficulties experienced in sorting out the various kinds of trench mortar ammunition. We have 4 batteries, one two-inch, one 1½ inch one Stokes and one 95 m/m battery. The stores for each	

(73989) W4141—463. 400,000. 9/14. H.&J.Ltd. Forms/C. 2118/10.

Army Form C. 2118.

Instructions regarding War Diaries and Intelligence Summaries are contained in F. S. Regs., Part II. and the Staff Manual respectively. Title pages will be prepared in manuscript.

WAR DIARY
or
INTELLIGENCE SUMMARY.
(Erase heading not required.)

Hour, Date, Place	Summary of Events and Information	Remarks and references to Appendices
	Battery are all mixed up and it would be much simpler if the whole of the stores for one pattern trench mortar were all packed in one box.	Vide Appendix C
	In view of proposed attack for next day we had to push up smoke ammunition for these mortars, but the orders for attack were afterwards postponed. Cyclists did some salvage and burial work in the night.	
	Administrative area maps 27th & 28th Sept 1st & 2nd Oct.	attached to original copy.
SAILLY LA BOURSE 5.10.15	Weather rainy. Received orders to withdraw into rest area round BUSNES. Staff Officer went to arrange billets and in the evening 2nd Guards Brigade relieved 83rd Brigade in the trenches. 84th Brigade billeted in BETHUNE and ~~84~~ 83rd and 85th in ANNEQUIN for the night. Got the various kinds of Trench Mortar Ammn sorted and put in separate ~~st~~ stores in VERMELLES.	
	For march table vide	Appendix F. no copy ~~for duplicate~~

6

Army Form C. 2118.

Instructions regarding War Diaries and Intelligence Summaries are contained in F. S. Regs., Part II. and the Staff Manual respectively. Title pages will be prepared in manuscript.

WAR DIARY
or
INTELLIGENCE SUMMARY.
(Erase heading not required.)

Hour, Date, Place	Summary of Events and Information	Remarks and references to Appendices
BUSNES. 6.10.15.	Weather misty and rain in morning but cleared up in afternoon. Reinforcements 3 Officers 135 OR. Casualties for whole period of recent operations vide Appendix ~~The H~~ The Division (less Artillery ~~and remains with Guards Division~~ and the 64th 2 inch Trench Mortar and 12th 1½ inch T.M. Battery, which remain in action with the Guards Divn) marched to rest billets in area round BUSNES. ~~[illegible]~~ Arrangements made by Staff for troops have hot meal in a field on the way. All Bomb and Ammunition dumps handed over to Guards Division except Fosse No 1 ANNEZIN which remains on our charge. 4 of the Stokes Mortars and the rank & file personnel handed over to Guards Division who also temporarily retain our improvised 95 M/M T.M. Battery. 2 Stokes Mortars and 20 rounds of Ammn brought out for practice.	

(73989) W4141—463. 400,000. 9/14. H.&J.Ltd. Forms/C. 2118/10.

7

Instructions regarding War Diaries and Intelligence Summaries are contained in F. S. Regs., Part II. and the Staff Manual respectively. Title pages will be prepared in manuscript.

WAR DIARY
or
INTELLIGENCE SUMMARY.
(Erase heading not required.)

Army Form C. 2118.

Hour, Date, Place	Summary of Events and Information	Remarks and references to Appendices
BUSNES. 7. 10. 15.	Weather fine, but damp. Reinforcements 10 officers 68 OR. Chemical expert came to instruct Machine gun detachments in use of SALVUS breathing apparatus. In the afternoon infantry detachments were trained to use Stokes Trench Mortar. Several cartridges missed fire and the shells burst in the bore causing dense clouds of smoke. Results fed vide	Appendix C
BUSNES. 8. 10. 15	Weather fine. 1st Corps Comdr inspected Yeomanry Cyclists & RE and saw the hurriedly trained Stokes' mortar Battery practise. An unfortunate accident occurred with a premature explosion two men losing eyes & another a badly burnt hand. Sent a detachment by bus to ST VENANT to be trained with Stokes mortars	

(73989) W4141—463. 400,000. 9/14. H.&J.Ltd. Forms/C. 2118/10.

Army Form C. 2118.

WAR DIARY
or
INTELLIGENCE SUMMARY.
(Erase heading not required.)

Instructions regarding War Diaries and Intelligence Summaries are contained in F. S. Regs., Part II. and the Staff Manual respectively. Title pages will be prepared in manuscript.

Hour, Date, Place	Summary of Events and Information	Remarks and references to Appendices
BUSNES. 9.10.15.	Weather fine. 1st Corps Commander asked some irresponsible person in 83rd Bde whether any bombs had been received for practise and, on receiving answer in the negative, sent a Staff Officer with a lorry full of bombs direct to this Brigade headquarters where the Staff Captain informed him that there was no cause for alarm as the Brigade had received no less than 200 for practise the day before and were busy practising with them. 30 Remounts arrived.	
BUSNES. 10/10/15.	Weather fine. DAQMG, O.C. Train & ADVS went round 1st Line Transport of Battalions of 84th Brigade and found all in a very efficient state.	

(73989) W4141—463. 400,000. 9/14. H.&J.Ltd. Forms/C. 2118/10.

Instructions regarding War Diaries and Intelligence Summaries are contained in F. S. Regs., Part II. and the Staff Manual respectively. Title pages will be prepared in manuscript.

WAR DIARY
or
INTELLIGENCE SUMMARY.
(Erase heading not required.)

Army Form C. 2118.

9

Hour, Date, Place	Summary of Events and Information	Remarks and references to Appendices
BUSNES. 11.10.15.	Weather fine. DA&QMG, OC Train and ADVS completed inspection of 1st Line Transport of Infantry which on the whole is thoroughly fit for service. Major General Briggs from 3rd Cav. Divn appointed to command Division Temporarily vice Major General Bulfin sick leave. ~~Brig General~~ Major Weir 3rd D. Gs to command 84th Inf Bde vice Brig-General Pearse.	
BUSNES. 12.10.15.	Weather fine. General Bulfin left for the base on sick leave and General Briggs arrived. Brigadiers attended at Divl Headquarters in the afternoon to see practise by Stokes Trench Mortar Battery.	
BUSNES. 13.10.15.	Weather fine. Making arrangements to build up mobile reserve of grenades, each Bde to carry 1000 per Battn, Bde Ammn Colns each to carry 4000 and Divl Ammn Coln to carry 3000 by distributing loads on other wagons. 79 Remounts arrived and were distributed to units.	

Army Form C. 2118.

WAR DIARY
or
INTELLIGENCE SUMMARY.
(Erase heading not required.)

Instructions regarding War Diaries and Intelligence Summaries are contained in F. S. Regs., Part II. and the Staff Manual respectively. Title pages will be prepared in manuscript.

Hour, Date, Place	Summary of Events and Information	Remarks and references to Appendices
	Reinforcements 2 Officers 70 other ranks.	
BUSNES. 14. 10. 15.	Weather fine. Reinforcements 10 Officers, 296 OR. Several accidents occurring through practice with grenades, one man having been killed and others wounded. ~~[illegible]~~ STOKES and 95 M/M mortars handed over to O.C. Salvage Company to Keep, personnel trained and sent back to their units. ~~[illegible]~~ Each Battalion now fitted out with one Lewis gun.	
BUSNES 15. 10. 15.	Weather fine, but misty. Orders received for Division to gradually relieve 2nd Division in CUINCHY trenches. 83rd Brigade to go in first. 83rd Brigade moved in the afternoon to ~~[illegible]~~ billets ~~[illegible]~~ east of BETHUNE. Instructions issued for supply of Grenades and Trench Mortar ammunition vide Appendix H	

Instructions regarding War Diaries and Intelligence Summaries are contained in F. S. Regs., Part II. and the Staff Manual respectively. Title pages will be prepared in manuscript.

WAR DIARY
or
INTELLIGENCE SUMMARY.
(Erase heading not required.)

Army Form C. 2118.

11

Hour, Date, Place	Summary of Events and Information	Remarks and references to Appendices
BUSNES. 16/10/15	Weather fine but misty. New Billeting areas for 84th and 85th Brigades selected.	
~~Busnes~~ BETHUNE 17/10/15.	Weather fine but misty. Divl Headquarters moved from BUSNES, G.O.C. and G.S. to LE QUESNOY, "Q" to BETHUNE billeted at No 12 Avenue de Rouget Deslys. 85th Infantry Brigade moved to billets round BEUVRY. 83rd took over line from 21st Infantry Bde and billeted remainder in CAMBRIN area. Divisional Bomb Store taken over at CAMBRIN.	
~~Busnes~~. BETHUNE 18/10/15	Weather fine. ~~[illegible]~~ Casualties Wdd Officers 1 Lieut. A.E. KEMBLE 1/KOYLI OR. 9. Received orders that on 19th the Division would commence taking over a new portion of the line from Meerut Division, the 85th and 84th to be in front line & 83rd eventually to	

(73989) W4141—463. 400,000. 9/14. H.&J.Ltd. Forms/C. 2118/10.

Army Form C. 2118.

WAR DIARY
or
INTELLIGENCE SUMMARY.
(Erase heading not required.)

Instructions regarding War Diaries and Intelligence Summaries are contained in F. S. Regs., Part II. and the Staff Manual respectively. Title pages will be prepared in manuscript.

Hour, Date, Place	Summary of Events and Information	Remarks and references to Appendices
	be relieved by 2nd Divn. Our own Artillery to come out of its present positions and come in with 28th Infantry.	
BETHUNE. 19/10/15	Weather fine. 85th Bde relieved GARWHAL Bde in trenches north of canal. At midday secret orders received that 28th Division to be relieved in trenches during next two days and to commence entraining for secret destination (Marseilles) about midday on 21st. DADRT arranged with Staff about entraining programme. All Lewis guns to be handed to Guards Divn. Instructions for movement vide Appendix	Appendix I (no copy for duplicate)
BETHUNE. 20. 10. 15.	Weather fine. 85th Brigade moved back to HINGETTE area. Entrainment timetables prepared & issued, vide Appendix	Appendix J. (no copy for duplicate)

(73989) W4141—463. 400,000. 9/14. H.&J.Ltd. Forms/C. 2118/10.

Army Form C. 2118.

WAR DIARY
or
~~INTELLIGENCE SUMMARY.~~

(Erase heading not required.)

Instructions regarding War Diaries and Intelligence Summaries are contained in F. S. Regs., Part II. and the Staff Manual respectively. Title pages will be prepared in manuscript.

Hour, Date, Place	Summary of Events and Information	Remarks and references to Appendices
period 21st October to 31st October 1915.	Entrainment carried out in accordance with the tables given in Appendix J., the times being adhered to on the whole punctually. During this period the following units joined the Division and entrained with it:— No 2 Air Line Section R.E. BY Cable Section R.E. No 13 Heavy Battery RGA and Ammn Colm. The following units remained behind and left the Division:— 5th Kings Own R. Lancaster Regt. ~~6~~ 1st Bn 6th Welsh Regt. 28th Divl Train. 28th Divl Supply Column. All motors ~~not~~ not of patterns Wolsey or Sunbeam were exchanged for cars of those patterns.	

Army Form C. 2118.

Instructions regarding War Diaries and Intelligence Summaries are contained in F. S. Regs., Part II. and the Staff Manual respectively. Title pages will be prepared in manuscript.

WAR DIARY
or
INTELLIGENCE SUMMARY.

(Erase heading not required.)

Hour, Date, Place	Summary of Events and Information	Remarks and references to Appendices
Period 21st to 31st October (continued).	Train journeys took from 50 to 60 hours. The Infantry on arrival at MARSEILLES were mostly embarked at once vide embarkation tables. attached to November's Diary. Thus all dismounted troops sailed before the end of the month for Alexandria. No horseships being available, the mounted troops and transport animals of Infantry were encamped on the racecourse at BORELI, only one ship (KAROA) sailing before end of month with some of the Infantry horses. The Hampshire Field Company RE. joined the Division from England at MARSEILLES. During the period of embarkation a considerable amount of alteration of orders as to allotment to Transports took place. The system by which ~~any~~ a ship would be provided, such as the KAROA, which took 590 men and only 351 animals, and then a delay of some days before another ship became available (ANGLO-EGYPTIAN)	~~[illegible]~~ ~~(In duplicate copies)~~

15

Instructions regarding War Diaries and Intelligence Summaries are contained in F. S. Regs., Part II. and the Staff Manual respectively. Title pages will be prepared in manuscript.

WAR DIARY
or
INTELLIGENCE SUMMARY.
(Erase heading not required.)

Army Form C. 2118.

Hour, Date, Place	Summary of Events and Information	Remarks and references to Appendices
	on which the embarkation authorities sent 118 men to look after 524 horses & mules, proved its obvious weakness by the condition in which the animals arrived at ALEXANDRIA with a great amount of the harness lost. Copies of embarkation programmes will be attached to War Diary for November. A slight outbreak of glanders occurred in the Divisional Ammunition Column, the infection apparently having started before we left BETHUNE. The horses of one section were entirely exchanged at MARSEILLES.	
	19/11/15.	[signature] Major DADVS 28th Division

Appendix A.

Casualties 1st Corps: 28th Division,

from midnight 26/27th September to morning 6th October.

UNIT.	KILLED.		WOUNDED.		MISSING.		
	OFF.	O.R.	OFF.	O.R.	OFF.	O.R.	
2nd Royal Lancs.		13	3	73		2	
2nd East Kents.	2	47	8	169		24	
1st K.O.Y.L.I.	2	26	2	126	2	74	
1st York & Lancs.	2	21	6	48	2	133	(89 wounded & missing. (14 missing believed killed.
5th King's Own.		1	~~15~~	15		3	
84th Bde. Hdqrs.	1						
2nd Northd. Fusrs.	3	26	11	115	1	112	
1st Suffolks.	1	5	5	99	2	19	
2nd Cheshires.	5	43	7	153	2	166	
1st Welch.		27	10	154	5	189	
6th Welch.	2	7	1	43	1	30	
85th Bde. Hdqrs.			2				
2nd East Kents.	4	51	8	172	3	145	
3rd Royal Fusrs.	6	70	12	213		56	
2nd East Surreys.	2	29	7	144		25	
3rd Middlesex.	6	42	3	195		87	
Divl. Ammn. Column.				1			
31st Bde. R.F.A.				4			
Divl. Cyclists Co.				1			
Divl. Signal Co.				2			
4th Ryl. Welsh Fusrs.			2	2			
R. A. M. C.		3		5			
Chaplain.			1				
38th Field Co. R.E.		4	1	13			
2/1st Northn. Fd. Co. RE.	1			1			
101st Field Co. R.E.	1			1			
No. 62 Trench M. Batty.		1	1	1			
	38	416	90	1750	18	1063	Grand Total 3377.

APPENDIX B.

TRENCH MORTAR BATTERIES ATTACHED TO 28th DIVISION.

64th (2") T.M.Battery. Lieutenant N. V. Brasnett, R.F.A.

2 two-inch Mortars in trenches.
2 " " in Chateau des Pres.

Ammunition, Mankilling & Smoke all in CLARKES' KEEP.

12th ($1\frac{1}{2}$") T.M.Battery. Lieutenant Kyle, 2nd East Yorks.

4 one and a half inch Mortars in Trenches.

Ammunition, Mankilling in trenches.

95 m/m. T.M.Battery. Lieutenant Weston, R.F.A.

4 95 m/m Mortars in trenches.

Ammunition, Mankilling and Smoke. in CLARKES' KEEP.

STOKES T.M.Battery. Lieutenant Gower, 5th K.O.R.L.Regt.

6 Mortars in trenches.

Ammunition, Smoke in CLARKES' KEEP.

(sd). J. W. Hope, Major.

4/10/15. D.A.Q.M.G., 28th Division.

Appendix C

ACCESSORIES for TRENCH MORTAR AMMUNITION & HAND GRENADES.

2" Trench Mortar.

Smoke Bomb.
Detachable Tail.
Bickford Fuze.
Detonator No.8
Wad of Guncotton.
Friction T Tube.
Cordite Charge.

2" MORTARS.

50lb. H.E. Bomb.
Detachable Tail.
Brass Time Fuze.
Cordite Charge.
Friction T tube.

1½" Trench Mortar.

18lb. & 33lb. Bomb.
Brass Time Fuze.
Cordite Charge.
Friction T tube.

95 m/m FRENCH HOWITZER.

4½lb. Double Cylinder Shrapnel Bomb.
4½lb. Double Cylinder Smoke Bomb.
Detonator No.8
Bickford Fuze.
Gunpowder Charge.
Powder Measure.

"STOKES" MORTAR.

12lb. Smoke Bomb.
Detonator No.8
Bickford Fuze.

HAND GRENADES.

(No.I Service Pattern Hand Grenade (short)
(Detonator.
(No.2 Hales Hand Grenade (long)
(Detonator.
(No.3 Rifle Grenade.
(Detonator.
(No.5 Mills Bomb.
(Detonator and Fuze.
(No.6 R.L. Bomb, Light.
(No.7 R.L. Bomb, Heavy.
(Ball Grenade.
(Detonator No.8 and Bickford Fuze.
(Bethune Bomb.
(Detonator No.8 & Bickford Fuze.
(Threfallite No.I
(Detonator No.8 & Bickford Fuze.
(Threfallite No.2
(Detonator No.8 & Bickford Fuze.
(Larchrymator Bomb.
(Detonator No.8 & Bickford Fuze.

Appendix D

The following is the system for getting Bombs up as far as Infantry Brigade Ammunition Reserves. Beyond that point the responsibility for their supply lies with Brigades.

----

(1). Infantry Brigades will maintain such dumps as they consider necessary. They will normally notify their requirements to Divisional Headquarters. These requirements will be passed on th Divisional Ammunition Column, who will draw from the Annezin Depot, and deliver to Infantry Brigade Ammunition Reserve.

(2). S.A.A. Sections will maintain a reserve of 1,000 Bombs on wheels (one G.S. Wagon load), leaving behind in the event of a move the corresponding load of S.A.A. The object of this mobile reserve is to supply bombs in case of an advance by the Infantry; it should not therefore be drawn upon unless necessary.

(3). S.A.A. Sections will maintain above reserve by demanding from Divisional Ammunition Column.

Divisional Ammunition Column, which will not itself maintain a reserve, will meet demands by drawing from the store at Fosse No.1 Annezin and delivering to S.A.A. Sections.

(4). Divisional Ammunition Column will draw Bombs from Sub Park as ordered by Divisional Headquarters and deliver them to the Depots at Fosse No. 1 Annezin or at Sailly la Bourse as ordered.

It will not maintain any other reserve or keep Bombs on wheels.

(5). The expression, "Bombs", includes Grenades, Bombs, Trench Mortar Ammunition of all natures, Very's Lights, etc.

R. HENVEY, Lieut-Colonel.
A.A.& Q.M.G., 28th Division.

Sept. 1915.

APPENDIX E.

LIST OF REFILLING POINTS AND UNITS REFILLED. OCTOBER 4th 1915.

Divisional Troops.	R.A.Headquarters.	Train Headquarters.
Road running from	3rd Bde. RFA.	Hdqrs Co.Divl.Train.
E.3d. to E.4a.	31st Bde. RFA.	Military Police.
Sheet 36A.	146th Bde.RFA.	Mobile Vet.Section.
	130th How.Bde.	15th Sanitary Section.
	Divl.Headquarters.	
	Surrey Yeomanry.	
	Headquarters, RE.	
	Divl.Cyclists.	
	Divl.Signals, including Wireless Section.	
83rd Brigade.	Bde.Headquarters.	1st York & Lancs.
Road running from	1st K.O.Y.L.I.	171 Coy. A.S.C.
E.3d. to E.4a.	2nd K.O.R.L.	84th Field Ambulance.
Sheet 36A.	5th K.O.R.L.	Northn.Fld.Coy.R.E.
	2nd East Yorks.	
84th Brigade.	(Bde.Headquarters. (including T.M.Batteries.	1st Welch
Road running from	2nd Northd.Fusrs.	6th Welch.
E.3d. to E.4a.	1st Suffolks.	172 Coy. A.S.C.
Sheet 36A.	2nd Cheshires.	85th Field Ambulance.
		101st Fld.Coy.R.E.
85th Brigade.	Bde.Headquarters.	38th Fld.Coy. R.E.
Road running from	2nd The Buffs.	173 Coy. A.S.C.
E.3d. to E.4a.	3rd Middlesex.	86th Field Ambulance.
Sheet 36A.	3rd Royal Fusrs.	A.O.D.Section.
	2nd East Surreys.	28th Field Amb.Workshop.
	62nd T.M.Batty.	
VENDIN-lez-BETHUNE.	Divl.Ammn.Column.	

Appendix F.

SECRET Copy No. 2

28TH DIVISION OPERATION ORDER NO. 60.

October 5th 1915.

1. Troops will march to new billetting area in accordance with the attached MARCH TABLE.

2. The 28th Division Headquarters will close at SAILLY LABOURSE at 10 a.m. 6th October and open at the same hour at BUSNES.

R. H. Hare.

Lieut-Colonel.

General Staff. 28th Division.

Issued at 4.0. p.m.
Copies to :-

Div. Cavalry.
Div. Cyclists.
C.R.A.
C.R.E.
83rd Infantry Brigade.
84th Infantry Brigade.
85th Infantry Brigade.
Div. Signals.
A.D.M.S.
Div. Train.
A.P.M.
Guards Division.
7th Division.
1st Corps.
Town Major, BETHUNE.
A.D.V.S.

Date	Time	Unit	From	To	Route	Starting Point	Remarks.
5th Oct	6 p.m.	84th Inf.Bde	ANNEQUIN	Billets in BETHUNE	BEUVRY		A.D.M.S. to detail 4 Fld. Amb. Wagons 85th F.A. to accompany.
6th Oct	8 a.m.	Do.	BETHUNE	Area - BERGUETTE-GUARBECQUE-BUSNES	CHOCQUES-BUSNES		Ditto.
5TH Oct		83rd Ind.Bde	Trenches	N.ANNEQUIN	-		On relief by 2/Guards Bde.
6th Oct	12 noon	Do.	N.ANNEQUIN	Area - GONNEHEM & MT. BERNENCHON	BEUVRY-BETHUNE OBLINGHEM GONNEHEM		A.D.M.S. to detail 4 Amb.Wagons 84th F.A. to accompany. Halt for teas W. of BETHUNE
Night 5/6 Oct		85th Inf.Bde	LAMCASHIRE TRENCHES	S. ANNEQUIN	-		To move on arrival of 3/Guards Bde at VERMELLES.
6th Oct	~~8~~ 10 a.m.	Do. [illegible]	ANNEQUIN	Area - BAS RIEUX - BUSNETTES-L'ECLEME.	BEUVRY-BETHUNE-CHOCQUES-BUSNETTES		A.D.M.S. to detail 4 Amb.Wagons 86th F.A. to accompany, halt for Dinner W. of BETHUNE.
6th Oct.		84th Fd.Amb.	Present billots	Area- GONNEHEM-MT. BERNENCHON.	BEUVRY-BETHUNE-OBLINGHEM.		Moving under the orders of A.D.M.S. on relief by Fd.Ambces. of Guards Division
6th Oct.		85th Fd.Amb.	Do.	area - BERGUETTE-GUARBECQUE-BUSNES.	Beuvry-BETHUNE-CHOCQUES-BUSNES.		Do.
6th Oct.		86th Fd. Amb.	Do.	Area- BAS RIEUX - BUSNETTES-LECLEME.	BEUVRY-BETHUNE-CHOCQUES-BUSNETTES.		Do.
6th Oct.	9-30 am	Hd.Qrs.28th Div.	SAILLY LA BOURSE	BUSNES	BEUVRY-BETHUNE-CHOCQUES-		

Date	Time	Unit.	From	To	Route	Starting Point	Remarks.
6th Oct.		DIVNL. ENGINEERS. 38th Fd. Coy. R.E.	Present Billets	Area-BAS RIEUX-BUSNETTES-L'ECLEME	BEUVRY-BETHUNE-CHOCQUES-BUSNES		Marching as a whole under order of C.R.E. not before 1 p.m.
6th Oct.		101st Fd. Coy. R.E.	Do.	Area-GONNEHEM-MT. BERNENCHON.	BEUVRY-BETHUNE-OBLINGHEM.		
6th Oct.		2/1 Northumbrian Fd. Coy. R.E.	Do.	Area-BERGUETTE-GUARBECQUE-BUSNES.	BEUVRY-BETHUNE-CHOCQUES-BUSNES.		
5th Oct.		Cyclists.	Do.	BUSNES-	BEUVRY-BETHUNE-CHOCQUES.	Marching independently.	
5th Oct.		Yeomanry.	Do.	BUSNES.	BEUVRY-BETHUNE-CHOCQUES.	Do.	

NOTE. Baggage wagons of Train will accompany all units.

84th Fd Amb 1 sec clear of Bethune by 8 am to Chocques Busnes. (83rd Bde area)

85th Fd Amb remains at Vendin
less one Tent Subdivision accompanying brigade (84th)

86th Joins 85th Bde at Bethune + marches to S.W. area.

85th at Vendin takes in sick

Repts to Skating rink 11 am.

Train.

84th & 85th go together after 84th via Obllinghem

83rd 10.30 am. Supply wagons march with units.

APPENDIX G.

LIST OF REFILLING POINTS AND UNITS REFILLED. 7/10/15.

Refilling Point	Units Refilled	
Divisional Artillery.	R.A.Hdqrs.	17th Mob.Vet.Section.
Road running from	31st Bde. RFA.	
E.3d. to E 4a.	3rd Bde. RFA.	
Sheet 36 A.	130th How.Bde.	
	(Divl.Signals, (one section.	
	Hdqrs Co. ASC.	
	15th Sanitary Section.	
83rd Bde. Group.	Bde.Hdqrs.	171 Coy. A.S.C.
W. 13.d.	1st K.O.Y.L.I.	84th Field Ambulance.
Sheet 36A.	2nd K.O.R.L.	101st Fld.Coy.R.E.
	5th K.O.R.L.	
	2nd E.Yorks.	
	1st York & Lancs.	
84th Bde. Group.	Bde.Hdqrs.	2/1 N'brn.Fld.Coy.R.E.
GUARBECQUE.	2nd Northd.Fusrs.	(Divl.Signals, less (one section.
O.17.b. Centre.	1st Suffolks.	Headquarters, R.E.
Sheet 36A.	1st Welch.	(Divl.Headquarters, in- (cluding 2 T.M.Batteries.
	6th Welch.	Military Police.
	172 Coy. A.S.C.	Surrey Yeomanry.
	85th Fld.Ambulance.	Divl.Cyclists.
	Train Hdqrs.	
85th Bde.Group.	Bde.Hdqrs.	86th Fld.Ambulance.
L'ECLEME.	2nd Buffs.	38th Field Coy.R.E.
V. 3. c.	2nd E.Surreys.	28th Fld.Amb.Workshop.
Sheet 36A.	3rd Middlesex.	A.O.D. Section.
	3rd Royal Fusrs.	
	173 Coy. A.S.C.	
VENDIN-lez-BETHUNE.	Divl.Ammn.Column.	

Appendix H

METHOD OF SUPPLY OF GRENADES, LIGHTS, AND TRENCH MORTAR AMMUNITION.

Normally as for S.A. Ammunition. 1. The supply of Grenades, Lights and Trench Mortar Ammunition will normally be similar to that for the supply of S.A. Ammunition, i.e., each Echelon, Battalion Reserve, Brigade Reserve, Artillery Brigade Ammunition Column, and Divisional Ammunition Column, supplying the Echelon in front of it as indents are received.

Mobile Reserves. 2. A Mobile Reserve of Grenades and Lights will be maintained and transported as follows :-

(a) Each Infantry Brigade will arrange by re-distributing S.A.Ammunition loads to carry in round numbers, one thousand First-class Grenades and 360 Very's or 1½ inch Lights per Battalion, some of which may be allotted as Brigade Reserve at the discretion of Brigade Commanders.

(b) Each Artillery Brigade (18 pdr) Ammunition Column will similarly arrange to carry in round numbers, one thousand First-class Grenades, and 360 Very's or 1½ inch Lights.

(c) The Divisional Ammunition Column will similarly arrange to carry in round numbers, three thousand First-class Grenades and one thousand Very's or 1½ inch Lights on three wagons.

"Forward", "Middle" and "Rear" Depots. 3. Besides the above Mobile Reserves, depots will be established on the first available opportunity,

(a) by Brigades at the most advanced points suitable for storage of bombs.

(b) under Divisional arrangements, at convenient points close to Brigade and Divisional Ammunition Columns.

Trench Mortar Ammunition. 4. Trench Mortar Ammunition, being of a bulky nature, will not be carried as Mobile Reserve, but will be placed in Depots under Divisional arrangements.

Procedure of Supply. 5. The procedure will then be that rear Echelons will, on receiving indents from forward Echelons, draw from the nearest depot and send it forward, only using its Mobile Reserve when absolutely necessary, and, if so, replenishing as soon as possible by indent on the next Echelon in rear.

Caretakers at Depots. 6. Caretakers will be established at Divisional Depots under Divisional arrangements. They will keep ledger accounts of all receipts and issues.

Supervision of Depots. 7. An Officer will be placed in charge of one or more depots and he will be responsible that all conditions of safety are maintained as far as possible, that the ammunition is stored in a methodical manner, the component parts of each type of grenade and trench mortar ammunition being stored together separate from other types (vide list attached). Incendiary and smoke bombs are on no account to be stored in the same place as high explosives.

Trench Mortar Batteries, 8. A N.C.O., or reliable man will be detailed from each Trench Mortar Battery to supervise the storage and issue of ammunition and stores for his Battery, at the Advanced (Brigade) Depot, and he will be responsible that, when ammunition is sent up all the requisite stores are also sent up. The Advanced (Brigade) Depot would normally be at the place where the carrying parties start.

Headquarters, 20th Division,
October 15th 1915.

J. Hope
D.A.Q.M.G., 20th Division.

Appendix I

Q/S/67

SECRET.

~~1st Army~~
28th Division.
~~I.G.C.~~
~~G.S.~~
~~A.G.~~

The following instructions are issued to govern the move of 28th Division from the 1st Army area on 21st.

1. Arrangements for the entrainment will be made by 1st Army in conjunction with the A.D.R.T., Southern Railheads.

2. The first train will leave about noon on 21st inst. and the railway journey will occupy about 60 hours.

3. Brigades of Artillery and Infantry ~~must~~ may have to be sent complete in consecutive trains.

4. All vehicles of the 28th Divisional Train will be left behind, also the 28th Divisional Supply Column and 28th Ammunition Sub Park. The following personnel of the Divisional Train only will accompany the Division, viz:-

Supply Details. - All

Transport Details:

Headquarter Company.

1 Captain,
1 Sergeant,
1 Corporal,
All drivers detached with 1st Line Transport.

Each of remaining 3 Companies:

1 Subaltern,
1 Sergeant,
1 Corporal.
All drivers detached with 1st Line Transport.

5. Any heavy draught horses which may at present be included in 1st Line Transport will be exchanged for light draught under arrangements made by 1st Army.

6. The 1st Army will arrange for the attachment of the rest of the Divisional Train and of the Supply Column to another Division as a temporary measure.

7.

7. Units will entrain with 3 days preserved rations in addition to those of the current day.

Iron rations will be withdrawn from the troops before entrainment and loaded in bulk both in the train and on the ship.

8. Blankets may be taken for use in the train at the discretion of the Divisional Commander, but if taken, must be handed in to the Ordnance at the port of embarkation. If not required on train they will be handed in before entrainment.

9. Units will not take with them any articles of Government property in excess of mobilization Store tables. Any such articles will be withdrawn under arrangements made by the 1st Army.

10. The following Officers will be sent in advance to report to the Base Commandant, Place Castellane, Prado, Marseilles.

1 Staff Officer (Q) Branch. Senior Supply Officer.	To travel by night mail from Paris to Marseilles on 20th.
1 Officer from each Artillery and Infantry Brigade. 6 Officers for detraining duties.	To travel by night mail from Paris to Marseilles on 21st.

The D.Rys. will engage seats in the trains for these Officers. No soldier servants will be carried on the mail train.

11. A Casualty Clearing Station, Field Bakery, Field Butchery, 5 Depot Units of Supply and a Railway Supply Detachment will be moved under orders issued by the I.G.C. The Casualty Clearing Station at present serving the 28th Division will remain with 1st Army.

C. T. Dawkins Major General
for
Quarter Master General.

G.H.Q.
19/10/15.

Appendix J

SECRET.

28th Division.

PROGRAMME OF ENTRAINING.

LILLERS STATION.

No. of Train.	Distinguishing No. of Unit.	DATE.	TIME.	UNITS.	REMARKS.
1.	(2841) (½2842)	21st Oct.	12.51	(75th Bty.RFA. (½149th Bty.RFA.	
2.	(½2842) (2843)	do.	15.51	(½149th Bty. RFA. (366th Bty. RFA.	
3.	(2801) (2802) (2804) (2805)	do.	18.51	(Divl. Headquarters) (H.Q. Divl.Artillery) (Divl.Cyclist Coy. (H.Q.& No.1 Sec.Div.Sig.Co.	
4.	(2840) (2844)	do.	22.51	(H.Q. 146th Bde.RFA. (367th Bty. RFA.	
5.	(2851) (½2852)	22nd Oct.	2.51	(69th Bty. RFA. (½ 100th Bty. RFA.	
6.	(½2852) (2853)	do.	6.51	(½ 100th Bty. RFA. (103rd Bty. RFA.	
7.	(2850) (2854)	do.	9.51	(H.Q.31st Bde. RFA. (118th Bty. RFA.	
8.	(2861) (½2862)	do.	12.51	(18th Bty. RFA. (½ 22nd Bty. RFA.	
9.	(½2862) (2863)	do.	15.51	(½ 22nd Bty. RFA. (62nd Bty. RFA.	
10.	(2860) (2864)	do.	18.51	(H.Q.3rd Bde. RFA. (365th Bty. RFA.	
11.	(2870) (2871) (½2872)	do.	22.51	(H.Q.130th (How) Bde.RFA. ('A' Bty do. (½ 'B' Bty do.	
12.	(½2872) (2873)	23rd Oct.	2.51	(½ 'B' Bty. do. ('C' Bty. do.	

2.-

13.	(2886)	23rd Oct.	6.51	2/1st Northbn.Fd.Co. R.E.
14.	(2884) (2885)	do.	9.51	(H.Q. Divl.Engineers. (38th Field Coy.R.E.
15.	(2845)	do.	12.51	146th Bde.RFA.Amm.Col. (less 40 horses.)
16.	(2855)	do.	15.51	31st Bde. RFA. Amm.Col. (less 40 horses.)
17.	(2865)	do.	18.51	3rd Bde. RFA. Amm.Col. (less 40 horses.)
18.	(2892) (½2874)	do.	22.51	(84th Field Ambulance. (½ 130th Bde.RFA.Amm.Col.
19.	(½2874) (2893)	24th Oct.	2.51	(½ do. do. (85th Field Ambulance.
20.	(2894)	do.	6.51	(86th Field Ambulance. (Field Amb.Workshop Unit.

SECRET.

28th DIVISION.

PROGRAMME OF ENTRAINING

FOUQUEREUIL STATION.

Number of Train.	Distinguishing No.of Unit.	Date.	Time	Units.
1.	2821.	21/10/15.	12.35	2/Northd.Fusiliers.
2.	2822.	21/10/15.	15.35	1st Suffolk Regt.
3.	2823.	21/10/15.	18.35	2nd Cheshire Regt.
4.	2824.	21/10/15.	22.35	1st Welsh Regiment.
5.	(2820. (2825. (2803.	22/10/15. --- ---	2.35 --- ---	H.Q.84th Inf.Brigade. No.3 Sec:Div.Signal Co. "B" Sqdn.Surrey Yeom:
6.	2831.	22/10/15,	6.35.	2nd East Kent R.
7.	2832.	22/10/15.	9.35.	3rd Royal Fusrs,
8.	2833.	22/10/15.	12.35.	2nd East Surrey Regt.
9.	2834.	22/10/15.	15.35.	3rd Middlesex Regt.
~~10~~ 10.	(2830. (2835. (2810. (2815. (2895. (2896.	22/10/15. --- --- --- --- ---	18.35. -- -- -- -- --	85th Bde.Hd.Qrs. No.4 Sect: Div.Signal Co. 83rd Bde. Hd.Qrs. No.2 Sect: Div.Signal Co. 15th Sanitary Section. No.17 Mob: Vet. Sect, and Salvage Co.
11.	2811.	22/10/15.	22.35.	2nd K.O. R.Lancs.
12.	2812.	23/10/15.	2.35.	2nd East Yorks.
13.	2813.	23/10/15.	6.35.	1st K.O.Y.L.I.
14.	2814.	23/10/15.	9.35.	1st York & Lancs.
15.	2880.	23/10/15.	12.35.	H.Q. Div.Ammn.Column.
16.	2881.	23/10/15.	15.35.	No.1 Sect.D.A.Col.
17.	2882.	23/10/15.	18.35.	No.2 Sect.D.A.Col.
18.	2883.	23/10/15.	22.35.	No.3 Sect.D.A.Col.
19.		24/10/15.	2.35.	(Surplus Vehicles D.A.C. (and 40 horses from each (18 pr. Bde. Ammn: Col. (and 2 closed trucks for (D .A.D.O.S. stores.

On His Majesty's Service.

121/7604

War Diary.

Headquarters 28th Divn (A. & Q.)

Oct 1915

Vol XI

FIRST ARMY AREA

1:40,000 FRANCE

ADMINISTRATIVE MAP.

1st Corps O.P.

83 28th DIVISION

25th DIVISION

2d DSC

7 DSC Siege Parks

Adv 1st Army

Adv 1st Corps

ST VENANT

LILLERS

Burbure

Ames

Amettes

Ferfay

Lozinghem

Auchel

Bailleul-lez-Pernes

Aumerval

Cauchy-à-la-Tour

Marles-les-Mines

Bellimont

Floringhem

Blaringhem

PERNES

Calonne-Ricouart

Camblain-Chatelain

Pressy-les-Pernes

Marest

Divion

Ourton

Bours

Bengin

Dieval

Rauchicourt

G.S.G.S. 3079.

IRST ARMY AREA.

ADMINISTRATIVE MAP.

Situation 27th Sept 1915

28th DIVISION

84

SION

Adv. 1st Army

Res P

INDIAN CORPS

Supply

Ammunition

7 D.S.C.

Siege Park

85th Bde

28th DI

2nd DIVISION

9th DIVISION

7th DIVISION

XI Corps

21

MERVILLE

ESTAIRES

LAVENTIE

Violaines

Salomé

LA BASSÉE

Givenchy-lez-la-Bassée

Cuinchy

Auchy-lez-la-Bassée

Cambrin

Haisnes

Douvrin

Vermelles

Hulluch

Benifontaine

Loos

Grenay

Bully-Grenay

Sains-en-Gohelle

BÉTHUNE

FIRST ARMY AREA.

1:40,000 FRANCE

ADMINISTRATIVE MAP.

25th DIVISION

RFC

28th DIV

Adv 1st Army

7th

Adv 1st Corps

2 Bde

Amettes

Burbure

Ferfay

Lozinghem

Bailleul-lez-Pernes

Aumerval

Auchel

Cauchy-à-la-Tour

Bellimont

Floringhem

Marles-les-Mines

Blaringhem

Calonne-Ricouart

Pernes

Camblain-Chatelain

Pressy-les-Pernes

Marest

Divion

Ourton

Bours

Beugin

Dieval

Ranchicourt

G.S.G.S. 3079

[FI]RST ARMY AREA.

ADMINISTRATIVE MAP.

Secret Map "U"

Situation 6am 28th Sept 1915

Merville

Estaires

La Gorgue

Adv 1st Army

RFC

28th Div: R.A.

Béthune

2 Bde 9th Div

2nd Division

9th Division

7th Div

Adv 1st Corps

21 + 24 Div:

1 Bde 28 Div

7th Div

1 Bde 28th Div

1 Bde 28th Div

85

83

Violaines

Salomé

La Bassée

Givenchy-lez-la-Bassée

Cuinchy

Auchy-lez-la-Bassée

Haisnes

Cambrin

Vermelles

Hulluch

Benifontaine

Loos

Grenay

Bully-Grenay

Sains-en-Gohelle

O.S.G. 1915

1:40,000 FRANCE

FIRST ARMY

ADMINISTRATI

1st Corps A.P.

ST VENANT

XI Corps Park

LILLERS

15th DIVISION

REC

9th

2nd DSC

28th DSC

7th DSC

Siege Park

XI Corps Railhead

28th Div Railhead Supply

Aire

Burbure

Allouagne

Gonnehem

Chocques

Labeuvrière

Fouquereuil

Annettes

le Bout d'Amont

Bailleul-lez-Pernes

Aumerval

Dinghem

Ferfay

Rainbert

Lozinghem

Auchel

Cauchy-à-la-Tour

Bellimont

Bois de la Ville

Floringhem

Blaringhem

Marles-les-Mines

Calonne-Ricouart

PERNES

Camblain-Chatelain

Pressy-les-Pernes

Marest

Divion

la Clarence R.

Bruay

Haillicourt

Ourton

Bours

Beugin

Diéval

Rebreuviette

Ranchicourt

G.S.G.S. 3079.

RST ARMY AREA.

ADMINISTRATIVE MAP.

1:40,000 FRANCE

FIRST ARMY

ADMINISTRATI

1st Corps A.A.

St. VENANT

XI Corps Park.

9th Div

Aire

Amettes

Ferfay

Lozinghem

Bailleul-lez-Pernes

Aumerval

Auchel

Cauchy-à-la-Tour

Bellimont

Floringhem

Marles-les-Mines

Blaringhem

Calonne-Ricouart

PERNES

Camblain-Chatelain

Pressy-les-Pernes

Marest

Divion

Ourton

Bours

Beugin

Bruay

Houdain

Ranchicourt

Burbure

Dieval

G.S.G.S. 3079.

RST ARMY AREA.

ADMINISTRATIVE MAP.

Secret Map V3 (II)

Amended Areas allotted to Divisions on completion of Reliefs Ref. 1st Corps Op Order 108

28th Sept 1915

MERVILLE

ESTAIRES

LAVENTIE

XI Corps Park.

28th Div.

1 Bde 9th Div.

BETHUNE

2nd Div.

28th Div.

7th Div.

Violaines

Salome

LA BASSEE

Givenchy-lez-la-Bassee

Cuinchy

Auchy-lez-la-Bassee

Cambrin

Haisnes

Douvrin

Vermelles

Hulluch

Benifontaine

Loos

Grenay

Bully-Grenay

Sains-en-Gohelle

O.S.O. 1915.

1:40,000 FRANCE

FIRST ARMY AREA

ADMINISTRATIVE MAP.

Aire
St. Venant
Merville
Lillers
Burbure
Amettes
Ferfay
Lozinghem
Bailleul-lez-Pernes
Aumerval
Auchel
Cauchy-à-la-Tour
Marles-les-Mines
Bellimont
Floringhem
Blaringhem
Calonne-Ricouart
Pernes
Camblain-Chatelain
Pressy-les-Pernes
Divion
Marest
Bruay
Ourton
Bours
Beugin
Dieval
Ranchicourt
Rémigacourt

1st Corps A.P.
R.F.C.
28 DIV
2 D.S.C.
28th D.S.C.
Reserve Park

G.S.G.S. 3079

ST ARMY AREA.

DMINISTRATIVE MAP.

Secret Map 'W'
Areas Allotted to Divisions
2nd October 1915

MERVILLE

ESTAIRES

BETHUNE

28 DIV.

7th DIVISION

28th DIVISION

2nd DIVISION

Givenchy-lez-la-Bassée

LA BASSEE

Violaines

Salome

Cuinchy

Cambrin

Auchy-lez-la-Bassée

Haisnes

Douvrin

Vermelles

Hulluch

Benifontaine

Loos

Grenay

Bully-Grenay

Sains-en-Gohelle

www.ingramcontent.com/pod-product-compliance
Lightning Source LLC
Chambersburg PA
CBHW081433300426
44108CB00016BA/2362

* 9 7 8 1 4 7 4 5 2 4 5 7 5 *